*T. S. ELIOT'S*

*POETRY AND PLAYS*

# T. S. ELIOT'S
# POETRY AND PLAYS

### A STUDY IN SOURCES AND MEANING

*By Grover Smith, Jr.*

 THE UNIVERSITY OF CHICAGO PRESS

*Library of Congress Catalog Number: 56-11001*

THE UNIVERSITY OF CHICAGO PRESS, CHICAGO 37
Cambridge University Press, London, N.W. 1, England
The University of Toronto Press, Toronto 5, Canada

© *1950 and 1956 by Grover Smith, Jr. Published 1956*
*Composed and printed by* THE UNIVERSITY OF CHICAGO
PRESS, *Chicago, Illinois, U.S.A.*

*TO MY PARENTS*

*Cum multa legeris et cognoveris, ad unum semper oportet*
*redire principium*

# PREFACE

This book analyzes T. S. Eliot's poems and plays and examines their sources, insofar as these have been identifiable. It does not show, in large, the relation of his poetry to his prose, nor, except in incidental fashion, does it attempt biography. It considers in particular the creative ideas behind each work and the literary echoes which enrich meaning; Eliot has always been a poet of the savored word, the historic connotation. Obviously, however, no book could or should exhaust all ultimate influences. The task of establishing origins is but secondary to the task of analysis, and, despite the great labor and large space that it demands, its worth is tested mainly by its contribution to this primary activity of the critic. Analysis, in turn, can only be judged by its fruits in understanding.

Although for the most part I have kept to chronology in commenting on Eliot's work, neither Eliot himself, after the lapse of years, nor anyone else seems to know precisely in what sequence the poems of 1915–19 were written, or, for that matter, those of 1909–11. Instead of attempting to dispose in a conjectural order the pieces within each of these two groups, I have arranged them to please myself, but I have dated the poems where I could. I think that in not more than one or two instances have I done violence to known chronology, except in grouping together the principal plays and in respecting the unity of *Ash Wednesday*. My close attention to the minor poems, especially those in quatrains starting with "The Hippopotamus," has been owing to their general interest and to my wish to neglect nothing that might clarify "the figure in the carpet."

I should be ungrateful if I did not register my indebtedness to several earlier books, namely, F. O. Matthiessen's *The Achievement of T. S. Eliot*, B. Rajan's *T. S. Eliot: A Study of His Writings by Several Hands*, Leonard Unger's *T. S. Eliot: A Selected Critique*, Frank Wilson's *Six Essays on the Development of T. S. Eliot*, Elizabeth Drew's

*T. S. Eliot: The Design of His Poetry*, Helen Gardner's *The Art of T. S. Eliot*, and Kristian Smidt's *Poetry and Belief in the Work of T. S. Eliot*. These were all in print before the substantial completion of my manuscript (except for my chapter on *The Confidential Clerk*) in the spring of 1952. Since that time I have seen E. J. H. Greene's *T. S. Eliot et la France*, D. E. S. Maxwell's *The Poetry of T. S. Eliot*, George Williamson's *A Reader's Guide to T. S. Eliot*, and the anonymous *On the Four Quartets of T. S. Eliot*. In S. Musgrove's *T. S. Eliot and Walt Whitman* I have found confirmation of views I expressed in *The Poems of T. S. Eliot 1909–1928: A Study in Symbols and Sources*, the forerunner of the present book.

For his attention to numerous queries I should like to thank T. S. Eliot. For other help I am indebted to Richard P. Adams, Conrad Aiken, Richard and Anne Ward Amacher, R. C. Bald, Merle and Helen Bevington, Travis Bogard, Elizabeth Bowen, Cleanth Brooks, Jr., Alan Willard Brown, Frank Caldiero, Elizabeth Drew, the late Irwin Edman, Brian Elliott, F. Cudworth Flint, Donald Gallup, Brendan Gill, Clarence Gohdes, Frederick L. Gwynn, John Hayward, S. K. Heninger, Jr., Aldous Huxley, Stanley E. Hyman, Edward B. Irving, Jr., Alfred L. Kellogg, Barnet Kottler, Roger Sherman Loomis, Emery Neff, Justin O'Brien, Robert T. Petersson, Martin Price, Dorothy Pound, Bernard Raymund, Bertrand Russell, Richard B. Sewall, Robert E. Spiller, Marjorie Strachey, William York Tindall, Lionel Trilling, Mark Van Doren, Henry W. Wells, Aubrey L. Williams, Jr., Clem Williams, Jr., Edmund Wilson, W. K. Wimsatt, Jr., and Phyllis, my wife. I wish to acknowledge the courtesy of T. S. Eliot and John Finley, Jr., in having allowed me to consult the Henry Ware Eliot collection at Harvard University, and the generosity of Dorothy Pound, acting for the Committee for Ezra Pound, in having sanctioned my use of an excerpt from an unpublished letter which I have transcribed by permission of the Yale University Library Committee. I wish to acknowledge also the co-operation of Kenneth Lash, formerly the editor of the *New Mexico Quarterly*, where in a different form some portions of my chapter on *Murder in the Cathedral* have appeared. Lastly, for having awarded me a grant toward publication, I desire to record my thanks to the Duke University Council on Research.

GROVER SMITH, JR.

# CONTENTS

## Part I. 1905–1919

1 The Individual Explosion     3
2 The Yellow Fog     9
3 Debate of Body and Soul     30

## Part II. 1919–1926

4 The Word in the Whirlwind: "Gerontion"     57
5 The Labyrinth     67
6 Memory and Desire: *The Waste Land*     72
7 Death's Dream Kingdom: "The Hollow Men"     99
8 Across the Frontier: *Sweeney Agonistes*     110

## Part III. 1927–1932

9 Visions and Revisions: the "Ariel Poems"     121
10 Lady of Silences: *Ash Wednesday*     135
11 The Turning World: *Coriolan*     159

## Part IV. Plays 1934–1953

12 Works and Days: *The Rock*     171
13 Action and Suffering: *Murder in the Cathedral*     180
14 Bright Angels: *The Family Reunion*     196
15 Hieronymo's Mad Againe: *The Cocktail Party*     214
16 His Father's Business: *The Confidential Clerk*     228

Part V. 1933–1948

17  The Complete Consort: *Four Quartets*                247

Notes and References                299

Index                329

# I *1905–1919*

# *1* THE INDIVIDUAL EXPLOSION

The early poetry of T. S. Eliot, before 1915, depicts attitudes typical also of the later. Postures of dejection in solitude, of grief for the unattainability of an ideal, bear witness to Eliot's romantic heritage. Some critics, catching at his techniques of style, have called him a classicist; they have been less precise than Eliot himself, for, as he has acutely said, "a poet in a romantic age cannot be a 'classical' poet except in tendency."[1] Certainly Eliot's first poems tended to counter sentimentality. All of his poetry has avoided romantic commonplaces, eschewed romantic pride, and banished romantic bluster. He began with the impersonal devices of monologue and aloof commentary, ridiculing emotional extravagance with the irony of common sense. But he was temperamentally a romantic, abhorring the gap between the actual and the ideal. Irony, though good camouflage, is no impenetrable mask.

Reared at St. Louis, with periodic holidays on the Massachusetts coast, Thomas Stearns Eliot grew up a member of a transplanted New England family of puritan origin and Unitarian faith. He has said little about his childhood reading. At the age of fourteen he discovered the *Rubáiyát* and was at once enchanted; about the same time he first read, with admiration, Rossetti's "The Blessed Damozel." At sixteen, having attempted Byron, he composed a piece of comic narrative verse in *ottava rima*, "A Fable for Feasters,"[2] which hints perhaps at a prior reading of "The Ghost," in Barham's *The Ingoldsby Legends*. Byron's influence persisted for twenty years or more. Characters in Eliot's own poems are seldom heroic, but they share with the heroes of Byron's Eastern romances a characteristic burden of blight and guilt, attributable, it may be, to a common Adam's curse of Calvinism. Any one

3

among Eliot's large troop of hollow men might say with Childe Harold himself,

> I look upon the peopled desert past,
> As on a place of agony and strife,
> Where, for some sin, to sorrow I was cast,
> To act and suffer,

and, although none could join Harold in "Spurning the clay-cold bonds which round our being cling," each along with him is a victim of the romantic distemper. For all, the world is out of chime.

That the romantic residuum in Eliot's poetry should have been pessimistic was owing to several causes, in part personal and in part educational. As a Harvard undergraduate he had come under the sway of the antiromantic Irving Babbitt. One cause, at least after 1912, was philosophical. From 1910 to 1915, Eliot concentrated his studies upon philosophy and logic. Upon being graduated after three years at Harvard, he went to Paris, where, during 1910–11, he was tutored by Alain-Fournier and attended Bergson's lectures. In the autumn of 1911 he resumed work at Harvard, investigating under the guidance of Josiah Royce the epistemological systems of Meinong and Bradley and trying to read Sanskrit.[3] In the spring of 1914, while an assistant in philosophy, he met Bertrand Russell, temporarily in residence as a lecturer. The following summer he spent some weeks on a fellowship in Germany, chiefly at Marburg, and from there went in September to Oxford, where at Merton College he finished his formal studies.[4] In 1916, or thereabouts, he completed the doctoral dissertation he had started at Harvard. He called it "Experience and the Objects of Knowledge, in the Philosophy of F. H. Bradley."[5]

From the monist Bradley, as Kristian Smidt has shown, Eliot derived certain assumptions about the nature of experience and carried their mark permanently.[6] Far from extolling the self like the romantics, Bradley, while affirming its importance, diminished its dignity. Reflected in Eliot's work is Bradley's view of the personality as a mere cluster of imperfections and delusions: even though perceptions can occur solely in the personality's timeless "finite center" of feeling, that is, in the conscious soul itself, that center has no unity and is but a vehicle for appearances. Still every soul is insulated from every other; this idea, reinforcing the romantic theme of isolation in guilt, seems to have deeply impressed Eliot. The one citation of Bradley in the poetry appears as a note to *The Waste Land* on the horror of solitude.

Eliot's undergraduate period holds a more generally recognized clue to his depreciatory handling of romantic optimism. In 1908, when he was twenty, he encountered *The Symbolist Movement in Literature*, by Arthur Symons, and there first heard of Jules Laforgue, whom with other French poets he then read.[7] Laforgue's own temperament was romantic, but his manner was cynical. He had a disposition to jibe clownishly at sentiment. This habit, though it shaded his poems with a subtle pathos, brightened them with a tinsel novelty all the more bizarre because of their slang. Splitting or "doubling" himself into languid sufferer and satiric commentator, he wrote poems deriding in one passage the tenderness of another.[8] Eliot accommodated this idiosyncrasy to his own needs; it helped him veil personal agonies with impersonal ironies.

Eliot resurrected the Laforguian evasions eight or nine years before delivering himself, in prose, of a doctrine about impersonality. "Tradition and the Individual Talent" dates only from 1917; not until 1924, in his introduction to Valéry's *Le Serpent*, did he state with full clarity how rigorously disciplined art should be: "One is prepared for art when one has ceased to be interested in one's own emotions and experiences except as material."[9] In the same place he repeated from the other essay the opinion that to make a work of art demands "surrender" of the appetitive self to the form being created. The regimen seems almost mystical, like the ethic of right action in his poetry of fifteen years later still. Eliot's spirit of dedication in such passages seems to have resulted not only from his disbelieving, with Bradley, that a man could have any personality worth expressing; it seems to have resulted from his inability to write poetry on any but these terms, from his shyness at the prospect of self-exposure. His more relaxed notion of impersonality—that it may consist in transforming personal experience into a "general symbol"—came in the 1930's.[10] Thus, in "A Note on War Poetry" (1942), he spoke of

> the point at which the merely individual
> Explosion breaks
>
> In the path of an action merely typical
> To create the universal, originate a symbol
> Out of the impact, . . .

and he testified to the possibility of

> private experience at its greatest intensity
> Becoming universal, which we call "poetry." . . .[11]

This view is not incompatible with the earlier one, but, in the light of *Four Quartets* (1935–42), it implies, as the other does not, that experience requires little masking. The difference lies in the nature of the later material itself, in the feelings aroused by it, and in the beliefs controlling these.

Eliot's poems of 1915–19, except "Gerontion," substituted for the dramatic monologue other impersonal devices such as semidramatic vignettes and allusive symbols. *The Waste Land* (1921) is a monologue embellished with mythology. Eliot's use of the Grail legend, and of the initiation pattern in rituals of death and rebirth according to Sir James Frazer's *The Golden Bough,* was intended rather to cloak the personal origins of the poem than to suggest a social meaning for it. He said in 1947, "I wrote *The Waste Land* simply to relieve my own feelings."[12] A vague remark, perhaps; but the adventures of the Grail knight metamorphosed into Tiresias retrace the obsessions of the romantic Prufrock and the forlorn Gerontion. The Prufrockian problem is highly adaptable to mythological treatment. Indeed, it might be instructive to read "The Love Song of J. Alfred Prufrock" as a parallel to the legend—putting the etiolated sentimentalist alongside of the quester who fails to ask the liberating question, the sea-girls alongside of the water-maiden bearing the life-symbol, the Grail itself alongside of the head of John the Baptist on a platter. (In the "Peredur" of *The Mabinogion,* the Grail talisman is in fact a man's bleeding head carried on a charger.)[13] Eliot, on the other hand, had found his lonely and dejected hero long before considering the applicability of the myth. "Prufrock" set forth Eliot's standard poetic theme: the idealist's quest for union with the vision forever elusive in this world.

The search charted in Eliot's mature poetry has, of course, not only a sexual but a spiritual motivation. The Grail legend helps illustrate this in *The Waste Land;* so do the references to Dante. Prufrock's ideal of love demands quite simply a perfect relationship grounded in sex. It is "romantic," in other words, without being "pure." His longing has all the force of a mystic's yearning for God, without any of the illumination. It is adolescent in content, unencumbered with religious motives; yet, in its fastidiousness, it is refined in contrast with love debased by actual success—hence the irony of his dream. Prufrock is but the first of Eliot's diffident personages frustrated by love. But with *The Waste Land* a new hero has fully emerged, still frustrated but cast in a more traditionally romantic mold. In him, the failure to find spiritual perfection, not in but through sex, inspires reflections on his spiritual exile.[14] Here, as in "The Hollow Men," Eliot's debt to Dante is notable for imagery, atmosphere, and the like; in short, for every-thing but the essential Dante of the *Commedia*, whose love transcended its fleshly origins. In *Ash Wednesday* Eliot's poetic voice is infused into a far more Dantean speaker. An ascetic alternative has mainly pre-vailed, and the Lady of that poem has come to symbolize chaste love as a mirror of the divine, the love beyond sex. But in later work Eliot's spokesman moves toward imitation of the negative mystics' severe denial of all human love, however idealized. Henceforth, except for a moment in "Marina," in "Burnt Norton," and again in *The Family Reunion*, there is to be no compromise with earthly desire. The search for God in the affirmation of creature-love gives way to a tormented negative progress: Dante yields to St. John of the Cross.[15] The only affirmation becomes that of art and worship.

The tragedy of Eliot's poetry is that, properly speaking, it shows no Beatrice. In the epigraphs to his unpublished Clark Lectures (1926), Eliot arranged a pertinent contrast. He first cited Dante's reply in the *Vita nuova*, XVIII, to the ladies' question about his love:

Madonne, lo fine del mio amore fu già il saluto di questa donna, di cui voi forse intendete; ed in quello dimorava la mia beatitudine, chè era fine di tutti i miei desiderii. ["Ladies, the end of my love was once the salutation of this lady whom you appear to mean; and in that dwelt my beatitude, which was the end of all my desires."]

And, then, in abrupt transition, he quoted lines from some popular ballad:

I want someone to treat me rough.
Give me a cabman.

Here might be represented in epitome the whole dilemma of spirit and flesh for one entertaining the ideal of their fusion and finding them, in reality, at odds. And for the would-be Dantean the conflict is hopeless.

The theme of love and the theme of redemption growing out of it were not Eliot's only concerns in his poetry after 1919. History—granted the typicality of the poet's own "finite center"—was as in-evitable a subject as it was to be for Joyce in *Finnegans Wake*. And poetry itself constituted a fourth problem. Eliot's "Whispers of Im-mortality" found an ingenious correspondence between the ideal of the poet and the ideal of the lover. At the close of *The Waste Land*, Tiresias was to ask, *"Quando fiam uti chelidon"* ("When shall I become as the swallow?"), thus phrasing at once the misgivings of thwarted lover, graceless seeker after faith, spokesman for a disinherited society, and inarticulate poet. The permutations of Tiresias' four categories of doubt were to become implicit in "The Hollow Men" and *Ash Wednesday* and were to supply four themes to *Four Quartets*. All four problems needed to be settled, and at length were settled in the same way.

# 2 THE YELLOW FOG

Eliot's apprentice work was imitative and slight. After several unimportant pieces, including "A Fable for Feasters," which appeared in the *Smith Academy Record* (St. Louis, 1905), he contributed nine poems, besides the Harvard class ode for 1910, to the *Harvard Advocate* between 1907 and 1910. Among them were three influenced by Laforgue: "Nocturne," "Humoresque," and "Spleen." But four more poems were unprinted until after "The Love Song of J. Alfred Prufrock" came out in *Poetry* (1915); these were "Conversation Galante" (1909), "Portrait of a Lady" (1909–10), and two "Preludes" (1909–10). In 1911 they were followed by the last two "Preludes," by "Rhapsody on a Windy Night," and by "La Figlia che Piange." Though several of the group were very good, none approached "Prufrock," which he began in 1910 while at Harvard and finished in 1911 during a visit to Munich in his Paris year. This superb dramatic monologue revealed him suddenly, to the few friends who saw his work, as an accomplished craftsman; the "Portrait," the "Preludes," and the "Rhapsody" helped ratify their judgment. He showed his manuscript poems to Conrad Aiken and others at Harvard and, undoubtedly, also to Jean Verdenal, the new friend he encountered at Paris. It was Verdenal, lost in the Dardanelles expedition of 1915, whom Eliot was to memorialize in his dedication to *Prufrock and Other Observations*.

The descriptive monologue "Portrait of a Lady," apparently the result of a Cambridge friendship with a lady since described gratuitously by Aiken as a "précieuse ridicule," is unequal to "Prufrock" because it is less incisive. "Prufrock" uses Laforguian devices to create a tragic satire; the "Portrait" does not communicate tragedy through feeling. The lady is at once pitiful and odd; the young man inept and

9

supercilious. Subtly, the derision in which he holds her turns back upon himself—more subtly than is usual in Laforgue, whose general influence is discernible.[1] But, although the lady is doomed to solitude and futility, so that she can say,

> But what have I, but what have I, my friend,
> To give you, what can you receive from me?
> Only the friendship and the sympathy
> Of one about to reach her journey's end,

she has experienced no tragic discovery; she is merely an object for detached contemplation. The young man himself is only discomfited; of course, nothing tragic has happened to him: he is abashed but is too thick-skinned to be hurt. She, characterized through her prolix and weary speech rhythms, is too much resigned in her decorum to realize her potentiality for despair. He, though in a position to see her as she is, is preserved by his egotism from being fretted except by his own difficulties.

To this refined spinster, for whom the relationship, however meager in promise, is a "last chance," the young sophisticate has shown civil but idle attentions. After becoming superficially involved, though more deeply than he has calculated, he finds himself without the diplomacy for a break. At length, having the excuse of a projected foreign tour, he pays the lady a final call to take his leave. When, with placid understatement and only half in reproach, she deplores that they "have not developed into friends," he suffers the mortification of seeming in the wrong and goes away shaken though not contrite. This poem, like its successor "Prufrock," deals with the psychological impasse of the sensitive person from whom life has been withheld. Since, however, it also takes a masculine point of view, it focuses rather on the chagrin of the witness, the young man, than on the agony of the lady. She, being not only the cause but at present the reflector of the young man's unwilling choice between becoming her "friend" and abruptly deserting her, is characterized solely through his own emotions. Yet her character is conceived in rounder form than that of any other Eliot personage who is not a "central intelligence." A Laforguian contrivance of one-sided dialogue (to be exploited again by Eliot in *The Waste Land*), by which the lady is made to speak and her visitor to comment silently, turns the scenes into episodes of observation and analysis—the analysis being expressed through his self-revealing soliloquy each time he escapes from her company. Since the young man's behavior would be impossible if he were attuned to anyone's feelings but his own, the portrait of him is consistent with Eliot's other work in the period. Other poems depict sad sensitives who cannot get what they want; the "Portrait" merely exhibits one perplexed about how to keep unscathed while rejecting what he has no use for. His problem, after his original involvement, is above all to save appearances, and to do so he injudiciously protracts his acquaintance with the lady until he cannot go free without embarrassment and cruelty.

The poem has three parts, or quasi-dramatic scenes, timed by the seasons. Each, constructing a different stage in the young man's attitude, takes its dominant tone from a particular pattern of imagery. There is first a foggy December afternoon of after-the-concert tedium; then an April twilight of pathos and unease; and, lastly, an October night of crisis when he can no longer dissemble but must act upon the disclosure that he and the lady have nothing in common. Part I opens in the depressing atmosphere of the lady's parlor, lit by four candles, "An atmosphere of Juliet's tomb" aptly presaging the hopeless end to which the "affair" is destined and yet establishing only a tragic-comic tone. As the setting appears false and theatrical, so does the bond of acquaintance. The pair have become allied through a snobbish interest in music (the bored young man describes satirically a long-haired virtuoso in a Chopin recital). The lady's attempt to compose emotional harmony between them on the pretext of such intellectual sympathy is so unattractive to her companion that he hardly takes it seriously. He hears in the yearning music of her voice the wearisome thin wailing of "violins / Mingled with remote cornets"; and upon this he imposes the counterpoint of his own irritation, the refractory throb of a tom-tom in his brain, "Absurdly hammering a prelude of its own" and ignoring with its primitive rhythm of impatience the meaning of the lady's pathetic tune.[2] For she speaks to him as to a possible lover, "a friend who has these qualities . . . / upon which friendship lives." His Laforguian nudge to himself, "Let us take the air, in a tobacco trance," delivers him, relieved of strain, into a world of male freedom where he can readjust to the trustworthy time scale of "the public clocks."

In Part II, despite his ennui, he has continued his visits, perhaps because the lady is enough of a curiosity to have afforded in the implied interim a certain intellectual amusement. At any rate, his confidence in the success of his game with her is staggered as he realizes that their intentions are colliding: she is hoping for an emotional liaison. The imagery of spring flowers here objectifies her frustration and his own pricked certitude. The seasonal cycle in the poem begins with winter, and after the brief scent of spring it declines again to the dead season; thus the quiver of life in lilacs and hyacinths is futile. But precisely through his confrontation with the hidden personal values in the cycle, as he becomes troubled by her attention to these tokens of awakening life, the young man is forced to experience the psychological climax of the affair. He plunges helplessly into an emotion compounded of embarrassment and of something which might pass for scruple but which is more like arrogance. Though he does not succumb to pity, he loses his casual freedom to release himself at will, for if he should accept her disparaging estimate of herself he could not cast her off without appearing boorish. On the other hand, he cannot pretend to desire intimacy. The lady has no power of attracting him. Plucked and artificially arranged, the April lilacs will quickly die, the sooner as her tense fingers crush them:

> "Ah, my friend, you do not know, you do not know
> What life is, you who hold it in your hands";
> (Slowly twisting the lilac stalks)
> "You let it flow from you, you let it flow."

Truly she lacks the very vigor of spontaneous life that she is invoking. But her rebuke to him is valid also: the incidentally erotic value of this imagery betrays his own waste of spirit, his own apathy. Her appeal, moreover, to her "buried life, and Paris in the spring" conveys to him an unmanageable fact, that she is no mere instrument of monotonous music but a wasted human heart. Matthew Arnold's poem "The Buried Life" contributes to her phrase the sense of the incalculable, unconscious vital principle, the essential humanity beneath all appearance. But equally there is the sense of a lost past, a vanished joy. (It is interesting, by the way, to speculate on Eliot's possible debt here to Henry James's *The Ambassadors*, where Lambert Strether visualizes his own recovery of life as the springing-up of dormant seeds: "Buried for long years in dark corners . . . these few germs had sprouted again under forty-eight hours of Paris."[3]) When she finishes by ingenuously granting the young man his right to independence and good fortune, and by sacrificing herself and foregoing the impossible return of youth, she has him morally outargued.

Still, even though his understanding of her position is precise enough to disquiet him, it has not mastered his assurance that he is innocent; it has not driven him to accept responsibility. To him, she remains only a "case," as before; but now he cannot deal with her. His conviction that the problem is merely how to save face only makes him puzzle about how to "make a cowardly amends" for what she has *said;* he is not worried by her motives for saying it. In private he can still distract himself with his cynical perusal of "the comics and the sporting page," with which he associates reports about an unconventional English countess (a comedy type for the lady herself), a brawl at a Polish dance (an antidote to the intensity of the Polish musician), and a bank defaulter's confession (a matter-of-fact settlement of a treason worse than his own). That this aloofness is under attack appears from his changed reaction to music: until the lady's attitude begins to disturb him, he has still been able to hear her voice as boredom, "the insistent out-of-tune / Of a broken violin"; now, as the sound of "a street piano, mechanical and tired," comes

> With the smell of hyacinths across the garden
> Recalling things that other people have desired,

he momentarily loses his haughty aplomb. But he recovers at once. Asking himself: "Are these ideas right or wrong?" and thus reaffirming the purely rational nature of the difficulty, he eludes emotional capture.

Yet he is detained, if not by generosity or even pity, then by his own inertia. Committed to the falseness of his position, which he can neither rectify nor evade, he feels compelled to come back, as he does in Part III, like a reluctant pilgrim to a shrine. Already worsted in the contest, he is about to be humiliated. He has at last obtained the pretext which will extricate him: he is going abroad. If only she will let the rupture be tranquil, if only she will rest content with the formality of a promise to write, appearances can be saved. Now, however, she brings the issue to a head. Why have they not "developed into friends"? To her hope that "Perhaps it is not too late" he can answer nothing; the feigned rationality of their acquaintance has dissolved. Having lost the self-possession, the dignity of his pose, the young man is stripped of his whole intellectual resource. He stands convicted in his own eyes of having seemed unmannerly, and can only resort to instinctive turns of voice and gesture to fend off her resigned disappointment. The imagery in the section—especially the figurative mounting on hands and knees, the smile falling "heavily among the bric-à-brac," and the mental shape-shifting to bear to parrot to ape—suggests a kind of dehumanization, as if through his abashment the crestfallen young man had become a bungling animal.

After so bad a quarter-hour, he would appear to have little chance of refurbishing his prestige. But his resilience is excellent. Instead of feeling justly scolded, he interrupts his flippancy only to condescend. Grudgingly he pays the lady's cause a tribute. It is a concession not to her point of view but to the victory she might be entitled to celebrate if, by carrying out her "threat" of dying, she should snatch away his right to the last laugh. That he could have the effrontery to conceive himself as having the right to smile is hardly more shocking, one feels, than the fact that all he would grant her, even *in extremis*, is a possible "advantage." He has not a word of remorse for his conduct; nor has he a motive for understatement. From the evidence in the poem, it is true, one would be hard put to demonstrate that he had been wilfully brutal. One would hesitate, furthermore, to impute to him any active responsibility for their sterile relationship: an emotion cannot be coerced. On the other hand, he is guilty of having been obtuse. His proneness to believe that he is responsible for nothing; that the error, if there was one, has consisted in letting himself be discomposed; and that the lady, despite her undeniable merit, is tedious by nature makes him intolerable and indeed despicable. Having assumed, even at the last, a privilege of analysis rather than a duty of compassion, he here indorses his original scorn. His levity hitherto has not done him credit; least of all does it avail him now when, before his equivocal last line, he recurs frivolously to the musical comparison in imagining her death.

The epigraph to the "Portrait" (from Marlowe's *The Jew of Malta*, Act IV, scene 1) at first glance looks anomalous. It cannot be announcing a literal fact; the young man and the lady have certainly not "committed fornication." It becomes clearer if taken as Eliot's blunt but probably afterthoughted chiding of the young man's attitude. For, though exaggerative, its bravado corresponds in moral callousness to the surface tone of the poem itself. By penetrating to the depths of the lady's lonely and empty life, the young man has committed a psychological rape; this is far worse than fornication, for he has not respected her human condition. Now, one of the remarkable things about this poem is its innocence with respect to the young man's moral duty. Except for the epigraph, it could not be said to dictate judgment of his character. Indeed, one can imagine a reader willing to accept him at his own valuation, if only because of his ceremonious trust of reason. And the young man is entirely reasonable by "social" standards. It would be interesting to know, therefore, whether Eliot did want the point of view suspected; if so, the poem would constitute evidence, unlike "Prufrock," against the charge of mere self-masking.

"The Love Song of J. Alfred Prufrock" raises fewer questions. Eliot, writing in 1916 to Harriet Monroe, who had published it in *Poetry*, thought it better than his other poems of 1909–11.[4] It has the best architectonic design, and it adapts Laforgue's self-irony to comparatively serious uses. As a monologue it owes a good deal to Browning. It is, furthermore, very Jamesian—more so even than the "Portrait"—if not in its ideology, then, at any rate, in its verbal mannerisms. Henry James's "Crapy Cornelia," published in 1909, may have suggested to Eliot the outlines of his poem. This is the story of White-Mason, a middle-aged bachelor of nostalgic temperament, who visits a young Mrs. Worthingham to propose marriage but reconsiders owing to the difference between their worlds. It could have contributed, especially from its opening chapters, a number of ornamental details and, from its ending, the crucial point of White-Mason's understanding with his widowed friend Cornelia: "I'm old."[5]

Eliot's Prufrock is a tragic figure. Negligible to others, he suffers in a hell of defeated idealism, tortured by unappeasable desires. He dare not risk the disappointment of seeking actual love, which, if he found it and had energy enough for it, still could not satisfy him. The plight of this hesitant, inhibited man, an aging dreamer trapped in decayed, shabby-genteel surroundings, aware of beauty and faced with sordidness, mirrors the plight of the sensitive in the presence of the dull. Prufrock, however, has a tragic flaw, which he discloses in the poem: through timidity he is incapable of action. In contrast with the lady in the "Portrait," who feels that she might come alive with lilacs in the spring, he has descended, because of his very idealism, into a winter of passivity. To pursue the tragical analogy, one might call Prufrock's idealism the "curse" which co-operates with his flaw to make him wretched. Alone, neither curse nor flaw would be dangerous; together, they destroy him. Prufrock's responsiveness to ideal values is something theoretically good in itself, an appanage of virtue; yet it partakes of impiety, for it is sentimental instead of

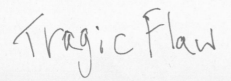

Tragic Flaw

ethical. His values are inherited from the romantic-love tradition, a cult of the unreal and consequently of the inapprehensible. But since he is consciously unheroic, as a comparison of his own with Hamlet's dilemma convinces him, Prufrock should seem comic rather than tragic did not precisely his awareness, his sense of proportion, counter laughter with a virtual admission that his case makes much ado about nothing. A comic discovery would set all to rights; Prufrock's discovery of his flaw,

> . . . I have seen the eternal Footman hold my coat,
> and snicker,
> And in short, I was afraid,

reminds one that no problem is trifling to the man it grieves and that the more ridiculous its revelation would seem to others, the more it may distress him.

The drama of the poem is presented through soliloquy, the action being limited to the interplay of impressions, including memories, in Prufrock's mind. A rather curious device complicates his reverie. By a distinction between "I" and "you," he differentiates between his thinking, sensitive character and his outward self. It may be that the poem contains traces of a medieval *débat*, as in "The Body and the Soul"; but Prufrock, in saying "you," is not speaking only to his body. He is addressing, as if looking into a mirror, his whole public personality. His motive seems to be to repudiate the inert self, which cannot act, and to assert his will. In a strict sense it is not this mirror image which is a *Doppelgänger* but the ego supervising the *monologue intérieur*. The ego alone "goes" anywhere, even in fantasy; the other, at the risk of being rebuffed with "Oh, do not ask, 'What is it?'" merely originates objections, though unfortunately this self finally decides his failure. Being no image of the heroic Prufrock he would like to be, but his own spindling, wispy frame, it necessitates his refusal of an action in which it, and not he, would be the real agent. The man of feeling can treat with no one except through his physical and psychological mask: through it he is interpreted and by it he is condemned. Nor can the ego survive disgrace of the personality; at the end of the poem it is "we" who drown.

The epigraph to the poem expands the context of Prufrock's frustration. Guido da Montefeltro, tormented in the eighth circle of the

*Inferno* (XXVII) for the sin of fraud through evil counsel, replies to Dante's question about his identity:

> If I thought my answer were to one who ever could return to
> the world, this flame should shake no more;

> But since none ever did return alive from this depth, if what
> I hear be true, without fear of infamy I answer thee.

His crime has been to pervert human reason by guile; like Ulysses he is wrapped in a flame representing his duplicity in his former life, when he knew and practiced "wiles and covert ways"—"Gli accorgimenti e le coperte vie." To Prufrock's own life this reply is also applicable. He, like Guido, is in hell, though, unlike Guido, he has never participated in the active evil of the world, so that this resemblance is as ironic as the resemblance to Hamlet. But in this also there is a core of substantial truth. Prufrock is similar to Guido in having abused intellect; he has done so by channeling it into profitless fantasy. By indulging in daydreams (the soliloquy in the poem itself), he has allowed his ideal conception of woman (the sea-girls at the end) to dominate his transactions with reality. He has neither used human love nor rejected it but has cultivated an illusory notion of it which has paralyzed his will and kept him from turning desire into action. His self-detraction when he confesses that he is only a pompous fool, a Polonius instead of a Hamlet (and recognizing this fact, partly a wise Fool too), accompanies his realization that the dream itself has been only a snare, though he cannot get out of its meshes.

> I have heard the mermaids singing, each to each.

> I do not think that they will sing to me.

Failing to abandon the illusion or to be content without physical love, he despairs of life. He has advanced beyond naïve sentimentality in discovering its emptiness, but he has found nothing to replace it. His tragedy remains that of a man for whom love is beyond achievement but still within desire. His age, his shyness, and the somewhat precious and for America, at least, esoteric quality of his name, with its obtrusive initial *J* (recalling the signature T. Stearns-Eliot which Eliot used), underscore his demureness. The name Prufrock, which sounds like the man, was borrowed for him by Eliot from a St. Louis family.[6] It was a good choice.

Prufrock's thoughts start with a command to the self designated as "you" to accompany him to a distant drawing-room. His object is to declare himself to a lady—though to precisely which one of the roomful, he never specifies and perhaps has not decided. The opening image symbolizes through bathos the helpless Prufrock's subjective impression of the evening, which is like an anesthetized patient because he himself is one.[7] By the meditated visit he might escape from the seclusion, both physical and psychological, oppressing him. That he cannot thus escape, first because of hesitancy and then because of despair, means that he will not stir from his spot at all. As the imagery shows, his world is a closed one. Various oppositions convey Prufrock's sense of impotent inferiority or isolation: the evening against the sky and the patient on the table; the streets and the room; the fog and the house; the women's transfixing eyes and the victim wriggling like a stuck bug;[8] the white, bare arms of cold day and the sensuous arms of lamplight; the proper coat and collar and the informal shirt-sleeves; the clothing and the feeble limbs; the prim manners and the amorous appetite; the prophet and the ignobly severed head; the resurrection and the grave; the prince and the emotional pauper; the bright world of singing mermaids skimming the waves and the buried world of death in the sea-depths of fantasy. These all set down a record of Prufrock's longing to reach out, like grasping claws, and take life into his embrace and of his inhibition by the discrepancy between wishes and facts.

In his tentative urge toward action he betrays the fruitlessness of his search: the streets, stifling "retreats" with cheap hotels and with restaurants ("sawdust restaurants" in more than one sense, perhaps) littered with oyster shells like the sea floor of his emotional submersion, could lead only to a question as overwhelming to the lady as to him. And the women meanwhile are talking, no doubt tediously and ignorantly, of Michelangelo, the sculptor of a strength and magnitude with which Prufrock cannot compete.[9] From the prospect of his visit he distracts himself by considering the yellow fog which sleepily laps the house and then by musing that he has plenty of time to "prepare a face," whether in order to lay a plot of momentous effect or to make small-talk over a teacup. But the recurring thought of the women leads him to speculate on their reaction to him, to the baldness he might betray if he beat too hasty a retreat, and to the ill-disguised thinness of his arms and legs. At this point he admits his first doubt, namely, whether he "dare / Disturb the universe"—a hyperbole illustrating his terrified self-consciousness. Immediately after he thus reveals his want of easy terms with life, he shows his distaste for the women as they are; both circumstances result, it appears later, from absorption in day-dreams. Rejecting the voices, the eyes, and the arms (all impersonal, all monotonous, hostile, delusive), he can think of no formula of pro-posal but one humiliating to himself—a presumptuous obsequiousness:

> Shall I say, I have gone at dusk through narrow streets
> And watched the smoke that rises from the pipes
> Of lonely men in shirt-sleeves, leaning out of windows?

His horror of being dissected, of being "pinned," makes him recoil to the wish that he had been

> a pair of ragged claws
> Scuttling across the floors of silent seas.[10]

With this image, just before the climax of the dramatic structure, Pru-frock perceives his lack of instinct, of mindless appetite, which would have given him a realizable aim and which, of course, would have made him at home in those depths where at present he exists abnor-mally.

He has already spoken of the fog and smoke as if it were a cat (a Sandburg cat, no doubt) curling round the house. He now refers to the drowsy afternoon (which, correcting himself, he realizes is evening after all), saying, it "sleeps so peacefully," "stretched on the floor"—or, like his etherized self, "malingers." He is again confronting the difficulty of action rather than its unpleasantness. The difficulty lies in dread of personal inadequacy, maybe even of sexual insufficiency—"the strength to force the moment to its crisis." The climax of his reverie is shaped as he compares himself, in his feeling of being de-capitated (perhaps, in effect, of being unmanned), to John the Baptist; and yet at once he disclaims the dignity of a prophet, seeing himself instead as the butt of a lackey's derision, as the butt of snickering Death. Having confessed his cowardice, he knows that it is too late for him to go, and indeed that it always was.

The remainder of the poem moves toward the image of drowning, a counterpart to the undersea image in the "ragged claws" lines. Hence-forth Prufrock speaks of what *would have* happened and affirms the improbability of a favorable issue to his suit. He would have had to "bite off" and "spit out"[11] his question in some graceless way; he would have had to "squeeze the universe into a ball" (an image in part borrowed from Marvell's "To His Coy Mistress," where it has sexual value); he would have had to rise like Lazarus from the dead (the comparison was suggested to Eliot by Dostoevsky's *Crime and Punishment*[12]) and "tell all," as Dives implored in the parable of the other Lazarus. And, at that, the answer of the lady might have been a casual rebuff. In view therefore of these impossibilities, of their clash with decorous commonplaceness and, above all, of their unacceptability because they would have brought exposure, "as if a magic lantern threw the nerves in patterns on a screen," he disclaims his pretensions. He cannot even dignify his *accidia* by associating it with that of Hamlet. Consequently he resolves, in the only positive decision he can make, to go down upon the seashore, where for a while he may masquerade in his dandyishly cuffed white-flannel trousers. He will perhaps part his hair to conceal his baldness and risk the solaces of a peach, the sole forbidden fruit he is likely to pluck. The happy mermaids, at least, will not insist that he wear a morning coat and tie. But even the mermaids, alas, will not sing to him. His vision of them has been a delusion into whose waters he has sunk deeper and deeper until, recalled to the intolerable real world by human voices in a drawing-room, he has waked and drowned in his subjective world of dreams. Like legendary sailors lulled asleep by mermaids or sirens and then dragged down to perish in the sea, Prufrock has awakened too late.[13]

Eliot's four "Preludes" belong to the "Prufrock" era; the first and second were written at Harvard, the third at Paris, and the fourth upon Eliot's return. During his year abroad he became interested not only in Dostoevsky, who influenced "Prufrock," but in Charles-Louis Philippe, for one of whose novels, *Bubu de Montparnasse,* he composed a Preface when it was published in English in 1932. This book, besides perhaps contributing a phrase to *The Waste Land,* supplied the subject for the third of the "Preludes"—the morning awakening of a woman in the slums. The principal passage from which Eliot took imagery for his poem reads, in Laurence Vail's translation, as follows:

At noon, in the hotel room of the rue Chanoinesse, a grey and dirty light filtered through the grey curtains and dirty panes of the window . . . and there was the unmade bed where the two bodies had left their impress of brownish sweat upon the worn sheets—this bed of hotel rooms, where the bodies are dirty and the souls as well.

Berthe, in her chemise, had just got up. With her narrow shoulders, her grey shirt and her unclean feet, she too seemed, in her pale yellowish slimness, to have no light. With her puffy eyes and scraggly hair, in the disorder of this room, she too was in disorder and her thoughts lay heaped confusedly in her head. These awakenings at midday are heavy and sticky like the life of the night before with its love-making, its alcohol, and its torpid sleep. One feels a sense of degradation in thinking of the awakenings of former days, when ideas were as clear as if they had been washed by sleep. Once you have slept, my brother, you too will have forgotten nothing.[14]

From another of Philippe's novels, *Marie Donadieu*, Eliot drew further inspiration. The sordid connotations of the third "Prelude" are explained by Philippe's preoccupation with streetwalkers. Marie Donadieu herself is not much better than Berthe; it is Marie who, strolling on the pavements, has

> . . . such a vision of the street
> As the street hardly understands.[15]

To both novels Eliot owed much of the atmosphere found not only in "Preludes" but in "Rhapsody on a Windy Night"—the down-at-heels, almost sinister atmosphere of a meaningless society, very different from the more polite and less sullied air of Boston described, a few years later, in "Aunt Helen" and "The *Boston Evening Transcript*." In composing the fourth "Prelude," he may have remembered from *Marie Donadieu* a description of Marie's lover, Raphaël, smoking his pipe.[16]

The "Preludes" are better unified than Eliot's method of composing them might seem to have permitted. Indeed, the first and second, written in close succession, not only complement each other but together lead into an epistemological concept entertained in the third and fourth; and all four agree in imagery. They illustrate a practice tested in "Prufrock" and followed again in the "Rhapsody," namely, of depersonalizing character by talking about bodily members such as feet, hands, eyes, fingers. Eliot's imagism was of his own contriving, for he was not in touch with the contemporary experiments of T. E. Hulme and F. S. Flint. The first "Prelude" begins with winter nightfall in an urban back street; from indoor gloom and the confined odor of cooking it moves outside into the smoky twilight where gusts of wind whip up leaves and soiled papers, and a shower spatters the housetops. Such adjectives as "burnt-out," "smoky," "grimy," "withered," "vacant," "broken," and "lonely" carry the tone. Reversing the direction, the second "Prelude" begins in the street, as morning (with a hang-over, one might almost say) "comes to consciousness" of stale-beer smells and coffee fumes; and the piece ends in contemplating house windows where, "With the other masquerades / That time resumes," hands are "raising dingy shades." The third "Prelude" exposes one of the "thousand furnished rooms" where a not overclean woman, sluggishly struggling awake and preparing to get out of bed, starts her own return to consciousness for resumption of life's masquerade. Since this masquerade (a "thousand sordid images") constitutes the woman's soul, just as in the fourth "Prelude" the transitory show of fingers, newspapers, and eyes constitutes the soul of the personified street, the hidden human reality it masks is itself neither soul nor "conscience" but a kind of register upon which the images have impinged as upon a *tabula rasa*. At the same time both woman and street are individual substances, so that each peculiarly registers the images they share. The woman can accordingly have "such a vision of the street / As the street hardly understands"—an intuition contrasted with the street's assurance "of certain certainties," equated somewhat ungrammatically in the fourth "Prelude" with a cocky masculine readiness "to assume the world." Woman and street alike are earthbound: she supine in bed, "he" trampled under foot; and in their hypothetical aspirations upward, when her soul's images flicker overhead and his soul is "stretched tight across the skies," they but mirror the degraded nature of their conscious selves.

Eliot's virtual repetition, in the fourth "Prelude," of the imagery from the opening lines of "Prufrock" supports this renewed treatment of the ideal and the actual or, rather, this review of the Prufrockian problem; for here his premise is not that these personages are spiritually superior to external actuality but rather that they have no images distinguishable from it. Prufrock, while cringing immobilized before the actual, does not relinquish the preferable ideal; but the woman and the street not only do not have any such ideal in reserve but, indeed, cannot have—for their consciousness and the external scene are identical. In other words, they cannot be, in the manner of Prufrock, romantic idealists because their consciousness embraces only what their senses can confront. There may be something illogical in Eliot's having endowed the woman with a "vision," though not if this means only experience or perception; clearly, while aware of the images making up her soul, she need not divine her lack of images more attractive.

One may surmise a partial debt to Bergson, whom Eliot had been reading at Paris. In Bergson's *Matter and Memory* an "image" is indifferently definable as a perception or as the perceived thing itself, so that subject and object merge. The perceiver, by coming into contact with the material world, absorbs images into his consciousness, where they persist as memories. In the aggregate, memories thus form a *durée,* considered by Bergson to be creative, since, as he explains in *Creative Evolution,* they affect the perception of things in the perceiver's future. Eliot's poem, however, holds up to view a set of images so disagreeable, or at any rate so empty of charm, that an optimism like Bergson's must appear implausible: what vital impulse can animate either the woman or the street, however impatient for creative action, if the consciousness of each is downtrodden and spiritless? Thus the fourth "Prelude" turns to pity, to a "notion of some infinitely gentle / Infinitely suffering thing" incarnate in these depersonalized images and, therefore, in the souls comprising them. But at once it shows cynical revulsion from sentimental fancies ("Wipe your hand across your mouth, and laugh"), as much as to say that such an existence is contemptible.

> The worlds revolve like ancient women
> Gathering fuel in vacant lots.

The plight of the woman and of the street collectively—the people whose souls are mere congeries of fugitive appearances—points up the meaninglessness of the universe, no living entity proceeding by instinct toward an appointed goal but a worn-out mechanism with parts stiffly toiling as, without destination, it moves in endless epicyclic paths. And yet, of course, this closing image intensifies that pity against which the spectator has been warned. For the "ancient women" are not to be derided; if perhaps in one moment they seem ludicrous, they seem in the next distressed with the bleakness of destitute old age, ignorantly condemned to privation. With the pathos of "brightness falls from the air," there lingers in the poet's mind the memory of an ancient golden age. Seeing the world as tragic in its very meanness, he manages to suggest, in retrospect, some pity even for the woman and the street.

"Rhapsody on a Windy Night" (1911) has a similar theme as well as some of the same origins. *Bubu de Montparnasse* provided again the atmosphere of loneliness, demimondaine sterility, and cultural desolation. Eliot's spectacle of a young man alone in a metropolis, where prostitutes solicit custom in the streets, reflects approximately the world of Philippe. The memories, the sight of street-lamps in iron rows, the glimpse of a woman in a doorway, the awareness of smells— all came from the novel; and though some Laforguian diction and lunar imagery went into the making of the poem, along with a personal recollection since mentioned by Eliot in *The Use of Poetry*, it depicts the Paris of Bubu and Berthe.[17] *Marie Donadieu* appears to have furnished the "Rhapsody" with a modification of the phrase "des odeurs de filles publiques mêlées à des odeurs de nourriture"[18] ("Smells of chestnuts in the streets, / And female smells in shuttered rooms"). A less recondite source, Oscar Wilde's "Ballad of Reading Gaol," along with a Laforguian geranium image, seems to have inspired Eliot's lines about a madman. Wilde had written:

> But each man's heart beat thick and quick
> Like a madman on a drum![19]

Beyond the sources of imagery there remains the Bergsonian philosophy which may have influenced the rationale of the poem. The "lunar incantations," or nocturnal voices that in the "Rhapsody" ensorcell the stroller's midnight ramble while the moon hypnotizes the deserted street, are Laforguian; but the dissolution of orderly thought into an irrational, almost surrealistic collage of discontinuous mental impressions obeys the laws of instinctive consciousness according to Bergson. Mingling as fluid perceptions, kaleidoscopic images pour into memory, the organ of time, the "floors" of which break down to enable their total synthesis. This dreamlike process, the quintessence of the nonintellectual, works by free association rather than by logic. From the meanings borne by the word "rhapsody," the reader of this poem might pick out several appropriate to an understanding of its title; perhaps the most suggestive meaning is the musical one, implying here the irregularity and diversity attendant on the principle of association. On the other hand, Eliot's images are not altogether random.

The "Rhapsody" has for speaker a man who, experiencing a "vision of the street," soliloquizes in response to visual images. His is the consciousness, corresponding to that of the woman in the "Preludes," which marshals the flickering images into a pattern of subjective *durée*. In the poem there is also, it is true, a clock-time structure (or, as Bergson would say, a "spatial" structure), divided by the hours announced at the beginning of the strophes—"Twelve o'clock," "Half-past one," and the rest. This structure is spatial more particularly because the times are synchronized with the speaker's pauses at street-lamps. But as each lamp mutters an "incantation" to direct his gaze toward new spatial images, these pass into his memory and unite with memories already there to make up subjective time where space is non-existent. The rhapsody of consciousness moves like a musical composition by introducing, abandoning, and returning to set themes scattered in time. Among its recurrent motifs are *irrationality* (the dissolving of "divisions and precisions," the madman shaking the geranium, the lapping tongue of the cat, the automatic gesture of the child, the vacancy behind the child's eye, the instinctive reflex of the crab, the moon's loss of memory) and *decay* or *inanimation* (the dead geranium, the pin, the twisted driftwood and the rusty spring, the mechanical toy, the paper rose, the reek of airless places, the bed waiting for its occupant). Depressing images besiege the speaker's consciousness, for he cannot evade them: what is more dismaying, they constitute his soul, for he is similar to the woman in the third "Prelude." It is not surprising therefore, in view of the "Preludes" and "Prufrock" as well, that the "Rhapsody" ends bleakly. The withdrawal of the speaker into his solitary room, as the last lamp shows him the way, furnishes no escape from a world within. "Memory!" the lamp reminds him: "You have the key"; and memory *is* the "key" to the imprisoning life for which his repose shall prepare—not the memory of what the intelligence can learn, like the number on the door, but the memory of what arbitrarily exists, the unalterable reality. And so the pity that in the fourth "Prelude" can be diverted to the slums and their creatures comes back to the poet, or to the mask through which he speaks, in the shape of terror for his own trapped human situation, and the knowledge pierces him with a "last twist of the knife."

Although the "Preludes" and the "Rhapsody" may deserve a less Bergsonian reading, the philosophical gloss is useful to suggest how thoroughly, both then and later, Eliot has considered the problem of relating consciousness to externality; obviously he was at odds with Bergson from the outset. Nor does such a reading obscure the similarities between these poems and the "Portrait" and "Prufrock." As has already been observed, the themes of dejection in solitude and grief for the unattainability of an ideal are common to Eliot's early work; the "Bergsonian" poems differ thematically from the others in their implicit doubt whether ideals are valid at all. They do not in this regard, like the "Portrait" and "Prufrock," point the direction of Eliot's subsequent work. They resemble the two longer and more dramatic poems in analyzing the plight of the isolated heart. The Laforguian influence, on close examination, does not appear dominant in Eliot's better poems of this period, in spite of its importance to his colloquial style and use of irony. The memorable thing is rather a psychological method that one might ascribe to a close study of Henry James, a study which could have affected, as strongly as imitation of Laforgue, the dramatic organization of Eliot's verse. Where this method is eclipsed, as in the "Preludes," the influence is as likely to have come from Dostoevsky, Philippe, or Bergson as from Laforgue, though certainly wherever the speaker in a poem serves as his own detractor one may suspect that Laforgue gave the cue. Geraniums aside (and the infirm moon), the peculiar vocabulary of Laforgue shows up more in the Eliot of half-a-dozen years later. Yet to detect Laforguianisms in the "Prufrock" period is easier than to identify Eliot's largely imaginary debt in that period to the metaphysical poets of the seventeenth century, sometimes ranked with Laforgue as significant models. Laforgue, in fact, decisively influenced one minor, not to say trumpery, poem besides the three printed in the *Harvard Advocate*. This was "Conversation Galante," a variation on Laforgue's "Autre Complainte de Lord Pierrot."[20]

The "Conversation" is a poem of seriocomic banter: a young man of rapid wit engages the attention of an extremely bewildered lady with playful poetic speculations on the moon as "Prester John's balloon" or as a misleading "old battered lantern"—an imaginative exercise which she does not follow. More soberly, and by way of a new start, he next essays to spiritualize his poetic mood; but when, attributing his own "music" to a superior Muse, he speaks of "Someone" who

> frames upon the keys
> That exquisite nocturne, with which we explain
> The night and moonshine; music which we seize
> To body forth our own vacuity,

she bridles slightly or is puzzled at the last word: "Does this refer to me?" Hastily he assures her, with mild irony: "Oh no, it is I who am inane." Then, to comment on her utterly blank, indeed crass, failure to co-operate, he characterizes her in a polite lecture as "the eternal humorist" because she will not countenance his poetic fancies. The implicit reasoning is sheer paradox: since her literalness makes her confute his "mad poetics," she is the "enemy of the absolute," which (in a metaphysician's sense) he has just suggested is the ground of art; and if she opposes the absolute, she is a humorist because she must embrace the mutable. To cap this perfection of ironic reversal, she ends by again objecting: "Are we then so serious?"—confirming that in his terms she is, though still unconsciously, "the eternal humorist." He seems to her to have modified his "fantastic," "vagrant," "inane," "mad" position by becoming critical and to have thus adopted undue seriousness. Her protest, betraying the eternal feminine spirit of contradiction, is a shift on her own part which proves his argument true. Poor lady! The poem was probably not worth including in Eliot's collected editions; its excessive difficulty does not hide its insignificance. But those who admire Laforgue find it successful.

"La Figlia che Piange," usually interpreted as the description of a lovers' parting, has a known origin helpful in surmounting its perplexities. While Eliot was traveling in Europe in 1911, he visited a museum in Northern Italy possessing a *stele* designated, according to a friend who suggested that he take a look at it, "La Figlia che Piange" ("young girl weeping"). For some reason, when he searched for this tablet he was unable to find it.[21] The subject of his resulting lines being nameless, he understandably in reprinting the poem used as an epigraph the phrase from Aeneas' address to Venus: "Maiden, by what name shall I know you?" (*Aeneid* i. 327). The girl depicted on the grave-monument should presumably be visualized as a conventionally sculptured libation-bearer in a posture of sorrow. This much being clear, it is nevertheless probable that in the imaginative drama of the poem the girl is real; it is difficult to see here any trace of the original conception. But the detail of Eliot's having failed to see the *stele* has a certain importance. In the poem there are three personages: the girl, the man who leaves her (the "lover"), and the poet himself, in whose mind the parting assumes dramatic intensity. Now the clue of the *stele* incident should be considered together with the fact that one of the Laforguian devices involves doubling the poet's personality. Here the lover, so-called, is the poet's own self (on the evidence of the poem's genesis) in his imaginary parting from a girl whose attitudes and gestures he, as director of the scene, is trying to fix in dramatic form. Thus he bids her,

> Stand on the highest pavement of the stair—
> Lean on a garden urn—
> Weave, weave the sunlight in your hair,

and then declares in explicit terms,

> So I would have had him leave,
> So I would have had her stand and grieve.

The situation reveals that there never was any such event; that the poet is simply making it up. When he affirms his poetic role by saying,

> I should find
> Some way incomparably light and deft,

he is talking about precisely this creative process, the act of inventing a leave-taking, but he is also talking about the way which he, in the role of the lover, should find to bid farewell. A cruel way, unhappily, "Simple and faithless as a smile and shake of the hand." (This is an echo of Laforgue's "Pétition": "Simple et sans foi comme un bonjour.") Though the poet goes back to the dramatic moment to remark, "She turned away,"[22] he is presently musing again on "how they should have been together," the topic engrossing him. But he ends with a Laforguian shrug, implied in his use of the word "cogitations" for his quasi-sentimental thoughts.

This much-praised poem unquestionably meant a good deal to Eliot, in view of his having assigned it the terminal position in his first collected volume. And it is among the best of the shorter pieces. Its tone will recall "Portrait of a Lady" and the relationship set forth there. The influences bearing upon it were various: Rossetti's "The Blessed Damozel" and, very likely, too, some characteristic imagery and romantic postures from Tennyson's *Maud*.[23] From Laforgue, Eliot drew not only the trick of doubling but the apologetically ironic manner at the close. One would not, however, call the poem an imitation; and the surest testimony to the significant influence exerted by Laforgue on Eliot lies in just this casual introduction of irony where the incidents are not peculiarly Laforguian—an effect instanced by the Prince Hamlet passage of "Prufrock." Laforgue acted as a stimulus to Eliot's verse rather than as a consistent model; it was Eliot's practice to emulate more often than to imitate, and he did so to more enduring profit.

The principal poems of Eliot's early twenties established a standard of theme and method by which his later efforts are measurable. The clichés about his impersonality and classicism are all sterling on the outside, but they have a core of pewter. Naturally no young writer who esteemed Laforgue could be initially free of sentimentality or could seem to be—unless it be a quibble to argue that Laforgue's affectation of antiromanticism was itself romantic. Eliot learned from Laforgue some sensible techniques for disguising ordinary romantic material. It is unlikely that Eliot could have foreseen the question whether these techniques expressed or concealed a point of view or in what proportion they did each. He wrote as he could, and learned by doing. But he had preoccupations none the less romantic for his elaborate cloaking of them. They amounted to more than disgust at the futilities of urban life; the clutter of drawing-room and dustbin, a scornful substitute for the pretty-pretty, was only the apparatus, or as someone has aptly called it, the décor, of Eliot's early poems. Squalor itself was not his bane; he did not aspire to found a "junkyard" school of poetry. What perturbed him was the helplessness of sensitivity and idealism against matter-of-factness. Playing, nevertheless, at man of the world, he adopted a satiric defense, and he did not give it up until, writing "Gerontion," he finally abandoned the manner of Laforgue.

But in some of the poems written between 1915 and 1919, without quite vindicating the shyness deplored in "Prufrock," he was to suggest, in effect, that the Prufrockian "spiritual" temperament is the victim not only of itself but of the aggressive crudity of its opposite. He wagged his head over shocking sensualists like Sweeney and Mr. Apollinax. The Prufrockian temperament, however, does not come off well when put alongside the champions of fleshly joy; and they, in turn, are scarcely annihilated at the satirist's hands, or, if done in at last, as Sweeney is, they fall in the pathetic likeness of Prufrockian tragedians. In general they survive better than Prufrock; and, being as much poetic masks as he, they appear to be treated tolerantly if not respectfully. There results a kind of deadlock between moral indignation at brassiness and admiration for vitality. In "Mr. Eliot's Sunday Morning Service," for example, Sweeney fares much better than Origen, the Prufrock of the moment, though neither is the whole man who, in the world of that poem, should be compounded of both. Although the poems of the second period are nothing for Eliot to be proud of, and form (one had almost said "articulate") the skeleton in his poetic cupboard, they help one to understand *The Waste Land* and poems later still. They present the clash between the fleshly and the spiritual, the antinomies of sex and love. If arranging a happy marriage of these two was at length to be a fruitless task, it was worth while for Eliot in the meantime to speculate on the ironies of the conflict.

# 3 DEBATE OF BODY AND SOUL

For three years after 1911 Eliot wrote almost no poetry. Although he is said to have preserved a few drafts of verse dating from that period, or at any rate from 1909–17, these have not been published and have been inaccessible ever since he turned them over to the New York book-collector John Quinn in 1922 or thereabouts. About 1913 a piece called "The Ballade of the Outlook" was seen by Conrad Aiken. For critical purposes, there is a gap, except for the trifling "Ballade of the Fox Dinner" (1909), from "La Figlia che Piange" to the poems of 1915. After completing his graduate studies at Harvard and going abroad for the second time, Eliot began to investigate new techniques of composition under the stimulus of Ezra Pound; but the first products of that association, included in *Prufrock and Other Observations* along with his previous work, were unimportant. The earliest of these, "Morning at the Window," was inspired by the neighborhood of Russell Square, where Eliot stayed in the autumn of 1914. Having passed the summer in Germany, he went from Marburg to London after the declaration of war and, before removing to Merton College, Oxford, lodged for a time at 28 Bedford Place. From there he wrote his brother, Henry Ware Eliot, on September 8, 1914, a letter referring to the street before the house, to an old woman who had sung "The Rosary" for pennies, and to a housemaid engaged in conversation at the area gate. The poem may date from the following year. "Morning at the Window" tries to recover the atmosphere of "Preludes" and the "Rhapsody"; its vocabulary is similar, but the effects are inferior owing to the imprecision of its verbal conceits. The image of the housemaids' "damp souls," being barely plausible (the unfortunate sound of the phrase had best be ignored), detracts from the visual accuracy of "sprouting," which has a fungoid connotation

30

appropriate to "basement kitchens." On the other hand, "An aimless smile that hovers in the air / And vanishes along the level of the roofs" is inept, not because the smile is torn away by the fog (the Cheshire Cat apparitional quality is good), but because in relation to the speaker "the level of the roofs" is undefined.

This was the first poem in which Eliot showed any indebtedness to Ezra Pound, if its slight resemblance to "Les Millwin" can be called that. Pound thought so, for he remarked in a letter to Marianne Moore in 1918 that Eliot "first had his housemaids drooping like the boas in . . . 'Millwins,' and it was only after inquisition . . . that he decided, to the improvement of his line, to have them sprout."[1] Pound had forgotten that the Millwins' souls were "lying." Actually the text of "Morning at the Window" published in *Poetry* (1916) describes the housemaids' souls as "hanging," so that the line underwent at least two revisions. Few other passages in Eliot's work have a direct relation to Pound's own.[2] He first visited Pound on September 22, 1914 (Pound wrote to Harriet Monroe later the same day that he thought Eliot had "some sense"),[3] and was under his close critical surveillance off and on until after 1921, when Pound settled in Paris. Pound it was (after Aiken's negotiations with Austin Harrison and with Harold Monro failed) who spent six months persuading Harriet Monroe to publish "Prufrock" (for which she paid Eliot eight guineas) and who, with John Gould Fletcher, deserves credit for its coming into print in *Poetry* (1915).[4] Miss Monroe objected to the Laforguian Prince Hamlet passage, surviving from Eliot's earliest draft, and to the over-all Jamesian manner of the poem.[5] Except for a possible echo of "The Age Demanded" from "Mauberley," in Part II of "Burnt Norton," an obvious echo of "The Return" in Part V of "Little Gidding," and a few other reminiscent lines, Eliot has seldom imitated Pound.

Other poems written in 1915, "The *Boston Evening Transcript*," "Aunt Helen," "Cousin Nancy," and "Mr. Apollinax," recall Pound faintly, but "Portrait of a Lady" also is satirical; Eliot did not need Pound to teach him satire. These studied ironies were evidently aimed at particular people, and one would not have to look far for the possible origins of names like "Ellicott" and "Slingsby." The latter occurs also in Edward Lear.[6] The poems contain an element missing from those of the Laforguian period—a kind of levity like Pound's own in such poems as "The Bath Tub" and "Phyllidula." The device of bathos, exemplified also in the opening lines of "Prufrock," is typical

of Pound's work in *Lustra;* with Eliot it becomes prominent in poems
depending on ironic contrasts:

> Wakening the appetites of life in some
> And to others bringing the *Boston Evening Transcript.*

> Now when she died there was silence in heaven
> And silence at her end of the street.

> Matthew and Waldo, guardians of the faith,
> The army of unalterable law.

The trick (superimposed in the first instance upon a rhetoric imitated
from Baudelaire's "Recueillement") becomes magnified through literary allusions. "Silence in heaven" (Rev. 8:1) and "The army of unalterable law" (Meredith's "Lucifer in Starlight") contrast the important with the trivial: the apocalyptic with the departure of an apparently garrulous old lady who, with her parrot, might have originated in
the pages of Flaubert's "Un Coeur simple"; and (by satiric climax in
this case) the everlasting with the oblivion of two neglected heretics.

"Mr. Apollinax" is not only a longer poem but a more energetic one.
Eliot aimed this satire at Bertrand Russell, under whom he had studied
at Harvard in the spring of 1914. Russell and Eliot first met at a tea in
the mansion of Mrs. Jack Gardner, where a certain Harvard professor
of literature or rhetoric was also present with his wife. Two years later,
on better acquaintance, Russell was to describe Eliot as his best
Harvard pupil.[7] In "Mr. Apollinax" Eliot's wit is so mercilessly cut-
ting that the subject (described as ebulliently vigorous) appears the
more foolish the more he is mythologized. The techniques of exaggerative contrast, Eliot's stock in trade for the next few years, found here
their ideal material: an apparatus of mythical figures to be ranged
against a modern one—with damage to both. Mr. Apollinax is thus
deflated through an incredible identification with Priapus, with the old
man of the sea, with a faun (who is hardly of marble), and with a
galloping centaur; and, yet, he thereby acquires a quasi-supernatural
character which must be humbled by the image of the foetus and of the
head grinning like John the Baptist's in Laforgue's "Salomé," and by
the remark about unbalance. The eeriness of this character, however,
tends to dominate the portrait, and the laughter of the poet, though
fortified with moral disapproval, is rather like that of Mr. Apollinax
himself, not only unbalanced but a little hysterical. As matters turn out,
the poem most nearly demolishes Mrs. Phlaccus and the Channing-

Cheetahs, who are drearily genteel. Mr. Apollinax, a blend of Apollo and Apollyon, is Dionysian rather than Apollonian.[8] As Priapus, he is the opposite of Fragilion, who, lurking shyly somewhere among birch trees, sounds thin, graceful, and pale, and who has affinities with the reticent speaker's own Prufrockian sensitivity. This sensitivity is typi-fied further by the "worried bodies of drowned men"—an image which, as E. J. H. Greene has shown, came to Eliot from Rimbaud's "Bateau ivre."[9] The juxtaposition of flesh and sentiment is reminiscent of Prufrock's debate between action and suffering. "Mr. Apollinax" allows one to laugh at both values. Eliot, when he wrote the poem, had probably seen Gaudier's fine phallus-shaped, and hence Priapean, marble of Ezra Pound, which was then on Ford Madox Hueffer's lawn at Notting Hill and which Pound was much later to take away to Rapallo.[10] The epigraph, from Lucian's "Zeuxis or Antiochus," Eliot had found as a quotation in Charles Whibley's *Studies in Frankness*.[11] It implies here simply that any novelty, however ridiculous, will draw a crowd. In "Hysteria" (1915), also concerned with laughter, there is none of the implicit Laforguian self-detraction, but there is an exposure of the speaker's own excitability. It is he, not the lady, who is hysteri-cal: "I decided that if the shaking of her breasts could be stopped, some of the fragments of the afternoon might be collected, and I con-centrated my attention with careful subtlety to this end." This piece of prose induces by its concluding sentence a kind of horror not wholly relieved by the reader's hope that perhaps the situation is funny after all. "Mr. Apollinax" remains humorous rather than perturbing.

Besides those already enumerated, Eliot wrote another poem before 1917, never intended for publication. "King Bolo and His Great Black Queen," a ballad he may have started about 1911, or perhaps later, and which he kept expanding for several years (Pound wondered ribaldly, in one of his letters to Eliot about *The Waste Land*, whether Eliot should show the poem to James Joyce), was *risqué*.[12] Eliot has reserved comment on it except to say darkly that King Bolo and his Queen were friends of Christopher Columbus. A great deal of light verse has come from Eliot since that time, including *Old Possum's Book of Practical Cats*; some miscellaneous verses, in assorted lan-guages, in *Noctes Binanianae* (1939);[13] *A Practical Possum* (*ca.* 1937); and an unpublished draft of a comic poem about a pig named, like a character in *Nicholas Nickleby*, Mr. Pugstyles. At Harvard there is a typewritten copy of this last effusion with the holograph of "Usk"

(1934) on its reverse. The verses contain a parody of Wordsworth's "The Reverie of Poor Susan."

"The Death of Saint Narcissus" was submitted through Pound to *Poetry: A Magazine of Verse* in August, 1915, but was withdrawn after proof sheets were ready. It is virtually unknown but appears in Eliot's *Poems Written in Early Youth*, privately printed at Stockholm in 1950. Eliot must have written it in 1915, by which time he would have read Pound's *Ripostes*, which had appeared in 1912 but to which Eliot probably paid little attention until he met Pound two years later. *Ripostes* contains "The Seafarer" and "The Return," both subsequently praised by Eliot, as well as two poems influencing "The Death of Saint Narcissus": Pound's "A Girl" and T. E. Hulme's "Conversion," the latter printed together with four other poems in an appendix as "The Complete Poetical Works of T. E. Hulme." Eliot's poem, an alternative title of which has been given by Aiken as "The Love Song of Saint Sebastian," is much longer than either of these; it comprises thirty-nine lines in a loose, irregular meter, unrhymed, and anticipating very roughly the kind of verse he later used in "What the Thunder Said." It is surprisingly close in diction to Hulme's "Conversion," which must have been fresh in Eliot's recollection. The hyacinths of Hulme have disappeared, or have been assimilated to the Narcissus of the title, but the walking, the cloth, the stifling, and the river are all present. Eliot was attempting to absorb the lessions of Imagism, whose prophet Hulme had been (his "Complete Poetical Works," which were not complete, had been written simply as models) and whose chief propagandist was Pound himself up to the summer of 1914. Eliot's use of Pound's "A Girl" was more incidental; he perhaps used also "The Tree," an early piece of Pound's published in *A Lume Spento* (1908). "The Death of Saint Narcissus" resembles "Conversion" in contrasting a joyous experience with what follows, but Eliot's poem does not end on quite so bitter a note of ignominy as Hulme's. In describing this experience, the speaker imagines a series of metamorphoses, one of them a tree metamorphosis like that of Pound's Daphne, but now recalled as something past. The lines introducing the metamorphoses form that is known to students of early Welsh and Irish bardic literature as an "I-have-been" sequence, with the difference that here the third person occurs instead of the first. The poem is also interesting for the several lines which after extensive revision have appeared in later works by Eliot. Its opening lines approximate to the passage about the shadow and the rock in *The Waste Land,* and it contains certain phrases reappearing in "Gerontion," *Ash Wednesday,* and elswhere. The metamorphoses somewhat resemble those in one chorus of *Murder in the Cathedral.* The poem seems unrelated to Paul Valéry's treatment of the Narcissus theme, but it may have some source in Fokine's *Narcisse.*

Eliot's four collected French poems (1916–17) laboriously combine effects from old and new sources. "Le Directeur," a touchingly radical, or perhaps only humanitarian, view of the social gulf between the reactionary director of the *Spectator* and a tattered little girl who is standing in a gutter, is similar in subject, though not in manner, to Rimbaud's "Les Effarés." The short lines, though they plunge ahead more rapidly, and one might say with greater ferocity than Laforgue's, are perhaps ultimately traceable to the style of "Complainte du vent qui s'ennuie la nuit."[14]

In "Mélange Adultère de Tout" Eliot turned to the "Épitaphe pour Tristan-Joachim-Edouard Corbière, Philosophe: Épave, Mort-Né," from the opening line of which he took his title. The poem owes more to Corbière than this, however, for it duplicates with some skill one of his favorite devices, the catalogue of diverse or paradoxical qualities embodied in one man or several. "Le Renégat" has the most noteworthy example, though its speaker is a good deal fiercer and more versatile than Eliot's.[15] Eliot's imaginary African adventure in "Mélange" was perhaps owing to Rimbaud.

"Lune de Miel" and "Dans le Restaurant" develop in French an equivalent to Eliot's "free" verse in English.[16] The former, an idyll of two bugbitten honeymooners at Ravenna, attempts free alexandrines. Besides employing the ironic contrast between squalor and magnificence already used after a fashion in "Le Directeur," it invokes a contrast between splendor and cultural apathy, already suggested in "Cousin Nancy" and "Mr. Apollinax" but here for the first time integrated into the scene itself instead of being merely the subject of an external ironic comment. The church of Sant' Apollinare en Classe, a few miles from Ravenna, belongs to the incidents of a honeymoon tour by Baedeker; whereas Matthew and Waldo and the old man of the sea are not only intellectually but geographically irrelevant to the doings of Cousin Nancy or Mr. Apollinax. As in this poem, so in several to follow, Eliot silhouetted his characters against a scene with an internal contrast. "Lune de Miel," opposing the fleshly interests of the honeymooning couple to the spiritual values of the Sant' Apollinare and the inexpensive Milanese restaurant to Leonardo's "Cenacolo" ("Last Supper"), creates another debate between body and soul in which the values of "Terre Haute" seem to triumph. The diction of the poem is reminiscent of Corbière, as is the play on words in the opening bathos ("Pays-Bas" and "Terre Haute").

In "Dans le Restaurant" drowning becomes for the third time a symbol. The old waiter in the poem, remembering "un instant de puissance et de délire," when in childhood he took shelter with a little girl beneath a willow in the rain, blubbers as he recollects that he ran away when a big dog came bounding at them. His fear and cowardice call up in the mind of the narrator, a client in the restaurant, a thought of his own bitter past. The waiter is like himself in paying dear for experience. There rises the image of Phlébas, a Phoenician sailor, drowned in youth and borne away by the tides.[17] The tone, though the cadences recall Corbière, is like that of certain epitaphs in the Greek *Anthology*. But "Dans le Restaurant" is full of puns and ironies; for example, "les rides" are not merely smears or wrinkles but the ripples of waves stripping clean the sailor's bones, and "la salle-de-bains" anticipates the climactic image of the murderous sea. The closing lines recall ironically the sarcastic admonition to the waiter, as if to a fretful and bad-mannered child, to wipe the streaks of tears from his face; to pick his head clean with a fork;[18] and, lastly, to go take a bath. For the word "vautour," having already half-suggested "vautre" ("welter"), permits "décrasse-toi le crâne" to carry the full meaning of "strip the flesh from your skull," as a vulture would do. The vulture belongs with both the waiter and the narrator through its relation to the myth of Prometheus. Eliot in *The Use of Poetry* referred to Gide's *Le Prométhée mal enchaîné*, the source for the dramatic situation of "Dans le Restaurant." "As André Gide's Prometheus said, ... *Il faut avoir un aigle*."[19] In Gide, Prometheus brings his eagle into a restaurant, where he shows it to a *garçon*. It is a symbol for the secret obsessive agony of the artist, from whom only cruel suffering can exact his art. Gide's *garçon* has no eagle; Eliot's is provided figuratively with a vulture (an alternative tormentor of Prometheus)—the frustration symbolized by the child's flight from the dog.

The situation remembered in the first part of "Dans le Restaurant" is fairly close to an incident in Philippe's *Marie Donadieu*,[20] but its literary source, if it had one, is more likely to have been Rimbaud's

"Les Poètes de sept ans," in which, however, the scene is not rural.[21] The version of "Dans le Restaurant" printed in *Ara Vos Prec* (1920), moreover, lacks the line "J'éprouvais un instant de puissance et de délire" and has instead "Elle avait une odeur fraîche qui m'était inconnue,—" which corresponds to Rimbaud's "Remportait les saveurs de sa peau dans sa chambre." Only in Eliot are failure and shame paramount; in Philippe and Rimbaud there is neither dog nor terror. Eliot produced an echo of Rimbaud's "Le Coeur volé"[22] in the line "Je te prie, au moins, ne bave pas dans la soupe" and of Laforgue's "La Première Nuit"[23] in the phrase "vieux lubrique."

*Ara Vos Prec* contains one poem, too significant to be ignored, that Eliot will not allow to be reprinted. This, entitled "Ode," reflects the influence of Laforgue, though it dates from about 1919; it owes to Laforgue elements of its subject matter but little of its tone. Its freely grouped rhyming octosyllabics indicate the general influence of Gautier. Eliot drew upon Shakespeare's *Coriolanus* (Act IV, scene 5, lines 72–73) for his epigraph:

> To you particularly, and to all the Volscians
> Great hurt and mischief. . . .

He used Catullus' "Hymen o Hymenaee," which is related to one subject of the poem, made what seems to be an allusion to Whitman, and adapted a passage in *Macbeth*, "The deep damnation of his taking off" (Eliot said "cheap extinction") and one in *Julius Caesar*, "Now lies he there." The model for his concluding section was Laforgue's "Persée et Andromède."[24] "Ode" is a poem of twenty-two lines arranged in three sections, each introduced by a key word: the first by "Tired," the second by "Tortured," and the third by "Tortuous." In the opening section the subject is the decay of poetry: "The sacred wood" is silent, and the "profession of the calamus" is "retired." In the second, as in "Prufrock," the subject is the agony of love. There is an ironic contrast between the children in the orchard, singing, like Catullus' youths and maidens, a prothalamion (the line appears again with a slight change in "New Hampshire"), and a deflowered bride, degraded to a "succuba."

The first two sections have some relationship to Laforgue's poem "Cythère," with its "bois trop sacré."[25] "Cythère" is exceedingly cryptic, but what light it sheds on "Ode" reveals that Eliot's own sacred wood may represent a kind of Avalon as well as a grove of the Muses, from which, however, there are no voices disclosing its mysteries; the only voice sends a derisive laugh from underground, perhaps from hell. There rises the stench of a "mephitic river," an Acheron which should perhaps be a Hippocrene (the fountain of Pegasus) but which is "uninspired." When in the second section of "Ode" other voices are raised, they only celebrate the ugliness of sex. The third section of the poem seems to contrast with this ugliness the happy union of Andromeda and her transformed dragon, who, after the petulant departure of Perseus in Laforgue's story, make off together from her island prison. There is evidently also an allusion to the myth of Danae's shower of gold: here it is a "golden apocalypse," in the etymological sense of an "unveiling." Once more there is a debt to Laforgue, for Perseus, the son of Zeus and Danae, with his necklace of gold coins, carries a memento of his parentage. He, like the bridegroom in the second section of "Ode," is careful to adjust his hair, and it, too, is golden. How all these circumstances combine in "Ode" is a little perplexing. The tone in the final section is one of disappointment; there is some kind of supplementary contrast between the dragon as beloved by Andromeda and the dragon "indignant," in the spirit of the traditional myth, "at the cheap extinction of his taking off." The concluding image in this deliquescence appears to show him vanquished, like Coriolanus, Duncan, and Caesar, by the wounds of his struggle, and changed into a discontented constellation beneath Charles' Wagon.[26]

It is just as well to begin with "Ode" in considering Eliot's Gautier period, which followed his tentative experiments with original French verse and his brief flirtation with Imagism. In "Ode" one sees a liberal modification of Gautier's tetrameter line after Eliot became proficient in manipulating it; the influence of Gautier is casual and, like the influence of Laforgue here, somewhat anachronistic for Eliot. The poem is Eliot's nadir; mediocre as some of the quatrain poems are, they are all better than this. From 1917 to 1919 he based his technique more on Gautier than on anyone else. Pound having disastrously encouraged him to study Gautier's *Émaux et camées*, he set to work being amusing.[27] The future, when it thinks of Pound and Eliot, will not overlook certain paradoxes. Pound, the finest contemporary critic of texture in poetry, seems to have exerted an adverse influence on Eliot's work. It is difficult to entertain any doubt at all about the relative excellence of the two poets' writings between 1915 and 1921. Pound's "Homage to Sextus Propertius," his translations and variations in *Cathay*, the cantos published in *Quia Pauper Amavi*, and his "Hugh Selwyn

Mauberley" were superb, whereas Eliot's poems, except "Gerontion," were merely learnedly clever. Pound never wrote anything as good as "Prufrock" and "Portrait of a Lady," poems of Eliot's youth, or *Ash Wednesday* and *Four Quartets*, poems of Eliot's middle life, but at the time when he was trying to enlighten Eliot's benighted Muse with the borrowed radiance of Gautier, he himself was at a zenith of poetic talent that Eliot could then but dimly rival. It is true that Eliot, having lost his original facility, was obliged to learn his art again. But it is improbable that without Pound's approval he would have enameled it with such preciosities as clutter it in this period. His verse in quatrains is largely an exhibition of functional plagiarism, a triumph of mystification. For the epoch in which the two poets were most together, Pound may have the last word.

> All things are a flowing,
> Sage Heracleitus says;
> But a tawdry cheapness
> Shall outlast our days.[28]

Adopting Gautier's quatrain, Eliot used it in seven of the poems in *Ara Vos Prec*. At the same time he made another innovation by flaunting a quasi-scientific vocabulary that mimicked Laforgue and, to some extent, Rimbaud. Words like "anfractuous," "epileptic," "miasmal," "polyphiloprogenitive," "phthisic," "superfetation," "piaculative," "arboreal," "feline," and "polymath" are as bold as Laforgue's "syncope," "analyse," "mammifère," "téléscope," and "autochtone." "The Hippopotamus" (1917), evidently the earliest of these poems, is the only one adopting Gautier's quatrain with two rhymes; the rest omit rhyme in the first and third lines of each stanza, as in ballad measure. It is also closer in subject to Gautier than are the others, being obviously referable to "L'Hippopotame" in *Poésies diverses*.[29] But whereas Gautier compares himself to the hippopotamus in invulnerability and freedom, Eliot makes the animal represent the weakness of the natural man, lukewarm in religious zeal but more acceptable to God than a disingenuous episcopacy. The latter is, in effect, "the church of the Laodiceans"[30] to which, through his epigraphs, Eliot directs the message of St. Ignatius to the Trallians—to revere the deacons, the bishop, and the priests of the Church, without whom there can be no Church on earth. The hippopotamus is, so to speak, a Trallian; doubtless he has not obeyed the injunction of St. Ignatius. But how much more should the Church itself, lukewarm as it is, heed the word touching the very justification for its mundane presence. The hippopotamus, though perhaps quite cold in faith, has ultimately more favor with God than apathetic Christians who "can sleep and feed at once." The Church, if spiritually asleep, is incapable of good; the hippopotamus is awake at least part of the time, and, though capable of error, he is also capable of reform—he will even be welcome in heaven. Eliot transformed Gautier's pleasant comparison into a modern *Physiologus*, maintaining didacticism in irony. The poem defends the flesh against the strictures of the hypocritically austere and is thus the antithesis of "Lune de Miel"—though only approximately so, for here the issue is moral, and there it is mainly aesthetic. "The Hippopotamus" is a better poem than its immediate successors, for it is logically independent of specific literary sources; one does not need to recognize the echo of Cowper's *Olney Hymns*, or the possible relation of the imagery to "Lycidas" or to Bishop Bramhall's "Answer to the Epistle of M. de la Milletière."[31] Nor, though the connection, if any, is beguiling in view of Eliot's days at Lloyds Bank, does one need to remember Lewis Carroll's *Sylvie and Bruno:*

> He thought he saw a Banker's Clerk
> Descending from the bus:
> He looked again, and found it was
> A Hippopotamus:
> "If this should stay to dine," he said,
> "There won't be much for us!"

"Whispers of Immortality" (*ca.* 1918) is much more complex than "The Hippopotamus." Among other peculiarities the punctuation of one important stanza (the third) varies from edition to edition, so that there is considerable leeway among possible interpretations. *Ara Vos Prec* has no punctuation after "sense" and a comma after "penetrate"; *Poems 1909–1925* has a semicolon after "sense" and a comma after "penetrate"; and *Collected Poems 1909–1935* has a comma after "sense" and a semicolon after "penetrate." Eliot's last change may have been influenced by the commentary of William Empson in *Seven Types of Ambiguity* (1930). Certain facts about the poem are evident enough. It contains echoes of Gautier and John Webster, and, perhaps, of Donne. It forms a suspicious parallel with D. H. Lawrence's "Hymn to Priapus." The rhythm of "Grishkin is nice: her Russian eye . . ." comes from Gautier's "Carmen,"[32] and the imagery of the grave may owe something to his "Buchers et Tombeaux" and *La Comédie de la mort.*[33] The flowers growing from a skull derive from

Webster's *The White Devil* (Act V, scene 4, line 130). The juxtaposition of body and thought in Eliot's second stanza shows the ability for which, in his essay "The Metaphysical Poets" (1921), he was to extol Donne and his contemporaries—the power to "feel their thought as immediately as the odour of a rose." The absence of such ability in some later poets he deplored as "a dissociation of sensibility."[34]

One way of reading "Whispers of Immortality" is as a criticism of this dissociation.[35] Eliot in this poem contrasted the unity of thought and feeling in metaphysical poetry with the disunity of these elements in modern poetry. His device, moreover, was metaphysical wit, which he was much later to define, in his "Note on Two Odes of Cowley" (1938), as almost precisely what in "The Metaphysical Poets" he called "a direct sensuous apprehension of thought, or a recreation of thought into feeling." In the later note he was to emphasize "balance and proportion of intellectual and emotional values,"[36] found at their best, perhaps, in the metaphysical conceit.

"Whispers of Immortality," taking as its subject the "direct sensuous apprehension of thought," shows by a conceit (emerging no doubt from this same operation) how thought and the senses may be unified. The governing metaphor takes the intellectual knowledge of death as an instance of thought and the sexual embrace as an instance of sensory function. The poem becomes a statement about sex as a means of attaining this knowledge of death—a means only possible, however, to such a lusty age as the Jacobean. The initial observation that

> Webster was much possessed by death
> And saw the skull beneath the skin

makes the word "possessed" mean obsessed and, at the same time, embraced: Webster saw in the most intimate connection a reminder of the "breastless" and "lipless" dead. ("Death," in the seventeenth century, was frequently a sexual term.) Beneath the flesh the shape of death was visible. Marvell wrote, in "To His Coy Mistress,"

> The grave's a fine and private place,
> But none, I think, do there embrace.

Webster might feel this even when there was an embrace, and be conscious of the grave in the embrace. It follows therefore that the sexual act gave him an intellectual insight: it illuminated death. The living head could already be visualized as a skull buried in the earth:

> Daffodil bulbs instead of balls
> Stared from the sockets of the eyes!

Eliot's seventh and eighth lines supplement the previous stanza: a human being is a skeleton clothed in thought; moreover, lusts are produced and augmented by thought, twining about them like the roots of flowers in a skull.

If sex can paradoxically do the work of thought,

> Donne, I suppose, was such another
> Who found no substitute for sense,
> To seize and clutch and penetrate.

Sense, in the context, means a sensuality able to penetrate the mystery of sex and therefore of death; equally, it means an intellectuality able to penetrate the mystery of death and therefore of sex. But neither can thought assuage the lusts of the flesh nor the embrace of love allay "the fever of the bone," the longing deeper still. The ambiguity of lines 7–8 and 15–16, however, makes this reading inadequate: "dead limbs" are not necessarily bones of a corpse, now acquainted with the embrace of death itself, nor are they necessarily the bones of the living frame—they may be members covered with flesh devoid of sensation. To the impotent flesh no contact is possible, and hence "the fever of the bone," awakened by sensual imagination, causes an incurable torment. The stress has thus moved from the objective contemplation of bones and flesh to the assertion of what agony "our lot" must bear.

No matter which reading one adopts for the first part, the second half of the poem clearly depicts the flesh which might vouchsafe intellectual insight, but which the shy sufferer, even as Prufrock, must forego. Grishkin,[37] unlike "breastless creatures," has "a friendly bust" and catlike charm for the "Abstract Entities" circumambulating her— people like the archbishop in Gautier's "Carmen." If in the final lines "our lot" is taken to include Webster and Donne, then the statement recurs to Webster's vision of "the skull beneath the skin": to make love to Grishkin, who, after all, is also "dry ribs," is to learn the realities of death and the inadequacy of any embrace. If, more probably, it should be taken to exclude them because no contact like theirs is here possible, the lines make an ironic criticism of the earlier motives of the poem, which have sought in poets of the past, themselves long since "possessed by death," the scant comforts of a knowledge reached through the senses but transmissible only through the intellect. Webster and Donne, for their part, were able to learn through the senses a truth inseparable from physical experience; for they commanded the unity of thought and feeling.

The Church and Christianity, already assayed through the satiric didacticism of "The Hippopotamus," provided also the subject of "Mr. Eliot's Sunday Morning Service" (*ca.* 1918), which recalls Rimbaud's "Les Pauvres à l'église." In this poem of Eliot's there is not, any more than in "The Hippopotamus," a ribald or even scornful condemnation of Christianity; there is, however, a good deal of impatience with fruitless formalism. The epigraph, from Marlowe's *The Jew of Malta* (Act IV, scene 1, line 21) alludes to a scene in which Barabas the Jew and Ithamore his servant, themselves guilty of having just poisoned a convent of nuns, are reviling the morals of ecclesiastics. When the two friars, the "religious caterpillars," appear, Barabas, because they know of his crimes, offers to become a Christian, to do penance, and, what is more to their liking, to hand over his riches to them. Eliot's poem takes from this imbroglio a double hint: that the clergy (here presbyters) are insatiate of gain and that they are immoderate in their fleshly lusts. Being "Polyphiloprogenitive" they add by their marital conduct an ironic gloss to the words of Christ: "Suffer the little children to come unto me, and forbid them not." They are only too glad, moreover, to pass a gaping collection plate among the pews where adolescents, "red and pustular," are "Clutching piaculative pence." As they are likened not to caterpillars but to neuter bees, their proper reproductive function, that of conveying pollen of truth to their spiritually unfertilized parishioners, is thwarted by religious sterility.

Against them is set the physically sterile example of "enervate Origen," who castrated himself for pious reasons and who disseminated "polymath" spiritual doctrine—which is said to have denied, as if to rebuke the flesh, the bodily resurrection of the dead. In contrast both with the presbyters and with Origen stands the Word, the Logos. Eliot in his second stanza (intelligible as punctuated in the *Little Review*, where it was initially published with a comma after the first line) called the Word "Superfetation of τὸ ἕν," apparently in reference to a blasphemous canard that the Son, being coeternal with the Father, was superimposed upon His own prior existence in being also begotten. At any rate, the begotten of God might, in similar logic, be offspring from a sexual act; and surely through Christ's Incarnation God must have affirmed certain values of the flesh. Origen (a product of the Word doctrinally because his theological teachings constituted a reaction to Christ's own, and physically because Christ was the Creator) frustrated God's sexual affirmation not only by mutilating himself but allegedly by distinguishing between the eternal Word as consubstantial with God and the human Jesus as subordinately created by God—and in effect thus nullifying the mystery of Incarnation. Eliot's third and fourth stanzas, however, confute both the presbyters and Origen. The Word is neither a catchpenny commodity to be peddled by Pharisees nor an austere and intangible power to be disputed over. The human form of the Word made flesh, whose "unoffending feet" shine through the baptismal waters, puts such foolishness to shame.[38]

The second half of the poem returns to the "sapient sutlers" as they tread the church aisle while the youthful members of the congregation wait to atone, their faces being as far from immaculate as the soul of Barabas, and their own souls dim like weak ghosts. The irony of the sixth stanza is heightened by the allusion to Vaughan's "The Night," which, after remarking Nicodemus' visit to Christ under cover of darkness, ends with the paradox of God's darkness. Eliot's poem shows darkness of a different sort, wherein Christ's exhortation, to which Vaughan referred, to "be born of water and of the Spirit" (John 3), is patently ignored.

The seventh stanza, introducing the neuter bees whose "hairy bellies" spread pollen, "Blest office of the epicene," characterizes the work common to the presbyters and Origen. This is, namely, to pass as intermediaries between the stamen of the Logos and the pistil of humanity and thus (needlessly) achieve a union already consummated in the Incarnation. If the presbyters ignore the spirit as Origen rejected the flesh, both values being requisite, these functionaries and the misguided theologian alike betray their task. Eliot's verbal conceit, established upon a natural opposition between the masculine principle and the feminine or the epicene, was evidently adapted from Laforgue's "Ballade":

> Une chair bêtement staminifère,
> Un cœur illusoirement pistillé.[39]

The foregoing stanza leads up to the image in the closing lines, the hairy male shape of Sweeney in his bathtub. According to Conrad Aiken, the model for Sweeney may have been a Boston Irishman named Steve O'Donnell, who gave Eliot boxing lessons and once a black eye;[40] in the Boston directories published during Eliot's Harvard period was listed a Stephen O'Donnell, pugilist. Eliot, however, has called Sweeney a composite of several people, one of whom, if an excellent conjecture by Robert Payne is to be credited, may have been the fictional Sweeney Todd of penny-dreadful fame. Todd, the Demon Barber of Fleet Street, created by T. P. Prest in the 1840's, was a shock-headed villain in the trade of butchering his clients to make meat pies. Lowering them into the cellar through a trap door beneath his barber's chair, he converted them into veal to supply the pie shop adjoining.[41] Eliot's Sweeney, be it noted, wields a razor in "Sweeney Erect" and prates of cannibalism in *Sweeney Agonistes*. The present poem shows him as the human counterpart to Eliot's hippopotamus. He is the fleshly antithesis of Origen but lacks the hypocrisy of the presbyters. This fact, along with the aquatic inclinations he shares with the hippopotamus, allies him with the intermediate symbol—the baptism of Christ. Whereas both Origen and the presbyters have been pictured as diverging from the example of the Word, Sweeney, in caricature, emulates it. Rhetorically the stanza balances the phrases "shifts from ham to ham" and "controversial, polymath," which correspond roughly to the earlier themes of physicality and spirituality. Through Sweeney therefore the poem contrives, by means of the bath symbol, a kind of vindication of the brawny natural man, with his carnal appetites, against duplicity and asceticism. Unhappily, the poem is obscure, precious, and bombastic.

The most obvious fact about Eliot's best-known Sweeney poem, the Hogarthian "Sweeney among the Nightingales," written in 1918, is that it relates to the *Agamemnon* of Aeschylus.[42] The epigraph in Greek, "Alas, I have been struck deep a deadly wound," echoes Agamemnon's cry when Clytemnestra smites him. That Eliot's Sweeney has recently been shown taking a bath may have prompted this citation, for Agamemnon was murdered in his bath. The nightingales, however, migrated into Eliot's concluding stanzas from the grove of the Furies ("bloody wood") in Sophocles' *Oedipus at Colonus*.[43] Another epigraph, from the anonymous *Raigne of King Edward the Third* (Act II, scene 1, lines 109–10), was prefixed to the poem as published in *Ara Vos Prec*; it alludes to the Philomel myth: "Why should I speak of the nightingale? The nightingale sings of adulterous wrong."[44] According to F. O. Matthiessen, Eliot once said that "all he consciously set out to create in 'Sweeney among the Nightingales' was a sense of foreboding."[45] But if the foreboding is evident, not so the circumstances that give rise to it. In plot, setting, and characters this poem is opacity itself. Sweeney apparently is being threatened with violence by two women in a tavern or dive. Their motive is unknown, as is their identity, except that one of them is named Rachel (née Rabinovitch). Perhaps, in view of their informal behavior, they themselves are "nightingales"—in low slang, harlots. Besides Sweeney, six people are present, including the host and the waiter; but of these only a certain "silent man in mocha brown" smells out a conspiracy. Since nobody murders Sweeney in the poem, the foreboding is unrelieved save by the final imagery.

Several details suggest that the vague ominousness may be due to Sweeney's being asleep, witnessing the confusions of a disjointed nightmare. He, it is said, "guards the hornèd gate," the gate of horn through which from the classical underworld true dreams emerge. If he is dreaming of some dreaded misfortune, it may be that the concluding lines reveal its nature. The approaching disaster is possibly sexual. The fruits mentioned, as well as the activity of the man in brown, have sexual connotations,[46] and "the hornèd gate," in a vulgar sense, likewise reinforces the suspicion. The song of the nightingales, their "liquid siftings" staining "the stiff dishonoured shroud," recalls narratives with various sexual significance: the murder of Agamemnon by his adulterous wife (Eliot really brought in the nightingales from Sophocles by mistake); the adultery of Tereus and the metamorphosis of Philomel; and some such incident as that recounted of clandestine lovers in Boccaccio's *Decameron* (Day V, novel 4), where the joke turns on the indecent meaning of the phrase *cantar l'usignuolo* ("to make the nightingale sing"). Through the suppressed epigraph, the oblique allusion to the Philomel myth supports the theme of sexual infidelity and brutality implied in the reference to Agamemnon.

Many critics regard the poem as an implicit criticism of the modern world, a nostalgic rebuke to drab materialism in contradistinction to the vanished glories of a remote epoch when culture rested on ritual and religion, on piety and faith.[47] Others read the crucial last two stanzas not as a contrast between Agamemnon and Sweeney, the heroic and the ignoble, but as an identification of Sweeney with a heroic prototype—so that the analogy dignifies his dismal fate into tragedy.[48] Both interpretations are misleading in so far as they assume that the Agamemnon of the poem symbolizes untarnished grandeur. The second is the more accurate if it allows for the circumstances stimulating the comparison. For Sweeney and Agamemnon are alike, but only in shame: a dead lion is as truly carrion as a dead dog, and the dog, if that is any consolation to it, is most lion-like when both are dead. (By the same token, Sweeney in prosperity could best be assimilated to Agamemnon by a recital of their common defects. The tragedy in each case has arisen from a base intrigue among men and women; and Sweeney's disaster, whether actual or dreamed, resembles the death of a Greek princeling who was burdened with a hereditary curse and who was at the peak of form when adulterous, murderous, and proud.)[49] A natural difficulty with rejecting the interpretation as a contrast of persons is that in other poems Eliot put such contrast to use: "Mr. Apollinax" and "Mr. Eliot's Sunday Morning Service" illustrate the inveterate conflict between spiritual and fleshly man. But in "Sweeney among the Nightingales" Agamemnon does not represent the aesthetic values opposed, for example, to Grishkin in "Whispers of Immortality" or to Mr. Apollinax or Cousin Nancy. On the contrary, he and Sweeney are cast in the same mold: they suffer alike. Both somehow traduce the values, aesthetic or spiritual, of the pure song and the convent. With these values, therefore, they are contrasted jointly. And since it is the nightingales that are here figured as having befouled Agamemnon's corpse with an indifferent shower of bird droppings, the immortal song itself portends for Sweeney, as for the conventional hero, not merely catastrophe but humiliation. The tragedy of Sweeney is indeed devoid of glory if he can share with greatness only its pollution. Yet the tragedy draws from his identification with Agamemnon a pathos surpassing any that might result from a simple contrast of the two men.

"Sweeney Erect" (*ca.* 1919) has less horror but an amusing whimsicality. The epigraph from *The Maid's Tragedy* (Act II, scene 2) by Beaumont and Fletcher calls up a scene in which Aspatia is lamenting that her lover has abandoned her. Seeing the resemblance of her plight to that of Ariadne in a tapestry that her attendant women are weaving, she bids them use her as their model. She then strikes an attitude of grief and speaks the lines quoted at the head of Eliot's poem. "Sweeney Erect" has its own Aspatia, a nameless epileptic who has hysteria when Sweeney gets out of bed and starts to shave. (Here Eliot may have got a hint from Poe's "The Murders in the Rue Morgue," where the mischievous orangoutang, after watching its master shave, steals the razor and lathers its face in front of the mirror. That incident precipitates the murders. Sweeney, at least in this poem, if not in the background of *Sweeney Agonistes,* is somewhat milder.) The epileptic is compared with Nausicaa, and Sweeney with Polyphemus, to produce an incon-

gruous pairing, reminiscent of the adventure in which the worthy but
unclad Odysseus, creeping from the undergrowth, accosts Nausicaa
beside the sea. Being gross and unkempt, he, like the naked Sweeney,
is as awful as Polyphemus. Nausicaa, however, is not one for hysterics;
but surely Odysseus never looked so grim as Sweeney. (The description of the epileptic in Eliot's fourth stanza evidently imitates a passage in Shelley's *The Triumph of Life* [ll. 182–88]; the same was used
also by Beddoes.) "Sweeney Erect" succeeds in being ludicrous, not
because the past was glorious, but because the present is not. Since
Ariadne is a wronged damsel, like Aspatia, the joke of the poem is that
the ungainly Sweeney has the role of heartbreaker. For the rest, "Sweeney Erect" raises more than one grim note to subdue the humor: the
sharp razor, the epileptic, and Sweeney's callous and slightly malevo-
lent reaction. Mrs. Turner and the "ladies of the corridor" introduce
by their own dubious presence in the "house," a hint that propriety
may be not quite the usual commodity there at all. The poem, with a
sly reference to Emerson's "Self-reliance," maintains an almost exact
balance between mirth and repugnance.

"A Cooking Egg" (*ca.* 1919), written in the first person, presents
only two major difficulties. The first lies in the meaning of the title,
which seems to designate the speaker himself: he is an "old egg"—one
not quite gone bad but far from new—which had better be used for
cooking. The second lies in the identity of Pipit. I. A. Richards once
conjectured that Pipit, sitting at a distance, was an old nurse to whom
the speaker had sent *Views of the Oxford Colleges* as a gift when he
attended the University.[50] Edmund Wilson would have it that she was a
"very mild, dull spinster."[51] F. O. Matthiessen, on the other hand, rejecting both the hypothesis of Richards and an unlikely possibility
(which nobody else had publicly suggested) that Pipit was "the poet's
mistress," argued from her name that she was perhaps a little girl.[52]
Despite his moralizing about Richards' error, Matthiessen was wrong,
though, like Wilson, he was on the right track. The proper inference
seems to be that Pipit, who was once a little girl with the name of a little
bird, and whom the speaker remembers, no doubt, as a childhood play-
mate, is now, like himself, grown up; and he, at length having paid her
a visit, is now reflecting, perhaps in a restaurant, on the changes that
divide them. There is more than a physical distance between the two:
there is the distance of time; between childhood and maturity lie the
Oxford colleges and the years that a spinsterish habit of knitting im-

plies—the interval between the prime of their elders, in whose youth daguerreotypes were fashionable, and the present day of the poem. A lapse of, say, twenty years is sufficient for a man of thirty to feel hopelessly estranged from what was probably a sweetheart of his childhood. Eliot alluded therefore through his epigraph to another retrospection, that of François Villon, who at thirty had "drunk up all his shame,"[53] and who similarly was "a cooking egg." Following Villon's *Testament* and the whole *ubi sunt* tradition, he wrote:

> But where is the penny world I bought
> To eat with Pipit behind the screen?
>
> .    .    .    .    .    .    .
>
> Where are the eagles and the trumpets?

They are buried under mountains of snow that cannot melt away. The speaker is in the same position as the old waiter in "Dans le Restaurant." He is paying for experiences the penalty of regret for a moment of joy in childhood and the penalty of something like remorse for the intervening years. The "penny world," a treat to be shared with Pipit as if to signify the ease with which the great world itself should yield to "the eagles and the trumpets" of his triumphant maturity, has disappeared, bearing with it not only those dreams but the mirth and pleasure of the moment behind the screen. The screen, whether intentionally or not, serves to evoke the famous indiscretion which causes Voltaire's Candide to be expelled from Thunder-ten-tronckh castle. There, too, was an Edenic innocence soon to be spoiled (like an egg) by time. In place of innocence now are the middle-class neighborhoods of London, with "red-eyed scavengers" (reminiscent of Villon's career) and A.B.C. restaurants where one can get all that Pipit herself is prepared to offer—"buttered scones and crumpets."

Heaven itself offers no consolation for this loss of childish illusions. The middle stanzas of the poem enumerate in an ironic tone the delights the speaker has been deprived of—Honor, Capital, Society, Pipit herself. And, of course, these things have all been overrated, so that in the other sense of "want" he will not desire them. The imagined greatness and charm of the past, with the renown of heroes, financiers, "vampires," charlatans, and saints, have been choked by the smoke of the present. (Of the people mentioned, Sir Alfred Mond suggests money in gas and nickel; Madame Blavatsky, the occult sciences [her book *The Secret Doctrine* is full of sevens]; and Piccarda de Donati, the ascent of Dante into the first heaven of space [*Paradiso* III—a favorite canto of Eliot's]).

The third stanza was evidently in part suggested to Eliot by George Wyndham's *Essays in Romantic Literature*, which he reviewed in the *Athenaeum* the day after this poem was first published.[54] The fourth contains a parody of Rossetti's "The Blessed Damozel," which may have come into Eliot's mind because Rossetti had translated "The Ballad of Dead Ladies" from Villon's *Testament*.[55] And in the sixth, Pipit and the Blessed Damozel and Lucrezia Borgia become identified, according to Matthiessen, with Rose la Touche, whose death painfully affected Ruskin. Ruskin wrote to Susan Beever: "But Susie, *you* expect to see your Margaret again, and you will be happy with her in heaven. I wanted my Rosie *here*. In heaven I mean to go and talk to Pythagoras and Socrates and Valerius Publicola. I shan't care a bit for Rosie there, she needn't think it."[56] When at the end of this stanza the speaker turns away from his futile memories and prospects, it is with the feeling that

> What might have been is an abstraction
> Remaining a perpetual possibility
> Only in a world of speculation.

The theme of "A Cooking Egg" is the ravages of time and, as in "Prufrock," the disease of unfulfilled love. The "weeping multitudes" personate the whole world caught in the same trap.

The allusive technique in "A Cooking Egg" is simple in comparison with the extravagances of "Burbank with a Baedeker: Bleistein with a Cigar" (*ca.* 1919).[57] The underlying theme is similar in the two poems: a sad dreamer has lost his chance for love in a world where sensitivity is no match for hard fact. Neither poem deals, naïvely, with the decay of a glorious past but, like "Sweeney among the Nightingales," with the disparity between the way things are and the way an idealist thinks they might be. "Burbank" contains no literal opposition between childhood and maturity. Instead it stages, against a background of obsolete Venetian splendor—what Venice looks like in Burbank's Baedeker—a modern drama contrasting the higher and lower worlds of man coexistent in the setting. Burbank takes to himself the artistic and spiritual values; he is the appreciative embodiment of the enduring spirit whose works are catalogued in the guidebook. Bleistein, on the other hand, typifies the commercial travelers, loitering like rats, or like the peasants in a Piranesi etching, among the towering monuments of creative intellect. The Baedeker and the cigar, each carried in the hand, symbolize the antithesis between soul (and *esprit*) and lumpish, fleshly greed and gluttony. Burbank, having come to Venice, "descends" (in several ways) at a small hotel, meets a Princess, and "falls." Whether this means that he falls unwisely in love or that he fails sexually, the Princess obviously does not remain with him but presently turns for other company to Sir Ferdinand Klein, who has apparently made his money in the fur trade.

Princess Volupine, as her very title and name connote, unites the proud illusions of aristocratic Venetian *esprit* with the palpable delights of flesh. Like Margareen in *Finnegans Wake* she is the feminine fusion of masculine contraries—here Burbank and Bleistein. Burbank, in making advances to her, is in effect trying to appropriate this fusion, to become a whole man, or, in other words, to compound flesh with spirit. Perhaps he has received the name of the American botanist precisely because of his desire to hybridize. But wretchedly he is abandoned by Hercules, the patron of vigor, who is no respecter of aesthetics. And Princess Volupine, who, though phthisic and debilitated, requires more than the artistic and impractical love of Burbank, disappears into the arms of Sir Ferdinand, her masculine counterpart. Sir Ferdinand Klein is the mean between the extremes of Burbank and Bleistein just as in "Mr. Eliot's Sunday Morning Service" Sweeney is the mean between Origen and the presbyters. The Jew of Venice is a parody of the simultaneously real and ideal unity of two worlds; even his name is partly aristocratic and partly commonplace and "little."

This poem contains more quotations and functional allusions than any of comparable length that Eliot has published. The majority, beginning with those in the epigraph, pertain directly to Venice.[58] In the epigraph, moreover, there is a series of bathetic contrasts between gaiety and sobriety, dignity and lust, nobility and decline. First there is a quotation slightly varied from Gautier's "Variations sur le Carnaval de Venise": "Tra la, tra la, la, la, la laire!"[59] and then a sober reminder in Latin, from an emblematic candle with an affixed, inscribed banderole in Andrea Mantegna's third painting of the martyred Saint Sebastian (in a Venetian collection): "Nothing endures unless divine, all else is smoke."[60] The second contrast, between beauty and vice, takes a description from *The Aspern Papers:* "The gondola stopped, the old palace was there. . . . 'How charming! It's gray and pink!' "[61]

This, evoking through the plot of the novel certain memories of Byron and Clare Clairmont, prepares for the "goats and monkeys," which are from *Othello* (Act IV, scene 1, line 274) and which further suggest Shylock's "wilderness of monkeys" in *The Merchant of Venice* (Act III, scene 1, line 128).[62] The next phrase comes from Browning's "A Toccata of Galuppi's," also with a Venetian setting:

> Dear dead women, with such hair, too—what's become of all the gold
> Used to hang and brush their bosoms? I feel chilly and grown old.

Eliot's combination suggests that the charming palace is tenanted by people who behave like animals. The third contrast occurs between this and a quotation having nothing at all to do with Venice; the lines are simply the final stage direction in John Marston's *Noble Lorde and Lady of Huntingtons Entertainement of their right Noble Mother Alice: Countesse Dowager of Darby the first night of her honors arrivall att the House of Ashby*.[63] The masque is a typical sample of lavish Renaissance hospitality; but now the noble countess has "passed on" like the old lady in *The Aspern Papers*, and with her has departed the glitter as well as the decorum. The presence of Niobe, the bereft, recalls Byron's phrase "The Niobe of nations" in *Childe Harold* (IV, lxxix), where it is applied to Rome; Byron has a lament for fallen Venice in the same canto. Eliot's epigraph was perhaps intended mainly to bowl the reader over.

The initial stanza of the poem itself, summarizing Burbank's misfortune, has a line modified from Tennyson's "The Sisters": "They were together, and she fell." In a topsy-turvy world it is the man who "falls," taking the place of the earl's corpse in the poem by Tennyson. In the second stanza, since Burbank's failure with the Princess is a kind of death, "defunctive music," borrowed from "The Phoenix and the Turtle," blends with music in the air and under the earth, heard in *Antony and Cleopatra* by Antony's soldiers when Hercules, his ancestor, abandons him to his fate before the battle:

> 'Tis the god Hercules, whom Antony lov'd,
> Now leaves him [Act IV, scene 3, lines 15–16].

The reference to Hercules seems to have evoked for Eliot a passage in the *Hercules Furens* of Seneca:

> ubi sum? sub ortu solis, an sub cardine
> glacialis ursae?

which he has three times compared with one of his favorite passages
in Chapman's *Bussy D'Ambois:*

> . . . fly where men feel
> The burning axletree, and those that suffer
> Beneath the chariot of the snowy Bear . . . [Act V, scene 4, lines 104–6].[64]

And of course the horses are identifiable both with those of the solar
chariot and with those of Saint Mark's cathedral at Venice; Eliot's description also distantly recalls Kipling's "Ballad of East and West."
The burning sun merges with Cleopatra's barge in *Antony and Cleopatra:*

> The barge she sat in, like a burnish'd throne,
> Burn'd on the water [Act II, scene 2, lines 196–97].

There is at the same time a re-echo of "A Toccata of Galuppi's," already used in the epigraph: "Balls and masks begun at midnight, burning ever to midday. . . ."

Bleistein registers no feeling, as "protozoic slime" might well not,
for "a perspective of Canaletto." The declining candle seems to come
into the poem from Mantegna's "Saint Sebastian." In the sixth stanza
a reference to the Rialto brings in the atmosphere of *The Merchant of
Venice* to equate the commercial Jew with Shylock, and again recalls
*Childe Harold* (IV, iv).[65] Not to Burbank does the Princess Volupine,
going a-Maying after strange merchants, extend her favors; just as
Cleopatra entertained Antony, but not as the Lord and Lady of Hunt-
ington entertained the Countess Dowager, the foxy voluptuary with her
guest disembarks from a gondola and enters the old palace. Eliot again
imitated Gautier:

> L'esquif aborde et me dépose,
> Jetant son amarre au pilier,
> Devant une façade rose,
> Sur le marbre d'un escalier.[66]

She alights, but no cry for "light!" goes up as when the Moor took
Desdemona from her father. There are no Desdemonas in Venice, and
the old Venetian lion, as in Byron, is somewhat battered.[67] Indeed, as
Gautier says, the patron of modern Venice is the alley cat.[68]

It is his own withered power that Burbank meditates among un-
Spenserian ruins of time and shattered lamps of architecture. Precisely
like "the cooking egg," he has discovered the horrible cleavage between the sensitive, subjectively oriented mind and the ugly facts of

life. One cannot help thinking that the poem ends with an irony pointed at Burbank, and that Eliot, far from concocting a hypothetical superiority of the ideal to the real, here ridicules, in a manner similar to the "self-irony" of the Laforguian period, the limitations of the Prufrockian temperament. But Burbank has a plea. Even if the ruins of time crumble only within himself, he deserves that possible fusion of the real and the ideal esteemed only by the idealist. Whatever may be said for Sweeney, nothing whatever can be said for Princess Volupine. As to Bleistein and Sir Ferdinand Klein, they figure only as straw men. (The question whether "Burbank with a Baedeker" was anti-Semitic is obviously not a pressing one. It suffices to say that this poem, like "Mr. Eliot's Sunday Morning Service," is in execrable taste.)

In the poems of 1910–19, Eliot was exploiting—abusing—the trick of literary allusion; and by 1919 he had formulated a theory concerning tradition: that a poet should be aware, and utilize his awareness, of both his own age and the past and of the past as a present reality.[69] This theory was probably at bottom Bergsonian.[70] But the persistent thematic contrast, the great debate between the spirit and the flesh, showed Eliot's main preoccupation, with the idealist crushed alike by the ineffectuality of his idealism and by the feebleness of his capacity for the real.

# II  *1919–1926*

## 4 THE WORD IN THE WHIRLWIND: "GERONTION"

  In "Gerontion" (1919) an old man's lost power to love and his lost hope of spiritual rebirth create a symbol of sterility and paralysis. The poem, a monologue like "Prufrock," combines with a kind of stream of consciousness the technique of allusion, already used in "Burbank," which fulfils Eliot's idea of the historical sense in poetry. To make the past seem present, because the memory of it exists in the educated consciousness, and at the same time to exercise awareness of "contemporaneity," are the technical intentions of "Gerontion," which thus shows in large the practical application of "Tradition and the Individual Talent" (1917). In writing this poem Eliot drew upon Elizabethan and Jacobean dramatists, whose iambic-pentameter variations influenced his own verse just as the past influenced his contemporary subject matter. Like the verse, the meaning is modern but is not independent of tradition; it is reinforced with meanings transmitted from Eliot's sources.

  It is through the verse itself that Eliot's debt to tradition most obviously appears in "Gerontion." Apart from borrowed subject matter, the poem contains more verbal imitations of Tourneur, Chapman, Middleton, Shakespeare, and Jonson than is usually recognized.[1] Through sources affecting chiefly the rhythms of the poem, "Gerontion" anticipated the *pasticcio* method of *The Waste Land*. But for an even more important reason the earlier poem may be considered prefatory. A stream-of-consciousness technique, the device of rumination, is utilized, though differently, in both. When the apparently disorganized flow of reminiscence in the mind of a single character provides narrative content, the present, supplying a process of thought, interacts with the past, supplying objects of thought. Yet the present with its narrow and immediate circumstance and the past with its multiplex forms transcending time and space strive for dominance. A work of art mimick-

57

ing the flow of consciousness must somehow settle the conflicting claims of present and past. One extreme, typified by much of Joyce's *Ulysses*, emphasizes the time of reverie itself—the present. Another extreme emphasizes the past, the source of memories, and tries to relegate the active process of remembrance, and hence the present, to a subordinate function. It shows past events not as recollected by present consciousness but as recalled to become present themselves, even though only memories. The dichotomy of the mind thinking and the object thought of vanishes: the events themselves flood the reverie, and, as in Proust's *A la recherche du temps perdu*, the barriers of time dissolve.

The method of Joyce has the advantage of enabling apparent realism in the stream of consciousness as such, whereas *A la recherche du temps perdu*, in its effort to vivify the past, makes no attempt to duplicate the way in which the narrator actually thinks. But Proust's method was more suitable to Proust's intentions. He wished to give the partial illusion of a thinking process while preserving all the advantages of orderly reminiscence without the artificiality of a memoir. Bergsonian *durée* posits that, since the past endures through memory into the present, all direct perception is modified by the survival of earlier impressions. *Durée*, Bergson says in *Creative Evolution*, "is the continuous progress of the past which gnaws into the future and which swells as it advances."[2] There is thus, in fact, to the Bergsonian no purely present consciousness: most of what one imagines one sees as externality is really memory. Hence, what is called sometimes the Bergsonian confusion between the subject and the object is actually an identification, which justified Proust's exploration of memory to recover the past as the subject's conscious world.[3]

An analogous technique informs *The Waste Land*, where the time of every action is its apparent time, not as a memory but as an objective reality. The past is made to seem present. Yet the actions in the poem are still only memories in the mind of Tiresias, the Proust of this inquiry. And his reverie, like every true reverie, seems not chronological but kaleidoscopic. This is not to say that the poem lacks narrative unity or that the "music of ideas" makes up its only structure.[4] It is true that schematically *The Waste Land* is far from the reminiscence technique of, say, Conrad's "Youth," but Tiresias' stream of consciousness, thought by some critics to be merely fragmentary, is highly selective and even orderly: there is a chronology in the poem, just as there is in *A la recherche du temps perdu*, but it is a chronology of symbolic incidents. For the "music of ideas" in its purest form one must turn to the *Cantos* of Ezra Pound, which have no story, only the duration of ideas and images.[5] The focus there rests upon the act of remembering and not upon what is remembered. Eliot's "Gerontion" stresses remembrance, but *The Waste Land,* memories.

It was perhaps in response to *Ulysses* that Eliot in "Gerontion" applied the dramatic soliloquy to an old man's meditations on the past. The influence of Bergson, except through his effect upon Eliot's theory of the living tradition, is no more conspicuous here than in "Prufrock," though it remains latent despite Eliot's rejection of Bergson's philosophy.[6] Eliot went beyond Bergson in founding his theory of tradition upon a *durée* of the whole literary past, not merely upon the survival of personal experiences in memory. His description in "Tradition and the Individual Talent" of how a new work of art affects the "existing monuments" supposes, however, a concept of creative evolution for which Bergson, as well as Gourmont, may have been responsible.[7] He did not approach Jung's theory of a collective unconscious, and, indeed, he only broadened Bergson's idea of memory to include facts that are learned, which Bergson had excluded from the content of *durée* itself.[8] The stream of consciousness in "Gerontion" does not resemble the types used by Joyce; it is too closely allied to Jacobean rhetoric to reproduce the way the protagonist thinks. What matters is the method by which the tension between past and present is resolved, and in this Eliot followed Joyce rather than Bergson and Proust.

In "Gerontion," through his imitations of Jacobean dramatists, Eliot recaptured the tone of a surviving past. The poem resembles *Ulysses* in suggesting through its meaning that history endures, with all its catastrophe and sin, as a heritage of care. Gerontion's nightmare is much bleaker than that of the groping but confident Stephen Dedalus in Joyce's "Nestor" episode. Upon the old man here lies the burden both of his own sins and of those antecedent to them; in a sense he is history itself, just as he is the "decayed house" in which he sits waiting to die. The poem lacks the optimism of *durée:* the enduring past urges no vital evolution through a creative present and instead hugs a vampirish immortality into a dead future. As in "Nestor," the focus rests upon present consciousness, but the more Proustian technique of *The Waste Land* is foreshadowed when Gerontion explains himself to the reader. "Nestor" was one model for "Gerontion," and from it Eliot took several suggestions for the reverie. Not only Eliot's "Vacant shuttles / Weave the wind" (combining Job 7: 6–7)[9] but his scurrilous portrait of the Jew may owe something to *Ulysses*. Stephen's reply to Mr. Deasy could have contributed a phrase also to *The Waste Land:* "A merchant, Stephen said, is one who buys cheap and sells dear, jew or gentile, is he not?"[10] Eliot's Jew in "Gerontion," another Leopold Bloom (who may possibly be considered to have migrated here—his name prompting the Belgian associations?) may be linked with Christ, though sarcastically. In the poem it is "Christ the tiger" who visits His wrath upon the slothful and lukewarm, among whom Gerontion numbers himself; the image and the situation both recall James's "The Beast in the Jungle." (Whether in his choice of an epithet Eliot was inspired by "The Tyger" or by Jonathan Edwards' comparison of God to an angry wild beast, *Ulysses* seems to lend color to the conjecture that Eliot's phrase alludes partly to Blake, for Stephen thinks of Blake while sitting in the classroom, and there is a quotation from "Auguries of Innocence" a little later in the "Nestor" episode.)[11]

The practice of allusion, justified in "Burbank" by the need to characterize the tourist, performs in "Gerontion" the function of condensing into decent compass a whole panorama of the past. If any notion remained that in the poems of 1919 Eliot was sentimentally contrasting a resplendent past with a dismal present, "Gerontion" should have helped to dispel it. What are contrasted in this poem are the secular history of Europe, which the life of Gerontion parallels, and the unregarded promise of salvation through Christ. Gerontion symbolizes civilization gone rotten.[12] The mysterious foreign figures who rise shadow-like in his thoughts—Mr. Silvero, Hakagawa, Madame de Tornquist, Fräulein von Kulp—are the inheritors of desolation. Against them is set the "word within a word, unable to speak a word"—the innocent Redeemer, swaddled now in the darkness of the world.[13] But Christ came not to send peace, but a sword; the Panther of the bestiaries, luring the gentler beasts with His sweet breath of doctrine, is also the Tiger of destruction. For the "juvescence of the year," in which He came, marked the beginning of our dispensation, the "depraved May" ever returning with the "flowering judas" of man's answer to the Incarnation. And so "The tiger springs in the new year," devouring us who have devoured Him. Furthermore, the tiger becomes now a symbol not only of divine wrath but of the power of life within man, the springs of sex which "murder and create." "Depraved May," the season of denial or crucifixion, returns whenever, in whatever age, apostolic or modern, the life of sense stirs without love. Eliot's *The Family Reunion* repeats the horror: "Is the spring not an evil time, that excites us with lying voices?" So now it returns and excites the memories of Gerontion. The source of his grief—the passionate Cross, the poison tree, "the wrath-bearing tree"—is both the crucifixion yew tree and the death tree of the hanged traitor, a token of Christ and Iscariot, redemption and the universal fall in Eden.

The futility of a world where men blunder down the blind corridors of history, guided by vanity and gulled by success, asserting no power of choice between good and evil but forced into alternatives they cannot predict—this is the futility of a labyrinth without an end. Someone has remarked that Eliot's obsessive image is the abyss. It is not: it is the corridor, the blind street, the inclosure; the "circular desert" and "the stone passages / Of an immense and empty hospital," imprisoning the inconsolable heart. At the center is the physician, the Word, enveloped in obscurity. But without is the abyss also, yawning for those who in their twisted course have never found their center. "Gerontion" points no way inward; it shows the outward, the *eccentric* propulsion of the damned, who, as Chaucer says, echoing the *Somnium Scipionis*, "Shul whirle aboute th'erthe alwey in peyne."[14] Alone in his corner, having rested, unlike Ulysses, from travel (and indeed having never taken the highways of the earth), the old man sits while the wind sweeps his world "Beyond the circuit of the shuddering Bear / In fractured atoms." The opposite movement, which discloses "a door that opens at the end of a corridor," opening, as one reads in "Burnt Norton," "Into the rose garden" and "Into our first world," leads to "the still point of the turning world," where, as Eliot put it in *Ash Wednesday*, "the unstilled world still whirled / About the centre of the silent Word." "Gerontion" describes only "the unstilled world," the turning wheel, the hollow passages—not "the Garden / Where all love ends," the ending of lust and the goal of love. The point at which time ends and eternity begins, at which history disappears in unity and the winding spiral vanished in the Word, is lost to the world of the poem. Yet the Word exists; it is only history which cannot find Him, history with a positivistic conception of the universe, a deterministic view of causation, a pragmatic notion of morals. As Chesterton's Father Brown remarks, "What we all dread most . . . is a maze with *no* centre. That is why atheism is only a nightmare." Eliot's symbol of the mazelike passages, or the clocklike wheel of time, or the whirlwind of death, the gaping whirlpool, is the antithesis of the single, unmoving, immutable point within. History is the whirlwind, for history is of the world, and history like the world destroys all that dares the test of matter and time.

The ruin toward which De Bailhache, Fresca, and Mrs. Cammel are whirled epitomizes the end foretold for the universe. The second law of thermodynamics sentences to death a world less and less subject to order, resolving at last into motionless particles. Gerontion's view of history as chaos, however, is referable to *The Education of Henry Adams*, the source of "May, dogwood and chestnut, flowering judas."[15] In formulating a theory of history as the dynamic interaction of mind and force, Adams proved to his own satisfaction that beyond the human mind there was only chaos, but a chaos in which motion was continuously accelerated. It was not that the universe was running down, but that forces were increasing so much in complexity that future history was predictable only as an ever greater contest between mind and nature. The increase of knowledge itself multiplied the unanswered questions; in the science of evolution, for example, every theory redoubled confusion: "In 1900 [the historian] entered a far vaster universe, where all the old roads ran about in every direction, overrunning, dividing, subdividing, stopping abruptly, vanishing slowly, with side-paths that led nowhere, and sequences that could not be proved."[16] But if the "cunning passages"[17] of history were chaotic, it appeared to Adams that matter was more so. The kinetic theory of gas established his belief that nature was without system.[18] Paraphrasing Karl Pearson, Adams testified to his own conviction: "The kinetic theory of gas is an assertion of ultimate chaos. In plain words, Chaos was the law of nature; Order was the dream of man."[19] And chaos, of course, would ultimately prevail. Meanwhile, man was obliged to impose, when he could, some pattern upon the flux, and he should try to harmonize this bewildering disorder. To Adams, man was a spider snaring forces in his web, conducting an operation to which, through the rhetoric of Tourneur, Eliot was to allude.[20]

That forces must at length subdue mind, that history must finish by reducing man to the same colliding molecules of gas that the kinetic theory discerns in nature beyond him, and that chaos itself must finally absorb humanity were conclusions which Adams did not dwell upon. The realization of Gerontion that within the flux of history man cannot but split into "fractured atoms" and that (in the image Eliot was later to use) permanence resides only at the center which now the darkness swaddles is a corollary of Adams' argument. But Gerontion is not at the center, cannot attain the center, and does not believe. He perceives with horror a disaster he cannot interrupt, because the Passion is "not believed in, or if still believed, / In memory only. . . ." Therefore he dramatizes himself in a tragedy which the common damned cannot even glimpse.[21] Like them he must be claimed by the gulf of death, the vortex that gaped for Phlebas.

In "Prufrock" the particular situation is both personal and general, but its social applicability has to be inferred. In "Gerontion," the overt statements about history weave a fabric of general meaning, a critique of civilization. Though one is never allowed to forget the presence of Gerontion, one never really knows what kind of man he is. Prufrock lives as a personality; Gerontion, as a recording memory. One is not tempted, nor should be, to say of "Prufrock" that it bewails the absence of spiritual vitality; it memorializes the man himself. "Gerontion" is more devious. The title and the opening lines reveal that an old man is speaking; he is described as in A. C. Benson's life of Edward FitzGerald, who also sat, "in a dry month, old and blind, being read to by a country boy, longing for rain. . . ."[22] A few lines later, after Gerontion has disclaimed a heroic career, there is another echo of FitzGerald, who wrote to Frederick Tennyson: ". . . I really do like to sit in this doleful place with a good fire, a cat and dog on the rug, and an old woman in the kitchen. This is all my live-stock. The house is yet damp as last year; and the great event of this winter is my putting up a trough round the eaves to carry off the wet."[23] One thinks, moreover, of Newman's blind Gerontius, of Molière's Géronte, of Samson led by a boy into the house of the Philistines, of Conrad's blind Captain Whalley in "The End of the Tether," and even of Kurtz in "Heart of Darkness," who in his last days said to Marlow, "I am lying here in the dark waiting for death."[24] The most vivid exemplar of Gerontion's impotence and despair is Samson, who, like Gerontion, is a symbol of betrayed religion as well as of shattered strength. Gerontion's frustration is both religious and sexual. But only his religious despair is immediately pertinent to the historical theme of the poem; the sexual agony here, instead of being linked with the spiritual sterility of the world, is vaguely extended as "unnatural vices."

It would be easy to overstress the sexual content of the poem; much of what Gerontion is saying on the subject must be understood as pertaining also to his spiritual state. Yet the phrase "such knowledge" (already used in "The Death of Saint Narcissus") seems to connote more than intellectual accomplishment. The "supple confusions," moreover, are surely not limited to history, and "She" is not history alone. Whatever the reference, it is covered by the lament that passion comes too late, when not believed in, and that there is given

> . . . too soon
> Into weak hands, what's thought can be dispensed with
> Till the refusal propagates a fear.

The ambiguity, referring as much to belief as to potency or love, tends to be puzzling when one reads the next section, in which, after the mention of the tiger, there is no longer any visible connection with the idea of secularism. Gerontion, now conceivably addressing a woman (who, of course, need not be present), is explaining that his actions ("this show") signify no renewal of passion; and at the same time he is blaming her for being unworthy of his passion:

> . . . why should I need to keep it
> Since what is kept must be adulterated?
> I have lost my sight, smell, hearing, taste and touch:
> How should I use them for your closer contact?

Passion is strongest in memory, and in the midst of his "chilled delirium" these thoughts

> Excite the membrane, when the sense has cooled,
> With pungent sauces, multiply variety
> In a wilderness of mirrors.

Their aphrodisiac power, like the lascivious mirrors of Jonson's *Alchemist*, stirs the impotent flesh. Gerontion, however, wants no rebirth of sex; he has given up everything to withdraw to his sleepy corner, where he waits for the real conclusion. The vital energy (symbolized by the warm rain)[25] that might have made him struggle, the possibility of becoming great through action, the heroic prospect of a Thermopylaean end—these are illusory desires which he has rejected. Unlike Prufrock he has not even an ideal of love, except the vanished union of sense and spirit, the spiritual bond which the secular world has destroyed. He can find neither faith through love nor love through faith.

Because Gerontion, though primarily a symbol, is still dramatic enough to remain a person, the poem tends to split between the personality, which nevertheless is undefined, and the argument, which is not intimately enough related to the old man's feelings. One is inclined to apply Eliot's statement about Hamlet (which almost paraphrases Byron's description of his Cain) and to say that Gerontion "is dominated by an emotion which is inexpressible, because it is in *excess* of the facts as they appear."[26] As a symbol he embodies the errors of history and is a kind of scapegoat suffering for his apathetic contemporaries—suffering for the world as it is, and not (for what is much less depressing) for the world as it seems to be. The symbolism of drought and rain is transparent enough, as is that of Gerontion's blindness. Both suggest, moreover, that in 1919 Eliot was already consciously leaning upon anthropological sources, perhaps including Frazer's *The Golden Bough*. Prufrock, Origen, and Burbank, symbols of sensitiveness and debility, are precursors of Gerontion; but the idea that he is waiting, though he cannot hope, for liberation seems to point to the Fisher King of the Grail legend and hence to the fertility rituals of paganism. His blindness certainly has analogues in ritual and myth; besides the maiming of Attis, Adonis, and Osiris, it brings to mind the slaying of Balder by the blind god. Whether that act typified the death of summer or the killing of the sun-god, it signified in every way a victory for darkness. Gerontion's blindness symbolizes both his fault and his punishment, which are inseparable. He is thus, in the light of Frazer and *The Waste Land*, a figure in whom a mythological role has been revived; the sterility, personal to him on the sexual level, comes from spiritual failure. The cold snows of Belle Isle and Cape Horn, as opposed to the tropic luxuriance of jungles in which he has not fought, are in their turn a symbol of the cold death of the spirit; the white feathers of the courageous sea bird an ironic symbol of cowardice and loss. As victim, Gerontion corresponds to the dying King of the Grail, wounded beyond power of healing, who waits for deliverance in vain.

Ezra Pound, writing to Eliot in 1922 about *The Waste Land*, dissuaded him from including "Gerontion" as a prelude to the whole. Eliot, after getting back the long manuscript, abridged by Pound's cancellations to about half its original length, had further inquired about certain criticisms which were unclear and had suggested not only prefixing "Gerontion" but omitting the episode of Phlebas the Phoenician. Pound strongly advised against either course.[27] If Eliot had decided notwithstanding to use the poem with *The Waste Land*, the essential identity of Gerontion with Tiresias would be plainer than it is, and the relation of the Grail legend to the earlier work would be more evident. Jessie L. Weston's *From Ritual to Romance*, cited in the notes to *The Waste Land*, was not published until 1920, but her previous study *The Quest of the Holy Grail* (1913) contains the substance of her theory about the origin of the Grail romances. Whether Eliot knew the work or not and whether he knew he was delineating a parallel between Gerontion and the Fisher King or even Frazer's dying god (he had certainly already read Frazer), one may perceive by hindsight the symbolic connection of the poem with both. In Frazer and Jessie L. Weston, Eliot discovered new materials to objectify a state already engaging him, to which "Gerontion" gave symbolic projection.

# 5 THE LABYRINTH

Gerontion, without metamorphosis of character, became the prophet Tiresias, an arresting symbol of spiritual acuteness and emotional impotence. Eliot supplanted the modern figure with a mythological one to unify the diversities of *The Waste Land*. The choice of blind Tiresias as the all-gathering memory may have been due to the link between "Gerontion" and FitzGerald, to whom Tennyson's "Tiresias" was dedicated, or to Pound's adaptations from the *Odyssey*, or to the then recent publication of Apollinaire's *Les Mamelles de Tirésias* (1918), in which Thérèse-Tirésias performs, like Madame Sosostris, as a *cartomancienne*. Since Tiresias is even more shadowy than Gerontion, most incidents in *The Waste Land* seem immediate, not recollected, even though they constitute his reverie. Eliot forged a Proustian effect by means of a stream-of-consciousness technique resembling Joyce's in being logically discontinuous. The premise that the past endures in memory he illustrated by jumbling together, though not undeliberately, a series of images, conceptual pronouncements, and dramatic encounters and by later referring to the collage as "what Tiresias *sees*."

Tiresias recapitulates the other characters, and in him as "spectator" all of them, as Eliot's note says, melt together. Although the notes that Eliot added to *The Waste Land* (at Roger Fry's suggestion and for the sake of a longer book) are to be deplored—both because their selectivity is misleading and because they vitiate the tone—they are inseparable from it. Eliot's own indictment of them, pronounced before an American audience in 1956, that they exemplify "bogus scholarship" is overharsh. At worst, they are confusing; the note on Tiresias is especially so. Here, Eliot seems to have overlooked the fact that Tiresias has to be considered not only a spectator but also, in the past, a participant in actions he now remembers. Tiresias is "I" as a participant in such flashback episodes as the fortunetelling scene, the scene in the typist's flat, and the desert journey; at the beginning, middle, and end of the poem he is a synthesizing commentator. Within Tiresias' mind alone can the characters commingle; in the world of past actions they and he are distinct. Even if they are viewed as in F. H. Bradley's system (an evident source for the scheme here; for Tiresias' consciousness forms "a circle closed on the outside," a private world peopled by appearances), there must be a difference between the perceiver and the perceived, imposed by time if by nothing else. On the other hand, the motions recalled in the poem appear as if outside time and within the maze of consciousness. The various personages have something in common with Lewis Carroll's Alice; Tiresias is the dreaming "Red King" of the poem.

Eliot composed *The Waste Land* in the autumn of 1921. He had been enabled through Ezra Pound's Bel Esprit fund to take a vacation for medical care, and he wrote most of the poem while recruiting his health at Lausanne.[1] Before returning to London, after an absence of three months, he visited Pound at Paris and left the draft with him.[2] Certain passages he had written even earlier, including what he revised from "The Death of Saint Narcissus"; a few lines, it is said, antedated his departure from Harvard in 1914, but it is improbable that those constitute much of the present text. About the end of 1922, Eliot transferred the original complete typescript with his own corrections and Pound's ruthless abridgments to John Quinn, since whose death in July, 1924, it has vanished despite efforts to trace it. Evidently the long draft contained in some form (to judge from one of Pound's allusions in the correspondence about it) the poem "Song to the Opherian," which was printed in Wyndham Lewis' *Tyro* (1922) before *The Waste Land* itself appeared in the October *Criterion*. "Song to the Opherian," as published, is a short piece of thirteen lines, signed with the bully pseudonym "Gus Krutzsch"; it is a primitive version of "The Wind Sprang Up at Four O'Clock."[3] One gathers that the draft contained also a quotation from *Purgatorio*, XXVI ("sovegna vos"), which Eliot was to use in *Ash Wednesday* and which he cited in his notes to "What the Thunder Said." For his epigraph he had taken the dying cry of Kurtz in "Heart of Darkness": "The horror! the horror!" Pound, however, objected that Conrad was perhaps not weighty enough for the purpose, and Eliot complaisantly removed the words.[4]

The epigraph that Eliot afterward adopted occurs simply as a chance remark in the *Satyricon* of Petronius. The passage (a prose original) had been versified by D. G. Rossetti as follows:

"I saw the Sibyl at Cumae"
(One said) with mine own eye.
She hung in a cage, and read her rune
To all the passers-by.
Said the boys, "What wouldst thou, Sibyl?"
She answered, "I would die."[5]

The sibyl of Cumae, besides being the guardian of a sacred cave from which she delivered oracles, was a gatekeeper of the underworld, as in the *Aeneid*. Aeneas' descent into hell by way of a cavern can be identified with the initiation ordeal to which novices were subjected in the mystery cults. The trials of spiritual initiation included, at least in areas influenced by the Cretan culture, a progress through a cavern, labyrinth, or maze, natural or artificial. Candidates descended and had a combat with death; that is, they were led through labyrinthine wanderings, and afterward were permitted to return, as if born again, to the light of day.[6] A labyrinth is actually mentioned in Vergil's description of the "temple of Daedalus," which stands outside the sibyl's cave; in Eliot's *The Cocktail Party* the image occurs along with the desert, the symbol of spiritual trial. An "archetypal" pattern of descent and ascent is symbolized in the *Aeneid* not only by the episode of the sibyl but by the entire quest of Aeneas from Troy to Italy. The ocean-voyage pattern of the hero-myth thus accompanies and dominates the narrower detail of his visit to hell and serves to unify the themes of sea-trial and grave-trial, necessary for symbolic rebirth.[7]

Since *The Waste Land* employs the primordial imagery of death and rebirth in accordance with the Grail legend, the sibyl belongs to the machinery of initiation in the poem; appearing in one of the Grail romances, she links the medieval legend to classical myth.[8] But her misfortune in the epigraph—to be shut in a cage and to wither away indefinitely, being preserved from death but condemned like Tithonus to grow old—symbolizes the motif of the waste land. The feminine power which should enable the protagonist to complete his quest for initiation cannot do so, and Tiresias himself, whom success would benefit, remains blind and impotent. The failure, however, is owing to him, so that the sibyl and the people in the poem itself are victims of his weakness. The sibyl here symbolizes death in life because the land is dead, and it is dead because Tiresias, the Fisher King, has been wounded and has not achieved, in the person of the quester, the goal of the quest. The sibyl (Madame Sosostris), the youthful Grail-bearer (the hyacinth girl), the quester (variously characterized, for example as "the young man carbuncular"), and the Fisher King embody facets of the one personality struggling to attain salvation. Had the quest been plotted to conform to C. G. Jung's prescription, it could not more exactly match it.

The Waste Land summarizes the Grail legend, not precisely in the usual order, but retaining the principal incidents and adapting them to a modern setting.[9] Eliot's indebtedness both to Sir James Frazer and to Jessie L. Weston's From Ritual to Romance (in which book he failed to cut pages 138–39 and 142–43 of his copy) is acknowledged in his notes.[10] Jessie L. Weston's thesis is that the Grail legend was the surviving record of an initiation ritual. Later writers have reaffirmed the psychological validity of the link between such ritual, phallic religion, and the spiritual content of the Greek Mysteries. Identification of the Grail story with the common myth of the hero assailing a devil-dragon underground or in the depths of the sea completes the unifying idea behind The Waste Land. The Grail legend corresponds to the great hero epics, it dramatizes initiation into maturity, and it bespeaks a quest for sexual, cultural, and spiritual healing. Through all these attributed functions, it influenced Eliot's symbolism.

Parallels with yet other myths and with literary treatments of the "quest" theme reinforce Eliot's pattern of death and rebirth. Though The Tempest, one of Eliot's minor sources, scarcely depicts an initiation "mystery," Colin Still, in a book of which Eliot has since written favorably (Shakespeare's Mystery Play), had already advanced the theory in 1921 that it implies such a subject.[11] And Tiresias is not simply the Grail knight and the Fisher King but Ferdinand and Prospero, as well as Tristan and Mark, Siegfried and Wotan. In his feminine role he is not simply the Grail-maiden and the wise Kundry but the sibyl, Dido, Miranda, Brünnhilde. Each of these represents one of the three main characters in the Grail legend and in the mystery cults— the wounded god, the sage woman (transformed in some versions of the Grail legend into a beautiful maiden), and the resurrected god, successful quester, or initiate. Counterparts to them figure elsewhere; Eliot must have been conscious that the "Ancient Mariner" and "Childe Roland" had analogues to his own symbolism.[12]

In adopting fertility symbolism, Eliot was probably influenced by Stravinsky's ballet *Le Sacre du printemps*. The summer before writing *The Waste Land* he saw the London production, and on reviewing it in September he criticized the disparity between Massine's choreography and the music. He might almost have been sketching his own plans for a work applying a primitive idea to contemporary life:

In art there should be interpenetration and metamorphosis. Even the Golden Bough can be read in two ways: as a collection of entertaining myths, or as a revelation of that vanished mind of which our mind is a continuation. In everything in the Sacre du Printemps, except in the music, one missed the sense of the present. Whether Stravinsky's music be permanent or ephemeral I do not know; but it did seem to transform the rhythm of the steppes into the scream of the motor horn, the rattle of machinery, the grind of wheels, the beating of iron and steel, the roar of the underground railway, and the other barbaric cries of modern life; and to transform these despairing noises into music.[13]

In *The Waste Land* he imposed the fertility myth upon the world about him.

Eliot's waste land suffers from a dearth of love and faith. It is impossible to demarcate precisely at every point between the physical and the spiritual symbolism of the poem; as in "Gerontion" the speaker associates the failure of love with his spiritual dejection. It is clear enough, however, that the contemporary waste land is not, like that of the romances, a realm of sexless sterility. The argument emerges that in a world that makes too much of the physical and too little of the spiritual relations between the sexes, Tiresias, for whom love and sex must form a unity, has been ruined by his inability to unify them. The action of the poem, as Tiresias recounts it, turns thus on two crucial incidents: the garden scene in Part I and the approach to the Chapel Perilous in Part V. The one is the traditional initiation in the presence of the Grail; the other is the mystical initiation, as described by Jessie L. Weston, into spiritual knowledge. The first, if successful, would constitute rebirth through love and sex; the second, rebirth without either. Since both fail, the quest fails, and the poem ends with a formula for purgatorial suffering, through which Tiresias may achieve the second alternative after patience and self-denial—perhaps after physical death. The counsel to give, sympathize, and control befits one whom direct ways to beatitude cannot release from suffering.

# 6 MEMORY AND DESIRE: "THE WASTE LAND"

## I. *"The Burial of the Dead"*

Part I of Eliot's *The Waste Land*[1] derives its title from the majestic Anglican service for the burial of the dead. The theme of resurrection, proclaimed through Saint Paul's subtly moving assurance that "the dead shall be raised incorruptible, and we shall be changed," finds here its counterpoint in the rhythmic annual return of spring, when once more "the cruelest month" of April touches "dull roots," and memory and desire blend an old man's inert longing and lost fulfilment.[2] Tiresias, who is speaking, has been content to let winter cover him "in forgetful snow, feeding / A little life with dried tubers." In the lines of James Thomson which Eliot put to use: "Our Mother feedeth thus our little life, / That we in turn may feed her with our death."[3] Blind and spiritually embittered, Tiresias wrestles with buried emotions unwittingly revived. In his mind "the floors of memory," as in "Rhapsody on a Windy Night," are dissolved. He is borne in phantasmagoria to scenes recalling the "Dixi, custodiam" of the rites of burial. They are scenes both of joy and of agony, and in memory they reveal that consciousness is death and that truly the speaker was alive only when he could forget. The death of winter and the life of spring usurp each other.

Memory takes him from the general truth to a particular event, to another springtime, in his youth, when warm days of the resurrection season brought rain, the water of life, with sunlight, and he was beside the Starnbergersee near the city of Munich.[4] A voice of a Lithuanian girl who recounted a childhood experience of terror, exhilaration, and freedom comes back to him. Against the double happiness of her memory and his, he must now set the present reality of the loveless,

arid desert within him. He thinks of Ezekiel, the "son of man," chosen
to turn the Israelites in their captivity back to God, and hence of
Christ, the "Son of man," whose temples, like his own, are now in
ruins. In this waste land Tiresias is the Fisher King, a type of all the
mighty who are fallen. It is too late for the message of Ecclesiastes,
who besought men to remember God before the time of the grasshopper
and the day of evil.[5] Ezekiel's solemn prophecy has been fulfilled
against the unholiness of the mountains of Israel: their altars are desolate and their images are broken.[6] "For," as in Bildad's words to Job,
"we are but of yesterday, and know nothing, because our days upon
earth are a shadow. . . . So are the paths of all that forget God; and the
hypocrite's hope shall perish. . . . He is green before the sun, and his
branch shooteth forth in his garden. His roots are wrapped about the
heap, and seeth the place of stones."[7] The desert nourishes no roots;
the spirit of vegetation, meaning love, cannot survive; the Fisher King,
like the suffering Job, is a withered plant—in the phrase of the Lord to
Isaiah "a dry tree," spiritually a eunuch.[8]

The only temporary refuge from the parching sun is a red rock,
which emotionally recalls the Grail (sometimes figured as a stone) and
Chrétien's castle of ladies, "la roche de Sanguin." It is an obscure
symbol—altar-like and sacrificial, the rock of St. Peter, the grotto of
the sibyl—which the protagonist remembers as the scene of his failure
in the Grail quest, as the entrance way to an intense revelation of
death:

> . . . something different from either
> Your shadow at morning striding behind you
> Or your shadow at evening rising to meet you.

The mystery is "fear in a handful of dust." Man who "fleeth as it were
a shadow, and never continueth in one stay" stands face to face with
his fall. There are echoes here of "The Death of Saint Narcissus,"
where the glow of firelight turns a gray rock red and where the poet
"shows" the dead Narcissus; and of Donne's "A Lecture upon the
Shadow," or of Beaumont and Fletcher's *Philaster* (Act III, scene 2),
where Philaster hurls at Arethusa his angry complaint against woman:

> . . . how that foolish man,
> That reads the story of a woman's face
> And dies believing it, is lost for ever;
> How all the good you have is but a shadow,
> I' the morning with you, and at night behind you
> Past and forgotten. . . .

In some tangential way the symbol of the shadow relates to sex and to the woman with whom the quester fails. Tiresias is recollecting an incident of his past, when in his vigor he played the part not of Fisher King but of Grail knight. A kind of death occurred in a garden. Fear vanquished him; the reality of love with which the hyacinth girl confronted him was overwhelming.

In the Grail legend the sacred talismans, as Jessie L. Weston tries to demonstrate, may have been sexually symbolic. The Grail, either a cup or a dish, represented the female; the lance or spear with it, the male.[9] The goal of the quest was never ostensibly to obtain these objects but rather, by asking the proper question, to liberate the Fisher King from his distress. Indeed, so far as can be seen, the various talismans had no essential connection with the story itself; they were symbols of the life principle behind the Grail legend. Since in the romances they lost much of their original meaning and became misunderstood, they were interchanged, omitted, or described inconsistently from version to version. In *The Waste Land* Eliot avoided the ambiguities attached to the cup and lance and substituted for these things other symbols.

The memories of Tiresias as the Fisher King contain no more important event than his failure with the hyacinth girl. Whether she is the Lithuanian or not is immaterial. She is the Grail-bearer, the maiden bringing love. As in the legends, he has met her in a place of water and flowers,[10] the Hyacinth garden. The function of the Grail-bearer is dual: first, she directs the quester to the place of his initiation or blames him for his failure there; second, she appears in the castle and bears the Grail into the great hall.[11] It is she whom, if his quest is completed, he marries; she would be in Frazer's terms the consort of the wounded and resurrected god, and she universally appears in proximity to the water symbol. At his meeting with the hyacinth girl in *The Waste Land*, Tiresias as the quester has omitted to ask the indispensable question of the Grail initiation. Evidently he has merely stood agape while she, bearing the sexual symbol—the spike-shaped blossoms representing the slain god Hyacinth of *The Golden Bough*[12]—has awaited the word he cannot utter:

> —Yet when we came back, late, from the Hyacinth garden,
> Your arms full, and your hair wet, I could not
> Speak, and my eyes failed, I was neither
> Living nor dead, and I knew nothing,
> Looking into the heart of light, the silence.

Eliot diversified the pattern slightly, for the hyacinth is a male symbol, and then, too, the quester himself has given the flowers to the hyacinth girl. But the effect is the same as in the Grail narratives. The quester becomes like the King, "neither living nor dead."[13] In fact, he is the King only from this point, for Tiresias in *The Waste Land* is merely what his own folly has created.[14]

The hyacinth girl occupies the position of the "word within a word" in "Gerontion," but with a sharp difference in emphasis. She symbolizes centrality; and in her, so to speak, the spokes of the turning wheel converge, just as the wheeling procession or dance of youths and maidens in the legend turns toward the Grail. But she is not for this quester the Word through whom at length he can rest content; his search must go on until he finds the Word by some other way. For she embodies romantic love, the promise of fleshly joy. About her there hovers the kind of spiritual air that romantic poets discern in the presence of the beloved. It is perhaps not the spiritual grace which is sometimes associated with Dante's young adoration of Beatrice. But, like Dante at the beginning of the *Vita nuova*, the quester trembles. And somehow he falters in confronting her. *The Waste Land* is only repeating the old pattern of disaster which overcame the child in "Dans le Restaurant" when the big dog frightened him in the rain.[15] Still, the moment has been one of joy, bringing together the two worlds of flesh and spirit. Though attended with disappointment, it contains, transitory as it is, values proceeding from the unmoved center and cited as the sustaining hope in Eliot's later poetry.[16]

Two citations from *Tristan und Isolde* outline further the drama of love and death. In the opera Tristan, having been mortally wounded, dies before Isolde, hastening to reach him, can restore him through her powers of healing. Like the Fisher King, Tristan languishes from an injury curable only through the lovers' reunion. Of the quotations appropriated by Eliot, the first occurs at the beginning of Wagner's action, when Tristan is bringing Isolde from Ireland to Cornwall, where she is to become his uncle's bride. The song is sung by a sailor at the masthead, and though it does not refer to Isolde herself, she hearing it supposes for a moment that it does. The ship bears her to her destination, but not before she and Tristan, through a magical potion, have fallen in love. After reaching Cornwall, they meet in a garden of Mark's castle, and it is there that Melot, who has betrayed them to Mark, wounds Tristan upon a bank of flowers. After the scene in the

garden—virtually equivalent to Eliot's Hyacinth-garden passage—
Tristan is taken to Brittany, where he awaits Isolde's coming. As he lies
wounded, a shepherd enters to report that her ship is not in sight—
that the sea is waste and void, "Oed' und leer das Meer!" The desolation in this second quotation used by Eliot contrasts with the fresh
breeze, a portent of happy love, in the first.[17] Just so in Eliot's poem
the love and hope at the beginning shatter in bitterness as the quester
fails. He receives his own wound in the garden, and, like Tiresias, he
becomes blind; the hyacinth girl vanishes, but he himself lingers to
meditate on his ruins.

Except for the moment in the Hyacinth garden Tiresias sees in his
memories only a dreary travesty of the initiation into love. The remainder of the poem up to the second initiation into the mystery of
the Chapel recounts his past wanderings through the waste land of the
"Unreal City." The other characters, base imitations of the Grail
actors, include Madame Sosostris, appearing immediately after the
hyacinth girl as if to reinforce a contrast. Oddly, she has a masculine
name. Sesostris, whose exploits are narrated by Herodotus, was a great
king of Egypt in the twelfth dynasty. Eliot's acknowledged source for
the name is an amusing scene in Aldous Huxley's *Crome Yellow*
(1921), where the crocodilian Mr. Scogan, for a Bank Holiday charity
fair, dresses up as a gypsy woman to tell fortunes and advertises himself as "Sesostris, the Sorceress of Ecbatana."[18] The episode, by contributing to the theme of female impersonation, supports Eliot's note
on Tiresias. But Eliot presumably worked also from the petition for
foresight in the burial service ("Lord, let me know mine end"), which
with *Crome Yellow*, the sixth book of the *Aeneid*, Apollinaire's *Les
Mamelles de Tirésias*, and Jessie L. Weston's references to the Tarot
could have provided the substance of his synthesis.

Though Madame Sosostris is presumably not young, she partly symbolizes rebirth, for she is a "wise woman" or midwife (*sage-femme*).[19]
She is a caricature of her predecessor the hyacinth girl. In her hands
she holds a group of symbols identical in value with the hyacinths.
Since her Tarot cards are considered Grail talismans, she is unmis-
takably another type of the Grail-bearer. She is a charlatan, however;
her activities (even her midwifery, such as it may be) are sadly deca-
dent and have nothing to do with the solemnity of her role in the Grail
legend. But in certain versions of the myth the young Grail-bearer becomes an old witchwoman after the quester fails in his test. In Wagner

the sorceress Kundry embodies Wolfram's Kondrie, the Grail-bearer as a hideous crone (the Loathly Damsel), as well as the water-lady Orgeluse, whom the Fisher King loved and in whose service he was wounded. Old or young, the Grail-bearer is not generally of her own accord hostile to the quester, whose success can restore her beauty as well as the King's virility. When in *The Waste Land* the quester fails, Madame Sosostris, occupying the sibyl's place in the initiation pattern, falls victim to a general desolation.

The Tarot pack, discussed by Jessie L. Weston, contains in its four suits—cup, lance, sword, and dish—the life-symbols found in the Grail narrative. Whether, as Jessie L. Weston contends, the designs shown on the face cards (the *atouts*) ever appeared in a calendar used for predicting the rise and fall of the Nile, the names of the four suits themselves recall the sexual talismans.[20] The twenty-two *atouts*, numbered from zero to twenty-one, are used in fortunetelling. There seems to be little evidence that the pictures on the *atouts* of the Tarot compare in antiquity with the Grail symbols. Some of the personages look like characters in particular myths, including the Grail legend, but the resemblances seem fortuitous. Among the *atouts*, Jessie L. Weston mentions only the Pope, who in the set to which she refers shows the influence of the Eastern Church, for he has a beard and holds a triple cross; and the King (otherwise the Emperor), who wears the headdress of a Russian grand duke.[21] Both of these may have been alluded to in *The Waste Land:* the former as "the man with three staves" and the latter as the archduke, mentioned near the beginning. The Tarot contains no drowned sailor or blank card; but the Wheel and the Hanged Man are authentic, though Jessie L. Weston says nothing about them. Eliot therefore had some other source for his knowledge. His one-eyed "merchant" is the Fool. He alluded also to the Tower, the High Priestess, the Moon, the Lovers, the Hermit, and the Star, which is identified by A. E. Waite, in *The Pictorial Key to the Tarot*, with Sirius, the Dog Star.[22] Belladonna, in "A Game of Chess," is perhaps the Empress.

The drowned Phoenician sailor and the Hanged Man symbolize respectively the loveless "death" ("Here, said she, / Is your card") and the potential healing or rebirth of Tiresias; but the Hanged Man, Christ who suffered and rose again, is a stranger to Madame Sosostris and to the spiritual state of the unsuccessful quester. Tiresias must go into the depths from which there is no return; he is denied the death,

longed for by the sibyl, into a new life. The "crowds of people" whom
Madame Sosostris sees are turning on the Wheel, the Wheel of Fortune
in the Tarot, broadly interpretable as a symbol of life in the world, like
the great wheel of Buddhism. These people, spiritually sterile, describe
a purposeless circle. They are ironically similar to the Grail procession
displaying the talismans in the legend. When they flow in a crowd over
London Bridge, each man's eyes fixed before his feet like the old men's
in Baudelaire's "Les Sept Vieillards," they go past the church of St.
Mary Woolnoth, typifying a Grail castle which the quester of the
romances would similarly have reached by crossing water. Nine o'clock
strikes: the hour to start work;[23] it condemns them to the tedium of
another futile day. Muted on the last stroke, the clock ends with a
"dead sound."[24] They, the ordinary people of the world, inhabit an
"Unreal City," the "Fourmillante cité" of Baudelaire's poem, cited in
Eliot's notes. This city is also a hell, for it is inhabited on the one
hand by the secular and on the other hand by the spiritually ignorant, like those characterized in the third and fourth cantos of the
*Inferno*.[25]

Stetson, the modern representative of "him who from cowardice
made the great refusal" (*Inferno*, III), is another counterpart to the
quester. The corpse he has planted in his garden is the dead god, of
whom he has knowledge, but whose life he rejects, choosing to remain
a "trimmer." The sprouting of this god, the quickening of the slaughtered Osiris (the triple phallused, the man with three staves),[26] would
be tantamount to a spiritual revival; but, like Marcello in Webster's
*The White Devil* (Act V, scene 4), the deity lies murdered and can
live again only through a power still withheld. This corpse is also Tiresias, the Fisher King, and his sprouting, as of the dead "grain" in the
burial service, would effect the restoration of love destroyed by his own
cowardly refusal in the Hyacinth garden. The "sudden frost" that may
have disturbed the bed of the corpse is analogous to his numbing
failure in the initiation. And the Dog (which has troubled many) is
whatever wrenches forth the buried disgrace of the past instead of letting it send up sprigs of life. The symbols, with the levels of reference,
are mixed: as the corpse is the god, its brutal disinterment would
correspond to an act of sacrilege; as it is Tiresias, its exposure would
repeat his incapacity in the Hyacinth garden. The Dog connotes his
terror, his shame, and even, perhaps, the lusts that later sections of the
poem suggest may have abused him. In the Tarot a dog accompanies

the Fool (Eliot's Mr. Eugenides). Eliot's change from Webster's "wolf" adjusts the symbolism to that of "Dans le Restaurant"; it also secures an allusion to the Dog Star, the star of lust and polestar of the Phoenician navigators, to Stephen Dedalus' joke about the fox and his grandmother,[27] and, even more curiously, to the tradition of the dog and the mandrake. If the anthropomorphic mandrake, which can safely be pulled out of the ground only by means of a dog and a piece of string, was itself a god (or, as J. Rendel Harris thought, the primeval Aphrodite),[28] then it supplies a workable analogue here. The mandrake, according to Frazer's *Folk-Lore in the Old Testament*, is sown from the body of a man hanged on a gallows.[29]

There is danger lest multiplied allusions, adventitious or not, should defeat meaning. It might be wisest for a cynical critic of this passage simply to regard the Dog as himself scratching away in the poem as in a great charnel graveyard.

> "Oh keep the Dog far hence, that's friend to men,
> "Or with his nails he'll dig it up again!
> "You! hypocrite lecteur!—mon semblable,—mon frère!"

For Eliot's quotation from "Au Lecteur" in Baudelaire's *Les Fleurs du mal* was an insulting one. The second book which Eliot is known to have reviewed, James Huneker's *Egoists: A Book of Supermen* (1909), contains the statement that after reading Griswold on Poe, Baudelaire asked, "Who shall keep the curs out of the cemetery?"[30] That is a problem indeed.

## II. *"A Game of Chess"*

The subject of Part II is sex without love, specifically within marriage, just as the subject of Part III is the same horror outside it. For people who must be continually excited and amused if they are not to be overwhelmed by boredom, sex is merely escape, and when it palls it converts marriage into tedious bondage. "A Game of Chess" reveals the working of this process in two classes of society. Having lost the hyacinth girl, the quester finds himself joined with a neurotic, shrewish woman of fashion, who is probably Belladonna, the "lady of situations."[31] She is to be contrasted chiefly with the hyacinth girl herself. Unlike Madame Sosostris, a mysterymonger who pretends to find some meaning in life, she stands merely as a symbol of lovelessness. Yet she too has something of the sibyl's role, for she has introduced the quester to the mystery of sex. She is enthroned, like the queen in *Antony and Cleopatra,* in a bedchamber or *Rape of the Lock* boudoir resembling that of Imogen in *Cymbeline* (Act II, scene 4, lines 87–91), as described by Iachimo:

> The roof o' th' chamber
> With golden cherubins is fretted. Her andirons—
> I had forgot them—were two winking Cupids
> Of silver, each on one foot standing, nicely
> Depending on their brands.

The andirons became Eliot's "sevenbranched candelabra," doubtless because the cherubim suggested the adornments of Solomon's temple, and the cupids, assimilated to the cherubim (but still coy), became golden. The same scene (ll. 68 ff.) contains a comparison with Cleopatra, whose barge is depicted on a tapestry hanging against the wall. The chimney piece is carved with "Chaste Dian bathing"—a clear contrast with the corresponding rape of Philomel "above the antique mantel" in *The Waste Land.* Two scenes earlier (Act II, scene 2, lines 18–21), where Iachimo visits Imogen's chamber, there is another passage that Eliot must have noticed:

> 'Tis her breathing that
> Perfumes the chamber thus. The flame o' th' taper
> Bows toward her, and would under-peep her lids
> To see th' enclosed lights . . .

and a few lines further on (ll. 44–46):

> She hath been reading late
> The tale of Tereus; here the leaf's turn'd down
> Where Philomel gave up.

But Belladonna has neither Cleopatra's exuberant sprightliness nor Imogen's tranquil chastity. However ecclesiastical her room may look, with its candlesticks and its perfumed smoke rising like incense into the *laquearia,* she is only, as the ceiling itself seems to show, a burning Dido, wronged perhaps, but faithless to her household gods. Yet here the lines preceding her spoken words have a darker implication. The sexual relation she represents is, if love be absent from it, little better than a rape. In one sense she herself has been the victim, untransformed into an "inviolable voice." But the real victim is the quester, who in the garden became the Fisher King through a failure symbolically equivalent to the crime of Tereus; it is he who has been silenced and, so to speak, spiritually mutilated. He is both Tereus and Philomel, and she a projection of his suffering upon the people of the waste land.

The fate of Bianca, seduced by the duke in Middleton's *Women Beware Women* (Act II, scene 2), while her mother-in-law's attention is diverted by a game of chess, resembles that of Philomel. Eliot's title for Part II came from that scene, which served also to reintroduce the theme of blindness. Livia, the duke's confederate, alludes continually, under color of talking about the game, to what is happening in the gallery above the old lady's head and in view of the audience:

> *Livia:* I've given three blind mate twice.
> *Mother:*                You may see, madam,
>    My eyes begin to fail.
> *Livia:*                I'll swear they do wench.

Eliot's subsequent reference to *The Tempest* reminds one that there too a chess game takes place, between Ferdinand and Miranda (Act V, scene 1, lines 172–75), which in its context betokens amity and love.

Blindness in "A Game of Chess," as in the Hyacinth garden, correlates with silence. Eliot's own reading of Part II differentiates carefully between the shrill, rasping voice of the lady and the detached, melancholy voice of her husband. The absence of quotation marks from the man's lines probably means that in reality he does not answer at all, and only meditates his thoughts. She first begs him to speak—but, as before, he cannot speak. Her nervous peevishness at the noise of the wind evokes in his mind the image of "rats' alley / Where the dead men lost their bones," for it was with a noise and shaking, and with a blast of wind, that the dead in Ezekiel's valley of dry bones received the breath of life and stood upon their feet. The wind itself recalls to him a line in Webster's *The Devil's Law Case* (Act III, scene 2, line 162): "Is the wind in that doore still?" which occurs, significantly, in a passage concerning a wounded man. She immediately mentions the wind, "What is the wind doing?" and he monotonously iterates "Nothing," which leads into the next question. His repetitions of the word are reminiscent (not without gross overtones) of Lear's warning to Cordelia, "Nothing will come of nothing. Speak again" (*King Lear*, Act I, scene 1, line 92), and of Ophelia's modest answer to Hamlet, "I think nothing, my lord" (*Hamlet*, Act III, scene 2, line 125). Mentally catching at "remember," the man, conscious that he has been blinded, that he is Tiresias, thinks of Ariel's song in *The Tempest* (Act I, scene 2, line 398), "Those are pearls that were his eyes. . . ." And his lady blindly pursues the motif: "Are you alive, or not? Is there nothing in your head?"[32] He is dead, and he has no eyes. His memory supplements her words with a parody of the question she might sarcastically put to him (in the words of some popular ragtime song) if she knew he was thinking of Shakespeare. His "O O O O" duplicates the hollow groans of Lear or Othello as Shakespeare represented them.[33] Afflicted with boredom, she thinks, again with unconscious irony, of rushing out and walking the street, much like the frenzied Dido in her palace at Carthage when Aeneas abandoned her.[34]

The chief symbols of this section—the sexual violation, the fiery hair, the chess game and the blindness, as well as the silence—are all more or less consonant with the Grail legend or other fertility myths. Cleanth Brooks has pointed out that the sexual violation occurs in one version of the Grail story.[35] The fiery points of the woman's hair present a Medusa-like contrast to the wet hair of the hyacinth girl; fire is here a symbol of lust; water, of love. The game of chess likewise means more than Eliot's note reveals. In the Grail romances the hero occasionally visits a chessboard castle, where he meets a water-maiden. In addition, chess has often been a symbol, notably with Elizabethan and Jacobean dramatists, for man's life and government in the world. Even putting aside the analogy between chess and the combats in ritual, one may discern in Eliot's use of the symbol a suggestion that the people in the waste land belong to a drama they do not understand, where they move like chessmen toward destinations they cannot foresee.

Blindness, as in the careers of Samson and Oedipus, symbolizes defeat and punishment, and at the same time it convicts the quester of moral inadequacy. The line from *The Tempest* foreshadows "Death by Water" and opposes to that death the regenerative "death" of Ferdinand's father, Alonso, whose eyes, according to Ariel, have been changed to pearls—there a symbol of rebirth. Indeed, Alonso has survived his shipwreck to become regenerate in the most practical sense; he repents and begs forgiveness of Prospero. The line, "Of his bones are coral made" presents the antithesis of "rats' alley / Where the dead men lost their bones," and there is no "sea change" in *The Waste Land*. The "lidless eyes," sleepless, imply the torture in which the man and woman live, waiting for the knock of death upon the door—or, it may be, for the Saviour who stands at the door and knocks.[36]

The ritual marriage, which should insure the restoration of life to the waste land, fails because the test of love has not first been passed.[37] Another side of the same picture comes in view through the second half of "A Game of Chess." The sordidness now is more candidly physical.

In these lines the pawns, Bill, Lou, and May, forgathered in a pub, hear about Lil's and Albert's misfortunes: Lil, having undergone an abortion, suffers from its effects and from the loss of her teeth; Albert, like Stetson, has been away at war. The tale is several times interrupted by the proprietor, who has to close up for the night, and in his urgent "HURRY UP PLEASE ITS TIME" most of the serious tone of this passage is compressed. The cry is an ironic warning to turn from this way of life. The pub itself recalls in the context that the Grail is associated with drinking and feasting; and, indeed, some of the best recent scholars identify the Grail solely with food-producing caldrons of Celtic mythology. The key symbol in the passage, however, is abortion, which advances the theme of unfruitfulness and sterility. The final line, grotesquely echoing a popular ballad ("Merrily we roll along"), Shakespeare's Ophelia, and Laforgue's Yorick, heralds "Death by Water," the death of those condemned for lust. Yet Ophelia, "the violet girl," is essentially a symbol of betrayed innocence; she is the Grail-bearer herself after the quester's failure, but her undoing, like that of Philomel, cannot be literally applied to the hyacinth girl; it indicates rather another aspect of Tiresias' wound, as does the physical decay of Lil, with whom Ophelia is immediately identified.

Up to this point and in Part III, just as the quester is distinguishable from the Fisher King, so, too, the female characters are divisible into two categories, corresponding to the metamorphoses of the Grail-bearer: on the one side is the hyacinth girl, as Imogen, Philomel, Bianca, and Ophelia; on the other is Madame Sosostris, Belladonna, or Lil, as Cleopatra and Dido. The change, occurring when the Fisher King receives his wound, is symbolized by rape. The pertinence of the deceived maidens from literature needs no further comment. Eliot's choice of analogues to Belladonna was not altogether a happy one; neither Cleopatra nor Dido nor, later, Queen Elizabeth I is mainly associated in the popular mind with lust but rather with grandeur. Hence "A Game of Chess" seems to invite the wrong interpretation as simple nostalgia for a golden age. Eliot's Belladonna, however, like Vergil's Dido, is a temptress, a Circe or Duessa who has trapped the quester in her toils, as in Tennyson's poem Merlin is enchanted to his doom.

III. *"The Fire Sermon"*

With Part III the Grail narrative turns once more to the quester standing disconsolately beside the river, figuratively the same water as in the Tristan and Isolde passage. The season is still winter, after the summer throngs have left the Thames, from which have long departed the fertility nymphs of Spenser's "Prothalamion." The attendance of nymphs at a marriage festival reflects disgrace on casual lovers by the Thames or "by the waters of Leman," the waters now of Lake Geneva, where Eliot, Byron-like, composed the poem, and of Babylon, where the exiled Hebrews sat down and wept. The analogue of Hebrew captivity has appeared once before, in the allusions to Ezekiel, and it appears again in Part V through the wanderings in the desert, which parallel the Exodus. Before the dramatization of lust in "The Fire Sermon," the earlier themes are recapitulated. The wind blowing across the dead land recalls Ezekiel, the prophet to whom was revealed in Babylon the ultimate restoration of the twelve tribes, the scattered bones in the valley. Here the wind is no Spirit of life, but a cold blast symbolizing death, "Time's wingèd chariot hurrying near" in Marvell's "Coy Mistress." The blight of time upon the waste land, the spiritual death, has make this a place of fetid decay. The rattling bones of the dead bring to mind details of the "Hades" episode in *Ulysses,* where on the way to Paddy Dignam's funeral Mr. Bloom repeats to himself a melancholy jingle: "Rattle his bones. Over the stones. Only a pauper. Nobody owns"; and where, crawling in the cemetery, is a rat among the other tokens of corruption.[38] The subject of gas in that episode arises first as the funeral procession stops for a moment near the Dublin gasworks:

> Mr. Bloom put his head out of the window.
> —The grand canal, he said.
> Gas works.[39]

Eliot's quester chooses a spot behind the gashouse from which to fish in "the dull canal." Having long since become the Fisher King, he is seeking, so that he may be redeemed from his torment, the primitive religious symbol of the fish, synonymous with the Grail.[40]

Simultaneously he becomes identified with Ferdinand in *The Tempest* (Act I, scene 2, lines 389–91), through another echo of the meeting between Ferdinand and Ariel:

> Sitting on a bank,
> Weeping again the King my father's wreck,
> This music crept by me upon the waters.

It is once more possible (though Colin Still's book may have affected the passage) that Eliot was following James Joyce; for in the "Proteus" episode Stephen, thinking of a man who has been drowned, quotes to himself Ariel's "Full fathom five" as well as a line from "Lycidas."[41] But Eliot expanded Ferdinand's words to:

> Musing upon the king my brother's wreck
> And on the king my father's death before him.

Cleanth Brooks explains the change as the forging of a link between the quester and the hermit (the brother of the Fisher King) in Wolfram's *Parzival*.[42] Yet such an association seems unconvincing; Eliot's adaptation chiefly concerns Ferdinand in *The Tempest*, and since he and Phlebas the Phoenician, as the note on Tiresias says, are "not wholly distinct" from each other, the symbolism of drowning must apply to them. In *The Tempest* it is the king, Alonso, who Ferdinand thinks has been drowned, so that a further identification makes the "death" of Alonso the "death" of Ferdinand as well. The quester is consequently in some sense about to re-enact his own father's misfortune. One may here detect the rudiments of a cyclical pattern: what happens to the father happens to the son (as in *The Family Reunion*), and, by inference, it happens to each generation of human brotherhood. This is not the world of *The Tempest*, where neither father nor son is drowned and where both survive to experience redemption—Alonso through penitence and Ferdinand through love.

Among the bones and the naked bodies of the dead,[43] the quester hears another kind of rattle, "The sound of horns and motors," heralding the prediction that in the spring the cycle of life, or rather death-in-life, will revive as Apeneck Sweeney visits Mrs. Porter. The entrance of Sweeney propels into *The Waste Land* another symbol of the rebellious flesh. He has already, like Agamemnon, suffered foully through too implicit faith in a woman, in "Sweeney among the Nightingales"; in "Sweeney Erect" he has played Theseus to the epileptic's Ariadne and, more ludicrously, Polyphemus to her Nausicaa. Presently he is to become the Cyclops again, Mr. Eugenides, the one-eyed merchant. His vernal encounter with Mrs. Porter is simply a new travesty of the scene in the Hyacinth garden; John Day's lines, which Eliot parodied, depict Actaeon's fatal meeting with Diana when he saw her bathing naked in a pool. Like the quester with the Grail-bearer, Actaeon suffered the punishment of his folly. He was turned into a stag and was pulled down and slain by his dogs, being an unlucky prototype of the waiter in "Dans le Restaurant."

As for Mrs. Porter, she is first of all Diana ("O the moon shone bright on Mrs. Porter"),[44] who was a fertility goddess before she was the chaste huntress. Doubtless there is also something of Hecate about Mrs. Porter. Both she and her daughter soak their feet in a bicarbonate solution. (Eliot has emphatically denied that the soda water here is anything but water with soda in it—"Not White Rock," he has said.) According to Robert Payne, the original ballad was an "eighteenth-century street-song." Eliot had probably heard "The moon shines bright on Charlie Chaplin," and "Red Wing," the common melody of which is traced by Payne to Schumann's *The Merry Peasant*.[45] Several versions of "Mrs. Porter" were current during World War I. C. M. Bowra states that the song was sung by Australian soldiers at Gallipoli in 1915, but he follows a red herring in alleging that Mrs. Porter herself "seems to have kept a bawdy-house in Cairo."[46] Although her reputation is still green in Australia, she is a mystery even there. Eliot has asseverated that she and her daughter "are known only from an Ayrian campfire song of which one other line has been preserved: 'And so they oughter.' "[47] Actually the words are well known "down under":

> O the moon shines bright on Mrs. Porter
> And on her daughter,
> For she's a snorter.
> O they wash their feet in soapy water,
> And so they oughta,
> To keep them clean.[48]

Payne's text omits the feet:

> The moon shines bright on Mrs. Porter
> And on her daughter:
> She washes out her —— in soda water,
> And so she oughta,
> To keep it clean.

The bath of Diana in her sacred grotto recalls also the ritual washing of feet in Wagner's *Parzival*. The quotation, however, comes from Verlaine's sonnet "Parsifal," where the knight, having mastered the temptations of lust, including sodomy, and cured the King of his wound, adores the Grail and afterward hears "Ces voix d'enfants chantant dans la coupole." The symbol in *The Waste Land* is practically equivalent to that of the children singing in Eliot's "Ode." But the blackguardly intentions of Sweeney, now the quester, have overcome the abstinent spirit of Parsifal, and what follows is again like the situation in "Ode":

Philomel is ravished, though her song is heard once more with the phrase from "A Game of Chess," "So rudely forc'd."[49]

The Tarot Fool, Mr. Eugenides, well born but fallen on evil days, is a cosmopolite, speaking demotic French (not demotic Egyptian) and selling currants in London. The Smyrna question, culminating in the expulsion of the Greeks from Smyrna in 1923, was already of topical interest when *The Waste Land* was written; the merchant is from a city in turmoil, another "Unreal City," perhaps connoting the decay of the Hellenic fertility cults and the Seven Churches of Asia. The very currants of the one-eyed merchant's trade hint that the joyous grape has shriveled up in the waste land. The dried fertility symbol which he transports is equivalent to knowledge of the sacramental Grail mystery, for Jessie L. Weston points out that the cults of Attis and Mithra were spread throughout the Roman Empire partly by Syrian merchants (as well as by soldiers, of whom Albert, the consort of Lil, is a modern representative); and, undoubtedly, Mr. Eugenides, uniting Phlebas the Phoenician sailor and the Fisher King in his boat, is a type of these.[50] His invitation, supposed to be a homosexual one,[51] is a travesty of that which usually the Fisher King makes to the quester outside the Grail castle. It is prepared for by the context of the line from Verlaine.

The one-eyedness of Mr. Eugenides accords with various forms of initiation ritual or myth. Sometimes the one-eyed man is as at this point a symbol of death or winter—the monster whom the primitive hero fights in his lair. In the Grail legend the symbol is uncommon, though the hero of the Welsh "Peredur" meets a one-eyed man at a house of chess players.[52] In other myths the one-eyed man is likely to be a sage magician befriending the hero in his quest; Odin himself is regularly described as one-eyed. Eliot in *The Cocktail Party* assigned to his Falstaffian "vice," Sir Henry, an innocuous version of the popular ballad of "The One-eyed Riley"; in doing so he may have been influenced by a remark of Dr. O'Connor's in Djuna Barnes's *Nightwood*. But Sir Henry, like Mr. Eugenides, is an initiator. It may be observed that in the song "one-eyed" is purely euphemistic. Mr. Eugenides, if not the ritual fool and physician of drama, is sexually ambiguous. He corresponds, moreover, to the chief actor in Frazer's account of the ritual "ride of the beardless one"[53]—which links Mr. Eugenides with the Hanged Man and even explains partly why Mr. Eugenides is unshaven. Either he has no beard to shave or he lets his beard flourish like the bearded Eastern patriarch of the Tarot—the man with three staves and hence a double for the Fisher King. As a businessman Mr. Eugenides frequents a commercial hotel in the City and spends week ends at the famous Brighton Metropole. Whether the quester accompanies him is largely an academic question. Tiresias, appearing next again in his own person, has yielded himself to profane loves and has "foresuffered all" either as a man or as a woman. He has twice changed his sex, according to Ovid's story.[54]

Having already alluded to Actaeon and Diana, Eliot did not follow the alternative myth, used by Tennyson in his "Tiresias," that the prophet was blinded because he saw Pallas Athene naked in her bath, but he apparently drew on Swinburne's "Tiresias" for the phrase "I Tiresias," thus gaining an added identification with Dante, who figures in that poem.[55] The scene contains reminiscences of still other poets. The allusion to Sappho's "Hesperus" is acknowledged in Eliot's notes, but the bit about the sailor comes from R. L. Stevenson's "Requiem," and "Out of the window perilously spread" seems to owe something to Keats's "Ode to a Nightingale." The line anticipates through one word the quest of the Chapel. There seem to be few other imitations in the passage, though "as he guesses" is obviously Chaucerian, and "When lovely woman stoops to folly" comes from Goldsmith's *The Vicar of Wakefield*.

"What Tiresias *sees*" at this point, the fornication of a clerk and a tired typist, summarizes the theme of lust in the poem, besides furnishing in the Grail pattern an episode of the quester's attempted seduction by maidens. Moreover, the act of love, debased through the absence of love into a kind of chemical reaction, implies the very opposite of the ritual prostitution in witch covens and fertility cults, where it is a symbol not of sapped but of created vitality.[56] The "young man carbuncular" is the quester himself; the food laid out in tins is a kind of Grail repast which the Loathly Damsel has prepared. The sailor home from sea (the Syrian merchant again) is the quester after he has crossed the water into the Grail castle, from which he must descend by the stairs into the infernal waste land. Tiresias recognizes in this affair the endless repetitions of vice, his own agony and his own guilt. Here is the worst distortion of the whole mystery. Yet because he has not forgotten the Hyacinth garden, there are times when the old symbols recapture their meaning, when music and the voices of fishmen (though not fishermen) and an old church bring back the tranquillity of an era before his failure. Thus even the shrill gramophone echoes the music heard by Ferdinand in *The Tempest* (Act I, scene 2, lines 391–93):

> This music crept by me upon the waters,
> Allaying both their fury and my passion
> With its sweet air . . .

—the reference to which recalls the image, "A rat crept softly through the vegetation." The mandoline of a street musician is "pleasant," and even the Thames fishmen are hardly like Tiresias the Fisher King; they have what seems a truly symbolic occupation, close by the church of Magnus the Martyr at the foot of London Bridge. The church, rebuilt after the Great Fire destroyed the one for parishioners dwelling on the bridge itself (it had been known as "St. Magnus ad pontem"), was especially the fishmen's church, erected, in fact, on Fish Street Hill, opposite the site of the Fishmongers' Hall. "Fish," "Martyr," and vestmental "white and gold" form a complex link with the Saviour and the ritual of Easter.

The Thames-daughters, counterparts to Woglinde, Wellgunde, and Flosshilde, the Rheintöchter in the *Götterdämmerung*, are a triad like the Moirae or Norns. The place of the latter has already been taken by Madame Sosostris. The river nymphs suggest also the sirens of the *Odyssey*, and in this capacity they are evil powers who lure the quester from his way; like Prufrock among sea-girls he is about to be drowned. Like the Rheintöchter, the Thames-daughters are the victims of fraud; each has her own story of lust and outrage, so that they symbolize rather the plight of the androgynous hero of "The Fire Sermon" than the enticements of harlotry. Their song is in two parts, which they sing together, each part concluding with the cry of the Rheintöchter, "Weialala, leia, Wallala leialala." Afterward they speak, one after another, and describe what has happened to them. It has been observed by Elizabeth Drew that Eliot's description of the Thames barges seems to have been modeled upon the beginning of Conrad's "Heart of Darkness," where the Thames, contrasted and compared with the dark Congo, is an important symbol.[57] The river, sullied with slicks of oil and tar and crowded with drifting debris, flows past Greenwich Hospital on the south bank, where formerly stood old Greenwich House, the birthplace of the first Queen Elizabeth and the palace in which she entertained the Earl of Leicester. Thus after a brief reminder of the earlier theme of the Dog, through a reference to the "gashouse district" of the Isle of Dogs, the song turns in its second part to Elizabeth and Leicester. Idling in their barge, probably to be associated with that of Cleopatra on the Cydnus, they typify the sterile lovers previously encountered.[58] Queen Elizabeth I, another Cleopatra, is practically indistinguishable from Mrs. Porter, for both are subservient to lust. The song trails off with a mention of the ancient stronghold, the White Tower of the Tower of London.

The three daughters correspond approximately to personages already introduced. The first, though from Highbury, is conversant with Queen Elizabeth's favorite Richmond and Kew; at Richmond she has fallen. She resembles the unhappily married La Pia in Dante's *Purgatorio* (V, 130–36). The second, whose feet are perhaps those of Mrs. Porter or her daughter (one would here presume the latter), is a habituée of Moorgate, in the City, and unlike the erstwhile Diana she has not the moon but her heart under her feet. The third, with broken fingernails, apparently deceived at Margate, is doubtless the typist again.[59] These three, whom lust has defiled, have as it were been deprived of their magic gold; so in the *Rheingold* of Wagner the treasure is taken by Alberich from the river nymphs and is withheld until in the *Götterdämmerung* they pull it from the extinguished pyre on which Brünnhilde has joined Siegfried in death.

The symbolism of fire, with analogues in the *Ring* and, indirectly, through the Church of St. Magnus, in the Great Fire of London, unites, as Eliot's note declares, "two representatives of eastern and western asceticism."[60] Both the Buddha and St. Augustine characterized the lusts of the flesh as a burning fire. When Augustine came to Carthage, he found there "a cauldron of unholy loves."[61] The Buddha in his "Fire Sermon" described all things as burning, the only refuge being such an aversion for life that one becomes free of desire and "knows that rebirth is exhausted."[62] That is to say, the goal of the Buddhist ascetic is nirvana. Augustine, too, exhorted his readers to shun the avenues of sense that lead the flesh to sin. Later in the *Confessions* he singled out, in his chapter on visual temptations, the eyes as fetters to evil-doing and rejoiced that God would pluck him from the snare they spread.[63] Eliot seems to have had in mind the words of the prophet Amos (4 : 11), "I have overthrown some of you, as God overthrew Sodom and Gomorrah, and ye were as a firebrand plucked out of the burning: yet have ye not returned unto me, saith the Lord."

The closing lines of Part III make sundry allusions beyond the message of asceticism. The very caldron of Augustine's metaphor usurps the Grail, which Jessie L. Weston tries diligently to show was not a Celtic caldron of plenty, an identification that here the phrase brings irresistibly to view.[64] The Grail should not be unholy, but so it is in "The Fire Sermon." Carthage itself takes one back to Stetson and "the ships at Mylae," to Dido burning on her pyre, and to the Phoenician traders. The Buddha, as Jessie L. Weston remarks, is sometimes pictured in the attitude of a fisherman, called in the Mahayana scriptures "the Fisherman who draws fish from the ocean of Samsara to the light of Salvation."[65] Augustine himself (or more probably Augustine of Canterbury, though here the coincidence of names suffices) belongs in the Grail quest through the curious circumstance, which Jessie L. Weston relates, of there being a Chapel of St. Austin in the *Perlesvaus* (*Perceval le Gallois*). This Chapel, a source of Jessie L. Weston's material for her theory of astral initiations, is a form of the Chapel Perilous common to many versions of the legend.[66]

"The Fire Sermon" is the cardinal turning point of the poem. Up to Eliot's "collocation" of St. Augustine and the Buddha, the quest to be reconciled through love and the fusion of body and spirit has reached nothing except disappointment. But asceticism is a way of reaching the terminus of union with Love itself. If what goes by the name of love can only draw one further downward into the hell of the waste land, with its seething caldrons of lust, then one must reject all burning; if one cannot be brought through love into the center, one must seek the center by another road. Yet *The Waste Land* does not realize a full victory for Tiresias, and no later work of Eliot disregards some importunate echo of love calling through flesh, even though the voice of the divine darkness becomes clearer, calling for the negation of all burning things.

## IV. *"Death by Water"*

The death of Phlebas writes the epitaph to the experience by which the quester has failed in the garden. In one sense it resymbolizes that failure, just as the closing lines of "Dans le Restaurant" recapitulate the terror there. But inasmuch as in *The Waste Land* the inability to love signifies the ascendancy of lust, Phlebas the Phoenician, the joint incarnation of Mr. Eugenides and an unsaved Ferdinand, drowns for the same reason that the quester in another guise becomes a buried corpse. He is not resurrected, nor does the corpse sprout. Instead he is sucked into the whirlpool, and, in a manner of speaking, he has been on the whirling wheel all the time, performing the same nugatory transactions of life that obsess Hakagawa, the connoisseur of Titian, for example, and the others whose furtive pleasure it is to divide Christ "among whispers." Now it is Phlebas who disintegrates in "fractured atoms." He is still, as Buddhists say, "bound to the wheel."

> As he rose and fell
> He passed the stages of his age and youth
> Entering the whirlpool.

His drowning, against which Madame Sosostris has warned him, re-enacts the rise and fall in the flower garden and the rise and decline through which, headed for death, he has passed his life; and as he dies the same movement returns, passing, in accordance with the superstition, as an instantaneous memory through his mind.[67] And yet, on an ironic level, he is like Christ; he is the sacrificial god descending into the waters. Jessie L. Weston (following an account based on Lucian) describes the annual rite of casting into the sea at Alexandria a papyrus effigy of the head of Adonis, to be borne by a current to Byblos, and after seven days to be fished out jubilantly by votaries of the cult.[68] But for Phlebas the baptism is a descent followed by no emergence; his seven days have lengthened into a fortnight; he is no Lycidas, "sunk low but mounted high," and his eyes like those of Tiresias have not been turned to pearls. His death resembles that in Part IV of "The Dry Salvages." If it hints also at the physical death beyond the death-in-life of the waste land, it certainly offers no hope of immortality, or of an escape from the wheel, but rather a lapse into hell or the endlessly recurring avatars of suffering in the flesh. Lastly, or perhaps more properly, first of all, Phlebas dies in the capacity of a Syrian merchant, carrying, according to Jessie L. Weston's theory, the Grail mystery to Britain—the merchant with his blank card.[69] The lines intone a defunctive music, regretful and admonitory, counseling everyone who turns the wheel, "Gentile or Jew," to renounce the traffic in worldly things and the lusts of the flesh which sunder men from love.

## V. "What the Thunder Said"

After the quester's wound in the garden, his immersion in the sea of lust, he languishes in a desert; and though now he should understand that salvation can redound from nothing and no one trapped there with him, the struggle not to desire, to accept and not to will, still imposes agony. The ascetic way, pointed to in "The Fire Sermon," he has not adopted. By a second initiation in this quest he attempts to achieve peace by turning directly to religion; but, just as love has failed because he has not affirmed it, religion fails because he does not make the requisite denial—the denial of self permitting an affirmation of self-discipline.

The opening lines of Part V, alluding to Gethsemane and Golgotha and to the failure of the quester's search for love, say, in effect, that death has not been conquered:

> He who was living is now dead
> We who were living are now dying.

The desert, like the wilderness of Sinai, contains no water, nor is there anyone to bring forth from the rock of life such a stream as Moses summoned with his rod. The rocks are dry like the rotten teeth of a skull. The region of the quester's wandering is a place of torture; hence the image borrowed from low, narrow cells of medieval dungeons.[70] In the midst of the physical waste land, where the cicada, like the grasshopper in the twelfth chapter of Ecclesiastes, is a burden, the quester longs for even the illusion of dripping water, for the voice of the hermit-thrush which would symbolize the Hermit of the Grail legend and, thus, spiritual redemption. He longs for the pine trees, sacred to Attis, the hanged god.[71] Now he is climbing up into the mountains, a place of thunder but no rain. The geographic location of this journey is not specified; it is partly in Palestine and partly in the foothills of the Himalaya,[72] just as the spiritual quest is partly in the Western and partly in the Eastern tradition. The travelers to Emmaus also passed through a waste land of defeat. Just as, when Christ appeared to the two disciples, they did not see that He had risen, so here the protagonist's blindness prevents him, as always, from seeing that life may come through death. His own death in the garden and in the sea has been analogous to the Hanged Man's sacrifice, but it has not merged with that sacrifice itself. Tiresias is a wounded god who is not God; he can be healed only by the unfound Redeemer. Like the disciples he believes that "He who was living is now dead"; the supposition is true of himself, but not of Christ, who still walks half-seen on the other side.[73]

Although the line "I do not know whether a man or a woman" refers to the visitant, as it must rhetorically, the uncertainty mirrors Tiresias' variable sex and supplies an allusion to the emasculate Attis. But perhaps the visitant is not Christ alone. The weird event forms an interesting parallel to a Buddhist legend in H. C. Warren's *Buddhism in Translations*, which may have influenced the passage. According to the story, a wise man, meeting a woman on the highway, begged alms of her. She only laughed at him, but since as she did so she displayed her teeth, he was enabled to achieve sainthood through realizing the essential impurity of her body, whose naked bones he had glimpsed; and a little later, meeting her husband in search of her, the saint replied to his question:

> "Was it a woman, or a man,
> That passed this way? I cannot tell.
> But this I know, a set of bones
> Is traveling on upon this road."[74]

The application to the quester's problem is obvious.

The women weeping for Christ and the women weeping for Tammuz, Osiris, and Attis blend together, their cry being a "Murmur of maternal lamentation." And on the plains are "hooded hordes," partly barbarians from the steppes, threatening to sweep over Europe, partly Tibetan tribesmen, perpetuating after a fashion the traditions of Buddhism. The nightmare of civilization in chaos mingles with a view of falling churches in the unreal cities. The Grail Chapel falls as the religious and cultural capitals are falling, the cities of the plain.

In approaching the Chapel Perilous and the Perilous Cemetery the quester as in the romances has to confront apparitions and terrors, of which the collapse of the cities is one. The Grail initiation at the Chapel Perilous constitutes what Jessie L. Weston calls "a journey to the Worlds beyond,"[75] like that of Owain Miles to St. Patrick's purgatory. It is in effect—and the mortuary atmosphere is indication enough —a descent into the grave, into the regions of the dead, so that the initiate may achieve spiritual knowledge. Jessie L. Weston attaches to the experience a mystical meaning. In *The Waste Land* the quester hardly wishes to penetrate to a deeper hell than the one he is already in; but he must try to make a spiritual descent which shall be a spiritual ascent similar to his search in the Hyacinth garden but now abjuring the flesh. For, as in the scheme which Eliot was to adopt much later, "the way up and the way down are one and the same."

The trial here incorporates fragments from previous encounters—the hair, the violet light, the towers, and the bells.[76] These last represent not only the unheeded church bells of London but the bell to be rung after a successful initiation at the Chapel Perilous.[77] The confused, unnatural imagery of the lines (ll. 379–84) was partly inspired, according to Eliot, by a painting from the school of Hieronymus Bosch.[78] Possibly he meant the panel entitled "Hell" (sometimes called "The Sinful World") forming a diptych with Bosch's "The Deluge." The relevant detail depicts a batlike creature, with dull human features, crawling head first down a rock wall.[79] Hieronymus Bosch was the painter, par excellence, of degradation translated into nauseous anatomical horror. The malformations of his subjects are man's own singular vices objectified. The quester in *The Waste Land* has encountered content of his own mind and through it the real state of the world outside him—the spiritual corpses of "all the lost adventurers," his peers. In direst plight perhaps is the Chapel itself, a symbol of the Church, through which he is seeking comfort. Its decay and desolation amount not merely to the conventional delusions besetting the quester in the romances; they are the actual ruins, the "dry bones," of formal religion in the Western world.

The cock, crowing enigmatically in Portuguese while perched on the rooftree, is the power to disperse the darkness and the shapes that walk by night.[80] A bird of sacrifice and good omen, it symbolizes the living Spirit beyond the dead Chapel, able even now to pour rain upon the land if the quester succeeds. The sunken river and the dry foliage await the outcome of the test; the approaching rain will fall if the quester gives assent to the three commands of the thunder. But this he cannot do. The test, like that in the garden, is one of worthiness. The voice of the god Pragâpati utters in the sound of the thunder the three cryptic syllables "Da Da Da," that is, "give, sympathize, control."[81] If the quester could reply, "I have given, I have sympathized, I have controlled," he could end his vigil and achieve restoration and spiritual rebirth. But because it is no more possible to answer the question affirmatively than to have asked another question among the hyacinths, he can only fail the second initiation like the first. Thus the voice of the cock becomes an ironic symbol, for, like Peter, who three times denied his Lord before the second crowing, the quester has abandoned the Hanged Man and has held back the longed-for rain, not at this moment alone, but throughout the quest. The "freeing of the waters," the pristine object of the fertility ritual in the *Rig-Veda* to which Jessie L. Weston traces the symbolism of the Grail legend, must wait.

The quester's three negative aswers deny not the self but the means to redemption; they are the wrong denials, refusals to descend and submit. They are expressed as replies to the three commands, and, since they form one of the most oblique passages in the poem, their dramatic connection is difficult to grasp. The first surely concerns the sexual blunder to which Tiresias has already confessed. The surrender has involved no acceptance of love, of the demands of life, but a yielding to lust—a choice which "an age of prudence can never retract." This alone, the craven surrender to a tyranny of the blood, has secretly dominated the quester's whole existence, though it is "not to be found in our obituaries." Joined with him in disgrace is someone else, the conjunct partner in a lust now become bondage. Whether this surrender denotes more or less than the failure in the garden, it is symbolically identical with it. The echo of Webster's *The White Devil* is to the point:

> —ô Men
> That lye upon your death-beds, and are haunted
> With howling wives, neere trust them, they'le re-marry
> Ere the worme peirce your winding sheete: ere the Spider
> Make a thinne curtaine for your Epitaphes.

The second denial, that of sympathy, has proceeded from the same cause. Like the traitor Ugolino, the speaker is shut in the horrible tower of his own loneliness, and he has also lost sympathy through his surrender to the imprisonment. The introduction of another traitor, Coriolanus, who betrayed his country and those who loved him, characterizes the quester as a renegade from his own land and traditions. The questing knight traduces the land when he fails in his initiation.

The third denial, that of control, refers to the hyacinth girl again, to Tristan and Isolde, and, ironically, to the line "My nerves are bad to-night" in "A Game of Chess." Eliot may have had in mind Arnold's "Dover Beach" and the entreaty, "Ah, love, let us be true / To one another!"—an appeal which is now unavailing, regardless of what "would have" been.

With this first and last failure the initiation concludes. The arid plain stretches behind Tiresias, who is still fishing and still wounded. He has found no love or redemption, for he has turned his back on both. He is like King Hezekiah, hearing in his sickness the bidding of Isaiah (38 : 1): "Set thine house in order: for thou shalt die, and not live." But this Fisher King has little left to set in order; his domains are stricken and the bridge to salvation at the Grail castle—London Bridge near St. Magnus the Martyr—has fallen down. The song "London

Bridge," and the game dramatizing it, are said to be folk survivals of the primitive rite of the foundation sacrifice—of the slaughter of a victim to avert evil from a newly built bridge or other structure. The scapegoat is represented in the song by the prisoner behind the stones:

> Take the key and lock him up, lock him up, lock him up,
> Take the key and lock him up, my fair lady.

Belladonna, the fair lady, has locked Tiresias up in a tower of morbid enslavement. Yet, again like King Hezekiah, Tiresias may even now come back to life and through prayer and patience avert from himself the general destruction. By self-restraint through the triple law of the thunder he must prepare for "a deeper communion," attainable not through fleshly love or through the ruined Chapel but through abnegation of his will. The remedy is that of Arnaut Daniel (who symbolizes the lusts of Mr. Eugenides), to accept voluntarily the refinement of the cleansing fire. From purgation and from the placid acceptance of what life can offer will ensue the transformation of the ravished spirit silenced in the garden, the metamorphosis into an "inviolable voice," like that of Philomel (the swallow in the form of the myth borrowed here from the *Pervigilium Veneris*).[82]

Meanwhile, disinherited, even as "Le Prince d'Aquitaine" in Nerval's "El Desdichado," Tiresias waits in a cruel April for his own spring to return beside the demolished tower, the Tower in the Tarot pack. This Tower, which the card calls "La Maison Dieu" ("the Hospital"), is a dismal pile of crumbling masonry, struck by a thunderbolt, with two figures, a man and a woman, hurtling from its summit. It is evidently a symbol of the shattered marriage in "A Game of Chess," the prison where the quester's surrender locked him up with Belladonna. Yet its broken ruins have not set him free; it is broken and not broken, and the surrender is irrevocable. Tiresias is alone spiritually, but not otherwise.

The difficult references to *The Spanish Tragedy*—"Why then Ile fit you" and "Hieronymo's mad againe"—have the function both of summarizing the poem and of universalizing the symbols. The first quotation from Kyd (Act IV, scene 1, line 69) pertains to Hieronymo's scheme to kill the murderers of his son while they enact a play for the entertainment of the viceroy. Balthazar and Lorenzo have asked him to help them, and he promises to fit into their plans while intending to make them fit into his own. The second quotation echoes the subtitle of *The Spanish Tragedy* in the quarto of 1615. The most obvious connection between Hieronymo and *The Waste Land* is that at the end of the tragedy the old man bites out his tongue; but Hieronymo, besides serving for another allusion to Philomel, corresponds to Tiresias in a further way. He is an inspired madman, a prophet, who oversees the destinies of the other characters and who must, like an ancient prophet, be mad in order to do so.[83] In *The Spanish Tragedy* the business of Hieronymo is to avenge the hanging of Horatio; in *The Waste Land* the business of Tiresias is to restore his youth, which, in a manner of speaking, has been slain like the Hanged Man on the tree. Hieronymo succeeds; Tiresias fails: but at least the destruction prophesied by Tiresias will also come to pass. The fragments he has shored against his own ruins fit equally well the ruins of all society; the quotation says, in essence, that you too, "mon semblable, mon frère," have your ruins: you too are the Fisher King in need of the prescribed cure. In proclaiming his madness, Tiresias is announcing that he has become a prophet to warn the crumbling world. Over against the prospect of its irremediable calamity stands the counsel of the Aryan myth, to give, sympathize, and be controlled, that all may come at length to peace.

The poem has ended with the focus again upon the present Tiresias. What his memories have dramatized is his past effort to appease the gnawing of fleshly and spiritual desire. They have summed up the crucial experiences that leave him unable to participate, through his interior life, in the April renewal of earth. Yet he has his fragments—touchstones, Matthew Arnold might have called them. Without words of hope to prop his mind Tiresias would be Empedocles on Etna; with them, attentive to their suasion, he may exorcise despair. His quest through his private waste land, the poet's quest through the poem, has achieved nothing that either fertility religion or the ascetic traditions set as a positive goal. His quest for love has failed; his quest for spiritual knowledge remains only inceptive and must still proceed, not through a mere formality of religion, but through inward conversion. But the very act of recognition, the deliberate acknowledgment of humility, points toward ultimate triumph, if not for society, nevertheless for himself. He can expect, if not the joy of Ferdinand, then at any rate the liberation of Prospero.[84]

# 7 DEATH'S DREAM KINGDOM: "THE HOLLOW MEN"

*The Waste Land,* in the possible release it sug-
gests from the quandary of intractable flesh contending with reluctant
spirit, is in one way more akin to the recent poetry of Eliot than to
"The Hollow Men" or *Ash Wednesday.* It sacrifices along with love the
feminine image which in a more nearly Dantean pattern would be-
token salvation. It gives up the quest through action and accepts the
quest through suffering. Admitting that in the midst of life we are in
death, it pronounces its hope that this world of death may disclose a
means of life. It turns hell into purgatory. The alternative it thus exhibits has affinities with the negative mysticism of St. John of the
Cross, though this exerted no influence upon Eliot until several years
after 1921, and had no dominant philosophical influence until the writing of "Burnt Norton" in 1935. The poems from "The Hollow Men"
to "Triumphal March" (excluding the skit *Sweeney Agonistes*) adhere
more than *The Waste Land* to the archetype revealed in "Prufrock"
and elaborated in "Gerontion." That is, they depict static despair confronting the true "center," sometimes of love, sometimes of faith, and
sometimes of both. With the single exception of "Marina," which almost by deceit ends happily, they express either pitiful rebellion against
death or tranquil resignation to it. They do not show submissiveness to
a protracted death-in-life. Even *Ash Wednesday,* Eliot's nearest approach to Dante, utilizes the "patience" theme from St. John of the
Cross ("to care and not to care") almost entirely as an interim refuge
until the protagonist and his symbolic Lady can perhaps be reunited.

"The Hollow Men" was the outgrowth of several years' experimenta-
tion. In symbolism it shows the influence of Dante, as does "The
Burial of the Dead," but metrically and rhetorically it produces an almost wholly new effect. Like "Gerontion" it employs the drama of the

99

speaking voice, the voice of one of the hollow men, in a soliloquy of irregular rhythms and abrupt images reminiscent of Imagistic practices. The growth of the work is traceable in some detail. In the autumn of 1924 three poems, "Eyes That Last I Saw in Tears," "The Wind Sprang Up at Four O'Clock," and "This Is the Dead Land," appeared in the *Chapbook* under the general title "Doris's Dream Songs." The first of these and Part II and Part IV of "The Hollow Men" (as finally organized) were published in the *Criterion* for January, 1925, and the first three parts of "The Hollow Men" alone in the *Dial* two months later, Part I ("We are the hollow men") having previously appeared with a French translation by St.-J. Perse in *Commerce*. Part V of "The Hollow Men" was first printed in *Poems 1909–1925*. It is impossible to say whether "Eyes That Last I Saw in Tears" or the middle three parts of "The Hollow Men" were in *The Waste Land* before Pound edited it. But it is probable that some lines of "The Hollow Men," especially of Part III, had occurred in that manuscript. The "stone images" in the "cactus land" might well be those of "The Burial of the Dead." As for "Eyes That Last I Saw in Tears," it has some affinity, through one image, to "Song to the Opherian," though certainly much less than "The Wind Sprang Up at Four O'Clock." "The Hollow Men," one suspects, was constructed upon fragments retrieved from *The Waste Land,* and it assuredly began from "Doris's Dream Songs." Only the third one of those appeared in the completed "Hollow Men"; the others were relegated to the limbo of "Minor Poems."

Like *Sweeney Agonistes* (1924–25), "Doris's Dream Songs" revive the rather enigmatic Doris of "Sweeney Erect"; and though obviously songs to Doris, not songs of Doris, they conceal her identity too well to justify particular conjectures. "Eyes That Last I Saw in Tears," which is better disciplined than "The Wind Sprang Up at Four O'Clock," seems in isolation an almost meaningless chant, but it has a source in the Lamentations of Jeremiah, derided by Judah for whose afflictions he wept, and it thus belongs with the complaints of "The Fire Sermon" and "What the Thunder Said."[1] Since the poem avoids explaining its predominant emotion of wretchedness, it needs a dramatic context. Although "The Hollow Men" with its "kingdoms" exhibits a similar landscape, one cannot say precisely what the speaker has lost that he may not find again. He remembers weeping eyes, but he cannot recapture the vision of sympathetic tears or hope to meet with other than derision when he meets those eyes after death.[2] The poem is not unconnected with the hyacinth-girl passage of *The Waste Land*; perhaps, indeed, it amounts to the quester's mourning for the "golden vision" in the garden. The Pre-Raphaelite manner of "La Figlia che Piange" does not carry over into this poem, which yet hints at a division between lovers as in "The Blessed Damozel."

"The Wind Sprang Up at Four O'Clock" incorporates about half of "Song to the Opherian" but omits all the details of resemblance between this and "Eyes That Last I Saw in Tears." The subject of love has disappeared; what remains is a kind of nightmare vision. This was apparently suggested both by the tumult of savages in Conrad's "Heart of Darkness" and by Kipling's "La Nuit Blanche"; "the Tartar horsemen," however, who do not occur in "Song to the Opherian," are of indeterminate origin. Perhaps they came from Huysmans' *A rebours*. Eliot has remarked on how one image in Kipling's poem appears also in the story "At the End of the Passage."[3] A "Face . . . blind and weeping," which "couldn't wipe Its eyes," is different in connotation from Eliot's image of "a face that sweats with tears," but it is comparable in visual effect. The face in Kipling's lines "whistled shrill with wrath," like the audible bats in "What the Thunder Said." For "Song to the Opherian" Eliot very likely adopted one of his images from Supilaw-yat's kissing the idol's foot in "Mandalay," and, if so, he conceivably took his bells from the same source. The final line of "The Hollow Men," "Not with a bang but a whimper," brings to mind Eliot's praise for the effectiveness of "whimpers" in "Danny Deever": " 'What's that that whimpers over'ead?' "[4] The title of "The Hollow Men," he has stated, was arrived at by combining "The Hollow Land," from William Morris, with "The Broken Men," from Kipling.[5] That sounds so ingenious and improbable that the explanation might be a joke.

"This is the Dead Land," the last of "Doris's Dream Songs," seems to contain nothing borrowed from Kipling; instead it has a paraphrase of two lines from James Thomson's "Art" (Part III). In *The Use of Poetry and the Use of Criticism* Eliot has cited the passage.[6] Thomson had written:

> Singing is sweet; but be sure of this,
> Lips only sing when they cannot kiss.

In writing,

> Lips that would kiss
> Form prayers to broken stone,

Eliot perhaps had also in mind Juliet's line ". . . lips that they must use in prayer" and the whole sonnet-dialogue between her and Romeo at their first meeting (*Romeo and Juliet*, Act I, scene 5, lines 95 ff.).

In 1924 Eliot contributed an Introduction to Paul Valéry's *Le Serpent*. In discussing some other poems that had attracted him, he quoted two stanzas of Valéry's "Cantique des Colonnes," and in so doing disclosed a model for two lines of "The Hollow Men," written a few weeks before the edition appeared:

> Shape without form, shade without colour,
> Paralysed force, gesture without motion.[7]

He had fitted a phrase of Marlow in "Heart of Darkness"—"a vision of grayness without form"—describing Marlow's feelings after the death of Kurtz,[8] into the cadences of Valéry:

> Servantes sans genoux
> Sourires sans figures,
> La belle devant nous
> Se sent les jambes pures.

Again, Part V of "The Hollow Men" reflects the influence of Valéry's "Le Cimetière marin," from which Eliot culled the line "Entre le vide et l'événement pur," comparing it in his Introduction with a speech of Brutus in *Julius Caesar* (Act II, scene 1, lines 63–65):

> Between the acting of a dreadful thing
> And the first action, all the interim is
> Like a phantasma or a hideous dream.[9]

Eliot's "Between the motion / And the act" echoes the words of Shakespeare, but the rhythm recalls Valéry; and "Between the idea / And the reality" makes an approximate translation.

The stylistic sources of "The Hollow Men" and of the short poems grouped with it do not in themselves provide many clues to the pattern of meaning. In *The Waste Land*, whatever it may have been before Pound dismembered it, one sees a body of separate images and vignettes, unified chiefly not by logical joints but by the anatomical chart of the Grail legend; and yet these details of structure, being dramatic, succeed in looking interrelated. But in "The Hollow Men," since its drama mainly depends on a continuing voice, nothing like a plot is visible, and the images are simply disconnected. Despite the dramatic postures—the hollow men "Leaning together," the "tree swinging," the lips praying to "broken stone," the groping shapes beside "the

tumid river," and the despondent shuffle round "the prickly pear"—
there are no dramatically motivated actions. There are no beginning
and middle, only an end. "The Hollow Men" is not unique among
Eliot's poems in being about a state—"Prufrock," "Gerontion," and
*The Waste Land* deal each with the state of its own protagonist (in the
manner which Pierre Legouis has defined as the "psychologically
dramatic").[10] But these all imply a past which, having brought about
such a state, furnishes some dramatic pretext for its emotions. From
"The Hollow Men" are absent any illustrative memories to epitomize
the sequence by which the speaker has sunk to his misery; there is not
even the reasoning process of "Prufrock." To have dramatic clarity, the
poem would need either a passage explaining the speaker's dilemma in
facing the past or else, perhaps, a scheme of consecutive allusions, a
myth. It would then be very different, losing no doubt the symbolic
intensity conferred by its mysteriousness but at the same time gaining
in dramatic force. That Eliot saw the problem is clear from his inclu-
sion of two epigraphs, each of which alludes to a quasi-dramatic pattern, and from his use of certain other echoes with a like function. But
"The Hollow Men"—and the influence of Valéry is relevant—marked
one of Eliot's nearest approaches to *la poésie pure,* though one need
not imagine that the poem held no denotative unity for Eliot himself.

The epigraphs indicate two lines of analogy drawn by "The Hollow
Men." " 'Mr. Kurtz—he dead,' " from "Heart of Darkness," is the
black servant's contemptuous announcement that the remarkable white
god of the Congo has expired.[11] "A penny for the Old Guy" is the
formula by which children solicit money for fireworks on Guy Fawkes
Day, the fifth of November. The connection between Kurtz and Guy
Fawkes is that both are "lost / Violent souls" commemorated only as
"the hollow men / . . . the stuffed men." Indeed, Marlow calls Kurtz
"hollow at the core."[12] That in another aspect Kurtz and Guy Fawkes
are not completely hollow, since the one, as Marlow acknowledged, attains an affirmative victory by recognizing the "horror" and the other
commits himself to action, serves but to reduce by comparison the dignity of Eliot's own hollow men. Part I of the poem (originally dated
November, 1924) depicts the scarecrow-like effigies of "poor Guys" in
the modern waste land.[13] One of these is the speaker himself, waiting
among the other straw dummies for the consuming fire. To this state
he has come, apparently through his refusal of the vision; like Tiresias
or Dante's Ugolino at the last, he is sightless.

Although "The Hollow Men" is not a mere appendage to *The Waste Land*, it may most profitably be read as an extension of the same design of quest and failure. The quest has already failed once when the poem opens. The history of Kurtz in "Heart of Darkness" conforms to the general pattern. Conrad may often be understood best through the study of primitive rituals of succession, initiation, and fertility. That Kurtz has been initiated into the tribe, becoming its shaman, its "rain and fine weather" maker, and that he has been ceremonially worshiped and appeased, seems an express symbol of his disastrous descent into the dark places. The gracious figure of his "Intended," from whom he has turned to immerse himself in the shadows, represents the light which Marlow, shaken by his own knowledge of the horror, is scarcely able to credit, except as either an illusion of the innocent or an ideal of the courageous. What happens actually to Kurtz happens figuratively to Marlow, who voyages into a hell so dreadful that he comes back unconvinced of any other reality. The sheer Manichaeism of the revelation only narrowly fails to overwhelm with darkness Marlow as well as Kurtz. Kurtz, after undertaking to combat darkness and devils, yields to them and is installed in the midst of them and, despite his final relative victory of self-knowledge, cannot avert his damnation. The whole design approximates that of hero-myths, but it combines with curious subtlety the quest to subdue evil with a quest to restore the god overtaken by death in the guise of life. In a sense Kurtz is like the Fisher King and Marlow is like the quester, but Kurtz has been a quester too.

The main parallel between "Heart of Darkness" and "The Hollow Men" consists in the theme, implicit throughout the latter, of debasement through the rejection of good, of despair through consequent guilt. In Part II of the poem the speaker confesses the impossibility of facing "the eyes," even in dreams, in the dream kingdom of his world; and in his imagination he encounters only their symbolic counterparts —sunlight, a tree, voices in the wind. The sunlight, however, shines only on "a broken column" among the broken desert images.[14] His inability to return and brave the eyes resembles Tiresias' state after the scene in the Hyacinth garden. In *The Waste Land* the lost eyes are those of the protagonist himself; here they are the upbraiding eyes of one incarnating his lost redemption. The speaker takes refuge in apathy; he desires to think of himself only as a scarecrow. He shrinks from everything but concealment among the other hollow men and wears, with them,

> Such deliberate disguises
> Rat's coat, crowskin, crossed staves
> In a field.

What he cannot contemplate is the reproach of

> . . . that final meeting
> In the twilight kingdom,

when at length he may meet the eyes in the real world of the dead.

The scarecrow symbol (like Hawthorne's "Feathertop") is appropriate to designate not only the ineptness and spiritual flaccidity of the speaker but, like the "tattered coat upon a stick" in Yeats's "Sailing to Byzantium" (1927), his inability to attain love. If one turns back to *The Golden Bough* and to some of the most ancient as well as most persistent rituals of pagan Europe, it is the straw man who seems to have functioned in certain of the fire festivals as a sacrificial representative of the vegetation spirit or as a scapegoat ridding his folk of accumulated ill-chance.[15] The commemoration of the fifth of November itself reflects the custom of burning in effigy the bearer of local guilt; the accident of the season—for Guy Fawkes Day shortly follows All Souls' —may have suggested kindling traditional autumn fires for the modern culprit. A connection between the straw man and the Fisher King will be easily apparent, for Eliot's hollow men re-enact the distress of the mutilated Tiresias.

The figurative straw dummies of the poem suffer both physically and spiritually. How they themselves have erred, the poem does not demonstrate. It is plain enough, however, that they are all but damned; and not for nothing is there an allusion here, as in "The Burial of the Dead," to the third canto of the *Inferno,* where those who "lived without blame, and without praise," are doomed to abide at Acheron without crossing into hell. But it is meaningful that the hollow men are not bound to such a torment as theirs: to follow the whirling ensign, goaded by hornets and wasps. Instead they are like the throng awaiting (with "pennies for the Old 'Guy' ") the barge of Charon to ferry them across to their everlasting sorrow in the depths. The eyes, terrible and unrelenting, even resemble the glowing coals of Charon's eyes, as described in both the *Aeneid* and the *Commedia,* or the streaming eyes of the demon in Kipling's "At the End of the Passage." But the very possibility of descending, of not being forced to remain on the hither shore, paradoxically signifies hope. Miraculously, the eyes that may reappear beyond the river portend salvation. As commentators have recognized, they are comparable to the eyes of Beatrice in the *Purgatorio* (XXX–XXXI). For the pattern of descent and ascent implies that having plunged into hell, the hollow men may find paradise. Part IV of the poem establishes a geography: the scarecrows, loitering beside "the tumid river" (a fixture also of "Heart of Darkness"), are trapped in Ezekiel's valley of bones, where, as in the "circular desert" of *The Family Reunion,* their suffering seems futile. Theirs is the "dream kingdom" where the eyes are but a memory. They must invade the "other kingdom," the "twilight kingdom" of actual death, which, after further purgatorial trial, may vouchsafe to them, through the eyes of pain and joy, a way upward, even to the "multifoliate rose" of the final cantos of the *Paradiso*,[16] to "the perpetual star," a symbol of the Holy Virgin. The way up and the way down are the same; the landscape is not Dantean except in so far as its moral and emotional processes match the allegory of the *Commedia.* And here, apparent hell is potential, though unrealized, purgatory.

In "Heart of Darkness" as in the *Commedia,* the feminine symbol, a prototype of the eyes in "The Hollow Men," charts the quester's pilgrimage into the region of pain; Kurtz's descent is irretraceable. But Dante's leads finally upward to his vision, beyond the eyes, beyond even the celestial spheres. And "The Hollow Men" has a similar pattern; moreover, as Genevieve W. Foster has shown in her Jungian analysis, the eyes, the rose, and the star are equivalent to the "Grail" of *The Waste Land.*[17] So, too, is the tree, recurring in *Coriolan* and "New Hampshire," and, through the children in the leaves, in "Burnt Norton" also.[18] (Here it ironically reminds one of Kurtz, "a tree swayed by the wind.") "The Hollow Men" would re-express the affirmative way by abjuring lust, the false center, the "prickly pear" of Part V, circled in a whirling or whirlpool motion, and by declaring the speaker's hope for the eyes. (In the negative way, the abandonment of lust would have to be ratified by renunciation of the affirmative symbol and by evacuation of desire.) But attainment of the vision, according to "The Hollow Men," is remote indeed. The agony of "Lips that would kiss," the unalleviated "anguish of the marrow / The ague of the skeleton," lacerates the heart with proximate desire.

The first four lines of Part V parody "The Mulberry Bush," substi-

tuting for the fertility symbol connoting love (as in the legend of
Pyramus and Thisbe) an image purely phallic. And echoing the chant
of the May games, "Here we go gathering nuts in May . . . At five
o'clock in the morning," with its reminiscence of the Maypole dance
and the "country copulatives," they underscore the sexual nature of
the plight with which the poem deals. In this terminal section, one is
back, so to speak, in the marriage chamber of Eliot's "Ode," where sex
has gone wrong. And in spite of the plain statement that the hollow
men must remain "sightless" unless the rose reappears, love, along with
powers of creation and repentance, is still sought in the world of nightmare.

With every effort to make the potential become actual a "Shadow"
interferes. This, whatever its private value, has in the poem no clear
conceptual reference. It implies Prufrockian inertia incapable of con-
necting imagination and reality, a defect of *kinesis*, in part a volitional
weakness and in part an external constraint. Deathlike, it hinders even
the attempt at prayer through which the speaker might come into the
"Kingdom" of pure actuality beyond. Eliot's threefold grouping of
contrasts between prospect and fulfilment comprehends three failures.
The oppositions of potentiality and actuality are not the Aristotelian or
Thomistic ones; they blur as the enumeration passes from "potency"
and "existence" to "essence" and "descent," but each constitutes an
antithesis compatible with Aristotelian dialectic. Even "motion," normally actual, can fit into the potential category through its special
meaning of "initial impulse," by which it contrasts with "act." Each of
the three groups (by ambiguities) recapitulates the preceding, until by
accumulation all three groups combine in the third, just as, according
to Aristotle, the soul includes in its highest powers those of the inferior
species. Perhaps the first group chiefly connotes sex; the second, sex
and creation; the last, sex, creation, and salvation.

The tripartite character of the problem, if never unambiguous, is
discernible in such words as "act," "creation," and "descent." The
emotional act of love is an emotional act of creation; the act of creation
is an act of incarnation. In a punning logic, comparable to the rationale of Book IV of Pope's *Dunciad*, the creative difficulties experienced by the poet parallel the spiritual difficulties of accepting the
descending Spirit of God. In *Ash Wednesday* and "Burnt Norton" the
double value of "word" and "Word" is almost as evident as in Pope.
Here—in connection with Eliot's recurrent disquiet, which he phrased

in 1947 as a fear "of never again writing anything worth reading,"[19] and with the fact of his religious conversion in the middle 1920's— these two latter aspects of the struggle seem quite personal to Eliot himself. It is not too fanciful to guess that the lines refer partly to the writing of this poem. Like Valéry, he was interested in the poem as a process;[20] his allusion to that interest resembles Gide's device in *Les Faux Monnayeurs*. Simultaneously Eliot was stating a general impediment to poetic creation. Coleridge in "Dejection" insisted that the imagination must be nourished by joy, exactly what is missing in the world of the hollow men.[21] But "The Hollow Men," like "Dejection," *was* written; creative inability is as inspired a subject for poetry as any other. The three problems, along with that of history (barely suggested as a general symbol in "The Hollow Men"), compose the substance of *Four Quartets;* "Burnt Norton" designates the triad as "the world of sense," "the world of fancy," and "the world of spirit."

Eliot, during his graduate studies at Harvard, applied himself for two years to Charles Lanman's course in Sanskrit and spent a year, as he has remarked, "in the mazes of Patanjali's metaphysics" under James Wood. The experience, though it left him "in a state of enlightened mystification,"[22] may possibly have percolated through to "The Hollow Men." The Hindu Trimurti, Siva, Brahma, and Vishnu, who respectively embody the powers of reproduction and destruction, of creation, and of preservation or salvation, might almost be the patrons of the three ideals. The power of Siva is the power in sex and in the cycle of death and rebirth; that of Brahma, God the creator of the world, is the power in mind; that of Vishnu, incarnate as Saviour, is the power in the descending Spirit that preserves men from evil. Vishnu, in Hindu mythology, is described as having assumed nine incarnations to deliver mankind and as being destined, in his tenth and final incarnation of the white horse, to destroy the earth. His *atman* is his essence; his *avatara,* his descent. In every avatar essential *atman* takes on flesh, and the supreme Avatar is the descent of Vishnu to unite the divine and the created. It is difficult, nor should it seem desirable at this point, to discriminate precisely between Eastern and Western modes of thought. For the hollow men no redemption is effectual.

The poem thus ends with a new formulation of the typical agony. Just as "Mr. Eliot's Sunday Morning Service" criticizes indirectly the cleavage between Origen and Sweeney, so, through abstract oppositions, "The Hollow Men" criticizes the failure of the will in attaining its objects. The interposition of the "Shadow" between essence and descent symbolizes the inability to reconcile spirit and flesh, word and deed. The symbol of the shadow, repeated from the garden scene of *The Waste Land*, is emotionally, though perhaps not denotatively, equivalent to the shadow cast in "Sweeney Erect" by Sweeney himself, the sensual man rearing up against the light. Since the conclusion of "The Hollow Men" corresponds to the last lines of "Gerontion," with the sufferers turning in the wheel whose center holds for them neither the Word, the eyes, the star, nor the rose, it seems to leave them in the condition of Dante's "trimmers" and almost to cancel the "hope" of Part IV. The whole poem is dominated by the horror of an earthly hell where, since "Life is very long," the hollow men must wait for death to liberate them into the twilight of "that final meeting."

# 8 ACROSS THE FRONTIER: "SWEENEY AGONISTES"

Eliot's *The Use of Poetry and the Use of Criticism* contains the remark: "The ideal medium for poetry, to my mind, and the most direct means of social 'usefulness' for poetry, is the theatre."[1] By 1933, when that sentence was written, he had already scrutinized the problem of the verse play in his Introduction to Charlotte Eliot's *Savonarola* (1926) and in his "A Dialogue on Dramatic Poetry." In this Introduction, pursuing a narrow inquiry into the limits of dramatic form, he adopted the premise that such form "may occur at various points along a line the termini of which are liturgy and realism"—the former being associated with the incantation of poetry and the latter with a "prosaic" mode of speech.[2] Through one of the speakers in "A Dialogue on Dramatic Poetry" Eliot reiterated his opinion that the relative merits of liturgy and realism in drama depend on the time: "When the age has a set religious practice and belief, then the drama can and should tend towards realism, I say *towards*, I do not say arrive at. . . . The more fluid, the more chaotic the religious and ethical beliefs, the more the drama must tend in the direction of liturgy."[3] His intention as of the late 1920's was to justify the renaissance of poetic drama by suggesting that the theater is socially most useful when it returns to its origins in liturgy, where poetry most profoundly touches the emotional life. In 1936, after the moderate success of *Murder in the Cathedral*, he generalized further by saying, in a broadcast talk, that he believed poetry to be "the natural and complete medium for drama." That talk, discussed by Matthiessen in his masterly survey of Eliot's dramatic theories, revealed that Eliot considered poetry preferable to prose because it provides, "underneath the action," the advantage of "a musical pattern which intensifies our excitement by reinforcing it with feeling from a deeper and less articulate

110

level."[4] In more recent years Eliot has stressed this argument and has said little about liturgy. Enlarging on his concept in "Poetry and Drama," read at Harvard in 1950, he has suggested that although in some plays prose or natural speech may be "dramatically adequate," in others a verse form of such range is needed that it can at one moment, while "saying homely things without bathos," affect the audience unconsciously through its rhythms and at another moment become "poetry"—"the only language in which the emotions can be expressed at all." And at its greatest intensity dramatic poetry enables one to "touch the border of those feelings which only music can express."[5]

If at times in his handling of verse in his plays, as in certain of his poems, Eliot has re-created the incantatory rhythms of liturgy, he has also duplicated by plot symbolism the conditions of myth and occasionally of ritual acts. He has never done so, however, without trying to respect the demands of contemporaneity. His verse, whatever the symbols, has a modern vocabulary and cadence, and it preserves the mean between liturgy and the common speech. So, too, the narrative elements of his plays involve ordinary people in such a way that what is mythic or ritualistic in the events is on a different level from the simple realism apparent on the surface. Eliot described in his essay on John Marston (1934) a quality also discernible in his own plays.

It is possible that what distinguishes poetic drama from prosaic drama is a kind of doubleness in the action, as if it took place on two planes at once. In this it is different from allegory, in which the abstraction is something conceived, not something differently felt, and from symbolism (as in the plays of Maeterlinck) in which the tangible world is deliberately diminished—both symbolism and allegory being operations of the conscious planning mind. In poetic drama a certain apparent irrelevance may be the symptom of this doubleness; or the drama has an under-pattern, less manifest than the theatrical one. We sometimes feel, in following the words and behaviour of some of the characters of Dostoevsky, that they are living at once on the plane that we know and on some other plane of reality from which we are shut out: their behaviour does not seem crazy, but rather in conformity with the laws of some world that we cannot perceive. . . . In the work of genius of a lower order, such as that of the author of *The Revenger's Tragedy*, the characters themselves hardly attain this double reality; we are aware rather of the author, operating perhaps not quite consciously through them, and making use of them to express something of which he himself may not be quite conscious.[6]

Surely Eliot's work in the drama exemplifies, in his sense of the words, "genius of a lower order" more often than genius such as that eulogized earlier in his paragraph. How consciously he has set out to appeal to different levels of sensibility or education in his audience is evident from the account of *Sweeney Agonistes* given in *The Use of Poetry*. Despite his efforts, however, Eliot has not always fully succeeded in putting his characters themselves on a double plane. On the other hand, Eliot has usually produced a happy doubleness of action, whether by deliberate symbolic allusion, as often in his poems, or by an accidental and unconscious archetypal substructure. The symbolism is not that of Maeterlinck; its naturalistic immediacy keeps it within the symbolistic limits of Yeats's last plays or of Eliot's friend Charles Williams' novels. Certainly it does not come far at times from Eliot's definition in the Marston essay of "a pattern behind the pattern into which the characters deliberately involve themselves; the kind of pattern which we perceive in our own lives only at rare moments of inattention and detachment, drowsing in sunlight."[7]

The most signal failure among Eliot's attempts to have a character function on more than one plane occurred in his skit *Sweeney Agonistes,* the example he has cited.

My intention was to have one character whose sensibility and intelligence should be on the plane of the most sensitive and intelligent members of the audience; his speeches should be addressed to them as much as to the other personages in the play—or rather, should be addressed to the latter, who were to be material, literal-minded and visionless, with the consciousness of being overheard by the former. There was to be an understanding between this protagonist and a small number of the audience, while the rest of the audience would share the responses of the other characters in the play.[8]

One thinks directly of the Fool and poor Tom in Shakespeare's *King Lear.* J. Isaacs has observed that Eliot was probably influenced by the example of Aristophanes; *Sweeney Agonistes* is subtitled "Fragments of an Aristophanic Melodrama." According to this scheme the character chosen—Sweeney himself—has to exist on a level of understanding or experience beyond the comprehension of some thickish members of the audience. But actually Eliot devised a character who utters certain gnomic statements about life and death without convincing one that he knows more than such people about what he is saying. Sweeney is Eliot's mouthpiece, and as such he indirectly hints at some of the ideas, moral and ethical, familiar to readers of the poems; but the undeniable doubleness of the action or theme seemingly does not extend to his awareness. To give a typical instance, when Sweeney says "Death is life and life is death," there is no evidence whatever that he attaches to the words any meaning that the other characters miss or that the audience as a whole, notwithstanding the "gotta use words" passages, cannot grasp. The statement is a paradox commenting on the horror of existence. If there are people in the play or in the audience whom the mystical overtone eludes, how is one to say that it does not escape Sweeney too? The "understanding" is between Eliot and the intellectual elite; it need not implicate Sweeney at all. Even the possibility that Eliot is on one level, Sweeney on another, and Doris and the rest on a third still lower would not alter matters unless one could be assured by internal evidence that Sweeney had higher intelligence than his friends and their counterparts in the audience. His mere possession of the facts making up his anecdote proves nothing. His ability to initiate quasi-philosophic remarks is admittedly suggestive; it gives evidence of Eliot's intention, but it does not bespeak acuteness.

The unfinished *Sweeney Agonistes* (a melodrama in the sense that it is embellished with songs among the dialogue), which Eliot seems at one time to have called "Wanna Go Home, Baby?" consists of two scenes, "Fragment of a Prologue" and "Fragment of an Agon." It has several times been acted and has been converted by Richard Winslow into a chamber opera, produced at Columbia University in 1953. In October, 1924, having drafted a version of the piece, Eliot sent it to Arnold Bennett with a request for criticism. He appears to have known Bennett for several years previously, at any rate since 1918, when Bennett provided him with a letter of reference while Eliot was trying to obtain a commission in the American army. Bennett returned the "scenario" within a few weeks, and on October 23 Eliot wrote to him again, saying that he was reconstructing it in accordance with Bennett's suggestions. But two years passed before "Fragment of a Prologue" was published in the *Criterion;* Eliot's writing was delayed by illness in the winter of 1924–25 and later by a trip of several months to rest in the south of France. Upon his return home at the end of 1925, he read, three times over, a copy of *The Great Gatsby* which F. Scott Fitzgerald had sent him, and he was probably struck by the intensity of Fitzgerald's own treatment of the contemporary waste land. When he wrote to thank Fitzgerald for the book on December 31, he had no reason to mention Fitzgerald's obvious indebtedness to himself.[9] But it is likely that before publishing *Sweeney Agonistes,* Eliot equalized the debt by incorporating a few hints from *The Great Gatsby;* in any case, the similarities are fairly prominent. As Menotti was to do in *The Telephone,* both Fitzgerald and Eliot introduced a telephone conversation to humorous effect. They both dealt with characters that illustrated the unconsciously tragic side of the vapid jazz age, and for good measure provided them with specimen songs of the period. The diminuendo chorus of the second song in "Fragment of an Agon" essentially duplicates the ballad quoted in chapter v of *The Great Gatsby*. The name Klipstein is very much like Fitzgerald's Klipspringer; in their choices of names Fitzgerald and Eliot alike drew upon the exotic and serio-comic. Eliot's Horsfall, a distinguished name with which incongruously may be associated a type of rubbish incinerator; his Krumpacker, which invites a silly pun; and his Wauchope, a name with military traditions for "the Loot," all have something in common with Fitzgerald's Endives and Fishguards and Swetts and Hammerheads.

Regardless of any actual connection between these two works, there can be no doubt that the world of Eliot's play is fundamentally the same as that of Fitzgerald's novel. But although Nick Carraway stands apart from the erratic society surrounding Gatsby, he never attains as *raisonneur* for Fitzgerald the same height of ironic commentary as Sweeney for Eliot. Nick's observations are conscious and unambiguous; Sweeney's are ambiguous and unconscious. Since the "Agon" presupposes a deeper philosophy of life than Sweeney himself seems to have, the poet takes a more obvious hand in the drama than Fitzgerald does in *Gatsby*.

*Sweeney Agonistes* is obscure because it was sent out before its time, "scarce half made up," and all attempts, however ingenious, to reconstruct the plot from internal data are necessarily disappointing. T. H. Thompson's amusing tour de force, "The Bloody Wood," is a creditably fanciful effort to write Sweeney's history from "Sweeney Erect" on.[10] But the truth is that Sweeney never had any history. Eliot's overgrave and perhaps rather sportive ("Possum") remark to Nevill Coghill that he thought of Sweeney "as a man who in younger days was perhaps a professional pugilist, mildly successful; who then grew older and retired to keep a pub" confirms Aiken's theory of Sweeney's origin; it has little to do with the earlier Sweeney poems.[11] Nor has the Sweeney of the play; for the moment that Sweeney becomes articulate he takes over, at least for a time, the role of Eliot's usual character who suffers, becoming Prufrockian or undergoing an amalgamation with the Prufrockian sensibility. Thus in *Sweeney Agonistes*, as in *The Waste Land*, the "action and suffering" motif of *Murder in the Cathedral* is prefigured.

"Fragment of a Prologue," where Sweeney does not appear, has just enough plot to convey easily, like "A Game of Chess," a sense of the superficiality of life on the everyday level. The characters, vulgar and rather boisterous, subsist in the realm of the "good time." No one can overlook the parallel with Madame Sosostris' cartomancy in *The Waste Land* or the allusions, hardly functional, to the Mrs. Porter of the ballad and the broad-footed Doris of "Sweeney Erect." From Eliot's point of view the fortunetelling with cards may be both a testimony to the characters' spiritual meagerness and a dramatic trick to foreshadow Sweeney's long harangue. Doris' cards ought to be predicting something, and perhaps they are, but not obviously. In one aspect they only make concrete certain unresolved anticipations; they dramatize the absence of events. In another aspect they make sense ironically, by concocting an inverse analogy between Doris' social set and the unfortunates in Sweeney's tale. What does not happen to Doris has happened to the girl in the bathtub. Possibly the card sequence parallels the content of the "Agon": Sweeney, the King of Clubs, is to attend a party where he will give Doris "news of an absent friend," Mrs. Porter, the Queen of Hearts. But owing to a quarrel Mrs. Porter will, alas, be dead. Naturally Doris, having "dreamt of weddings all last night" (a fatal portent), takes the two of spades as ominous to herself; her inference is that she too can expect a violent demise. The cards could have a serious connection with a latent ritual theme of sacrifice; they correspond to a means of casting lots for a victim. Poor Doris, or maybe Dusty, might be next—"Or it might be you." But the "Prologue," avoiding the issue, turns out to be no *Rape of the Lock*. It concludes with a fatuous dialogue between Klipstein and Krumpacker, whom Eliot might better have eliminated. This latter portion exemplifies Eliot's recourse to music-hall sources; the device of "bouncing" a line from one speaker to the next as in the "Do we like London" exchange is typical of these. If anything in the "Prologue" deserves commendation—and not much feeling runs through its nerveless plot—it is surely the jolly singsong and thump of the verse.

These characteristics are even more marked in "Fragment of an Agon," with its lively "King Bolo"-like opening about cannibals and missionaries. Apart from Eliot's having possibly got a few pointers from *The Admirable Crichton* or *The Moon and Sixpence*, there is not much to say about the island imagery; for although it is highly suggestive of a symbolic ritual pattern, this attains no development. The dead girl's case bears only superficial comparison with Celia Coplestone's in *The Cocktail Party*, a play in which the theme of her sacrifice or "devouring" is adjoined to the protagonist Edward's own spiritual reconciliation. But even here, after the dialogue of Doris and Sweeney, at least an intimation emerges of that necessity which so many of Eliot's characters accept—the need to negate. The epigraph from *The Ascent of Mt. Carmel* (Book I, chap. iv) applies to the case of the murderer in Sweeney's story, who might have been Sweeney himself. If "the soul cannot be possessed of the divine union, until it has divested itself of the love of created beings," what treatment of the thing one loves is more appropriate, hyperbolically, than to kill it? Thus the victim, Doris' predecessor of the bath, was the missionary who by her death could deliver the murderer from a death-in-life ("I've been born, and once is enough. / You dont remember, but I remember") and translate him, but only through the Dark Night of an awareness of sin, into a state of happiness beyond the terror of renunciation. What good all this may have done the victim is much less important; no doubt she was better off dead, for "Death is life and life is death." The episode of the recollected murder thus attains its meaning, not only on the conscious level of fear and remorse, identified in the epigraph from the *Choephoroi* and in the *Iolanthe*-like final chorus,[12] but on this exaggeratedly ironic, unconscious, figurative level implied by the epigraph from St. John of the Cross. On the one level, as in the ascent in Part III of *Ash Wednesday*, the psychological state is an aspect of hell; on the other, of purgatory. What Eliot seems to have meant is that a soul self-convicted of sin may be in a spiritual condition so like the Dark Night ("When you're alone like he was alone") that it is effectively the same; by murder the soul has destroyed its own unregenerate self. Murder as a metaphoric equivalent to negation was Eliot's own gratuitous addition to the analogy, but there is no doubt an ironic sense in which even St. John's words could bear this construction. Yet, although Sweeney speaks of his own "birth," like the mystic's spiritual rebirth, he gives no sign that he is aware how the paradox has arisen. That remains on the plane of Eliot's undramatized intention.

Sweeney's attitude toward the criminal resembles that of Othello toward himself in his final speech, described in Eliot's "Shakespeare and the Stoicism of Seneca" (1927) as an act of "*cheering himself up.*"[13] Eliot's observation that Othello "is endeavouring to escape reality," that "he has ceased to think about Desdemona, and is thinking about himself," is incisive commentary on Sweeney's own effort to "cheer up," perhaps as his "other self," the man that did the murder.

The reader is spared the embarrassing spectacle of a humiliated Prufrock or the painful one of a Samson enlightened by blindness, but "Fragment of an Agon" has at bottom an almost identical configuration. Neither Sweeney nor the murderer pities the girl who was "done in." Her death has brought horror and it may have brought purgation, just as the mystic's spurning of created beings brings him closer to God, but the selfishness is as ugly as that famous scandal of the anchorite, in his desert hermitage, slamming the door in his mother's face. When Eliot's characters turn away from their fellow creatures, they sometimes show a disagreeable tendency to do so out of contempt and pride, a surfeit of smug arrogance. So on the question whether the murderer loved or hated the girl he killed would depend the whole validity of Eliot's clever fable of remorse as a type of the Dark Night.

Eliot's adoption of his subject presents no mystery. For years—long before *The Waste Land*—he had been fascinated by the Byronic problem of man in isolation with a burden of guilt upon him. With Eliot it was a rooted obsession, this disquieted concern with those moments when, as he was to phrase it in "Literature and the Modern World" (1938), "a man may be nearly crushed by the terrible awareness of his isolation from every other human being" and be "alone with himself and his meanness and futility, alone without God."[14] Yet this is the perennial agony of the romantic puritan. Besides it the torment of the imprisoned Ugolino is almost anesthetic. One must turn to the picture of Svidrigaïlov among the dust and spiders of a rural bathhouse and to the image of hell imprinted on his mind as, with his pistol in his pocket, he walked the streets to the dark tower of his suicide. The knowledge of having stepped beyond the point of reparation, of having irretrievably committed "The awful daring of a moment's surrender," marks a succumbing to damnation, not to be palliated by accusing destiny or denying the freedom of the will. The awakening belongs to tragedy which discovers too late. In the first instalment of Eliot's "Eeldrop and Appleplex," a sketch contributed to the *Little Review* in 1917, there occurs a curious forecast of this theme as worked out in *Sweeney Agonistes*. Eeldrop is talking about the need to look upon people as individuals rather than as subjects for gossip or statistical classification:

> The awful importance of the ruin of a life is overlooked. Men are only allowed to be happy in classes. In Gopsum Street a man murders his mistress. The important fact is that for the man the act is eternal, and that for the brief space

he has to live, he is already dead. He is already in a different world from ours. He has crossed the frontier. The important fact that something is done which can not be undone—a possibility which none of us realize until we face it our-selves.[15]

The experience of such a man is not communicable; perhaps he him-self cannot fathom it. Sweeney at least understands the terror and is able to communicate his knowledge to the chorus, who interpret it as nightmare, but he fails to put over a feeling of "the eternity of punish-ment" for one who is "already dead," just as he fails to suggest the similarity between such punishment and the mystical descent.

It is hard to see Sweeney in the role of a criminal, and he ought not to be pushed into it. Possibly he is only a witness—like the "M'Swee-ney" that Dr. Crippen was never able to produce at his trial![16] He may be a witness testifying to a state of reprobate misery he does not fully comprehend except as an experience, and so cannot judge as a moral evolution. But behind the *fantoccini*, strings in hand, Eliot must have had a stark vision of the spiritual initiation of a Raskolnikov after the crimes of a George Joseph Smith. The state of misery Sweeney de-scribes creates something of the same impression as the Devil's con-frontation of Punch before the eyes of little Edmund Gosse. It can be compared in dramatic horror only to the last scene of *Dr. Faustus*. It is, nevertheless, different because of the other level, where, as in "A Game of Chess," the knock at the door may come from a redemptive power. (Is the hangman also the Hanged Man?) "Fragment of an Agon" is defective in execution (save the mark) because the farcical music-hall style, without any indication that Sweeney is deliberately talking down, is an improper vehicle for this serious theme. The sophisticate may be worse off than the uninstructed, for, although he may feel that Swee-ney's tale is tragic, not just sensational and brutal, he may for this very reason be supercilious toward the dilute mixture. Ideally, as Eliot real-ized, one should be able to remark in Sweeney a kindred superiority of awareness, so as not to despise him for a fumbling ignorance of the inner meaning. If, however, one does not notice the ironic parallel to St. John of the Cross, one will not fret over Sweeney's probable blind-ness to that meaning. The critic with no interest in Eliot's idea might find the work strained to grotesqueness by the subject matter, and the only audience likely to be gratified is a morose one with a taste for the frivolously macabre. Eliot's failure seems the more abysmal when the theory from which he was working is traced to its apparent model— De Quincey's essay "On the Knocking at the Gate in *Macbeth*."

# III  *1927–1932*

## 9 VISIONS AND REVISIONS: THE "ARIEL POEMS"

Eliot himself bears witness (1932) to the suggestion "that a dramatic poet cannot create characters of the greatest intensity of life unless his personages, in their reciprocal actions and behaviour in their story, are somehow dramatizing, but in no obvious form, an action or struggle for harmony in the soul of the poet."[1] This formula, which Eliot complained that the dramatist John Ford had neglected, might be useful to a playwright, though the words "in no obvious form," very strictly construed, could vitiate any outside critical judgments it inspired. Regrettably the ideal animating the formula is merely chimerical if a writer packs all the important conflict into one personage, substitutes declamation for drama, and leaves to the supporting characters no task but nugatory comment and static personification. Eliot has impressive success in conceiving a protagonist and bitter difficulty in manipulating the other actors so that they, and not simply the protagonist's utterances, carry on the dramatic movement. This is one reason his poems are better than his first plays. The "struggle for harmony in the soul of the poet" often traduces the other dramatic values by assuming objective form as a monologue more suitable for a poem.[2] That form dominates the work of Eliot's third period, from 1927 to 1932. None of the major poems except "Triumphal March," the worst of the lot, pretends to be anything technically but a meditation by a single voice; even "Triumphal March" has a strong monologue at the core. For the sake of his art at the time, it is fortunate that Eliot was able to keep away from poetic drama and exercise the skill he best understood.

The internal conflict in "Journey of the Magi" (1927) is typical for the period. This poem was Eliot's first contribution to Faber and Faber's "Ariel Poems" by contemporary writers. The numbers of the

series, he has remarked, "were published during four or five successive years as a kind of Christmas card. Nobody else seemed to want
the title afterward, so I kept it for myself simply to designate four of
my poems which appeared in this way."[3] These were "Journey of the
Magi," "A Song for Simeon," "Animula," and "Marina." His fifth
such poem, "Triumphal March," forms the opening of *Coriolan;* "The
Cultivation of Christmas Trees," a companion piece to "Animula,"
dates from Faber's revival of the series in 1954.[4] "Journey of the
Magi," though it seems a new version of "Gerontion," differs from it
thematically in ignoring the panorama of history. Hence its drama of a
bewildered, shaken man, despite remoteness from the contemporary
scene, appears more pertinent than that of "Gerontion" to Eliot's own
spiritual quest. Examined along with external evidence of his beliefs,
the poem seems to concern a more advanced stage of the religious
struggle already manifested.

Eliot's confirmation as an Anglican churchman occurred in 1927,
the year in which he became a British subject. His statement of his
tenets, in the Preface to *For Lancelot Andrewes* (1928),[5] followed by
two years the original publication of the title essay, itself a clue to his
position. His occasional reviews had also revealed an intellectual attitude toward Christianity consistent with his later profession of belief.
But the earliest hint of the direction in which he was set had presented
itself in his poems. These, however, had affirmed the emotional hollowness of the soul distraught between the demands of flesh and spirit;
they had implied nothing about the intellectual religious convictions
of their author. Eliot has remarked that rational assent to Christianity
may precede Christian sentiments; his conversion could have come
only at the end of a long period of vacillation.[6]

"Journey of the Magi" is the monologue of a man who has made his
own choice, who has achieved belief in the Incarnation, but who is still
part of that life which the Redeemer came to sweep away.[7] Like Gerontion, he cannot break loose from the past. Oppressed by a sense of
death-in-life (Tiresias' anguish "between two lives"), he is content to
submit to "another death" for his final deliverance from the world of
old desires and gods, the world of "the silken girls." It is not that the
Birth that is also Death has brought him hope of a new life, but that it
has revealed to him the hopelessness of the previous life. He is resigned
rather than joyous, absorbed in the negation of his former existence

but not yet physically liberated from it. Whereas Gerontion is "waiting for rain" in this life, and the hollow men desire the "eyes" in the next life, the speaker here has put behind him both the life of the senses and the affirmative symbol of the Child; he has reached the state of desiring nothing. His negation is partly ignorant, for he does not understand in what way the Birth is a Death; he is not aware of the sacrifice. Instead, he himself has become the sacrifice; he has reached essentially, on a symbolic level true to his emotional, if not to his intellectual, life, the humble, negative stage that in a mystical progress would be prerequisite to union. Although in the literal circumstances his will cannot be fixed upon mystical experience, because of the time and condition of his existence, he corresponds symbolically to the seeker as described by St. John of the Cross in *The Ascent of Mount Carmel.* Having first approached the affirmative symbol, or rather, for him, the affirmative reality, he has experienced failure; negation is his secondary option.

The quest of the Magi for the Christ child, a long arduous journey against the discouragements of nature and the hostility of man, to find at last a mystery impenetrable to human wisdom, was described by Eliot in strongly colloquial phrases adapted from one of Lancelot Andrewes' sermons of the Nativity:

> A cold coming they had of it at this time of the year, just the worst time of the year to take a journey, and specially a long journey in. The ways deep, the weather sharp, the days short, the sun farthest off, *in solstitio brumali,* "the very dead of winter."[8]

Also in Eliot's thoughts were the vast oriental deserts and the camel caravans and marches described in *Anabase,* by St.-J. Perse. He himself had begun work in 1926 on an English translation of that poem, publishing it in 1930.[9] Other elements of his tone and imagery may have come from Kipling's "The Explorer" and from Pound's "Exile's Letter." The water mill was recollected from his own past; for in *The Use of Poetry,* speaking of the way in which "certain images recur, charged with emotion," he was to mention "six ruffians seen through an open window playing cards at night at a small French railway junction where there was a water-mill."[10] In vivifying the same incident, the fine proleptic symbolism of "three trees on the low sky," a portent of Calvary, with the evocative image of "an old white horse" introduces one of the simplest and most pregnant passages in all of his work:

> Then we came to a tavern with vine-leaves over the lintel,
> Six hands at an open door dicing for pieces of silver,
> And feet kicking the empty wine-skins.

Here are allusions to the Communion (through the tavern "bush"), to the paschal lamb whose blood was smeared on the lintels of Israel, to the blood money of Judas, to the contumely suffered by Christ before the Crucifixion, to the soldiers casting lots at the foot of the Cross, and, perhaps, to the pilgrims at the open tomb in the garden.

The arrival of the Magi at the place of Nativity, whose symbolism has been anticipated by the fresh vegetation and the mill "beating the darkness," is only a "satisfactory" experience. The narrator has seen and yet he does not fully understand; he accepts the fact of Birth but is perplexed by its similarity to a Death, and to death which he has seen before:

> All this was a long time ago, I remember,
> And I would do it again, but set down
> This set down
> This: were we led all that way for
> Birth or Death?[11]

Were they led there for Birth or for Death? or, perhaps, for neither? or to make a choice between Birth and Death? And whose Birth or Death was it? their own, or Another's? Uncertainty leaves him mystified and unaroused to the full splendor of the strange epiphany. So he and his fellows have come back to their own Kingdoms, where,

> . . . no longer at ease here, in the old dispensation,
> With an alien people clutching their gods

(which are now alien gods), they linger not yet free to receive "the dispensation of the grace of God."[12] The speaker has reached the end of one world, but despite his acceptance of the revelation as valid, he cannot gaze into a world beyond his own.

"A Song for Simeon" (1928) derived its title from the "Nunc dimittis," or "Song of Simeon" in the Prayer Book. The prayer that follows the second lesson at Evensong is taken from chapter 2 of Luke, recounting the ritual presentation of the child Jesus at the temple. Eliot based his poem upon this passage. But in so doing he developed the character of Simeon into a parallel to that of the speaker in the previous monologue and, rather more conspicuously, to that of Gerontion. Simeon's spiritual crisis is not quite as in "Journey of the Magi"; like Gerontion's it looks into the future. What Simeon sees is the harassment and persecution of those, ironically enough, who, like himself, shall credit the vision now appearing. Whereas Gerontion in his "sleepy corner" sees destruction engulf the worldly or profane, Simeon, though awaiting a tranquil death for himself, sees the destruction, as the world accounts it, that must overtake the righteous. This is a necessary destruction if life is to come out of death, but Simeon himself is unprepared to face it. Here again is the renunciation of an old life without a concentrated search for "the ultimate vision." Simeon is not only a soul relinquishing the life of the senses, a Tiresias; he is a soul that through its greater prescience, as it were contagiously, bears the sufferings of men elected to encounter suffering through action. But in his own person he is not constrained to pass from the one realm into the other, from the old dispensation into the new. Thus like the Magi he is simply transient between two worlds; the difference is that like Tiresias he understands the movement from the one into the other. He has passed the stage of Gerontion, who has lost the Word, and that of the hollow men, who are not freed from the circuit of the prickly pear.

The monologue, a tired murmur of an old, old man, starts with a brief section displaying familiar symbols from "Gerontion" and *The Waste Land* to create a new statement concerning death and rebirth. The stubborn approach of spring, with hyacinths symbolizing pagan life and fertility, is contrasted with the stubborn duration of winter. Snow and flowers, as in "Gerontion" and "The Burial of the Dead," bring into opposition the two principles everlastingly alternating in the cycle, here again represented by an old man and a "depraved May." But the spring brings also the Child, and the hyacinths have a new meaning, in view of which the fertility cults of Rome belong with the "winter sun" that "creeps by the snow hills." For in the spring a new Light shines, to turn pagan death into life, making an end of the old life, "light . . . / Like a feather on the back of my hand"—recalling the final scene of *King Lear*. Meanwhile Simeon awaits "the wind that chills towards the dead land," partly the whirlwind of death in "Gerontion," partly the wind of the Spirit in Ezekiel, a breath restoring life to the dead through the death of Christ. The feather blown in the wind (contrast "White feathers in the snow") will thus be blown into the hands of God.

But the change itself imposes a terrible trial upon the human soul.

The surge of a new life, whether the sexual struggle of Gerontion and Tiresias or their spiritual struggle which is this narrator's as well, amounts to no placid awakening. Not for nothing is time's April "the cruelest month"; it arouses the spirit to decision. The Women of Canterbury, in *Murder in the Cathedral*, beseech the Archbishop to return to France, that they may be spared the new suffering. Simeon, too, that he may not outlive this beginning, not participate in the vitalizing growth of the new faith, prays for peace through "the still unspeaking and unspoken Word," the eternal countertype of strife. He resembles Gerontion or the protagonist of "Journey of the Magi"; for he too is unwilling to be caught up in a life inflicting violence and calamity. In plea for a tranquil death, he offers testimony to his past righteousness:

> I have walked many years in this city,
> Kept faith and fast, provided for the poor,
> Have given and taken honour and ease.
> There went never any rejected from my door.

It is precisely "honour and ease" that the future must withhold; his own "faith and fast" will not avail in "the time of sorrow." Like Christ, "despised and rejected of men; a man of sorrows, and acquainted with grief,"[13] his posterity will be driven, Christian and Jew, "to the goat's path, and the fox's home, / Fleeing from the foreign faces and the foreign swords."[14] Christ himself is to say, "The foxes have holes, and the birds of the air have nests; but the Son of man hath not where to lay his head."[15] The symbols here pertain to the Way of Sorrows and the Passion. Simeon is speaking of something which he cannot know about; what nevertheless assumes importance is not "the mountain of Zion, which is desolate, the foxes walk upon it" (Lam. 5:18), but the scourging of Christ, the Stations of the Cross, the weeping of the Virgin on Calvary, and even the day of the last "abomination of desolation" when the inhabitants of Judea shall flee to the mountains.[16] From such future vicissitudes, Simeon would be preserved through the peace of "the still unspeaking and unspoken Word."

This poem and "Journey of the Magi" are in one way simpler and in another way more intricate than "The Hollow Men." First, they omit the harrowing struggle with sexual desire. They have, it is true, "the silken girls" and the "Roman hyacinths"; these, however, symbolize what the old men have already put away from them (the hyacinths, unlike those in *The Waste Land*, connoting little more than the pagan and sensual aspect of rebirth, like the lilacs bred "out of the dead land") and no longer express the tension between lust and love that dismays Gerontion and Tiresias. Corresponding to the eyes of "The Hollow Men" and the hyacinth girl of *The Waste Land* are the Birth in "Journey of the Magi" and the Word in "A Song for Simeon." These poems, like the others, set up an affirmative, numinous symbol, uniting flesh and spirit, and show it to be inapprehensible. The sufferers in them, as much as the hollow men, must turn unfulfilled toward death. The difficulty here is that a new element has obtruded into Eliot's usual pattern: the soul vanquished not by sex or unbelief but by sheer spiritual incapacity. The fact that these men are old, Eliot having economically used the same symbol of age to suggest impotence and unbelief (Gerontion) and twisted desire (Tiresias), seems to point to the Pauline sense of "old man," the unregenerate. At any rate, the Magi and Simeon, like Gerontion, appear to symbolize the soul's enchainment to the past, and its inability to desert its bonds at the cost of a painful readjustment. These men are still in and of the world, still spiritually uncleansed of the human taint. It is this that makes them "old" men: "After such knowledge, what forgiveness?"

Though both of these poems depict the failure of affirmation, they do not explicitly praise the other way, of abnegation and martyrdom of spirit. But they draw up a pattern for *Murder in the Cathedral, The Family Reunion, Four Quartets,* and *The Cocktail Party.* The humility to which the Magi and Simeon descend is that of conscious ignorance and inadequacy. This humility, however, comes but a step before the deliberately chosen ignorance of the mystical Dark Night as Eliot has described it in "East Coker":

> In order to arrive at what you do not know
> You must go by a way which is the way of ignorance.

And that is the martyrdom of the "old" man in soul and mind; it, in turn, comes but a step before the full sacrifice of Thomas Becket at Canterbury. Thus "Journey of the Magi" and "A Song for Simeon" are not entirely poems of despair. They foreshadow the way in which purgation compensates for the debility of body and will and the scars of disappointment.

Except for "The Hollow Men," "Animula" (1929) is Eliot's most pessimistic poem. The state described and its symbolic configuration are the same as in "Journey of the Magi" and "A Song for Simeon."

> Wandering between two worlds, one dead,
> The other powerless to be born.

But those poems limit grief by pinpointing it in the dramatic contexts. They have a historical focus. Simeon and the Magi must endure an external necessity wherein they can know only the Incarnation, not the Atonement. It is not so much that their own potentialities are weak as that a superior order has confined them to a dispensation of law instead of love. The Atonement was retroactive without bestowing the consolation of perceived grace. These men have, but do not know, the benefits of Christ's still unrevealed sacrifice. They are joyless, and the more so because, Tantalus-like, they verge so close to what they cannot grasp. Curiously, in this one aspect, both poems are less, not more, intimate to the Eliot problem as such: detachment is mitigating. "Animula," on the other hand, makes so general a pronouncement, not about a single spiritual dilemma but about the helplessness of the whole human condition, that it contrives to be more dismal and more personal at the same time. In "Animula" the soul, despite its natural appetite for good, can do nothing whatever. By resistance and inertia, it misses an "offered good" and ignores the grace extended.

As a philosophic poem, "Animula" is prosaic in tone and traditional in meter. The rhyming pentameter is monotonously regular; the diction flat. One is dismayed to see in Eliot so cheap a phrase as "fragrant brilliance" and to be afflicted with the unintended overtones of so carelessly chosen a name as "Boudin."[17] But the technical disorders of the poem do not infect the treatment of its theme.

As usual the discovery of hollowness in the world of the natural man heralds no spiritual rebirth. In "Animula" the soul is kept back by the confused meshes of its past, by time, and can only live "first in the silence after the viaticum." The poem does not emphasize the desirability of death and contains no hint of an overwhelming experience which astonishes and arrests the eager soul in its progress. It suggests, however, something of the immobile hopelessness depicted in Part V of "The Hollow Men," though, again, it lacks even the memory of any symbol such as the eyes with their connotation of eternity coinciding with the temporal world. The only analogue to the obsessive lost experience is a gentle "whisper of immortality,"

> . . . pleasure
> In the brilliant fragrance of the Christmas tree,
> Pleasure in the wind, the sunlight and the sea.

In value this corresponds approximately to the pagan "Roman hyacinths" of Simeon's past and to the "regretted"

> . . . summer palaces on slopes, the terraces,
> And the silken girls bringing sherbet.

The new life toward which "Animula" points is "the warm reality, the offered good, / . . . the importunity of the blood," just as in the preceding poems the ideal is the Word and the Child. The inability to reach it is identified both with the breaching of childhood naïveté and with the invasion of this by adult perplexities, as in Vaughan's "The Retreat" or Wordsworth's "Ode on Intimations of Immortality."

> Full soon thy Soul shall have her earthly freight,
> And custom lie upon thee with a weight,
> Heavy as frost, and deep almost as life!

The title "Animula" recalls Hadrian's compassionate address to his soul;[18] the lines are now probably best known in Byron's translation. Pater took from them a chapter heading for *Marius the Epicurean*. Eliot began with an adaptation from *Purgatorio*, XVI, "Esce di mano a lui, che la vagheggia / prima che sia . . . / l'anima semplicetta" ("From the hand of Him who loves her before she is, there issues, in the manner of a little child that plays, now weeping, now laughing, the simple soul: who knows nothing save that, moved by a joyous creator, she turns willingly to that which gives her pleasure. First she tastes the flavor of a trifling good; by it she is beguiled, and after it she runs, if neither guide nor rein turn back her longing. Wherefore it was needful to put law as a curb, needful to have a sovereign who might descry at least the pinnacle of the true city"). Even though the soul takes its greatest pleasure in the search for God, toward whom its free will, stimulated by appetite, naturally moves it, it is easily deflected by frivolities and evils. "Animula" assumes that such distraction is inevitable. Blame for the soul's travail rests with the "pain of living and the drug of dreams," from which ensue the cramping of will, the inhibition and misdirection of desire. Stifled by all that "perplexes and offends," the soul takes refuge in barren learning. It becomes "irresolute and selfish, misshapen, lame," no longer exuberant, incapable of living. It seems to have no choice but denial, passivity. It can yield to the behest neither of flesh nor of spirit.[19]

Thematic resemblances in "Animula," not so much to the other "Ariel Poems" as to "A Cooking Egg" and "Dans le Restaurant," form a connective with an earlier period in Eliot's development. The image of "Floret, by the boarhound slain between the yew trees," re-creates in the closing strophe the situation of the old waiter alarmed in childhood by the "gros chien." But now the symbolism of the dog may imply a broader reference. Even though Floret, as Eliot has said in a letter quoted by Ethel Stephenson, "is so entirely imaginary that there is really no identification to be made . . . perhaps [he] may sug-gest not wholly irrelevantly to some minds certain folklore memories."[20] The figure is in some sort an avatar of the fertility god, here depicted between the yew trees of death and resurrection, slain and waiting for rebirth. Adonis, deprived of virility and life under the tusks of the boar, is as much his archetype as is the quester in *The Waste Land*, whose buried life is menaced by the nails of the dog. The fate of Ac-taeon, ruined by his vision of beauty too divine for mortal beholding, might best translate into mythological language the deliberately vague connotations of the image. And Dante's greyhound, the *Veltro*, would provide a helpful association: as a hound of heaven it embodies a para-dox of destruction and restoration, like the tiger in "Gerontion" and the leopards in *Ash Wednesday*. But Eliot cannot be above suspicion of having lifted the image from *The Hound of the Baskervilles*. The onomatopoeic Guiterriez and Boudin are those who, denying the blood and pursuing their ceaseless pattern in mockery of truth, "represent," according to Eliot, "different types of career, the successful person of the machine age and someone who was killed in the last war [i.e., World War I]."[21] At any rate they are exasperating. Eliot, having changed the men's names, has no legitimate reason to allege that they are in the poem at all; if they are in the poem, it is unfinished until the reader can identify them. The finely shocking terminal line of "Ani-mula," in substituting "birth" for "death," compensates slightly for this brummagem device.

"Marina" (1930) departs radically from the tone established in the three poems grouped with it. Although its protagonist confronts a symbol of vital restoration, the meeting signifies no transcendent com-munion impossible to him but, on a dream level, the benign and even triumphant realization of joy in a human relationship. The context designated in the title is that of Pericles' reunion with his daughter Marina in Shakespeare's *Pericles*. The recognition scene there (Act V, scene 1) has more than once been extolled by Eliot for its dramatic and symbolic force.[22] The incredible, yet miraculously probable, reunion of the lost daughter with the old king in the drama is like a rebirth of the king himself, a recovery of hope despaired of. Marina's birth at sea—virtually, one might say, of the sea—is perfected by her deliverance from shame and death. To Pericles, finding her alive whom he has thought dead, she seems the incarnation of a vision.

Against this almost beatific discovery Eliot set for his epigraph line 1138 of Seneca's *Hercules Furens,* "Quis hic locus, quae regio, quae mundi plaga?" ("What place is this, what land, what quarter of the globe?"). These words are the first clouded mutterings of Hercules as he awakes from the unconscious fit into which he has sunk overcome by madness. Having ascended from his labor in the underworld, where he secured the dog Cerberus, he has been driven to frenzy through Juno's jealousy of him as Alcmena's son. In his madness he has turned his envenomed arrows against his own children, and now, his senses gradually returning, he is about to recognize the enormity. The total situation, antithetical to that in *Pericles,* discloses, in contrast with the discovery of Marina in Eliot's poem, not only the horror of death but the horror of personal defeat suffered by Hercules. As the assassin of his children he has met disaster through a turn of Fortune's wheel, the reverse of that which has blessed Pericles; and whereas Pericles' daughter is alive, Hercules' children are lying slaughtered. The crime of Hercules succeeds a moment of overweening pride, the moment of his highest exultation; he has completed his twelfth and final labor and has killed the tyrant who abused his household, but he has incurred divine resentment. With such a career of arrogant boastfulness, leading to deprivation and ruin, Eliot contrasted the gracious experience of Pericles by a somewhat oversubtle mingling. In a letter written to Sir Michael Sadler in May, 1930, Eliot spoke of having used the scenes from the two plays so as to form a "crisscross" between them. "Marina" owes to Seneca the rhetoric of its opening line and the undercurrent of irony produced by the confluence of death and life.

The poem is a monologue, spoken precisely at the instant of recognition. Pericles is not sure whether he has crossed the boundaries of dream into reality. His experience belongs to a kind of halfway world, the atmosphere of which pervades his words. As in a dream, he is standing on the deck of a vessel approaching land, from whose granite shores are borne the scent of pine and the song of the woodthrush— images rising out of some buried recollection and made vivid as he becomes conscious of his daughter's presence. The images objectify the emotion stirring in him. They obliterate the memory of other images—those of men associated with the sins of envy, pride, sloth, and concupiscence, and with the state of death consequent upon habitual sin. These

> Are become insubstantial, reduced by a wind,
> A breath of pine, and the woodsong fog
> By this grace dissolved in place.

Marina's apparent restoration has conferred a grace, a life-giving and sin-purging benediction. His dream seems palpable; Marina seems a living creature in whom the idea, the figment, becomes objectively real and in achieving transformation both clearer and less clear, because different:

> What is this face, less clear and clearer
> The pulse in the arm, less strong and stronger—
> Given or lent? more distant than stars and nearer than the eye.[23]

She seems tangibly one who, as in *Ash Wednesday*, "moves in the time between sleep and waking":

> Whispers and small laughter between leaves and hurrying feet
> Under sleep, where all the waters meet.[24]

As a fulfilment, she surpasses even his pathetic fatherly yearning for lost "small laughter," without, in any measure, having the inadequacy of a mere substitute. The image latent in the dream world has been of something never heard, the sounds of children concealed in the leaves. Eliot's source was probably Kipling's "They," the story of ghostly children frolicking about the house of a blind woman.[25] In "Marina" the dream child comes with almost a religious epiphany, and it is hardly accidental that the phrase "Given or lent?" echoes Alice Meynell's line "Given, not lent" in her poem "Unto us a Son is given," referring to Isaiah, chapter 9.[26]

Marina is not the Child from "Journey of the Magi," but she is invested, for purposes of the poem, with the characteristics of flesh clothing a divine emanation. Thus at the instant of Pericles' recognition, although (and because) it is not clear to him whether the child really is "given," the images he associates with her are "stars" and "the eye." These are the same already adopted by Eliot in "The Hollow Men"; again, they are symbols, as are the leaves and the thrush, of the values inherent in the Grail of the romances. Marina is the focal center here, corresponding in a purer form to the hyacinth girl of *The Waste Land*. And for once the communion is not abortive. The meeting brings together, at least on one level of consciousness, a quester and the object of his quest, and there is no division or disappointment.

Such beatitude is far from typical of Eliot's usual symbolic scheme. But the happy nature of the experience in "Marina" does not violate the principle enunciated in his *After Strange Gods* (1934) that "ideals" are not the concern of poetry[27]—which can mean that poetry should not show unreal attainments as if they were true. Pericles' happiness occurs where the literal event is not actual and is not supposed to be actual, except as dream. The connection between the actuality of dream and that of waking is simply emotional; the experience has emotional authenticity. Eliot's use of the impersonal situation involved only a partial masking. The status of this poem among his other work is as if he had dispensed with the impersonal and had written about a dream of his own—actual in occurrence, ideal in content. If, instead, he had treated of the actual meeting of Pericles with Marina, he would have had to present as actually joyous the sort of experience which his work always shows as eclipsed and thwarted. His instinct not to rely on the impersonal, that is, rather to make the tension between the actual and the ideal internal to the poem, may well give evidence of an intimate personal symbolism in "Marina." As a personal symbol the poem could not have totally reported the mixed private emotion by abstracting merely the constituent of ideal feeling. As it is, in all but the contrivance of situation, it is most likely as personal as "Animula." The ground of this opinion would be firmer, of course, if biographical evidence were accessible. But three points are noteworthy: the identification of the speaker with Pericles depends almost wholly on the title; the emergence of the speaker from his dream state, in contrast with the awakening enjoyed by Shakespeare's Pericles, is incomplete; and, finally, in view of the epigraph, it is possible that the speaker is grievously mistaken. The underlying parallel with the Hercules recognition serves to qualify for the reader the flash of pure delight felt by Pericles. There is an irony superior to the poem, and even if inadequately transferred from the epigraph into the monologue, it works an effect.

In the last two strophes Pericles is associated with the decaying ship in which he now moves through the fog. What, "unknowing, half conscious," he has made his own is his life itself; it is a life paradoxically identifiable with "This form, this face, this life / Living to live in a world of time beyond me," that is, with Marina, and it becomes "The awakened, lips parted, the hope, the new ships." The semi-ambiguous, semi-visionary blending of the old with the new harmonizes with the dream world of the event. The vision, with the strange regularity of dream, embraces once more, without impairment of logic, the symbolism of the shores and the woodthrush, so that with the closing words, "My daughter," Marina has been merged into the obscure promise of the serene haven and the song of the bird. The thrush, not quite the same as in *The Waste Land*, connotes exultant life rather than the "deception" spoken of in "Burnt Norton." The setting has a New England look, and Eliot's boyhood memories of the Massachusetts coast (of which he spoke feelingly in a preface written in 1928) were laid under contribution for this poem. But the specific place he had in mind, and indeed mentioned in his original draft, was Rogue Island, lying at the mouth of the New Meadows River, Casco Bay, Maine.

Despite the differences between "Marina" and the other "Ariel Poems," it shares with them a quality looking back to the conclusion of *The Waste Land* as well as to the spiritual struggle in *Ash Wednesday*. The poem communicates its intuition that the obsolete desires and ambitions must be sloughed off before the soul can find its higher mode, its unequivocal unity with the vision. Thus "Marina" is more Dantean and Platonic than its predecessors. It aspires to transcend the agony of the soul entangled in its past, voiced in earlier poems; it aspires also to transcend the frustration of the soul striving, as in *Ash Wednesday*, to be reconciled; and it reveals, without dwelling on the process of rebirth through suffering, the emotional state which rewards devotion, a state conferring tranquillity and love. That this state is merely foreshadowed is plain from the fact not only that "Marina" unfolds as a dream landscape but also that Pericles articulates something like a prayer:

> . . . let me
> Resign my life for this life, my speech for that unspoken.

Since the poem has no past or future, one has perhaps no right to speculate on any for Pericles. But if one should imagine a future for him, it would have to be one in which he resigned the withered life for that heralded in his illuminative dream. Had Eliot not altered "word" to "speech" after his first draft, one might say something more about the creative and religious overtones of this line. What is crucial here is the possibility of putting the old life behind and moving upward, of "faring forward," transhumanized, to "the Garden / Where all love ends."

# 10 LADY OF SILENCES: "ASH WEDNESDAY"

Ash Wednesday was published in 1930, Part II having already appeared as "Salutation" in 1927, Part I as "Perch' io non spero" in 1928, and Part III as "Al som de l'escalina" in 1929. The first edition of the completed work contained a dedication to Mrs. Eliot.

Perhaps the main superficial defect of the poem is its disjointedness, a quality equally visible in The Waste Land and "The Hollow Men." But Ash Wednesday has dramatic unity and even more than The Waste Land a precise temporal focus. The time, from the point of view of the protagonist who "sees" the action, becomes established in Part I, returns at the end of Part III and at a transitional stage of Part IV, and is re-established in Part V and Part VI. As the title implies, the occasion is the beginning of Lent. Excursions of memory into the past occur in Part II, Part III, and Part IV; they are roughly analogous to the recollection scenes of The Waste Land (ll. 8–18, 31–422) in which, however, the time of the protagonist, Tiresias, seems to fluctuate as he loses himself in the past. Ash Wednesday depends on the unifying principle of consistency in point of view; its monologuist is a man plunged almost into despair. The poem thus belongs among Eliot's numerous tristia, and it explores familiar themes and symbolic patterns.[1]

Like earlier poems it predicates a conflict between the values of flesh and spirit, the one objectified as sensuous memories of a buried life, the other as a state of striving toward the grace of union with the Word. A symbol of the enlightenment of grace is the dream visitant in Part IV; although her identity is never disclosed, some of the imagery surrounding her is reintroduced both in the final prayer to the Virgin and in passages referring to another Lady, an earthly one, who "honours the Virgin in meditation." The figure in the vision may

135

therefore be supposed to bridge the distance between this Lady and the heavenly intercessor, and to personify the values of incarnation, the fusion of the divine and the human. The earthly Lady belongs to actuality rather than ideality; she is associated, at least by implication, with all aspects of human love, carnal as well as spiritual. There are thus three feminine types in the symbolism of *Ash Wednesday:* first, the Virgin representing the divine because she has access to the divine Word; second, her visional counterpart; and third, a Lady who, living in the immediate world, has been an object of desire and, as a symbol of spiritual succor, an object of reverence and thus an embodiment of the vision. To the protagonist of the poem this Lady is the only proximate guide for his ascent toward the divine. At the beginning of Part I and throughout the actual present of the poem, he is deprived of her presence and is unable to "turn" toward her again. This fact means for him that he can make no approach to either human or divine love. To judge from Part II, he has already renounced sexual love; and now he is obliged to renounce even the beloved presence with its quasi-spiritual powers.

After the four central parts of *Ash Wednesday*, exhibiting respectively the rejection of carnal love, the involuntary persistence of desire, the lost vision of light, and the inability of human weakness to reach the Word, the poem concludes with a renewed prayer to the Virgin for humility and for an end to the painful separation from grace. It is then that the peculiar role of the Lady becomes most clear, for the protagonist seems to address his prayer also to her, evidently in a plea for an end to their own division. She, having potentially fulfilled his heavenly vision, holds the only fulfilment of his spiritual desire; she is to all intents a direct intercessor. Thus by a daring and rather mysterious identification, at any rate within the poetic fiction, she becomes indistinguishable from the Virgin. If the word "separation" can be said to allude to the scattering of the bones in Part II, the protagonist is even ironically confuting his determination to renounce desire, but this reading is not of primary importance; it simply bears specific witness to an ambiguous undercurrent in *Ash Wednesday*. What is plain enough is that the whole poem exemplifies Eliot's conception of love as a spiritual but earthly power. The difference from *The Waste Land* consists in the removal of the Lady, on the chief level of interpretation, from a role such as that of the hyacinth girl, a symbol of fertility and sexual love, to the role of a Beatrice. In other words, although the Lady connotes sex, she also connotes spiritual stability in such a way that the sexual can be excluded, as in Part II, without obliteration of her spiritual function. In *The Waste Land* there is a more romantic idea: the hyacinth girl, once lost, is lost entirely; and the spiritual quest goes on, by way of the Chapel Perilous, without her. The Lady here becomes almost more than human, so that the desired reunion with her would constitute on its dominant, spiritual side a mediatory step toward the divine union itself. The poem might be read as a sort of allegory of man's relation to the Church. Yet the theme of her withdrawal reminds one less of the *Commedia* than of the *Vita nuova*.[2] She is like the Beatrice for whom Dante, separated by her death, long grieved before he wrote his great poem of reconciliation.

The plight of the protagonist is similar to Tiresias' and the hollow men's, except that he knows from the start what Tiresias does not learn until the end and what the hollow men never learn at all, that the quest for salvation may require the negative discipline of patience and denial, not merely in the rejection of carnality, but even in the loss of spiritual certitude. He therefore acquiesces in rejection and loss by pronouncing the words: "I renounce the blessèd face / And renounce the voice"; he has no alternative. Although Eliot in Part I and in other places, as Leonard Unger has pointed out, touches on the negative mysticism of St. John of the Cross,[3] *Ash Wednesday* adopts no thoroughgoing negative scheme which would dictate renunciation of the Lady even as a spiritual guide.[4] The poem makes clear that its protagonist merely seeks patience to endure until such time as the separation may be ended. His denials reflect no willing refusal, like that made by St. John, of the principle that spiritual exaltation is attainable through created beings. He is in reluctant exile from what might uplift him.

Because the poem is about suffering in exile, it tries to establish consolation upon the grounds tenable after the actual parting. As Eliot puts it:

> Because I cannot hope to turn again
> Consequently I rejoice, having to construct something
> Upon which to rejoice.

It finds abatement of despair in the analogy between such suffering and the purgatorial Dark Night described by St. John of the Cross. Eliot elected to draw upon St. John apparently in order to suggest a paradox in the Lady's role. In St. John's negative system the protagonist is neither renouncing enough, since the Lady still symbolizes the ideal, nor renouncing for the right reason, since if the Lady remained present he would presumably not renounce at all. The negative mystic, unlike Dante, would insist that the Lady could only deter spiritual progress. In the poem the affirmative ideal and the negative feelings are at cross-purposes. What Eliot achieved by citing both Dante and St. John was a composite that neither would have acknowledged. The affirmative pattern is dominant, but only through the device, foreign to Dante, of extinguishing the Lady's identity at the end by transferring her symbolic attributes to the Virgin. If one were seeking philosophic originality in *Ash Wednesday,* this is where one would detect it.

The Dark Night to which Eliot alludes is a condition of various stages in St. John's mysticism. Its keynote is detachment and emptiness. It is this which makes the advance toward God a negative process, for the soul advances toward perfection by being weaned from its desires. Not to hope for anything is at once a source of anguish and a token of increasing sanctity. According to St. John there are two major stages in the Dark Night, the active and the passive, which he deals with in *The Ascent of Mt. Carmel* and the unfinished *The Dark Night of the Soul.* The first comes early, after the novice has felt an awakening, perhaps an "intimation of immortality" or dreamlike intuition. (Such experience is discussed by Eliot in his essay on Marston and is represented at the beginning of "Burnt Norton" and elsewhere. It compares with Dante's first meeting with Beatrice.) Bliss yields to "aridity," a state of loss, during which the novice must undergo, by deliberate and voluntary effort, a purgation of will in the active Dark Night of sense and spirit. At the end of this stage he may be favored with heightened consciousness of grace, manifested at times through the phenomena of audition, vision, ecstasy, and rapture. This state, known as illumination, is the goal of the illuminative life. But still a further ordeal must precede the divine union. In the midst of his illuminative life the mystic becomes spiritually destitute, as if in reaction to his previous happiness. He is battered by temptation, doubt, terror. These plunge him into the passive Dark Night of sense and spirit, which, like the active one, is contingent on the "aridity" of spiritual callousness and emotional fatigue. By means of it, however, he receives a final, involuntary purgation and becomes prepared for his ultimate surrender to the unitive life.[5]

*Ash Wednesday* does not preach the efficacy of any mystical program; its eclectic negative and affirmative contents merely help to define the emotional temper. Part IV, by the paradisiacal vision, alludes to the awakening, here affirmative rather than negative. Part I and Part II exemplify the active Dark Night which follows privation, although this also has an affirmative origin. The only clue to an illuminative state is the joy of the bones in Part II, but this arises in separation from the Lady, and she, in Part VI, is involved with the unitive ideal which the illuminative should presage. It is evident that too narrow an application of mystical terms would be unwarranted. The structure of the poem mirrors, however, an emotional condition common both to negative and to affirmative mysticism.

The first day of Lent is a day of weeping and fasting and of repentance for the sins of the past, when Christians seek God's help to turn them back toward Him and away from the world. Eliot's poem employs a number of phrases borrowed from the ritual appointed for that day, according to the Book of Common Prayer or the Roman ordinal and missal. Proper psalms for Ash Wednesday are Psalms 6, 32, 38, 102, 130, and 143, each of which has some kind of echo in the poem. The lessons taken from Isaiah, chapter 58; Jonah; and Hebrews, chapter 12, are also relevant. The "Miserere . . . secundum" (Psalm 51 in the Authorized Version) provides crucial symbolism, as does the Anglican service of Commination, where this psalm also figures. References to Joel, chapter 2 (as the Epistle for Ash Wednesday), to further scriptural passages, and to ritual forms characteristic of Anglo-Catholic and Roman Catholic usage, occur at various points. Other important sources for imagery are the Ash Wednesday sermons preached by Lancelot Andrewes on Jeremiah 8:4–7 (1602), Joel 2:12–13 (1619), and Matthew 3:8 (1624).

## I. *"Perch' io non spero"*

*Ash Wednesday* commences with a brilliant specimen of prolonged ambiguity. This sets forth two major themes: the hopelessness of the return to joys of sense and the hopelessness of the return to God. Along with these is a minor theme, completing a triad as in Part V of "The Hollow Men": the artist's failure to create. Like the allegory of man and the Church, the periodically emergent subject of artistic striving is veiled here. But there is nothing surprising in its association with the more perspicuous themes of sex and religion, for there is a fine tradition, medieval and romantic, in which a Lady, invoked as an object of love, is honored with the Muses' title. Baudelaire, in what Eliot has called an "astonishing" letter, thus addresses his Mme Marie in a way that would be appropriate to the Lady of *Ash Wednesday:*

> Through you, Marie, I shall be strong and great. Like Petrarch, I shall immortalize my Laura. Be my guardian Angel, my Muse, and my Madonna, and lead me in the path of Beauty.[6]

There could be no more succinct characterization of one who stands proxy for all the higher ideals compactly gathered in Eliot's phrase, "the word." It is interesting also that, following the example of Baudelaire, the speaker in *Ash Wednesday* suffers and triumphs through the paradox that Eliot approvingly cites from Charles Du Bos's study of the French poet: ". . . . that contemplative desire which needs presence alone, and which truly possesses only because it does not possess." Absence from the Lady motivates grief, and yet it occasions the purgatorial trial that can end the speaker's separation from a greater spiritual value and stimulate an artistic revival.

The first theme begins as the opening line paraphrases Guido Cavalcanti's poem "Perch' io non spero di tornar giammai," where Cavalcanti, languishing in exile and despairing of return, bids the *ballata* take word of his sorrow and illness to his Lady in Tuscany. Despite thirteenth-century conventions of the *senhal,* Cavalcanti's Lady may be assumed to have been his own wife. Eliot's second theme is simultaneously introduced as the same line points to the motif of turning in the ritual of Lent—turning toward God in a spirit of contrition. The metaphor is from Joel, chapter 2: "Turn ye even to me, saith the Lord. . . ."[7] This provides irony, for, although the Lady must be regarded as the symbolic goal of this spiritual turning, there is an implicit negative limitation which makes her the wrong goal. The line "Desiring this man's gift and that man's scope," echoing Shakespeare's twenty-ninth sonnet (but recalling in this context also the seventeenth stanza of Arnold's "The Scholar Gipsy"), bears several interpretations. It presents a reason for the speaker's lack of hope, a desirable or undesirable condition of the turning, and a reason or condition of the striving or refusal to strive in the line that comes after. It carries overtones of the pain described in the sonnet, where the poet's grief vanishes with the memory of love, and his "state,"

> Like to the lark at break of day arising
> From sullen earth, sings hymns at heaven's gate.

This image of the soul liberated with the exultancy of a bird's flight parallels an image from Jeremiah, on which Bishop Andrewes commented in his Ash Wednesday sermon of 1602: "What then, shall I continually 'fall' and never 'rise'? 'turn away' and not once 'turn again'? Shall my rebellions be 'perpetual'? . . . Shall these swallows fly over me and put me in mind of my 'return,' and shall I not heed them?"[8] Eliot worked into *The Waste Land* the image of the swallow restoring the joy of spring; here he used the "agèd eagle," reminiscent of the fable in the bestiaries which says that in old age the eagle flies upward toward the sun and then plunges into a well which renews its vigor. The story has scriptural warrant, and St. John of the Cross alludes to it as a parable of spiritual regeneration for the "old man."[9] Dante's dream in *Purgatorio*, IX, of being borne up by an eagle to the sun is a variation on the Ganymede myth, symbolizing rebirth. Eliot's symbolism recalls also Gide's *Le Prométhée mal enchaîné*, supporting the third, minor theme; Gide's eagle connotes the secret agonies of the artist. (One incidental detail, amusingly pertinent to the eagle's stretching his wings, is that Eliot put the pseudonymous signature "Apteryx" ["wingless"] to several of his reviews published by the *Egoist* in 1918.)

Of the various kinds of turning (including "verse") considered at the beginning of Part I, the first two kinds (the turning to fleshly love and the turning to God) are either mutually exclusive or not, depending on how one reads the line adapted from Shakespeare. If desire for the "gift" and "scope" persists after loss of hope for the other turning, then the disappearance of hope is only relative: the speaker can seek flesh at the expense of spirit or spirit at the expense of flesh; or, perhaps, if these are equally impossible, art at the expense of both. Accordingly he may be able to rejoice in one construct because he wants the means to achieve another. It is at least plausible, moreover, to read the second strophe ("Because I do not hope to know again") either as a parallel to the first or as an answer to the question "Why should I mourn?" and similarly with the third strophe in relation to the second. In other words, the three strophes are either "in parallel" or "in series" or both. The overlapping of meanings is important. The despair of the speaker is not unmodified; it is a despair balanced by hope that is being vitiated by despair. The symbolism of trees and springs supports a dual application, to religious faith and to sensory joy, which cannot appear together and which may not appear independently. The "vanished reign" and the "infirm glory" partly have the tone of a passage in Wordsworth's "Immortality Ode"; but they also reformulate the plight of Prufrock.

Eliot's treatment of time and place concedes certain limits to human experience. The ideal of "turning," even if once actual or partly actual, has vanished from actuality in the present; and only the present of things "as they are" has validity. If this fact causes pain, nevertheless it means that the sins of the past are not actual either. By the same token the present torment need not determine the future. Boundaries of time and place justify not only grief but rejoicing. At this point the attitude toward the "nothing" of actuality, on its highest level the *nada* of the Spanish mystics, is sustained by the doctrines of St. John of the Cross. If renunciation of "the blessèd face" and "voice" is a resigned act of detachment from a human being, then it may create, from the negative point of view, the occasion for rejoicing in service to God. On the other hand, if it is a despairing rejection of a spiritual vision, whether embodied in a human being or not, it may signal a rejoicing which is illusory. St. John devotes several chapters of *The Ascent of Mt. Carmel* to the purgation of the will, which must be cleansed of the "unruly affections" of joy, hope, grief, and fear. The purgation of joy obliges the mystic to fix his rejoicing only upon the "spiritual fruit" of "serving God . . . with true charity" and not upon the pleasures or benefits of his own powers, spiritual or otherwise.[10] The true joy of mystical detachment verges on that sought by the psalmist in the "Miserere": "Purge me with hyssop, and I shall be clean: wash me, and I shall be whiter than snow. Make me to hear joy and gladness; that the bones which thou hast broken may rejoice." The other joy, an imaginative rejoicing in one's attachment to human desires, is that to which a man incapable of turning to God "with fasting, and with weeping, and with mourning" might be prone. Eliot's "Consequently I rejoice" is ambiguous enough to suggest both or either of these joys. The state objectified here is one of bewildered misery. The one possible act is "to construct something," yet to do that is to resist immersion in "nothing."

An echo of the "Kyrie," "And pray to God to have mercy upon us," alludes at the same time to the "Épitaphe Villon":

> Quant de la chair, que trop avons nourrie,
> Elle est pieça devorée et pourrie,

Et nous, les os, devenons cendre et pouldre;
De nostre mal personne ne s'en rie,
Mais priez Dieu que tous nous vueille absouldre!

Villon's moving lines, and those of the "Miserere," look forward to the symbolism of the bones in Part II and relate to the Ash Wednesday theme of penitence, reflected in the formula for the imposition of ashes: "Remember, man, that thou art dust and unto dust thou shalt return." From here to the end of Part I, Eliot treats of the need for patience and submission in accordance with St. John's warning against cleaving to distractions. The prayer, perhaps with a side glance at Psalm 131, beseeches ability to forget, and God's forgiveness of "what is done, not to be done again," of whatever is actual with the limits of actuality. The impotence of the eagle's wings, whether for passion or for devotion, has produced a chance to rejoice in new values, however dangerous, and a need to acquiesce in the loss of the irrevocable. For this reason, in the aridity of affections peculiar to the will, the speaker prays, "Teach us to care and not to care"; that is, to care for what can or ought to be and not to care for what cannot or ought not to be. He would learn to "sit still," to master what, according to Pascal, is the cause of all human unhappiness, the inability to remain tranquil.[11] He concludes his prayer with words from the "Ave Maria." In effect he is already at the hour of his death, in the sense that separation and exile, the hopelessness of turning, have ended a way of life. From later parts of the poem, and inferentially here because of the echo of Cavalcanti, one can identify the "blessèd face" as that of a Lady from whom in some way he is exiled. One does not yet know that the apparently conclusive prayer for negative patience is enforced by the context of exile and that the ideal of spiritual reunion, not by turning but by waiting, includes restoration to her face and voice on a transcendent plane.

## II. "Salutation"

Part II of *Ash Wednesday* celebrates the theme of joy in the acceptance of death. As in Part I the theme is the speaker's powerlessness to rise from his dejection (strongly suggestive of the Fisher King situation in *The Waste Land*), so here it is his contentment, because of his Lady's love, to submit to a death in which that love sustains him. The Lady is symbolically equivalent to Dante's Beatrice, and the original heading "Salutation" refers to the scene in the *Vita nuova:* "After so many days had passed, that the nine years were exactly completed . . .

this wondrous Lady appeared to me clothed in whitest hue, between two gentle ladies who were of greater age; and passing upon a way she cast her eyes to that side where in sore fear I was; and of her ineffable courtesy, which now is rewarded in the world above, saluted me with such virtue that I thought then to see all bounds of blessedness."[12] Eliot's canceled epigraph to Part II, "The Hand of the Lord Was Upon Me:—*e vo significando*," came from the "dry bones" chapter of Ezekiel and from the words of Dante to the poet Buonagiunta da Lucca in *Purgatorio*, XXIV: "Such a one am I who take note when love inspires me, and in what manner he dictates within me, go uttering it." The Lady here already tends to serve, like Beatrice, as a mediator between the downcast soul and the loving intercessions of the Virgin. But Part II opens with a description of the death from which the speaker has given up hope of returning; the events are all in the past. The main symbolism is that of the bones discarded by three white leopards, which have devoured his legs (suggesting strength of body), his heart (the organ of the emotions), his liver (the organ of sensuality), and his brain (the organ of sense perception). (The last three correspond to the vital spirit, the natural spirit, and the animal spirit in the Galenic physiological theory which sprang from Democritus. Dante mentions them in *Vita nuova*, II, when recounting the effect of Beatrice's first appearance to him. It is by an act of devouring, moreover, that in Dante's dream of "the lord of fearful aspect" Beatrice receives his heart.)[13]

Eliot's leopards have the same dualism of function, in what essentially is the allegory of this passage, as do the main levels of ambiguity in Part I. Being predatory, the leopards may well signify the world, the flesh, and the devil; St. John of the Cross lends a certain weight to such an interpretation by his emphasis, in *The Dark Night*, upon these three traditional enemies of the soul. Thus they occupy the place of the dog in *The Waste Land* or that of the leopard numbered among the three beasts met by Dante, and supposed to typify, both there and frequently in medieval symbolism, the filthy pleasures of the world.[14] Yet these almost heraldic beasts, whose color is the white not simply of uncleanness but of purity and faith, are also agents of purgation. Like "Christ the tiger" they have eaten up the old life, leaving the scattered bones to wait for symbolic resurrection. This death provokes joy for the potential renewal of strength and life (further paralleled in Grimm's story "The Juniper Tree," which Leonard Unger has identified as one of Eliot's sources).[15] The juniper tree, a rebirth symbol, adjoins the bones, as if to demonstrate, like the story of Elijah and the juniper tree in I Kings, the unity of life and death; "the cool of the day" recalls, with several species of irony, the Garden of Eden.

In symbolic terms, devouring is a variant of the descent pattern. It calls to mind many stories and rituals recorded by anthropologists. Eliot alluded, by the "gourd," to the tale of Jonah, who, swallowed up by a fish, became for theologians a type of the Christ inclosed three days in hell; Jonah is cited by St. John as a type of the mystic undergoing the trial of darkness.[16] Eliot's synthesis of the devouring symbolism with that of the bones resembles that made by Grimm in "The Juniper Tree," but it is supplemented by references to Ezekiel, chapter 37 ("Shall these bones live?"), where the bones represent Israel ("Our bones are dried, and our hope is lost").

The bones, despite their dryness, are able to emit a sound of life, thin and sad, because of the Lady's loveliness and devotion.[17] The next lines introduce from Part I the theme of renunciation, again concerning the lost powers; the "dissembling" of the speaker facilitates his search for "oblivion" (a word rich in literary memories, as for example of Sir Thomas Browne's "iniquity of oblivion") and enables the sacrifice of both his spiritual and sexual love.[18] Accordingly

> It is this which recovers
> My guts the strings of my eyes and the indigestible portions
> Which the leopards reject.[19]

From death springs life. "The strings of my eyes" alludes to the bond of love, with the imagery of Donne's "Extasie." The Lady, a woman in white as in *Vita nuova*, III, withdraws like Beatrice; she is to remain a spiritual presence only. Through concentrating upon his renunciation, the speaker will achieve forgetfulness of what is lost, and thus he may achieve rebirth—the bones' coming-together as prophesied by Ezekiel. The punning echo of Ecclesiastes, chapter 12 ("the grasshopper shall be a burden, and desire shall fail"), lets one hear the chirping of the bones as a resigned and therefore joyous celebration of carnality subdued. Their song, a litany to the Lady, is a counterpart to the Litanies of the Holy Virgin and, perhaps, to Gourmont's "Litanies de la Rose."[20] It reiterates the symbolism of the rose not only as applied to the Virgin ("la Rosa, in che il Verbo divino / carne si fece," of *Paradiso*, XXIII) but as utilized in medieval courtly-love allegory, where the rose is an emblem of the Lady for whose love the hero sues.

The Lady in *Ash Wednesday*, thus analogous to the central figure of such allegory, is the focus for a sublimation of human love.

> The single Rose
> Is now the Garden
> Where all loves end.

That garden is paradise regained; the Hyacinth garden of *The Waste Land* is paradise lost. Eliot's Lady is described in paradoxes: "Calm and distressed / Torn and most whole," and so on, which pertain equally to her two roles. What has already been noted about the centrality of the hyacinth girl is again relevant. Here active lust has fallen away; the "torment / Of love unsatisfied" has ceased with the "End of the endless / Journey to no end"—and the hollow men finish their insatiate turning. As it is to do in Part V, the symbolism of the "Word of no speech" reinforces the symbolism of this "Lady of silences."[21] The unspeaking voice of human love disappears into the placid center of the eternal rest.

Part II draws to a close with the singing of the bones, rejoicing at the death of their active hope. Fulfilling the prayer in the "Miserere" by their forgetfulness of desire, the bones are "united / In the quiet of the desert," the desert also of St. John's *Dark Night;* there the contemplative isolates himself for "dark contemplation" on the secret ladder of love.[22] Eliot's concluding lines substantiate that Part II is an allegory, not simply of the individual soul, but of the scattered body of Christian believers, analogous to the tribes of Israel and Judah in Ezekiel's valley of dry bones. The indebtedness of the bones to the Lady parallels that of Christians to the Church. Eliot's citation of the assurance given in Ezekiel, chapter 48 ("This is the land which ye shall divide by lot unto the tribes of Israel for inheritance, and these are their portions, saith the Lord God"), is deeply ironic; for whereas the inheritance of the tribes was to come in the glory of restoration, this inheritance is death—the "broken jaw of our lost kingdoms." But for the speaker, accepting an ascetic way, the legacy of the dead shall be regenerative.

III. *"Al som de l'escalina"*

Part II has exhibited joy because through sacrifice the blessing of the garden may be attainable. The poetry which follows, except in Part V, deals largely with the urgent pressure of the past. In one sense desire has failed and in another it is as importunate as before. This fact may be good if the desire, as in Part IV, seeks an ultimately realizable ideal; but time preserves sensuous memories, too. Though *Ash Wednesday* as a whole contains a less keen despair than "The Hollow Men," such memories linger beneath the speaker's ostensibly calm submissiveness. Memory is the "ague of the skeleton."

The winding stairs have caused an interpretational crux. The assumption of some critics has been that they are equivalent to the purgatorial ascent in the *Commedia* (or, rather fancifully, to the three steps at the gate in *Purgatorio*, IX) and to St. John's mystical ladder in *The Dark Night of the Soul*. It is true that they resemble these. That the speaker, after the denial of the flesh in Part II, should be shown in Part III as moving toward regeneration would conform to the stages in mysticism. As in St. John of the Cross, the act of renunciation should be followed by further temptation and suffering during which the aspirant made progress without realizing it. But here another element intrudes, that of retrospection. The protagonist is remembering an ascent according to nature, not purgatorial in actuality. That is, he does not leave the bones and at once rise upon the several flights of a spiritual staircase, but he is revealed in a place high up on the stair, from which he looks backward to a time, probably before dismemberment, when he was "climbing" in a manner not then spiritual. His present condition, defined already in the rejoicing of the stripped bones, is qualified by the duration of his past into his present with memories that presumably lessen joy. If the stairs epitomize purgation at all, they do so not like a present actuality but like a past one, purgatorial as a memory. They reveal the enigmatic process by which, after something has happened, its meaning alters through some interim event. (In the idea of time implicit in this passage may be discerned an analogue to Eliot's conception of "what happens when a new work of art is created." According to "Tradition and the Individual Talent," "The existing monuments form an ideal order among themselves, which is modified by the introduction of the new [the really new] work of art among them."[23] And according to *The Use of Poetry and the Use of Criticism*, there must periodically arise an "exhaustive critic" who will "review the past of our literature, and set the poets and the poems in a new order."[24] To Eliot, life is like art and criticism in being able, and indeed in being obliged, to revaluate its past; it is privileged to put old foundations to a new and better use and thus, in the phrase from Part IV of *Ash Wednesday*, to "redeem the time.")

The speaker's allegorical "turning" in Part III dramatizes his unregenerate life. He has a memory of himself in an earlier guise:

> The same shape twisted on the banister
> Under the vapour in the fetid air
> Struggling with the devil of the stairs who wears
> The deceitful face of hope and of despair.[25]

The "second turning of the second stair" blots out the remembered faces and envelops the protagonist in darkness. The simile of "an old man's mouth driveling, beyond repair, / Or the toothed gullet of an agèd shark," alludes to the "old man" of St. Paul.[26] Images supervening at "the first turning of the third stair" revive temptation and beguilement. The "slotted window," apparently a balistraria, gives a narrow view of a landscape where

> The broadbacked figure drest in blue and green
> Enchanted the maytime with an antique flute.

Eliot's imagery, featuring the symbolic blossom of May Day, the hawthorn, has a Pre-Raphaelite quality: the "broadbacked figure," itself almost floral, reminds one less of Dante's imagery than of Burne-Jones's. The symbolism of the may accompanies that of the window "bellied like the fig's fruit," which, with the flute, has an emphatic sexual connotation; the hair likewise, as in "Prufrock" and *The Waste Land*, supplies a romantic reference.[27] These things are "distraction," for not only do they infatuate, but they deflect the soul from any higher purpose. The speaker, still ascending, climbs with "strength beyond hope and despair" either of refusing the fading sensual vision or of recovering it. Accordingly the final lines of Part III, from the "Act of Humility" in the Mass, state his unworthiness to turn to God. (The prayer appears in the liturgy just before the communion of the celebrant; its source is Matthew, chapter 8.) At the same time, by a devious ambiguity, the lines pertain to the climber's inability to find that other "word of no speech," the word of human love characterized as "lost" at the beginning of Part V.

The present moment of the prayer derives its dramatic intensity from an implied contrast between the memories and a different kind of beatitude. The stress with which it is charged is comparable to that of Gerontion's "After such knowledge, what forgiveness?" The sexual content of these memories of knowledge is accentuated by the original epigraph taken from *Purgatorio*, XXVI, "Al som de l'escalina"—the ground of Arnaut Daniel's petition to Dante: "Now I pray you, by that goodness which guides you to the summit of the stair, be mindful in due season of my pain" ("Ara vos prec, per aquella valor / que vos guida al som de l'escalina, / sovegna vos a temps de ma dolor"). Arnaut's own sin stands for all lusts of the flesh, the importunity of the sensual man's desires, associated by Eliot with turning both here and in "The Hollow Men." In this context the circular movement, typifying sin and therefore hell, coincides with the other, the purgatorial circling: the sinners in *Purgatorio*, XXVI, go round about the mountain, bathed in fire; when Arnaut himself finishes speaking he plunges back into the refining flames ("Poi s'ascose nel foco che gli affina"). Eliot equates the experience of sin—the speaker's ascent among the false enchantments of time—with a hell having a false similitude of heaven, but he also hints that this, like the leopards' devouring, can be tantamount to purgation.

The potential merging of hell with purgatory, evident in the last section of *The Waste Land* and in "The Hollow Men," is to appear also in "Little Gidding." The turning, however, is now ended; the protagonist finds himself in the passive Dark Night, where both the wrong and the right kind of voluntary turning are impossible. He seeks the still center, the Word, but without some sort of turning this attainment must wait for extraordinary prevenient grace. The joy he is capable of now is only the joy of one tormented in the fire of memory and despair.

Part III recapitulates an initiation pattern. Both Dante and St. John by the stair or ladder (in Eliot it may have been borrowed from W. B. Yeats) symbolize an effort corresponding to that of the quester in the Grail legend. Jessie L. Weston remarks in *From Ritual to Romance* that the initiation scheme in Mithraism accomplished its ascent to the deity by seven ladders; this is a familiar concept. Eliot owed little of his imagery in Part III to either of his principal sources, though the blue and green of the flautist's attire deceptively recall the liturgical symbolism of the colors—the blue for heaven and the green for hope.

IV

Part IV, like the preceding, concerns memories, but no longer any of a sensual kind; the prospect from the window yields to the glorified vision of a Lady investing the scene with a light of grace. Here for the first time the personal sufferings of the protagonist become subordinate, so that the total emphasis rests upon the happy dream retrieved by consciousness. The Lady seems to float upward from a depth of yearning within him, from his own shaping of desire into an ideal embodiment. She is a symbol of the desire beyond desire and of the fusion of human and celestial. She, better than the vague ghost of "Lilac and brown hair," is the true countertype of the hyacinth girl, holding, with ephemeral intensity, the central focus of all impulse toward clarity and beauty. She lifts the speaker's aspiration above matter into a domain of pure form. Like all perfect things she can be manifested only in dreams; she is

> One who moves in the time between sleep and waking, wearing
> White light folded, sheathed about her, folded.

This spirit of a lost Eden receives his invocation in the words of Arnaut, "Sovegna vos"; emulating Arnaut, he articulates them from fire. It is she "Who walked between the violet and the violet," as Matilda in *Purgatorio*, XXVIII, "went singing and plucking flower after flower, wherewith her path was pied."[28] She is far more than a symbol of the vanished garden. The speaker's plea that she remember him explains his purgatorial state, by associating this with Arnaut's, and furthermore, because the apostrophe to her is very nearly devotional, exalts her to a heavenly dignity. Indeed, she goes dressed in "Mary's colour," the white and the celestial "blue of larkspur." Hers is the ignorance that those already redeemed from "eternal dolour" possess while yet understanding its agonies.

Between the protagonist's first vision of this Lady and his present suffering, the years have intervened,

> bearing
> Away the fiddles and the flutes, restoring
> One who moves in the time between sleep and waking. . . .

The years take away the transitory things of the flesh and in her restore them transfigured, almost apotheosized, as "White light folded." She irradiates the blindness and the spiritual darkness shrouding him, as in the *Commedia* the Lady Lucia shines with the light of illuminating grace. Through the Lady of the vision the lost years are themselves brought back—the years of lost creativity, lost love, and lost devotion. These years are now made capable of redemption. "Redeem the time" supports not simply the construction intended in St. Paul's use of the phrase, that a man favored with the light should maintain it against the evils of his age and should be, in another idiom, the leaven that leavens the whole lump. Eliot's protagonist seems to say that this vouchsafed light enables the remembered past as well as the present to be re-deemed. The years may thus find restoration by acquiring new mean-ing; and the memory, revived as in the "higher dream" of which Eliot spoke in his essay on Dante, imposes this new meaning upon them. The vision that in its first glimmer was misunderstood can now be "read." "We had the experience but missed the meaning," said Eliot in "The Dry Salvages"; in *Ash Wednesday* he contemplated an experi-ence merely human in its genesis and reinterpreted it as a spiritual awakening.

The line "While jewelled unicorns draw by the gilded hearse," mark-ing the climax of Part IV, contrasts with the preceding vision. It intro-duces gaudy ostentation, symbolizing death. To insist that "the gilded hearse" stood for any particular thing would be futile; it connotes the whole world of temporal pomp, but in the surroundings of dream allegory it corresponds partly to the car of the Church in *Purga-torio*, XXIX, partly to Blake's "marriage-hearse," and partly, as Eliza-beth Drew suggests, to the poetic past.[29] The present "triumph" is garish and unseemly; the unicorns of chastity and healing are now prinked up with jewels, like the gaily decorated beasts of a carrousel, and the coach they draw is vulgarly disguised with a coat of gilding.[30] The processional image, unmodified, may have originated for Eliot in the solemn tradition of medieval allegory, but in his handling it has be-come utterly different from Dante's; it has more in common with the progress of Lucifera in *The Faerie Queene*. The spectacle discloses nothing which, except most superficially, could find place in "the higher dream." It serves, by drawing attention from the ideal, to shift the per-spective through a symbol of human folly to the actual, waking world.

As the dream slips away, the speaker thinks of the "silent sister veiled in white and blue," *similar* to the Lady in the vision but existent corporeally in time and thus essentially the same as the Lady in Part II. The basis for her resemblance to the visitant is obscure. The main dif-ferences are that this Lady is silent and that she is "between the yews, behind the garden god" and not "between the violet and the violet." But, like the dream Lady, she embodies the genuine in a world of spuri-ousness. In a very general sense the yew trees on either side of her are symbols, as are the violets earlier, of the victory over death; but they contribute a divergent emphasis. The violets, with a peculiar mytho-logical association in the Attis cult, connote a perpetual flowering of life and a subsidence of death beneath the roots of immortality; the funereal yews suggest death and the life beyond it. The Lady, being *behind* the god Priapus, "whose flute is breathless," implies obliquely the relation between sex and love. The sexual meaning of the breathless flute is clear enough; the indicated privation bears some analogy to the dryness of the bones. The action of the Lady, who "bent her head and signed but spoke no word," defines both the power and the limitations of her love:[31] she has pointed to salvation, by the sign of the Cross or otherwise, but as a "Lady of silences" and of absence she has not spoken the longed-for word which should wholly release the sufferer. Apparently the curative word, "the word unheard, unspoken," is still only potential. But as the dream was the "token," its redemption will fulfil the reality, and the Lady's sign alone has been enough to evoke the jet of the fountain and the hopeful song of the bird, symbols portending rebirth.[32] The word will be spoken when the wind, a divine *pneûma*, or breath, of God, scatters the whispers from the yew tree of death. These, as usual in Eliot, are allied to both death and secrecy. But this wind is a cleansing one that will renew breath, that is, life or power; it brings immortality, not death, "after this our exile"—a phrase from the prayer "Salve Regina," supplicating the Holy Virgin.

## V

The Lady's failure to speak the word is consistent with her withdrawal and the protagonist's exile. It has been seen that his renunciation of her voice in Part I is complemented by the symbolic death recounted in Part II, and that these acts conform to an actual necessity imposed by the loss of hope. Part III and Part IV uncover memories of a past lost because the word is missing which, on the one hand, might nullify (or, alternatively, appease) his sensual torment and, on the other hand, might endow his radiant vision with actuality. In Part V, once more, he has to face his actual state: the intermediary word is gone, but the ultimate Word, the Logos, remains. Christ is still the center round which all things turn. The Infant Word and the whirling world, as in "Gerontion," here form the pattern of the center and the wheel subtending the pattern of conflict between spirit and flesh. The Incarnation, made known through the Epiphany, is the mover and goal of right desire. But, so long as desire is wrongly motivated, "the unstilled world" resists its Redeemer. The speaker in *Ash Wednesday* believes that he is in exile both, like a Cavalcanti, from the Lady herself, who speaks no word of love, and, like the parade of jeweled unicorns, from the Savior. Thus the line from the "Liturgical Re-proaches," "O my people, what have I done unto thee," echoing Micah, chapter 6, acknowledges the betrayed Christ's reproach to His people and reflects the exile's awareness of his own guilt. Eliot presumably remembered that Dante is said to have addressed to the citizens of Florence, from his asylum at Verona, a letter beginning with the same phrase: "Popule mi, quid feci tibi?" Though by quoting Christ's words the speaker rebukes the infidel world, not exempting himself, he also voices through them a continuing grievance against his private waste land.

The incantatory rhythms and rhetorical devices of sound in the next strophe produce a rapid and somewhat shallower current of symbols. The desperate plea for the word, with overtones of both "word" and "Word," conveys a quality of frantic agony. Without meditative si-lence in a Dark Night of noise and ignorance the speaker can discover "No place of grace."[33] Worldly distractions cause him to avoid "the blessed face," the face of the Lady, and beyond this, the face of the Redeemer. He requires the corrective intercession of the Lady, or of the Virgin, with whom the symbols gradually blend her. Meanwhile, he wavers among those "torn on the horn between season and season, time and time, between / Hour and hour, word and word, power and power." The metaphoric horn symbolizes both help and torment, com-bining the scriptural "horn of salvation" with Dante's shaking horn of flame (*Inferno*, XXVI). The "children at the gate" can neither receive nor spurn grace; and for them, who in bewilderment "chose and op-pose," the speaker would have the Lady utter her word, though it is she whom they offend in their hesitancy, dreading to surrender to the spirit. They

> . . . affirm before the world and deny between the rocks
> In the last desert between the last blue rocks
> The desert in the garden the garden in the desert
> Of drouth, spitting from the mouth the withered apple-seed.

The blue rocks seem equivalent to the gate and to the yew trees—the place of decision; they represent, therefore, even if not a literal death, a crisis of spiritual death and rebirth. The way of life passes through death, "the last desert," which the protagonist has entered in Part II. The blue rocks signify both the death of desire, the "desert in the gar-den," and the rebirth of the spirit, "the garden in the desert." They are obliquely analogous to the chamber of initiation or the sibyl's cave, though they contrast with the red rock of *The Waste Land*. But the rejection of the apple-seed means the casting-away of redemptive joy, even at this propitious place. Thus in Joel, chapter 1, the prophet grieves that "the pomegranate tree, the palm tree also, and the apple tree, even all the trees of the field, are withered: because joy is withered away from the sons of men."[34] Accordingly at the end of Part V there is still need for a prayer, a word. Of this the protagonist is still unworthy. He is half "a broken Coriolanus" and for the rest an unhappy victim of an apostate civilization, a realm of clamor and darkness. Neither the voluntary relinquishment of human desires nor the tentative revaluation of the "higher dream" has transformed him into a new man or, except happily in the artistic meaning, given youth to the eagle's wings.

## VI

In its conclusion *Ash Wednesday* exposes the same circumstances as in Part I, but it moves the stress from what the suppliant may actively do to what he must passively sustain. It makes explicit the relation between desire and memory. Also it changes "Because I do not hope" to "Although I do not hope," thus not only exploiting the dual meaning of Cavalcanti's "perché" but contriving a tribute to Du Bos's estimate of Baudelaire's analogous problem: ". . . every 'because' is doubled with a 'despite,' every cause carries with it the corresponding inhibition. . . ."[35] Unlike Part I, this final section elaborates the fact that for the speaker the process of learning "to care and not to care" is arduous because, although hope has flown, desire still tears the heart. His statement in Part I, echoed here, "I no longer strive to strive towards such things," reveals that the act of striving, or wishing, is involuntary or even unconscious. Part VI exhibits in some detail the nature of his besetting desires. Although he does not hope to turn again either to the flesh or to God and although he has renounced the face of the Lady, he cannot elude his unwilling wish to return:

> Wavering between the profit and the loss
> In this brief transit where the dreams cross
> The dreamcrossed twilight between birth and dying.

It may be that the two ideals, salvation and sensory joy, are meant by these dreams crossing in the twilight between two worlds; either would be profitable in default of the other. He speaks the confessional formula, "Bless me father," because, in so far as the poem is an *apologia* or self-appraisal, he has been confessing all the time the conflict obstructing his penitential duty. The distractions appeal to his human wish for beauty and love—for "the one veritable transitory power." So long as he succumbs to his human dualism of flesh and spirit, both of them susceptible of desire, these things before his mind's eye, the "white sails . . . seaward flying / Unbroken wings," remind him of the positive attainments he does not hope for. Most of the things viewed from the "wide window" imply, equally with the trees and springs in Part I, that his task is to abjure delights of sense. The joy he feels is that of a "lost heart" for a phantasm.

> And the lost heart stiffens and rejoices
> In the lost lilac and the lost sea voices
> And the weak spirit quickens to rebel
> For the bent golden-rod and the lost sea smell.

He remembers "the cry of quail and the whirling plover," birds flushed from covert to soar on wings stronger than his own. But it is all a delusion of "the blind eye," creating "empty forms between the ivory gates," the traditional avenue of false dreams.

The extent to which this whole remarkable passage concerns a stubborn longing for the presence of the Lady as a spiritual guide depends on correlation with Part I. Obviously the tone of such phrases as "quickens to rebel" and "empty forms" does not encourage such a reading. But since the delusion lies in his merely *dreaming* of the ideal, and since the natural imagery has been associated also with the visitant in Part IV, the possibility of this second meaning exists. Theoretically, then, the sensuous imagery here, after the pattern of the "Rose of memory" and the fountains and springs, reflects not only the specious ideal of "a slotted window" but the Lady's uncommunicated sanctity; it fuses Part III and Part IV. Nevertheless, the texture of images discourages the notion, partly because the Lady has become too much a spiritual power to be again symbolized so naturalistically, and, more fundamental, because it would be psychologically inappropriate to depict such a spiritual attraction as causing so much turbulence. A spiritually desirable thing would astonish, grieve, even soothe, but not excite. And it would not be, one surmises, so urgent a subject for confession. The symmetry with Part I is by no means absolute. The speaker is baffled by the unreality of the "empty forms"—the insubstantiality, one might say, of art as well as memory. The renewal of the "salt savour" is disappointing, whether it add pungency to the sand where the bleached bones of sense lie dispersed, arouse new vigor in the spiritual salt of the earth, or restimulate the poet's artistic endeavor. Affirmation of created things has to take them as they are, not as they were or might have been.

The protagonist has no recourse except the patience he elected at the beginning. His decision is crueller here than in Part I, for he is not bowing to fate but wrestling with it. Before, he was faced with the tolerable fact that the defeat of one attitude would mean the victory of another, the negative; now, even in this chosen triumph of negative resignation, he confesses that the issue is unsettled because the inappeasable longing will not be put down. Desire survives hopelessness. His state is compatible with Eliot's remark in *The Sacred Wood* about Francesca da Rimini, that "it is a part of damnation to experience desires that we can no longer gratify."[36] Caught in "the time of tension between dying and birth," at the point where, as it were, two fields of force have mutually canceling attraction; in a "place of solitude" where three ideals of attainment—the sexual, the spiritual, and the artistic—(and the three parts of time) are all present as dreams, and where the symbolic gates formed by the blue rocks and the yew trees wait for him to resolve the conflict of choice and opposition, the protagonist, like the soul in "Animula," seems powerless "to fare forward or retreat." The portent of his deliverance is the voice of "the other yew," evidently the voice of life and immortality, just as the whispers shaken from the first yew by the divine breath were voices of the dead past, hopeless desire, and death. But this voice does not achieve full utterance, which remains the goal of his petition: "*Let* the other yew be shaken and reply." Yet he himself gives an answer in the prayer itself. The will to receive negative discipline lies not far from the very state induced by such discipline—one of serene detachment. Through detachment he could become worthy of the life-giving presence, divine or human, from which he has borne separation.

Although he prays directly to the Holy Virgin, it is with a sense that she is not really other than the Lady veiled from his sight. The two are symbolically one:

> Blessèd sister, holy mother, spirit of the fountain,
>     spirit of the garden,
> Suffer us not to mock ourselves with falsehood
> Teach us to care and not to care
> Teach us to sit still.

The epithet "sister" recalls Eliot's remarks on Baudelaire's line "Mon enfant, ma sœur" from "L'Invitation au voyage," that "The word *sœur* here is not . . . chosen merely because it rhymes . . . it is a moment in that sublimation of passion toward which Baudelaire was always striving. . . ."[37] In Eliot's lines the plea echoes that of Part I, and rightly so. The protagonist, in the manner of Tiresias at the end of *The Waste Land,* is again confronting the present actuality with which he began. He is no longer revolving in his mind, as he has been doing throughout the central sections of the poem, the causes of his vacillation. Furthermore, he has experienced some change of mood. He does not ask that the Virgin pray "at the hour of our death" but that she help him not to be separated. First, however, he must submit wholly to God. In Dante's "la sua volontate è nostra pace,"[38] corresponding to the "Collect for Peace": ". . . whose service is perfect freedom," he finds a harmonious complement to the negativism of St. John of the Cross. Submission to the divine will dictates renunciation of the personal will, but it leads to the finding of life and to reaffirmation. The rocks themselves may paradoxically be "Exhausted and life-giving," and the divine will, which Dante calls in the *Paradiso* (III, 86) "that sea to which all moves," is not only the destroyer of the old but the source of the new. It acts through the Virgin Stella Maris, the "spirit of the sea." The words from the "Anima Christi," "Suffer me not to be separated," to which Eliot appended the ritual response "And let my cry come unto thee," ask for reunion after the hopelessness and seeming despair have become humility. This would be a spiritual reunion with what cannot be hoped for; paradoxically it would offer restoration of hope. Through the painful negative trial of separation, the protagonist may once more find even the Lady herself and be ransomed from exile.

It would be easy to overemphasize the influence of negative mysticism on *Ash Wednesday,* but its importance is subordinate. The affirmative mysticism of Dante is of greater moment to the poem. One might complain, in fact, that the Lady is so imperfectly realized that the feelings clustering about her draw most of their dramatic justification from the Dantean allegory. Certain of the attitudes in *Ash Wednesday* have a post-romantic quality, derived, perhaps, from Eliot's notion of Baudelaire, to whom he seems to have felt most akin spiritually in the late 1920's. One can hardly explain why Eliot made *Ash Wednesday* so cryptic or why he did not give it a more readily apprehensible structure. He said wittily in *The Use of Poetry* that he had thought of prefixing to a future edition of the poem some lines from Byron's *Don Juan* (which he thereupon misquoted). One may regard as sincere the protest that "I don't pretend that I quite understand / My own meaning when I would be *very* fine."[39] Anybody, moreover, can find more meanings than Eliot could have intended, while still, without some indispensable facts of biography, losing much of what he really meant. Eliot's treatment of formal structure betrays his main poetic weakness, and, apparently, despite the great store he sets by symbolic relationships, he has usually been content to let most of his "plot" grow out of allusions to other writers. *Ash Wednesday* is not innocent of what looks like wilful mystification. Its structure appears haphazard even where it is not, and its sheer verbosity at times is irritating. Yet to a reader willing to fortify himself with certain outside lore, the poem reveals part of its secret. To a reader content with the illusion that it exemplifies only *la poésie pure*, it communicates much by its brilliant texture of tone and imagery.

          In 1931 and 1932 Eliot issued for publication two sections of a poem, never completed, called *Coriolan*. The first was "Triumphal March." During his visit to Chicago in 1950 he said that he had meant the work to show "a sequence in the life of the character who appears in this first part as Young Cyril."[1] It is difficult to fathom all of Eliot's purposes from what he finished of this finely rhetorical though imperfectly dramatized poem. It seems that he was attempting to depict the career of Coriolan at different stages, dated by Cyril's growth from childhood to maturity, and to suggest a contrasting parallel between Coriolan and Cyril, the one a statesman and hero, the other a nobody. In "Triumphal March" at least, they are not only antithetical but in some ways, like many opposites, complementary as well. That the symmetry tended to dissolve in "Difficulties of a Statesman" may have been one of the reasons Eliot abandoned his project—another being that in 1933 he was lecturing in the United States and evidently had no time to spare for it. The milieu in the poem is a politically centered, secular culture where the "little people" look to Coriolan as the focus for their ideals. "Triumphal March" shows the populace of a great city craning their necks to glimpse their symbol of stability, the general riding godlike, behind flags, trumpets, and eagles, in triumph through the streets. "Difficulties of a Statesman" exposes the perplexities of the general, faced with the practical impossibility of embodying firmness and enlightenment when he himself can find no center of peace. Eliot, having partly a satiric motive, aimed his thrusts (a little unfairly) at the blank ignorance of the goggling rabble and (with rather more justice) at the pomposity of government as a substitute for this center.[2]

    Both sections suffer from obfuscation. In "Triumphal March" the monologue is spoken by a spectator of the triumph who possesses some unusual powers of sight. It is not precisely clear, however, which of the remarks are his own and which come from other people, especially from young Cyril, unable to peer over the heads of the crowd. It is unclear also whether the speaker gives a running account of the proceedings or simply his vivid recollection of them, for he is careless with the tenses of his verbs. All this difficulty could have been moderated by the judicious insertion of quotation marks. In allusiveness "Triumphal March" competes with *The Waste Land*, without so much dependence on functional sources. F. O. Matthiessen pointed out that the tone was indebted to a passage in Charles Maurras's *L'Avenir de l'Intelligence*, where a second-rate writer talks excitedly about a celebration in honor of some literary personage, for which generals, officials, musicians, and professors have all turned out on parade. The story is received incredulously: "—Et les soldats faisaient la haie?—Ils la faisaient."³ Some of Eliot's rhythms were undoubtedly suggested by that account. He also took a phrase or two from section 4 of Perse's *Anabase* and relied on Shakespeare's *Coriolanus* for some implicit historical background.

Coriolan's character is merely latent in "Triumphal March." From the other part of the poem, however, as from Shakespeare's treatment of Caius Marcius, one infers the hero's impatience with the people's fickleness and gullibility. The supreme irony intrinsic to Eliot's use of Coriolanus as a symbol is that the Roman general stands for arrogant betrayal of people who also betray him. Since the triumphal procession of magistrates, warriors, and Vestals is contrasted with Christ's entry into Jerusalem on Palm Sunday, the theme of betrayal strikes an ironic counterpoint to the people's feeling for Coriolan as a savior:

> O hidden under the dove's wing, hidden in the turtle's breast,
> Under the palmtree at noon, under the running water
> At the still point of the turning world.

Actually the symbols appropriate to Coriolan as a public figure occur in Eliot's admirable opening lines: "Stone, bronze, stone, steel, stone, oakleaves, horses' heels / Over the paving." The clang of armed troops, answered by the irregular clop-clop of steel hooves, resounds with a metallic coldness belying the claims of force as an instrument of peace. The spectators as well as the general typify a society barred from the spiritual values productive of peace.

If Coriolan is a counterfeit savior, so, from another point of view, is the child among the pilgrims who throng the way to the temple. The

Passover journey recorded in Luke, chapter 2, forms a relevant parallel to the scene. Standing by as one of the uncomprehending mass, young Cyril is a foil to the lordly hero. The name Cyril means "lord"; its pattern of consonants resembles that of the name Coriolan. The link is ironic in the light of what Cyril is and of what he is to become, a telephone operator at one pound ten a week. Cyril's being brought to see the sights retraces the pattern of his having been taken to church on Easter Day, when he mistook the Sanctus bell for the handbell of the crumpet man. Even the child—and "of such is the kingdom of heaven"—lacks touch with the mystery. All these people, childishly fixing their eyes on an earthly power, have taken one of the hollow men for their divinity. It is easy to see why: they are flux and he seems to be permanence. They honor him as "the still point of the turning world"; he, as is evident in "Difficulties of a Statesman," is tormented by the same longing for the hidden peace they imagine him to be lord of. "Triumphal March" is thus about the empty husk of a supposititious centrality, personified in a conquering master accorded a Roman triumph and, in the Roman fashion, crowned as a god with the oakleaves of Jupiter. This Coriolanus commands armaments denoting that he is modern as well as ancient—timeless like the city and its people. The setting might be anywhere: the pomp is simply a type of the universal secular adoration of the transitory and false in place of the eternal. Of course, the irony is unrealized by the narrator of the poem. Eliot's view of the mob was colored by the satiric appraisal of popular institutions in Aristophanes' comedies, perhaps especially by that in *The Knights*, which presents a cynical comparison of the politician Cleon with a vulgar sausage seller, Agoracritus, an advocate of peace and good government. Eliot has remarked that the sausages mentioned in "Triumphal March" came from Aristophanes;[4] they may suggest an identification of the crowd with the capricious, pliant Demos of that play. (They relate also to Roman religion, perhaps as phallic symbols, having been a regular feature of the Lupercalia and the Floralia, as they were in the religious dances from which Greek comedy began.) At Harvard there is a school copy of Aristophanes' *Acharnians*, in W. W. Merry's edition, with marginal notes by Eliot. It may have first stimulated the Aristophanic attitudes in his own poetry.

The spectators' perceptions as the cavalcade advances are necessarily limited. Eliot's ironic use of a line from Edmund Husserl's *Ideas* need not be allusively functional, although from its original context the line might imply that the people neither know what perceiving is nor are in any position to benefit from it. Assuredly they fail to know their leader. Husserl, recapitulating the opinion of the "Man in the Street," states that the average man thinks of perception as "an empty looking of an empty 'Ego' towards the object itself which comes into contact with it in some astonishing way":

> The natural wakeful life of our Ego is a continuous perceiving, actual or potential. The world of things and our body within it are continuously present to our perception. How then does and can *Consciousness itself* separate out as a *concrete thing in itself*, from that within it, of which we are conscious, namely, the *perceived being*, *"standing over against"* consciousness *"in and for itself"*?[5]

A naïve view of consciousness, as an immediate absorption of the perceived thing into the subject, must be inadequate. Husserl defines rather an amalgamation, through sensory experience, of multiple changing views of the object. Obviously, too, in Eliot's poem the people really see only what they are meant to see; they have no means of reaching the silent man behind the trappings. Yet to them the arrival of Coriolan conveys a sense of revelation, a sense of the immediacy of what is "hidden," from which they think to profit through their perceptions. Coriolan, however, from whom the light is also hidden, is an interloper into the people's famished search for eternal order.

Eliot's list of weapons and supplies was purloined almost verbatim from Ludendorff's *The Coming War* (1931), where it represents the munitions surrendered or destroyed by the Germans after Versailles.[6] This array, which "comes first," has several poetic purposes, including contrast with the undistinguished contingents which follow. The resort to bathos by ushering in the golf-clubbers, the Scouts, and the gymnastic society is, perhaps, too transparent for remark, but it is not unsubtle, for after "the Mayor and the Liverymen" Coriolan himself rides abruptly upon the scene, as if for the sake of being implicated in the more foolishly portentous part of the show. Nevertheless, Coriolan outwardly has a fulness of self-possession and authority. How far this may be ironic, the poem fails to communicate. Absence of interrogation from his eyes might mean vacancy; his indifference, exclusion of sympathy. Since the narrator can report only what he himself perceives, one cannot know the lurking reality here, the motives of Coriolan's gaze or the objects of his expectation. It may be that, just as the hero connotes peace to those about him, so over him there hovers at this hour a higher dream of escape into the shelter of "the dove's wing"

—the word "hidden" referring either to what the people falsely divine in him or to what, as in "Difficulties of a Statesman," he yearns for. Eliot's handling of this climactic moment reproduces something of the austerity which Yeats, in *A Vision* (1925), ascribed to Roman portrait sculpture in contradistinction to the flexible grace of the Parthenon frieze:

They could now express in stone a perfect composure, the administrative mind, alert attention where all had been rhythm, an exaltation of the body, uncommitted energy. . . . One sees on the pediments troops of marble Senators, officials serene and watchful as befits men who know that all the power of the world moves before their eyes, and needs, that it may not dash itself to pieces, their unhurried unanxious never-ceasing care.[7]

This frigid and essentially brutal, though perhaps to the sectaries godlike, posture is utterly different in value from the heartbeat of the dove or the refreshing and purifying water of life. The climax effects at once a juxtaposition and a polarization of the diverse symbols for centrality.

The sacrifice offered at the temple fulfils the ritual duty customarily paid to a *triumphator*. Roman triumphs originated as rites of devotion to Jove, whom a victorious commander was attired to resemble. There is a conspicuous similarity between a triumph and the installation of a priestly king as described in Frazer's *The Golden Bough*. Though Eliot made no point of this fact, it should be deemed implicit in the pattern of "Triumphal March" because of the spiritual, or in any event emotional, values attached by the populace to Coriolan. It means that the procession is not merely the unchristian but the pagan counterpart of Christ's own victory and triumph; it lends to the poem a formally ritualistic effect that deepens the irony and explains, better than the mere credulity of the people, the grounds of their homage. The poem combines the gravity of an ancient ritual with the inanities of a modern victory parade. As the section ends, the reader is aware that the spectators have never grasped the irony of the dust and glitter. Their vision, like young Cyril's on Easter Day, stops at externals, although the main speaker has articulated, somewhat precociously indeed, their emotional reaction to Coriolan's presence. The sausage that someone, presumably young Cyril himself, is about to throw away seems to correspond vaguely to the crumpets. Miss Drew's observation that the line hints at "the ignoring of the food of the spirit in favour of that of the body" cannot be improved upon, yet something might be added about arcane and sacramental properties which the people ignore in this object as Cyril ignores them in the Eucharist. The hobble is that an ordinary sausage could not have any such properties except for Romans; it ought not to have, qua sausage, any ironic value in modern terms. A side remark, "He's artful," apparently referring to Cyril, provides an unconscious characterization of the general. Eliot's concluding lines from Maurras seem to indicate that like a symbolic veil the ranked soldiers, by whom the people are awed, have blocked off all sight of the reality behind appearance and have obscured the nature of a "light" which is in fact darkness.

As "Triumphal March" presents an outward view of Coriolan, so "Difficulties of a Statesman" lays open the hero's inward thoughts. In *The Waste Land* Coriolanus appears as a type of the Fisher King. In the present poem his "wound" is a Prufrockian inability to deal with the world or to gain an affirmative goal. He seeks, like Prufrock and the quester in the Grail legend, to be redeemed by going back to a condition promising emotional repose. Through a retreat to his mother's protection, he would find the spiritual stability that in "Triumphal March" the people erroneously attribute to himself. Such a value, implicitly religious, is embodied again by the dove and the tree of noon; they represent a center isolated from the hurly-burly of his responsibilities. A close parallel to *The Waste Land* exists in the implication, here supported by the historical Coriolanus' estrangement from his mother, that Coriolan has gone too far ever to "turn again." Unlike the sufferer in *Ash Wednesday*, who resists separation, Coriolan hears at length only the bidding "Resign," a negative command that in one sense means to accede to his spiritual exile. Coriolan is almost the opposite of Coriolanus: instead of a stern, obdurate figure of pride, hardly amenable to his mother's entreaty for Rome and fully alive to the fact that her counsel may be "most mortal for him," he is a distraught, overburdened child crying "Mother mother" from shock and despair. Comparison with the lines "O mother, mother! / What have you done?" in *Coriolanus* (Act V, scene 3) shows the reversal to be complete. The modern Coriolan makes no such boast as:

> If you have writ your annals true, 'tis there
> That, like an eagle in a dove-cote, I
> Flutter'd your Volscians in Corioli;
> Alone I did it.

Instead he turns in imagination from the eagles, himself being now wingless, to the breast of the saving dove.

The initial lines came from Isaiah, chapter 40: "The voice said, Cry. And he said, What shall I cry? All flesh is grass, and all the goodliness thereof is as the flower of the field . . . but the word of our God shall stand for ever." The chapter proclaims the immeasurable power and majesty of God, to whom "the nations are as a drop of a bucket, and are counted as the small dust of the balance" and the inhabitants of the earth as grasshoppers. The prophet has been enjoined to cry to Jerusalem "that her warfare is accomplished, that her iniquity is pardoned. . . ." "Difficulties of a Statesman" starts with an ironic delegation of this task to the false Messiah Coriolan, whose pitiful mission it is to "cry crumpets," as it were, to satisfy the material not the spiritual demands of his small chirping constituents. The holders of decorations and the members of orders—"O Cavaliers!" in Eliot's Whitmanesque phrase sharpened by mockery—are "grass," but they are plainly not the sort of people to whom it is easy to play God. Coriolan wrestles with the routine of bureaucracy, with trivialities made ludicrous by bloated official language. Poor Cyril must be made a telephone operator "with a bonus of thirty shillings at Christmas." The irony is exquisite. So is the ironically more terrible irony of the rival committees' and commissions' squabbling about the merits of peace and war.

> Meanwhile the guards shake dice on the marches
> And the frogs (O Mantuan) croak in the marshes.
> Fireflies flare against the faint sheet lightning
> What shall I cry?

This passage illustrates Eliot's inveterate habit of alluding to a poetic dilemma along with a spiritual one. Coriolan has unexpectedly become comparable to the poet Sordello in *Purgatorio*, VI. Appearing to Dante, like the hero to the people of "Triumphal March," "in the movement of [his] eyes superb and slow," Sordello greets his master Vergil with the words, "O Mantuan, I am Sordello of thine own land."[8] By recalling this meeting, Eliot has caused the theme of the poet in purgatory to cut across that of the statesman; the trials of contriving speech among frogs and "small creatures" harass also the poet who in *Ash Wednesday* could find a voice among bones "chirping / With the burden of the grasshopper." When Coriolan borrows the prophet's "What shall I cry?" he exemplifies the poet trying to make poetry. There is contrast between the worker with fragments and the worker with stately hexameters as there is between the political discord besetting Coriolan and the harmonious Augustan order acclaimed by Vergil. It balances an implicit distinction between "faint sheet lightning" and the true thunderbolts of Jove. And, if to say so is not too rude, so does the relationship of Eliot's line "And the frogs (O Mantuan) croak in the marshes" to Vergil's "Et veterem in limo ranae cecinere querelam."[9]

Coriolan's bondage to a patrimony of unwanted leadership, symbolized by "the row of family portraits," is expressed as a fusion of monotony ("Remarkably like each other") and boredom ("a sweaty torchbearer, yawning"). A suggestion of Eliot's cyclic symbolism occurs in the detail of almost duplicate busts "lit up successively by the flare," as in the motif of the "sacred fire" in "Heart of Darkness." The world of *The Waste Land* is spectrally evoked by this parallel to the fatherson identification, whereby all generations merge in oblivion. "Difficulties of a Statesman" also continues Eliot's practice of using feminine symbolism for salvation and for rebirth from the dreary cycle. Eliot's work allows little room for puritanic emphasis upon the masculine values in the quest for salvation, but *Coriolan*, as much as *The Waste Land*, enforces the conclusion that for human needs those values (e.g., Coriolan's military prestige as well as his inherited rank) are fatal and that only feminine values (symbolized by the dove's breast and the flowers and sheltering foliage) can provide sustenance. The dualism in "Difficulties of a Statesman" revives the old flesh-spirit tension. Coriolan spurns the Sweeney-like powers of his station because he craves something maternal. Like "enervate Origen," in a manner of speaking, he abdicates manliness; he longs for his childhood. Eliot seems to have deliberately created an Oedipal character. Even in *Ash Wednesday*, where the intention was probably otherwise, the same lines of reasoning may be followed. And the infant "Word" of *Ash Wednesday*, in search of whom the protagonist would shuffle off his fleshly desires, is in one aspect a self reborn from all anguish of the world. The affirmative symbol, theoretically compromising between flesh and spirit, would, in fact, erase the "Sweeney impulse." "Difficulties of a Statesman" translates the problem from sex to politics without revolutionizing the emotional pattern.

After the reference to cyclamen and clematis, which respectively carry traditional associations of voluptuousness and virginity and thus maintain the polarity common to Eliot's symbolism of refuge, Coriolan intensifies the appeal to his mother. Fatigued, on the one hand, by the burdens of office, almost with aversion from his ancestors' strong necks and "Noses strong to break the wind,"[10] and, on the other hand, by the steady importunity of the "small creatures" that cry thinly through the darkness, he repeats his question "What shall I cry?" The multitudes cry to him, yet his own message, as he seems dramatically to apprehend, must be as uninspired as theirs. The conclusion punctuates the theme of betrayal with their shrill and ambiguously ironic crescendo, "RESIGN RESIGN RESIGN," echoing inversely, and perhaps by accident, the three diminishing "heartbeats" at the end of Beethoven's Overture to *Coriolan*.

# IV  *PLAYS*
*1934–1953*

# *12* WORKS AND DAYS: "THE ROCK"

Eliot's experiment with drama in *Sweeney Ago-nistes* constituted a false start. Not until 1934 did another such effort come to light, and that was so unfortunate—through no great fault of Eliot's own—that scarcely anyone could have predicted for him a successful future in theatrical writing. *The Rock,* it is true, is a pageant rather than a play, and largely a prose pageant at that, so that within the terms of his arrangement with the producers he had little opportunity to improve his theory of "levels." He did what he could, however. As his Preface explains, his duty was simply to fit words to a scenario prepared by E. Martin Browne for the Forty-five Churches' Fund. What Eliot wrote was subjected to criticism by various kinds of expert people, with the natural result that a good deal of it is mediocre at best. Eliot cannot be censured for having missed an adequate conception of characters he did not invent; but he may barely be acquitted, on grounds of piety, of having abused his talent with such hackwork. It could appeal only to people in want of no convincing. The stilted Cockney scenes, particularly the first with its embarrassingly naïve use of a song from *Hamlet* and with its incredible debate in sociology, insult a mature audience; they strain patience even before the entrance of Mrs. Ethelbert. Their diction fails utterly to give the illusion of life, and the sentiments of the speakers, even when least priggish, would be intolerable in never-never land. Ethelbert the foreman, whose devotion to his work would have gratified Carlyle or William Morris, has the verisimilitude of a Galsworthy American. The middle-class characters, Mrs. Poultridge, Millicent, and the Major, say indeed what might be expected of them, but they hardly become more than stock types.

Although in the historical scenes Eliot was more fortunate because stiff bookish didacticism is normally expected of dead saints and

171

bishops, these passages also show lapses. Against the suitable treatment of Bishop Mellitus, Rahere, Nehemiah, Bishop Blomfield, and St. Peter and the Fisherman one must set with a black mark the Victorian melodramatics of the Crusaders' parting and the chilly verbiage exchanged by Wren, Evelyn, and Pepys. Not even the importation from E. C. Bentley's clerihew, about Wren's dining with some men, saves the latter conversation from stodgy tedium. Eliot manifested good taste, however, in inserting a Latin ritual for the taking of the Crusaders' cross and in borrowing from Latimer's *Sermon of the Plough* and *Second Sermon Preached before the Convocation of the Clergy,* and apparently from elsewhere, his examples of iconoclastic preaching, though Thomas Hobbes could have contributed matter more valuable.[1] The suggestion of plot, wherein Eliot correlated Ethelbert's views on religion with those of the Saxons and his difficulties in erecting the modern edifice with those of Rahere (whose introduction as a ghostly visitant was apparently prompted, as Robert Graves has pointed out, by the circumstances of Kipling's "A Truthful Song"),[2] might better have been emphasized by having all the historical scenes make a similar revelation to the Workmen. Perhaps the Agitator scene fails to connect with the tribulations of Nehemiah because Eliot had a keen sense of the difference between ancient Jerusalem and an English church. Also it might have been too shocking to have the Agitator and the Crowd actually wreak their vandalism upon Ethelbert's brick walls, after the fashion of the invading Danes; but the shift of attention away from Ethelbert harms any unity of perspective afforded by the previous correlation. One never learns, by the way, whether the Crowd really damage the church; when the theme reappears in the iconoclasm scene, it refers not to them but to the remarks of the revolting Millicent.

The verse of the pageant is of seven or eight different types. One of these occurs uniquely in the Kiplingesque comic song sung by Ethelbert; this has a Savoyard or music-hall flavor like other light verse by Eliot. Another occurs in the "Builders' Song" (presumably indebted to Blake),[3] which sporadically interpolates into the action a reminder of the central theme, the contemporary need for the building of churches. A third occurs in the prologues spoken, in the manner of Gower's prologues in *Pericles,* by the Chorus Leaders before certain of the scenes, including the ballet *divertissement* of Dick Whittington and his cat. A fourth occurs in the verse assigned to the Plutocrat, and a fifth and sixth in the contrasting chants of Redshirts and Blackshirts in the same dialogue. Analogous to these chants but reminiscent of "The Hollow Men" and the *Landscapes,* is another type occurring in the chants of the Workmen (who therein reverse the menace of Isa. 28:20) and of the Unemployed (who sorrowfully echo Matt. 20:7). Lastly there is the type occurring in the choruses proper (spoken unapocalyptically, though by seven men and ten women) personating "the voice of the Church of God"; to it belong also the lines of the Rock himself. The effect of such variety, interspersed with a like variety of dumb shows, with prose speeches, and with music, would be more pleasing if more systematic or, at least, coherent.

Where verse is present, as in the only scene without prose, that featuring the Chorus, the Plutocrat, and the totalitarians, Eliot's genius flourishes. In that scene he mixed several styles so as to sharpen the contrasts between rival opinions. His lines for the Redshirts parody the clumsy unmusical free verse which he detested; those for the Blackshirts have a heavy, regular, foot-stamping beat. In both places the verbal ironies are crude, even more so than in the speeches of the Plutocrat. It is clear that Eliot was trying to denigrate these villains of the scene by making them as silly and vulgar in their talk as they are unchristian in their views. If in each case he relied too much on the effects of emotional prejudice among his audience, in a pageant such as this it would not do to give either the Redshirts or the Blackshirts the disruptive benefits of intellectual debate. Being present only as symbols of what has already been repudiated, they are hollow men. The Chorus' Greek tragedy recognition of the Plutocrat prepares again for disapproval. He, though hollow likewise, has a chance to argue his side. He is suave instead of militant, but he is for this reason all the more vile, and he will not be taken seriously when he grumbles about the salaries of the clergy, tithes, the Ecclesiastical Commission, and the difficulties of divorce. When at length he offers the Golden Calf, whose "real name is POWER," and makes the most coy pun in the language by saying "you'll find it very neat," his role is converted into a burlesque of anti-ecclesiastical criticism. To enforce the moral, Eliot had the scene end in an undignified scramble for the Calf. From the dramatic point of view the whole episode is not so crude as most of *The Rock:* it is mainly comic and dispenses with the idea of rationally convincing anybody about anything. In this respect some of the other scenes, pretending to weigh opinions, seriously err. To the purpose of the episode the Plutocrat's verse is exactly adapted; it sustains just the amount of stately pomp, enhanced by a mechanical blank-verse measure, necessary to make the bland triteness of his remarks sound foolish. Yet, despite the comparative excellence of this scene, most of *The Rock* causes one to regret that a certain anthologist was not right when he amusingly stated as a fact that the play did not exist and that the choruses printed in *Collected Poems 1909–1935* were all that there was. Musically, whatever their dramatic deficiencies, these rank among Eliot's best poems.

Throughout the work, the Chorus, assuming a Greek role of commentary, employs supple diction with a broad range of tone. Its speeches convey pleading and reproach, sorrow, wrath, and joy, at tempos extending from the slow calm of its prologues, through the irony and grief of its reflective passages and the intensity of its exhortations, to the quick jubilation of its hymn of praise. D. W. Harding, in a review published in *Scrutiny* in 1934, noted that the Chorus "succeeds in upbraiding those whom it addresses while still remaining humble and *impersonally* superior to them."[4] But this humility of tone may have been wrongly calculated; if the Chorus were not so restrained, it would command more respect. In fact, it is most dignified when, as in the lines beginning "Thus your fathers" it abandons the subterfuge of impersonal criticism and attacks its hearers directly. Among the most satisfactory features of its language is the agreeable mixture of Prayer Book English and blunt, unhackneyed colloquialism by which it maintains a traditional authority while reaching, sometimes with a shift into irony, the contemporary ear through a contemporary idiom. Occasionally it simply meditates biblical themes, as when, after the completion of Ethelbert's church, it apostrophizes the tabernacles of the Lord in lines molded after Psalms 84 and 132; more often it descends almost to parody, as in the paraphrase of Nehemiah 4:17:

> Remembering the word of Nehemiah the Prophet:
> "The trowel in hand, and the gun rather loose
> in the holster."

By their imagery the choruses frequently recall Eliot's other poetry, with numerous echoes of *The Waste Land* in particular. The choric verse shows great metrical diversity. Perhaps the standard measure, or "ghost behind the arras," as Eliot would say, is iambic pentameter, but this gives way repeatedly in passages of excitement or incantation to a kind of poetic prose of highly irregular stress involving anapestic substitutions; once, in the final chorus, there are lines with a distinctly

Swinburnean ring. Although in general the rhythms are heavily indebted to the Bible and Prayer Book, they reflect also, like those of *The Waste Land,* the influence of Jacobean drama. The outstanding example of an apparently deliberate imitation of this manner comes near the close of the passage reprinted as Chorus III, where the strictures on human ambition resemble a speech of similar tone by Meleander in Ford's *The Lover's Melancholy* (Act II, scene 2). Yet the rhythm is more rapid and, just as one might expect here, less conversational than that of the model, if it was a model at all. The same passage even anticipates in several places the four-stress verse pattern of *The Family Reunion.*

It is in the final chorus that the verse attains its richest lyric splendor. The theme is light—the light of the Church as a city set on a hill, shining against the darkness where "The great snake lies ever half awake, at the bottom of the pit of the world, curled / In folds of himself until he awakens in hunger," and where power is given to "those who prize the serpent's golden eyes, / The worshippers, self-given sacrifice of the snake." In a canticle of praise, the opening line of which was adapted from Francis Thompson's "The Kingdom of God," the Chorus glorifies the "Light invisible" and then, enumerating a descending hierarchy of lesser lights, offers thanks for the light of morning, the light of evening, and

> The twilight over stagnant pools at batflight,
> Moon light and star light, owl and moth light,
> Glow-worm glowlight on a grassblade.

In the next strophe it turns to the lights of man's worship, on altar and in sanctuary, "Small lights of those who meditate at midnight," and to light transpiercing, reflecting, refracted. Finally, speaking with the voice of small creatures whose succession in the cycle of life is as a candle extinguished and relighted—whose individual lives are as the explosions of a rocket—it joins the theme of the temporal, by the candles set on the altar, to the theme of the eternal, the Invisible Light in whom darkness and light are the same.

In contrast with the Chorus, which represents the Church in fields of action, the Rock himself is the spokesman for the Church as the eternal witness, the sufferer and martyr. Though at the end he stands revealed as St. Peter, the allegory seems to forbid too literal an identification. That is, he embodies rather the type of sainthood than any particular saint. He first enters "led by a boy," like Samson and like Sophocles'

Tiresias, and speaks the command of the Church to its martyrs: *"Make perfect your will,"* an application of the axiom from Dante to man's duty of right action. The dramatic role of the Rock is to prop the Chorus in its faith by encouraging humility and by painting the present difficulties of the Church as an immemorial contest forever continuing. In one aspect he is the protagonist of the pageant, for, though he divides with the Chorus leader or *coryphaeus* the function of narrator, the narrative itself concerns a past and present which coexist in his knowledge; he "has seen what has happened," and he "sees what is to happen." And the experience of the Church is his own, for he is the Church. Thus one has no need of the incidental analogy with Samson to compare the Rock with Gerontion, Tiresias, and even the Sweeney of "Fragment of an Agon," all being sufferers rather than actors, but all re-enacting the eternal martyrdom of history in the theater of their own consciousness. There are superficial resemblances between the Rock and Tiresias; both, though the dramatic machinery is different, bear witness through memory, and both hang "between two lives" (the Rock says also, "I have known two worlds of death," evidently the past and the present),[5] which in the pageant resolve themselves into the life of time and the life of simultaneous consciousness or eternity. These are the two worlds that, as the Rock declares, cross "In every moment of time,"

> In every moment you live at a point of intersection,
> Remember, living in time, you must live also now in Eternity.

The concept of eternity explored by Eliot is one of simultaneity as opposed to succession; it is a timeless state not in contradistinction to temporal events but in the absence of change. Eternity, from the purely human point of view, means the simultaneity and, as it did to Spinoza, the actuality of all times, as God would observe them; it is duration, not in the sense of Bergson, to whom the actuality of the past endured only as memory, but in the sense of a coincidence of all the parts of time, including the future, which to Bergson did not exist. The present, the "point of intersection," is the moment of our perception, a moment we instantaneously lose, but which to God remains present under the definition of eternity. To human consciousness—that of Tiresias, for example—the duration of the past is limited by the experience of memory; to divine consciousness the function of memory is taken over by perception. God cannot strictly be said to remember anything. Tiresias' view in *The Waste Land* is not eternal; theoretically the

Rock's view is. Of course, there is little dramatic difference. The Rock does not disclose the future, wherein a difference would matter, and in dealing with the past, since the action is for people to watch, he must show it as ordinary sequence.

The notion of simultaneity finds its complement in the idea that the future somehow repeats the past. Although simultaneity and recurrence are distinct from each other, since the latter derives wholly from a conception of cycles, they merge through men's belief that experience of simultaneity, as in the afterlife, would amount to re-experience of past events. Another sort of simultaneity appears in J. W. Dunne's serial universe, where a sequence of future dimensions exists already. This involves recurrence psychologically, that is, as Dunne says, through precognitive dreaming and the phenomenon known as *déjà vu*.[6] Both this theory and Nietzsche's faith in actual recurrence are independent of the commonplace that "that which is done is that which shall be done: and there is no new thing under the sun." When in *The Rock* Eliot's brickmason Ethelbert speaks of "some new notion about time, what says that the past—what's be'ind you—is what's goin' to 'appen in the future, bein' as the future 'as already 'appened," he is probably referring to simultaneity and not to recurrence. His speculation goes along with the Rock's view of eternity "crossing the current of time"; for the temporal activity of building the material edifice— Ethelbert's job and the Church's care—constructs the visible Church in the eternal dimension. This motif, crucial to the pageant, is expressed in the dualism of Chorus and Rock, of present and past workmen, and in the symbols of change and eternity.

To reconcile, by contemplation, the flux with the eternal is the task of sainthood:

> ... to apprehend
> The point of intersection of the timeless
> With time,

as Eliot was to phrase it in "The Dry Salvages." Everyone, by the very nature of time, constantly touches eternity, but without *apprehending* it. To lay hold of the moment, to know it, would be to know God in it. One may clarify the symbolism by identifying "the point of intersection" with the divine point that moves the wheel, "the Word within / The world and for the world." Man's present moment, then, is analogous to the "still point" of the Incarnation uniting two worlds and turning the wheel of time, which man experiences as succession and remembers as duration. Thus the philosophic structure gets support from Eliot's earlier imagery. The familiar antithesis of the wheel and the point is implicit in the *parodos* at the beginning of *The Rock*. The wheel means the sequence of human invention, action, and language ("words"), and the sequence of the natural cycles typified by the constellations of the Eagle and Orion the Hunter (a figure connoting the vegetation myths of love and death). The point itself means stillness and unmoved mover, the Word. In Chorus VII the same pattern recurs for a contrast between man's uncertain temporal gropings and the certainty of the Incarnation, and between this and man's later turning away from God to follow his own devices. Eliot's symbol for the Incarnation becomes here "a moment in time and of time,"

> A moment not out of time, but in time, in what we call history:
> transecting, bisecting the world of time, a moment in time
> but not like a moment of time,
>
> A moment in time but time was made through that moment: for
> without the meaning there is no time, and that moment of
> time gave the meaning.

Finally in Chorus IX, after a luminous treatment of Aristotelian causation in art, Eliot extended the previous dichotomy of nature and God, time and eternity, to cover also his old preoccupation with flesh and spirit in humanity:

> For Man is joined spirit and body,
> And therefore must serve as spirit and body.
> Visible and invisible, two worlds meet in Man;
> Visible and invisible must meet in His Temple;
> You must not deny the body.

It is not one of the motives of *The Rock* to suggest to the audience a negative way of sanctity through contemplation or martyrdom. The effort of the saint to transcend time by union with God differs from this affirmative law of service to the Church, and to Christ through the Church, by labors of body and mind which sanctify time "under the aspect of eternity." *The Rock* contains, in other words, a philosophy of using time rather than of escaping from it, of focusing upon the life of the wheel as the means to attain the point rather than of neglecting the wheel—nature and time and man's active life—for the sake of a more immediate communion. Yet ultimately both ways are the same if every moment under the aspect of eternity is synchronous with the moment of the Incarnation, which has redeemed all the moments of time that meet and become eternal in it; the saint's absorption in the moment of Incarnation brings him no closer to God than does the worker's absorption in the moment of his toil. But it is doubtful whether these themes, as handled by Eliot, furnish anything to the average public listener's understanding. They are hard to trace and compare even on close reading. One suspects that much of the choric verse could convey little meaning when recited; it would merely punctuate the shifts of action. These facts are regrettable, for this verse admirably fulfils the ambition of Eliot not only to make poetry have an auditory force but to put it where it is ideally heard—in the theater. Obviously the choruses, referring in their themes to serious and potentially very dramatic situations, contain also a comedy of time and eternity that latently unifies an irregular, episodic train of incidents.

# 13 ACTION AND SUFFERING: "MURDER IN THE CATHEDRAL"

For the Canterbury Festival of June, 1935, Eliot wrote his first independent full-length drama, *Murder in the Cathedral*.[1] Though, unlike *The Rock*, this play was a product of his own architectonic, it was not originally an independent venture into the competitive world of the theater. Assured of an audience to whom for the occasion the subject would appeal, Eliot was again able to indulge his affection for religious symbolism without calculating, as was needful with his later plays, the odds against success if he did not compromise with the public caprice. He could remain a poet writing about life on his own terms without unduly fretting over the fact that these were not the terms of most other people. *Murder in the Cathedral*, in other words, is just as much coterie literature as Eliot's earlier poetry. It has had a good deal of vogue among audiences picked for their religious sympathies, and, surprisingly, it even held the boards for some time before the curious at the Mercury Theatre in London and, subsequently, at the Old Vic. Its interest has been considerable also among university undergraduates in the United States, where it has several times been revived by subsidized amateurs. But when finally made into a film, which was given a *première* at Venice in 1951 and in London and New York in 1952, it failed to catch popular fancy. This fact contributes to the estimate that the play is hard for the public to understand.

There are six published versions of *Murder in the Cathedral*: the abbreviated and complete versions of 1935; three revisions, appearing in 1936, 1937, and 1938; and the film edition of 1952. The second edition (1936), which is the latest stage text to have been issued in the United States, and the film edition are adequate for most critical purposes. The other versions omit some speeches; they reassign a good many which had overburdened the Fourth Knight, whose part Eliot wanted doubled with one of the Tempters'; and they simplify and otherwise improve the Knights' prose apologies and the Archbishop's sermon. Only the film version contains important new material; this is detailed and explained, in the 1952 edition, by George Hoellering, producer of the picture and collaborator with Eliot in the screen adaptation. Besides the original introits (near the beginning of Part II), supplanted by a chorus in the 1936 edition, the film includes a preliminary speech by Becket to the ecclesiastics of Canterbury; a new chorus; a prose trial scene, showing Becket confronting King Henry, and an address by the Prior to the people in the cathedral. And, at the end, instead of the verbose declarations by the four Knights, it has three briefer statements, the last emphatically communicating what Hoellering oddly alludes to as "the main point of the whole play"—that the Knights rather than Becket best represent the views of an audience content that "the pretensions of the Church" should be subordinate to "the welfare of the State."[2] (Significant as this announcement is, it seems less important than the example set by Becket in making his will compliant with God's.) Although the film production, partly because of the professional portrayal of Becket by Father John Groser and partly because of Eliot's reading of the invisible Fourth Tempter's lines, is, despite its inherent deficiencies of action, vastly superior to any conceivable stage presentation, still the text itself by its innovations and by its exclusion of the final speeches of the Priests is less satisfactory as a unified and completed drama. The following account is, therefore, based chiefly upon the widely circulated second American edition.

Some of the cosmopolitan sophisticates at the Venice film *première* are said to have been disappointed when *Murder in the Cathedral* belied their expectation of a detective thriller. Their error was not much worse than one might have foreseen from the inappropriateness of the title which Mrs. E. Martin Browne originally suggested and Eliot adopted. The play, though certainly taking its theme from the murder of St. Thomas à Becket in 1170, is not about "murder in the cathedral" but about the spiritual state of a martyr facing death, the spiritual education of the poor women who are witnesses to his sacrifice, and the wilful opposition of secular to eternal power. If Eliot had called it, as he is reported to have meditated doing, *The Archbishop Murder Case*, the reference, though equally misleading, would have been less indefinite. (He seems to have had some difficulty with his choice, which superseded, according to Ashley Dukes, the tentative title *Fear[s]* in *the Way*,[3] a quotation from Ecclesiastes appearing also on one typescript draft of *The Family Reunion;* this has little to do, that one can see, with either play.) It is true that the historical personality of Becket gave the foundation to the plot. Eliot took a good deal of care to make the historical actions accord with the most trustworthy accounts by Becket's contemporaries, but, since the play concerns rather what happens through the man than what happens to him, such details are largely incidental—as is all the action properly so called—to verbal expressions of various attitudes. That is, Part I, establishing the context of the spiritual struggle by means of Becket's exchanges with characters who are projections of it—the Women of Canterbury, the Priests, and the Tempters—virtually lacks historical authenticity and in all but a few respects is simply a prologue to the historical action of Part II; yet it sets forth the whole of the psychological choice that the action is only to ratify. It presents the motif of suffering, through Becket's decision not to act; Part II presents the motif of action, through Becket's suffering the acts of others. The categories of action and suffering constitute the internal rationale of the drama.

The few historical facts which Part I incorporates are ordinary. The most interesting of these are Becket's secret longing for martyrdom and his political background, symbolized most effectively by the chess game accompanying, in the film, his dialogue with the First Tempter. In contrast, Part II reflects some precise study of the events immediately preceding the murder, as is evident from comparison of the play with the eyewitness narratives of Grim and others in E. A. Abbott's *St. Thomas of Canterbury*.[4] The scene in the cathedral is especially derivative. Historically Becket refused to have the door barred, exclaiming, as an anonymous chronicler reported, "Absit ut ecclesiam Dei castellum faciamus." In the play the terror of his adherents, who see the Knights as little better than "maddened beasts," recalls his exclamation, according to another report, against the "canes interfectores," or, it may have been, "carnis interfectores." When Eliot's Knights enter brandishing their swords and bawling, "Come down Daniel to the lions' den," in the manner of Lindsay's "Daniel Jazz," they make a jocular acknowledgment of the martyr's triumph, even while degrading themselves to beasts. Becket's retort in the play, "It is the just man who / Like a bold lion, should be without fear," translates the Archbishop's actual words, a quotation from Proverbs, chapter 28, in the Vulgate. If one ignores certain liberties taken with the sequence of events, it was

only in Becket's dying prayer that Eliot enlarged conspicuously upon
the early chroniclers. What Becket apparently said was that he com-
mended his soul and his cause to God and St. Mary, to the martyrs
St. Denis and St. Elphege, and to the patron saints of [that] church—
the last, of course, including St. Elphege. Eliot followed the priest
Grim in omitting Elphege from the prayer and including him in
Becket's sermon and concurred with still other authorities, possibly
the wrong ones, in understanding by the saints all the saints of the
Church; but he added gratuitously the names of John the Baptist and
the apostles Peter and Paul. The two last were the patrons of the
ancient abbey founded by St. Augustine of Canterbury.

Tennyson in *Becket* adopted the legend of a violent storm after the
murder; Eliot gave the storm symbolic treatment through the Chorus'
frantic cry beginning "Clean the air" and containing the words "A
rain of blood has blinded my eyes." Along with the symbol of rain he
introduced the image of bleeding boughs, taken from classical epic or
from II Esdras 5:3: "And blood shall drop out of wood, and the stone
shall give his voice, and the people shall be troubled." Afterward, in
the last speech of the Third Priest, he availed himself of the tradition
about the murderers' ultimate doom to exile, shipwreck, and death
among the infidels. (That same speech owes a great deal to purely
verbal sources. Opening with testimony to the enduring power of the
Church, it continues, ironically paralleling Heywood's *Hercules Furens*
["Goe hurtles soules, whom mischiefe hath opprest"],[5] with a condemnation of the Knights that has sometimes been compared with the
anathema in Baudelaire's "Femmes damnées: Delphine et Hippolyte,"[6]
though perhaps indebted rhetorically to the "axletree" passage in
Chapman's *Bussy D'Ambois*. In its second half the speech unexpectedly echoes the *Iphigenia in Tauris* as translated by Gilbert Murray.)[7]

*Murder in the Cathedral* surprises by two strong dissimilarities to
George Darley's and Tennyson's verse plays on Becket—by the quality
of its diction and by Eliot's novel and peculiarly unhistorical treatment of the protagonist's character. Instead of assuming the common
judgment of Becket as overweeningly arrogant, waging a battle of personal and ecclesiastical spleen with a foe hardly more impoverished in
spiritual attributes, Eliot depicts him as humbly submissive, accepting
death, not resisting it. Darley in his *Thomas à Becket* creates a proud
statesman, deceitful and greedy for dominion, a Machiavel who aspires
to rival the king and who, repeatedly occupied in blasting the ears of

his enemies, dies with a curse against his murderer: "Execrabilis esto!" Tennyson shows the prelate eschewing self-aggrandizement and exalting the Church, yet, for all his nobility, dying only as a statesman in a contest for power. Accordingly both emphasize the robust aspect of Becket: Tennyson in *Becket* shows him defending himself; Darley has him putting up a stout fight, after abusing Traci as a "vile reptile." Of course, Darley's play is egregiously silly, but Tennyson's, more scrupulously than *Murder in the Cathedral,* conforms to the estimate put by secular history upon Becket's quarrel with Henry II. The difference in Eliot arises from the abstraction of a two-sided conflict between princes of the Church and the State into a one-sided assault by pride upon sanctity. There is no doubt that Tennyson's hero has few marks of saintliness apart from fidelity to the rights of the Church; Eliot's, after quelling his confusion of will, is devoted less to the Church than to God— were divided allegiance possible. Eliot would have got into grave difficulties if he had made Becket rougher. Since in *Murder in the Cathedral* Becket speaks to the Knights sternly, without discourtesy or scuffling, he retains dignity and escapes arrogance. In the long view it is impossible to say that Eliot was wrong in his distortion, which may have created a Becket more like the "real" one than his apparent conduct ever revealed, a hero more deserving of sympathy than even the protagonist of Aubrey de Vere's urbane dramatic poem *St. Thomas of Canterbury.*

Because the Archbishop triumphs morally over both the Tempters and the Knights, it may be preferable not to call Eliot's play a tragedy. It is true that a morally victorious catastrophe occurs in Milton's tragedy of Samson. *Murder in the Cathedral* presents, moreover, certain parallels (as Louis L. Martz also has noticed) with Sophocles' *Oedipus at Colonus,* the finest classic tragedy of reconciliation through death. But in both this and *Samson Agonistes* the problem of evil is not only universal but individual, through the particular flaw generating ruin. Granted that remission of guilt, as well as retribution, comes within the scope of tragedy, one would still be nearly right in designating *Murder in the Cathedral* a comedy. For the death of Becket, though it results obviously from human sin, does not result from the only flaw the play ascribes to him—his pride as a prospective martyr. This he surmounts in time to reconsider; then he consents to martyrdom again in order to obey what he sees as God's will. The best analogue to Eliot's plot is the "moral-quest" theme of the moral interludes or the tribulation theme of the Book of Job. Indeed, Eliot could have borrowed his four Tempters from Job as easily as from late fifteenth-century drama. However, Becket's suffering comes after the temptation, and it really constitutes also the reconciliation.

*Murder in the Cathedral* is a drama of such symbolic relationships that the ingredients of tragedy are all present, but apportioned—in fact, allegorically—among the different characters rather than confined to Becket himself. There is a moral flaw, original and particular sin; there is (in the external view) a catastrophe, affecting the victim destined to expiation; there is justification. The first is manifested in the suggestions of the Tempters, the will and act of the Knights, and the suffering of the Chorus; the second, the martyrdom, is executed upon the sufferer, Becket; the third is fulfilled in the damnation of the Knights, the potential salvation of the Chorus, and the exaltation of the saint. The late Theodore Spencer aptly pointed out that the characters live on different levels of moral refinement: that is, Becket, the Priests, the Chorus of Women of Canterbury, and the murderers have, on a descending scale, distinct ideas of reality, ranging from the acute spirituality of Becket to the depraved worldliness of the Knights.[8] The cumulation of these, with a distributive allotment of dramatic functions, makes up the total movement sometimes called "tragic." But as in an obsolete pictorial convention, rejuvenated by the cubists, of depicting successive temporal states on the same spatial canvas (Duchamp's "Nude Descending a Staircase"), the different functions here coexist: the Knights are sin, the Chorus is suffering, Becket is martyrdom. This is "tragedy" *sub specie aeternitatis,* as it may appear to God. Francis Fergusson, remarking this quality in the play, compares the levels to the discontinuous "orders" of Pascal, discussed by Eliot in his Introduction to the *Pensées.*[9] But they are more than these. And the levels create something as distinguishable from Sophoclean tragedy as is a Greek frieze from the procession or battle it represents. In its "spatial" treatment of character *Murder in the Cathedral* is as static as a Grecian urn: it belongs almost to a genre which is pre-tragic, the ritual drama of sin and redemption, where all the components of strain and antithesis are externalized, discrete. The internal conflicts of Becket and the Chorus are, as it were, microcosmical.

The plot of *Murder in the Cathedral* has, therefore, two aspects: one in which the characters are static types and another in which they are persons capable of development. At the end of Part I, after dismissing the perfunctory temptations of worldly pleasure, subservience to the king, and alliance with the barons, Becket rejects the lure of conscious glory in martyrdom. In the first aspect this act is only an intensification, a validation of his status as an appointed martyr. The audience, though aware of his pride, knows nothing of his temptation until it is presented, and by then he is ready to spurn it. In the second aspect his moral struggle teaches him the meaning of martyrdom as the perfection of will. In like manner the Chorus is to learn the meaning of suffering. Becket's initial desire is imperfect: from this he rises to a greater good. In discovering that his grandiose will to be martyred is sinful, he allows the wheel of fortune to bear him materially down and morally up. (The parallel with *King Lear* in some ways is informative; the important structural difference lies in Eliot's having adopted the "imminent-horror" type of discovery praised by Aristotle with reference to the *Iphigenia in Tauris*.) Without the discovery it would not be easy for the audience to look upon the Archbishop as a human being at all, much less to see him as a real historical figure. Part I is necessary because unless Becket vanquished the Tempters it would be inexplicable that by his death he could vanquish the Knights. His inward conflict in Part I presages the outward conflict of Part II, where for him and the Knights the tension exploits physical power, not psychology, and where only for the Chorus does it still animate a spiritual combat. This tension, as the Women experience it, corresponds to the Christian drama of fall and regeneration; Atonement is symbolized by Becket. As martyr in Part II, Becket is a type of Christ, who also suffered temptation before entering upon the drama of action through suffering; as Becket's human temptations to sin, the Tempters are the whispering Adversary; as sinners and sufferers, the Women of Canterbury are types of fallen Adam, enacting the inward strife in imitation of Becket, who enacts it in imitation of Christ; and as persecutors, the Knights are Satan going to and fro in the earth and walking up and down in it. Becket, like Christ, is tested, slain, and exalted, not for his sin but for other men's. It goes without saying that Becket's early biographers did not neglect the comparison, by no means unusual in saints' lives, between this martyr and the Savior. But, of course, Becket does not really atone for others' sin, even though his death serves as a memorial example whereby the Women of Canterbury come to accept their lot. Despite the theme of the ritual scapegoat, to read literal Atonement into the events of the play would be to lift it wholly to the allegorical level.[10]

The ritual motif, aligning *Murder in the Cathedral* with *The Rock* through verbal effects reminiscent of liturgy and with *The Waste Land* through the theme of death and rebirth, endows this play with a kind of secondary pattern like that mentioned by Eliot in his essay on Marston. But, besides being deliberately allegorical, the pattern also functions through the transcendent character of Becket, who seems to achieve awareness beyond earthly experience. In his order of reality he faces something which neither the other characters nor the audience understands. Unlike Sweeney in *Sweeney Agonistes* he is not merely saying ambiguous words: he is reacting to a vision. His certainty of election to martyrdom depends on no omen comprehensible to his followers but on an interior refinement worthy to be called communion. His language when he talks of action and suffering, of the still wheel which turns, is that of one whose very sensibility gains mysterious access. This may all be dramatic illusion, arising in some measure from cryptic phrasing; but it is successful. To be sure, one might complain that Becket is a little too remote even in his most commonplace lines. Eliot bars the audience from Becket's innermost self.

In *The Rock*, there is more than a suggestion that the Rock because he is the Church in its eternal aspect represents the "still point" of communion with God and that the Chorus is the "wheel" of human active life in the world. So in *Murder in the Cathedral* Becket and the Women of Canterbury (like Tiresias and the forms populating his memory) typify the dualism of eternity and time, duration and flux, spirit and flesh, action by suffering and suffering by action. Here Eliot has uncovered a paradox: the sufferer suffers only because of the actions of himself or others. The Fourth Tempter says to Becket what Becket has already said about the Chorus:

> You know and do not know, what it is to act or suffer.
> You know and do not know, that acting is suffering,
> And suffering action. Neither does the agent suffer
> Nor the patient act. But both are fixed
> In an eternal action, an eternal patience
> To which all must consent that it may be willed
> And which all must suffer that they may will it,
> That the pattern may subsist, that the wheel may turn and still
> Be forever still.

What preserves this from utter self-contradiction is the statement "Neither does the agent suffer / Nor the patient act"; for, though by a shift of time the human agent may become the human sufferer, each role is distinct. One meaning of the passage is that every cause predicates an effect, and every effect a cause; they cannot occur independently. When Becket speaks to the Chorus he thinks of himself as the actor, the source of will, and of the Women as passive recipients of sorrows and benefits resulting from his choice of martyrdom. But when the Fourth Tempter (almost his *Doppelgänger*) flings the same words back in his teeth, Becket seems to realize that unless the sufferer refrains from willing to suffer and thus from soiling his hands with his own blood, he cannot be a true martyr. After almost blundering, Becket recognizes that not only the Women but he himself must be passive. He must only consent to the divine will, so that he shall suffer and shall become for suffering in others the involuntary agent. Both action and suffering come from God as the unsuffering "first agent" or first cause of action. Aristotle, in speaking of the nature of movement (analogous to action), compares the good, toward which desire moves, and by which it is moved, to the unmoved center which in a wheel imparts motion to the rim: "For everything is moved by pushing and pulling. Hence just as in the case of a wheel, so here there must be a point which remains at rest, and from that point the movement must originate."[11] Thus in the *De Anima*; and in the treatise *De Generatione et Corruptione* he uses another image to describe action and passion (i.e., passivity) which Eliot in part duplicated—the image of the physician, the curative diet, and the patient. A "first agent" (the physician) acts, without being acted upon, through a "last agent" (food), which, being acted upon, in turn acts upon a passive object (the patient).[12] So God as "first agent" acts through prevenient grace upon Becket; and Becket, as patient, consents. In like manner, because in this synergy his consent involves will, he also acts, but only as a "last agent," to afflict the Women of Canterbury with further suffering, which, when they consent to it, becomes an agency in their salvation. The consenting agent as such does not suffer, and the patient as such does not act: the former because he consents and is an instrument, and the latter (the Chorus) because it permits or "suffers" the benefits of the cure.

Obviously between God and Becket there is another "final agent," the Knights. Eliot does not, in this part of the play, expatiate on their function. It is related by inference, however, to the paradox of action and suffering. They, by malice, are to will what, despite them, is to bring about justice. Eliot owed to Spinoza, perhaps, the seeds of his concern with the aspect of eternity which makes "All partial Evil, universal Good." He abandoned Spinoza, it is true, over the very issue that would confirm the influence, for he has had no commerce with Spinoza's monistic denial of evil or with Leibniz' "best of all possible worlds." By the time he was ready to use the idea of universal reparation, he was under the sway of St. Augustine and the mystics, whose acknowledgment that "all things," as St. Paul understood, "work together for good to them that love God" does not exculpate sin, even though that, too, produces good.[13] This paradox of good through sin is subjacent to the Knights' defiance of God. When Becket first supposes that he has the right to precipitate his suffering he is aware that "the wheel may turn and still / Be forever still"; by a deeper intuition he knows that the still wheel, as God beholds it, incorporates all the pattern of interlocking good and evil which men can only view as flux. Confident that his cause is right, Becket proposes to act so as to vindicate the Church by bringing good from the evil will of his foes. There is no deflecting him from this purpose by temptations which involve compromise. But what he has forgotten is what he himself is easily able to object against a lesser temptation, that only the fool "may think / He can turn the wheel on which he turns." By making his own will the mover of action and suffering in himself, the Knights, and the Chorus, he would be attempting precisely this—and failing. For on the turning wheel, good as often produces evil as evil produces good; only with God are these resolved, without losing their peculiar character, into the perfection that man aspires to. Only God's will can be the criterion of right or wrong action and suffering. In supplanting God's will with his own, in electing to be the center of the wheel without God, Becket would be inviting, on his own responsibility, whatever evils might ensue from his choice: he would be committing the Knights' sins of pride and murder.

Aghast, he exclaims: "Can I neither act nor suffer / Without perdition?" While the Chorus, the Tempters, and the Priests counsel him to avert action, he comes to his awakening.[14] The only way in which he can reach the stillness of the turning wheel is to yield to the mover, the point that is not himself. Those who act, all but God, and those who suffer are inescapably on the wheel; those who consent with the will of God are as God. Confessing that he has been about to "do the right deed for the wrong reason," to give a sinful turn to the wheel, he explains that this temptation sprang from his will for good. "Sin grows with doing good," he says, like Milton in *Areopagitica* ("Good and evil we know in the field of this world grow up together almost inseparably"). Only by extinction of self-will can he avoid the mortal sin of pride at his moment of sacrifice. Accordingly he is content that he "shall no longer act or suffer, to the sword's end," for God, not he, is the only agent through whom good can proceed from evil, and what God wills brings neither pain nor suffering to one who accedes to it as to a vocation. The martyr, freeing himself from the wheel, can assist the ultimate redemption of time. Henceforth he will not act, for God will act through him; he will not suffer, for God will empower him to consent. He has made a "decision," he says later, "To which my whole being gives entire consent," a decision taken "out of time." In his Christmas sermon he is able to affirm to his people: "A martyrdom is never the design of man; for the true martyr is he who has become the instrument of God, who has lost his will in the will of God, not lost it but found it, for he has found freedom in submission to God." His is the Dantean faith: "La sua volontate è nostra pace."

"Burnt Norton," published in 1936, confirms the impression that Eliot was particularly interested in Aristotelian philosophy at about the time he was writing *Murder in the Cathedral*. Although it is possible that some of this came to him through St. Thomas Aquinas, the direct influence of Aristotle is traceable to Eliot's early studies in both Aristotle and Leibniz. To the same early period one may ascribe the formulation of the "body-soul theme" which the youthful poems had only foreshadowed. Aristotle's hylomorphism may have been much in Eliot's awareness at that time.

The Chorus in *Murder in the Cathedral*, though ostensibly active in the toils of life, can only be passive under the oppression of the State and the agony of personal sorrow.

> For us, the poor, there is no action,
> But only to wait and to witness.

But by consenting, as Becket himself consents, the women look ahead to an end of action and suffering. They occupy a circumference, so to speak, of which Becket is the center, for they rely on him as the source of the movement they participate in. When he is the point, they are the wheel, as he is the wheel when God is the point. It is their dramatic function to comment upon the events they witness. They fit the role of sufferers by being ordinary hard-working women with no pretense to power. They are like the crowds of people in *The Waste Land,* passively moved by what a Buddhist would call "Samsara," the wheel of life. Their direct antithesis, of course, is the quartet of Knights. Both the Knights and the Chorus, as human beings, are capable of action and suffering and both, in some senses of the words, exist by both conditions; but Eliot confined them to separate functions in their relation to Becket: he contrasted action with suffering—the masculine with the feminine, the violator with the violated, the beast with the prey. It is ironic that, being also upon the wheel, the Knights, too, should revolve round the Archbishop. Once Becket's will unites with God's, once he "conquers the beast" by submission, their sinful action, always contributory to the plan of God, proceeds from a mover who is the man Becket.

Through most of the drama the polarity of action and suffering finds correspondence in the imagery appertaining to the Knights and the Chorus. The principal examples are in the choruses themselves and in the speeches of the protagonist. Perhaps the most prominent imagery is zoölogical; it has two purposes, to characterize the murderers, in which application it joins with the imagery of sensation, and to associate the passive Chorus with unredeemed, elemental nature. But not less important is the imagery of nature in wider aspects—the cycles of day and night, summer and winter, spring and autumn; these identify the Chorus with the great turning wheel of creation and corruption, growth and ruin. Thus, too, as one might expect from Eliot's usual devices, there is an undercurrent of sexual imagery, so hidden as almost to elude remark, but springing up at times in the choruses. In this the antithesis between violence and passivity becomes one between male and female. The Women see the intrusion of Becket's struggle as a disturbance, a strain. They want to be let alone. They speak of "births, deaths and marriages," of girls who "have disappeared / Unaccountably, and some not able to," of "private terrors" and "secret fears." Gradually, as Becket's destiny—their doom, as they regard it—becomes perspicuous, the terrors increase until in the last chorus of Part I they have heightened their imagery to the point of speaking of "oppression and torture," "extortion and violence," "Our labour taken away from us, / Our sins made heavier upon us," "the young man mutilated, / The torn girl trembling by the mill-stream." And at this juncture they begin to name the beasts—leopard, bear, ape, hyena—the "Lords of Hell."

As the play lengthens toward its denouement (after the opening chorus of Part II, where the Women balance against the retrospective autumnal imagery of the start of the play an imagery that looks to the coming spring, still buried in winter) they reach the extremity of having to accept an overt embrace of the bestial. In the extraordinarily moving passage just after Becket's first wrangle with the Knights, they acknowledge that death has violated them through every sense—smell, hearing, taste, touch, and sight—whereby they have known, almost in the intimacy of beast with beast, the creatures of the earth and sea. This sensation, this identification, finds unequivocally sexual language when the Women succumb to "the shamed swoon / Of those consenting to the last humiliation," subdued, violated, mastered, "Dominated by the lust of self-demolition . . . / By the final ecstasy of waste and shame." The echo of Shakespeare's "waste of shame" is not needed for its sexual reference. The Chorus, when it resumes, faces the dread of being "foully united forever, nothing with nothing," of being no longer human, of being cast out into the Void behind the Judgment. Eliot objectified thus, in the most galvanic verse he has published, the nature of human consent to the will of God. Between Becket's submission to the acts of his murderers and the anguish of the Women's resignation to the divine will, of which the Knights are sinful instruments, this astounding imagery stands as a precise symbol of both. The passion of the Women comes later in Part I than the consent already ordaining Becket's tribulation; here in Part II, however, their spasm of suffering leaves him behind, and they have died in will before his blood spouts under the sword.

As the murderers hack at Becket's skull, the Women chant a tormented prayer for cleansing, for purification from defilement. Recalling that they "did not wish anything to happen," they utter a cry of dread at the unimaginable "instant eternity of evil and wrong" by which they are soiled, "united to supernatural vermin,"

> It is not we alone, it is not the house, it is not the city that
>     is defiled,
> But the world that is wholly foul.

Nature itself, as at the moment of Adam's fall in paradise, becomes contaminated by the Knights' re-enactment of primal sin. The world is in the spiritual Dark Night of despair. But to the Women Becket has spoken earlier of the reconciling joy that shall replace their pain:

> Peace, and be at peace with your thoughts and visions.
> These things had to come to you and you to accept them.
> This is your share of the eternal burden,
> The perpetual glory. This is one moment,
> But know that another
> Shall pierce you with a sudden painful joy
> When the figure of God's purpose is made complete.

The birth of peace is to follow the ravishment of will; a sword has pierced their hearts only that death may give life, as Becket knows it must. It is in obedience to his own words that the doors have been opened to the irruption of merciless force.

With the prospect of assured beatitude, recompense, redemption of time, the Women raise their voices once more at the end of the play in a "Te Deum" beyond resignation. They have learned that all things, and even their loss, are for the divine glory and that even in denial there is affirmation. Yet not only in "both the hunters and the hunted" is the glory manifested, but in both resides the guilt of primal sin: in those who act and in those who suffer. The song of praise, therefore, which has acclaimed the goodness of creatures that a little earlier would have symbolized bestiality, ends with a supplication for personal forgiveness. The Women assume the burden disclaimed by the Knights. This paradox—that the Knights should have affirmed by denying and that the Chorus should have denied by affirming—is but contributory to the more central paradox of the wheel turning and still. Now at the price of humility all is appeased and adjusted.

This terminal chorus is conspicuously indebted to Anglican ritual, including perhaps the English "Gloria in excelsis" and the "Benedicite, omnia opera." More than some previous choric passages it recalls *The Rock*. Since Eliot's verse in *Murder in the Cathedral* is not so miscellaneous as in *The Rock*, the feeling of structural orderliness is greater for the play. Much of the poetry spoken by the Chorus has a comparatively quick rhythm, despite the inevitable blurring of syllables which group recitation would cause; in actual staging, however, the lines are allotted to antiphonal voices. Because here the Chorus is not only an observer but a participant, at least in the moral progression of the work, its verse is often little different from that assigned to Becket. In the lecture "Poetry and Drama" (1950) Eliot explained that in his search for a "*neutral*" style, neither too modern nor in the wrong way archaic, he had "kept in mind the versification of *Everyman*, hoping that anything unusual in the sound of it would be on the whole, advantageous."[15] The influence of *Everyman* is more obvious in the verse than in the plot, although an image reported by the Chorus, "Death, God's silent servant," is suggestive of God's "mighty messenger." Eliot's principal debt appears in the rhyming passages of the Tempters' dialogues with Becket, where the sharp, irregularly assorted stresses, four to the line, mimic skilfully the meter of the old play. Going further, Eliot sometimes introduced alliteration. The four-beat measure, one of Eliot's favorites in the other plays and in the *Quartets* as well, he had already used in *Sweeney Agonistes*. After *Murder in the Cathedral* he cultivated simplification, retaining few of the mechanical barriers that here somewhat insulate the dialogue from ordinary speech. For choric purposes, his verse tends to be more dactylic in the plays than elsewhere. Obviously it is allied to Old and Middle English alliterative verse. Once in a while it gives way to a longer or shorter line. One of the most intelligible choric sections, to an audience straining its ears in the far gallery, is that in three-beat verses beginning "We do not wish anything to happen." Elsewhere Eliot got his measure by simple plagiarism: the stychomythic exchange between Becket and the Second Tempter came in part from Sir A. Conan Doyle's tale of Sherlock Holmes "The Musgrave Ritual."[16]

Over against the preponderantly metrical language of the play stand the sermon, preached on the historical Becket's text, and the prose speeches of the Knights, who, after the murder, step forth to harangue the audience. Ever cautious, Eliot admits only that in these speeches he *may* have been slightly influenced by Shaw's *Saint Joan;* it is hard to see how there could be any doubt. The purpose of the speeches is dramatically clear only in the film version. As Hoellering says in his Preface, in their earlier form they rather amuse the audience than shock it. The Fourth Knight's plea for "a verdict of Suicide while of Unsound Mind" causes all but the most attentive to forget that his predecessor has incriminated the audience itself by pointing out that modern society does not want the Church to be meddlesome and by showing how he and his confreres have made the audience' kind of world possible. Those who are not misled by the Fourth Knight into dismissing the quartet as mere zanies at this point will detect the acute sarcasm of the First Knight's concluding admonition "not to loiter in groups at street corners [or] provoke any public outbreak." The film version, hitting hard with the incrimination passage, is less subtle and, perhaps, too simple; but if this is a play to be watched and heard, not just read, the easier post-climax is preferable.

In any case, there is some danger lest this message should nullify the laboriously wrought thesis that the contest has been waged between brute power and resigned holiness, and suggest instead that, as in Tennyson, it has been fought merely between the State and the Church. Becket is superior to the latter sort of quarrel, which would suit the mentality of the Second Priest, who seems close in spirit to the Knights, just as the First Priest resembles the Women and the third Becket himself. The Second Priest typifies the potential moral strength of the Knights' immoral practicality. He is not bad; he is only unsaintly. If the conflict were up to him, he would use force when he did not need to lie low, and lie low when he could not use force. Although the Third Priest grasps the final meaning, he, in turn, does so as a spectator rather than as a participant like the Women. In the last analysis the struggle vindicates the Church, not as the priesthood represents it, but as the laity, the Women of Canterbury, reconstitute its purpose after Becket through humility has shown them the way. Through Becket the Church becomes the Women and ceases to be merely the Priests. Thus the Knights' addresses to the audience ought to make an appeal not just to those on the side of the self-willed State but also to those overprizing the temporal authority of the Church. By martyrdom Becket has shown that the power of the Church as well as that of the laity must, in the mystical sense, be negative. And the Women in their meager lives of action will compose a Church dedicated to humility. What *The Rock* communicates vaguely is here an illumination: that the suffering of the Witness and the action of the witnesses are one and the same thing.

## 14 BRIGHT ANGELS: "THE FAMILY REUNION"

Eliot's melodramatic tragicomedy *The Family Reunion* opened in London at the Westminster Theatre in March, 1939.[1] This play, although it contains some charming poetry, was not a success. It was, however, important to Eliot's development. The closing lines of *The Waste Land*, discovering a middle choice between despair and hope, find the only means of survival to be patience. The loveless desert, they proclaim, holds the fountain of a new life. If the poems of the 1920's are less sure of this premise, they yet conclude that the old life of desire and sensation, being irrecoverable, must be allowed to die, even if there remains a distant possibility, as in *Ash Wednesday*, of reunion with love. Now patience is suffering, which means the renunciation of action, though often, as in *Sweeney Agonistes*, it means the necessary consequence of action. But the inference from *The Waste Land* that suffering means purgation, and that this demands endurance of hell, anticipates the defiant announcement in *Murder in the Cathedral* that suffering and action are not different after all. To suffer or endure is to live; to live is inevitably to act. All who act rightly, moreover, are martyrs, witnesses; for right action requires humility, the refinement of will under oppression. This, in more covert form, is the theme also of *The Family Reunion*.

The textual problems littering the critic's path in *Murder in the Cathedral* are happily absent here. There is but one published version. The four typescript drafts preserved at Harvard it is not practicable to analyze; nor will it be until, at some unforeseeable date, they are printed. Yet they are valuable in occasionally illuminating Eliot's intention where the public text is merely allusive. They sometimes show what Eliot started to mean and kept in some rudimentary form in the finished work. Of these, the earliest, Typescript A, contains only Part

196

I; Typescripts B and C, however, cover the whole play, as does the unlabeled but obviously late draft belonging to Emily Hale.

The Family Reunion, like Murder in the Cathedral, depicts two different worlds. The larger, the "normal" world, is subdivided into different orders of reality according to the potentialities of the characters moving within it. Like the Knights, the people in this play whose vision is circumscribed by purely natural law are shallow, almost flat, lacking complexity. They see only events; they cannot interpret motives except by the selfish standards of profit and loss, expediency, private satisfaction. The strongest and best characterized of them is Amy, dowager Lady Monchensey, mother of Harry, Lord Monchensey, the hero of the play. The weakest are the obtuse and laughable Violet and Ivy, Amy's sisters. Amy's brothers-in-law, Harry's uncles Gerald and Charles, are the one very stupid and the other, the most redeemable of the whole family, deliberate and blundering. But Charles is neither quite down to the moral level of these others nor up to the rigidity of Amy's self-will; he has a streak of philosophic humor, which helps him to accept the astounding denouement of the play without being indignant or even entirely perplexed. (It was Charles, capable of surprise at the bulldog in the Burlington Arcade, whom Eliot intended as a partial counterpart to himself.)[2] Harry's two younger brothers, John ("not exactly brilliant") and Arthur ("rather irresponsible"), who, as if too negligible to be worth presenting to the audience, are detained from attending the family party at Wishwood, are dim projections of Gerald and Charles; the resemblances are apparent even in the slight news that the family receives of them. John has had a concussion: "A minor trouble like a concussion / Cannot make very much difference to John," says the tactless Harry. Arthur, arrested in Ebury Street some weeks earlier for what was obviously tipsy driving, is reported in the newspaper to have told the constable, "I thought it was all open country about here." His whimsey (though this detail of it was suggested to Eliot by a contemporary newspaper account) would be appropriate as much to Old Possum as to the sherry-drinking Charles. But the sensibility most patently identifiable with Eliot's own is that of Harry himself. This fact, perhaps accidental in the composition, explains somewhat the arbitrariness of Harry's strictures on his family and the uncritical tolerance the play accords this character in whom there is much to criticize.

The second, or "spiritual" world, has only one representative, Harry's Aunt Agatha, another sister of Amy. Agatha, if not exactly an inhabitant of the world of vital spirituality, is at any rate a guardian of its threshold; and she has looked within. Harry, the self-styled wife-murderer, does not submit to the authority of Amy and her world, as do his uncles, his two brothers, and all his aunts except Agatha. Nor does he yet belong to the world of which Agatha is the custodian. He exists rather "between sleep and waking," too sensitive and acute not to revolt against the dictatorship of his mother and the family who serve her, yet spiritually too childish without Agatha's guidance and, indeed, too ignorant without her instruction, to understand the preternatural messengers calling him away to purgatorial trial.

Amy lives in a pattern of timed moments, by the clock; like the works of a clock she is a machine. At the start of the play she grumbles that, now she is old, the clocks cannot be trusted; she fears that time will have a stop. As if in support of the characterization, the physician Warburton is made to say of her, at the beginning of Part II,

> The whole machine is very weak
> And running down. Her heart's very feeble.

Her last words as she dies in the final scene are "The clock has stopped in the dark." To Amy time is only succession and a measure of succession; the past and the future do not exist even as determining forces. Thus she is able to see life as order, controllable by the will. Nothing is unchangeable, nothing inevitable. Yet having long since, in her own life, halted "the normal change of things," she expects her dependents to be unchanging too, except under her control.

Against her mechanical self-possession there bursts Harry's turbulent, fluctuating disquiet; for his wheel of life, so to speak, is not the cold, precise pivot-wheel of the cosmic clock but an organic "burning wheel" of desire and memory. Like Lear he is on a "wheel of fire." Anne Ward has aptly pointed out that Harry's conception of time may well have come to Eliot from T. E. Hulme's modified concept of Bergsonian *durée*.[3] The view common to Hulme and Harry is a pessimistic one, of time in the natural order not as succession or as an index of creative evolution but as destructive duration which bombards order, preserving it only as the rubble of memory, still flaming with the suffering of the past. Just as Amy's perspective bears comparison with that of the Knights in the preceding play, so Harry's resembles that of the Women of Canterbury when aroused to consciousness by Becket. In the same manner as they, Harry knows the suffering imposed by action. But more shrewdly he has a sense of the coeternity of action and suffering, at least enough so that he can confirm Agatha's wise preliminary warning to the family: "The man who returns will have to meet / The boy who left." He declares:

> I am the old house
> With the noxious smell and the sorrow before morning,
> In which all past is present, all degradation
> Is unredeemable. As for what happens—
> Of the past you can only see what is past,
> Not what is always present. That is what matters.

He is a Gerontion, identifying himself with the house and its memories as well as his own.

The imagery of *The Family Reunion* is designed largely to support Harry's nightmarish impressions. Afflicted with horror because of the duration of his anterior life like the murderer's cancer mentioned by Warburton, he objectifies his feelings by talking of stench and contamination, of "the slow stain," "Tainting the flesh and discolouring the bone." He describes himself in the scene with Agatha as having been moving

> In and out, in an endless drift
> Of shrieking forms in a circular desert.

This is but a different picture of Agatha's insight into the same experience in her own earlier life,

> Up and down, through the stone passages
> Of an immense and empty hospital.

She, not Harry, has already learned that within the insane hell of despair exists in potentiality a state of reconciliation, of transcendence, and that suffering is the means for its attainment. That is a state which even she has not quite reached. In the same scene, when Agatha awakens him to acceptance of his destiny, Harry remarks:

> I have thought of you as the completely strong,
> The liberated from the human wheel.
> So I looked to you for strength. Now I think it is
> A common pursuit of liberation.

From her, Harry receives the commission, so to speak, to pursue his liberation from the wheel, not as his mother would have him do, by denying his past and starting again "as if nothing had happened," but by acknowledging with Agatha what he already believes, that "everything is irrevocable," "the past is irremediable," and "the future can only be built / Upon the real past." To brood pessimistically on duration is tantamount to lunacy; to believe that duration can somehow be neutralized, as the turning wheel in *Murder in the Cathedral* can be stilled in the unmoved center, marks the beginning of sanity.

Unfortunately, the play evades explanation of Harry's spiritual goal. An audience has the right to wonder in what way Harry's life after he departs from Wishwood will differ spiritually from his present condition. Though knowledge of Eliot's other work might give some people a sufficient hint, *The Family Reunion* needs an explicit equivalent to Becket's "make perfect my will," with some religious sanction for Harry's program, if only to define the future transcendence. The play has the wheel; it requires, in clearer fashion than by so casually introduced a symbol as "the single eye," a definition of the pivotal point. It is not enough that Harry should foresee deliverance; the audience wants to know precisely what vision he may encounter. He himself does not know. He says of it merely, when the moment of understanding comes:

> I feel quite happy, as if happiness
> Did not consist in getting what one wanted
> Or in getting rid of what can't be got rid of
> But in a different vision.

Eliot perceived when he wrote the play that the purgation was another story; he has since suggested that in leaving this a mystery he failed to respect "the rules of the game."[4]

Harry's inward plight arises out of strange events. The plot, as distinguished from the dramatic conflict of *The Family Reunion*, is singularly weak. For Amy's birthday, late in the transitional month of March, the family have assembled at Wishwood, Amy's house in the north of England. Before Harry arrives, someone remarks that he has been absent for eight years. A year ago his wife, of whom the family did not approve and whom Harry did not love, disappeared by accident or suicide from the deck of an ocean liner. Amy intends that Harry shall "take command at Wishwood," where she will help "contrive his future happiness." Harry presently enters, behaving strangely; his first utterance, concerning the uncurtained window, is followed almost at once by an agitated reference to apparitions looking in at him:

> Can't you see them? *You* don't see them, but I see them,
> And they see me. This is the first time that I have seen them.

(Unless the audience recognizes this as a paraphrase of Orestes' cry at the end of the *Choephoroi*, or consults the theater program, it must wait until the end of scene 2 to learn that Harry is being harried by the Furies, there visibly stretching forth their skinny claws.) After some fairly civil talk all at cross-purposes—Harry's portion of it would be flagrantly insulting from anybody else—he proceeds to outline obscurely, "in general terms / Because the particular has no language," his sense of damnation: "The sudden solitude in a crowded desert / In a thick smoke. . . ."

> One thinks to escape
> By violence, but one is still alone
> In an over-crowded desert, jostled by ghosts.

Then he startles everyone by saying, rather casually,

> It was only reversing the senseless direction
> For a momentary rest on the burning wheel
> That cloudless night in the mid-Atlantic
> When I pushed her over.

Afterward, he explains, he "slept heavily, alone." His phrasing here shocks his mother more than the story. "Then I recovered. I am afraid of sleep: / A condition in which one can be caught for the last time." (This allusion to Kipling's "At the End of the Passage" reinforces a parallel which the imagery has already developed with "The Hollow Men.") Harry is no better off with his wife dead than he was before; "She is nearer than ever." His present horror, furthermore, not only prolongs the tormenting revulsion he felt in his wretched marriage. He is suffering because of something deeper and earlier than the drowning of his wife. "It is not my conscience, / Not my mind, that is diseased, but the world I have to live in."

Eliot's debt to the *Oresteia* of Aeschylus is less even than most critics have conceded. It is certainly, however, more vivid than O'Neill's in *Mourning Becomes Electra*. In *The Family Reunion* as in the *Eumenides* the suffering of the hero is not caused by personal guilt. Although Eliot at one stage of the writing planned that Harry should be expiating the crime of having desired to kill his wife, the play conveys nothing of the kind. Harry is expiating a family curse, of which he is simply the victim. His father, now dead, plotted before the birth of Harry to murder his own wife Amy. As one gathers from Agatha's discovery of the facts to Harry in Part II, it was because of the father's clandestine infatuation with Agatha herself that this design took shape and because of Agatha's intercession for the unborn child that it did not take effect. The murder failed to occur; Harry was born; his father died abroad. The meditated crime set the curse in motion, very much as Adam's fall in paradise loaded his posterity with original sin. (The early drafts of the play take the curse back to a mad great-uncle Harry, a satanic Thyestes.)

The denial of Eden to Harry has been caused by something prior to his own acts. There is a noteworthy difference, however, between propitiation for this curse and for the original sin of Adam. Original sin makes every man at birth guilty of the primal fall; at the same time it predisposes him, by what is termed the *necessitas peccandi*, to commit sins of his own, of which he is guilty likewise. He can never directly atone for original sin: Christ has done that. All that man can do is to accept the vicarious Atonement and be penitent for sins his own will has concurred in. In Harry's case there is obviously no guilt for his father's sin: his father was not Adam. Harry has inherited merely the curse, the retribution never visited upon the father. This, in the manner of retribution for the original sin of Adam, includes both Harry's particular, personal sin, that of willing his wife's death (it is improbable that he really "pushed" her, though he can never be certain), and the rest of the suffering he has to endure in the play. But Harry is not guilty of his own sin, because it was determined by his father's. Harry is innocent. The play, as it issued from Eliot's hands, curiously asks the audience to sentimentalize Harry's own crime, for which he is not repentant, and to approve of Harry's expiating the curse in order to atone for his father's crime, for which he is not to blame. If he has been guilty of original sin, like the rest of the human race, that fact has nothing to do with the plot. The play shows him at the end departing without compunction in obedience to the Eumenides, the revaluated Furies, and thereby causing, as the physician Warburton has warned him a shock might do, the death of Amy his mother. And he is represented as thus starting to become saintly, even perhaps Christlike. His action is in the best puritan tradition of "Woman, what have I to do with thee?" Harry's advice to Amy is ridiculously unsatisfactory:

> You must just believe me,
> Until I come again.

Evidently Eliot had somewhere in mind the idea that on an allegorical level Harry could suggest by his conduct the role of Christ, for he is to symbolize redemption of the family from the paternal curse by being "Its bird sent flying through the purgatorial flame"; in other words, its scapegoat. Several details imply an analogy between Harry and the ritual hero of myth, such as the eight-year variant of the ritual term of wandering, the "birth-mystery" in Harry's question: "Tell me now, who were my parents?" and, indeed, the whole identification with Orestes. The trouble is that these latter obscure the Christian comparison and that it too vanishes in the mere muddle of literal and symbolic. Harry ought not to be, in quite this way, both agent and sufferer.

The nature of the curse which, as in Aeschylus, obsesses Eliot's hero is one of the most poorly dramatized details of the pattern. The curse, though it includes Harry's crime, comprehends far more, everything being related to the father's lapse as an effect to a cause. In its broadest aspect it is Harry's whole manner of life up to his conversation with Agatha; when revealed, this inheritance turns out to have been a blessing. The curse proceeds immediately from Harry's upbringing. Thus one would not be wrong to equate it approximately with what psychoanalysis calls fixations, inhibitions, and lingering traumas. A loftier art would term these his resented moral consciousness. The essence of the play is his discovery that this is good rather than bad. The curse, from the moment when its existence as a burden becomes known to Harry, is a benign guide. Through it the *felix culpa* promotes redemption. From Aeschylus, to objectify the duration of a beneficent vengeance, Eliot borrowed the Eumenides, whose vindictive role he supplemented by making them implicitly the inciters of Harry's crime. Although Harry is not aware of them until after the "murder" occurs, by all the logic of the play they personify his prior animosity toward both his mother and his wife. They have been visible first for some unexplained reason to Harry's faithful Pylades, the chauffeur Downing, who in the last scene assumes the role of a guardian Apollo. Then they appear to Harry at Wishwood, though they have always been at hand, whether "behind the nightingale's thicket," as if in the sacred wood of Colonus, or "Behind the palm trees in the Grand Hotel." Later they manifest themselves to Agatha and, then, in unspecified circumstances, to Harry's cousin Mary. There are two feasible explanations how they can be seen. They may be visible because they are in fact the classical Eumenides themselves, real goddesses, intended not as figments of the mythopoeic imagination but as real personages subsisting in their own world of light and shadow but sometimes pressing through the barriers to remind humanity of the order beyond. People may believe in devils and angels but not, at least nowadays, in Allecto, Megaera, and Tisiphone; therefore the credibility of the play breaks down whenever they appear. If they were really angels the case might be otherwise; but Harry's calling them "the bright angels" comes too late to do any good. This is the main reason they ought not to be visible to the audience—not, as Eliot argues in "Poetry and Drama," because they cannot be presented right.[5] The alternative explanation for their visibility is that, although they are called the Eumenides, they are really ghosts. *The Family Reunion* will support this theory, and one may suggest that the play makes complete sense only if the theory is right.

The justification for such an argument is that the Eumenides have an intimate connection with Harry's early life. Because they transmit the curse, they should have had a natural breeding place in his experience. Were they invisible, they could be explained psychologically as shapes from the unconscious mind. An audience would then accept their status without fluster. Now a visual illusion presumably emanates, purely or compositely, from forms seen in the waking world. If a man dreams, one says he dreams of what he has seen. If he dreams while awake, one explains the condition in the same way, only one says that he is diseased. This is the problem which in *Crime and Punishment* the haunted Svidrigaïlov puts before Raskolnikov.[6] And what if Harry's hallucination should be of the objectively real sort; what if, instead of only being ghosts from memory, the Eumenides should be ghosts from some earlier segment of the temporal dimension as it *externally* exists? Since they are honestly visible to others, they must be external ghosts; that is, if they proceed from Harry's natural experience at all. If they are not gratuitously supernatural, they must be rationally preternatural.

For what Harry has not perceived about duration, what Agatha understands, is that it may perhaps lodge both in memory and in the world. Past time need not be, as Bergson supposed, lost to all but the mind retaining its impressions; it may be concretely simultaneous with the present. A man is many selves: from one point of view there is no "becoming," for what he was is no longer he, unless preserved in simultaneous time.

> I turned and saw below
> The same shape twisted on the banister
> Under the vapour in the fetid air.

The past thus survives as an eternal present with the present and the future. One can remember it, and, perhaps, as J. W. Dunne contended, one can "remember" the future too: but the reality of other times is, at any rate, not merely subjective.[7] And just as one's own other selves exist, so also do those of everyone else. Other selves may come "here," or one may go "there," if permitted passage through the time barrier. The area of such speculation is recognizably that of science fiction; it is also the area of much serious inquiry into the nature of time. Without being committed to any final opinion, one may regard with interest such a testament as, for example, *An Adventure*, by Anne Moberly and Eleanor Jourdain, originally published in 1911 and re-issued by Eliot's firm, Faber and Faber, Ltd., in the 1930's, narrating a strange sensation of time travel from the twentieth century into the eighteenth. It is to this kind of experience, not essentially different, after all, from the reverse experience of "seeing ghosts," that Agatha refers when she speaks of "the loop in time." By this, one may under-stand some warping of the time dimension (a dimension pictured as a spiral describing a cone—the system of Yeats) which brings diverse times together, the ghosts of Christmas past and the ghosts of Christmas future. And the apparitions which *The Family Reunion* desig-nates as the Eumenides are possibly, even if only in a symbolic aspect, the past selves of the women to whom Harry's childhood was en-thralled.

Just before Agatha mentions this "loop in time" she alludes to "The Jolly Corner," by Henry James. Now it has been noticed—by F. O. Matthiessen, for one—that Agatha's allusion supports her reminder that Harry will have to meet at Wishwood the self he left there.[8] In the James story a certain Spencer Brydon returns to his old home in Amer-ica, a house which because of its associations he thinks of as "the jolly corner," and there, in pursuit of a tugging compulsion, he tracks down by night through its empty rooms the "ghost" of the maimed self he might have been had he remained in New York instead of following his European career. *The Family Reunion*, exchanging the roles of the good and bad selves, transfers the "might have been" to the relation between Harry and Agatha—to the imagined communion in the rose garden, where "what did not happen is as true as what did happen." Of Harry's meeting his actual or only potential self as a *Doppelgänger* the drama enacts nothing. But it confronts him with the Furies:

> When the loop in time comes—and it does not come for everybody—
> The hidden is revealed, and the spectres show themselves.

Harry's mother, unloved by her husband, became during Harry's child-hood a possessive despot. Talking with Warburton, Harry recalls that when he and Mary were children "The rule of conduct was simply pleasing mother; / Misconduct was simply being unkind to mother"; their holidays "were not holidays, but simply a time / In which we were supposed to make up to mother / For all the weeks during which she had not seen us." And when she saw them, he explains, she seemed more unhappy and they felt more guilty. (Guilt, it should seem, passed later into Harry's "anaesthesia." He does not feel guilty for things he does.) Even the children's pleasures, one learns from Harry's conversa-tion with Mary, were made artificial and orderly in accordance with Amy's genius for control. The psychoanalyst will understand what hap-pened both in Amy and in her son and why. It is small wonder that when in his adult life Harry flouts his mother's plans for him by marry-ing the weak woman the family hates, he is hounded by ghosts who, when they fully reveal themselves at Wishwood, are peeping old women. Indeed the draft labeled Typescript B directs at their last appearance that they shall be attired as for a journey, with luggage and shawls. Harry's inner restraint, the power of his mother, having haunted him through the miseries preventing tranquillity in his mar-riage, is reinforced by its alliance with the now tripled and externalized *imago* of that same power. The Eumenides of myth, as Eliot introduced them upon the stage, answer as much to the circumstances of Harry's upbringing as to the neurosis which these have induced. It is no acci-dent that in *The Family Reunion* the Chorus, soliloquizing dismally in unison, should be composed of the aunts and uncles who have given in to Amy's domination: in Aeschylus' *Eumenides* the Chorus comprises the Furies themselves.

By projecting Harry's childhood repressions beyond the human agent to blame for them into the conventional personification, the Furies, Eliot spared the already bewildered spectator the qualms he might feel in having to face two incarnations of Amy, a past and a present one. It is regrettable that despite "the loop in time," not needed by Aeschylus' real Eumenides, the relation of the specters to Amy should so easily elude notice. But Eliot had to manage things this way, for he wanted to show the Furies later as the benevolent Eumenides: that is, as a projection of Agatha rather than of Amy. It would have been awkward had Amy's ghost of the past suddenly yielded the stage to her sister's. The Furies have to symbolize mainly something abstract

—the moral climate of the house and family as both a creative and a harmful thing.

The play affirms that since the Eumenides can bring about good, Harry must seek instead of fleeing them. In one sense he has always sought them. Without consciousness of personal guilt, he has returned to Wishwood in the belief that he can escape suffering; but this "jolly corner" enshrines the suffering which he has all the time pursued. Almost as soon as he arrives, he understands this fact without being yet certain of it. His past, the house and family, and the Furies are all one. Before he is convinced, he carries on a dialogue with his cousin Mary, the childhood companion who, living with the family, was his ally against Arthur and John. Amy has kept her there as a future wife for Harry; he, being free now, might still marry her. For him to do so would be to accept Amy's scheme of continued domination (for as master of Wishwood he would be but the instrument of his mother) and to adopt Amy's notion of time—the notion that all potentialities are still open. The conversation discloses that Mary, having only an elementary idea of Harry's trouble, regards herself and Wishwood as supplying the solution; from her point of view he is only deceiving himself by his loathing and can make a fresh start there. The temptation—for such it is—presents itself through her cryptic, trancelike plea that the flowers which spring earliest, while the snow is still on the ground, suffer the least cruel of all painful rebirths. Harry responds, against his instinct that such escape is probably hopeless, by saying,

> You bring me news
> Of a door that opens at the end of a corridor,
> Sunlight and singing. . . .

Immediately, inducing in him an "apprehension" like "a sweet and bitter smell / From another world," the Furies stand revealed in the window. They return now as if to warn him off with the old restraints of the curse. In a rage, he boorishly tells Mary that she is of no use to him; and the specters, their work done, vanish again.

The corresponding scene in Part II, between Harry and Agatha, awakens him to the real outside causes of his unhappiness, but it should, one feels, also reveal to him the flaws in his own character. It ought to modify his previous statement that the world and not his conscience is diseased. Instead it leaves the audience dissatisfied with him because the evil of the past is shown too abruptly as an agency for good. At the climax the curse is revealed to have its cause in love and thus to be analogous to love; Harry with Agatha perfects in imagination his father's incomplete fruition of the "rose-garden," and, whereas Agatha really "only looked through the little door," they now figuratively commune in the garden itself. The terrible childhood is thus implicitly converted into a blessing, so that the Eumenides, now projected from the new "mother," Agatha, are "bright angels." None of this episode finds dramatic justification, even though it involves Harry's learning the truth about his father and, more important, his learning for the first time what the Eumenides are—the bearers of a curse, something outside him, which he must endure and turn to spiritual use. Such a discovery, which might if differently contrived make Harry sympathize with the family—he even admits that he might become more compassionate toward his mother, "But she would not like that"—simply strengthens his antipathy. The only thing that is changed is the recognized "meaning" of the past. The clue lies in the notion on which *The Waste Land* and *Ash Wednesday* shed some light, that past time is redeemable in so far as present knowledge redeems the memory of it. What *Ash Wednesday* does not imply is that because the past held the potentiality of this new meaning, now actualized, the redemption of the memory redeems the actual past, though ultimately "out of time" and in the domain of eternity, where all things are perfected in God. Thus is offered a final solution to the terrible discrepancy between "the idea and the reality." In the last two *Quartets* the concept is set forth with even greater clarity. "The Dry Salvages" puts it this way:

> We had the experience but missed the meaning,
> And approach to the meaning restores the experience
> In a different form. . . .

The redemption of wasted time is familiar from Shakespeare's *Henry IV*, Part I. But Shakespeare's Harry is characterized as deliberately redeeming time while ostensibly wasting it; Eliot's Harry redeems it, not only in reputation but in fact, after he has done harm. Eliot's doctrine is a tenuous one on which to hang the law and prophets of a play. The audience, if not just giddy by now, leaves the theater with perhaps a suspicion that it has been intellectually "had." The Furies, as Harry has come to understand them, were never entirely evil; his agony was not hell but purgatory—and all because of a sudden retrospective change of attitude.

> . . . in the end
> That is the completion which at the beginning
> Would have seemed the ruin.

Mary was paradoxically quite right in assuming that all Harry needed was to stop deceiving himself. His new direction, however, is to be in compliance with the past, not in resistance to it.

If it seems perverse that the play should offer justification for Harry's past and future instead of blaming him, it is merely that the plot abstracts for its use the deterministic elements of life. Harry is not a wholly voluntary agent.

> Perhaps my life has only been a dream
> Dreamt through me by the minds of others.

Eliot's mistake consisted in giving Harry so much irritability without making clear that the curse alone has been responsible for it. The side of Harry's personality which has resisted the curse ought to be likable. He is too exclusively possessed; all that an audience can see is the possession. His motivation should be split. If Harry were an obviously good man, devoted to the mother and the wife but driven by the curse to injure them against his will, and then reconciled by justification of the curse, he would be acceptable. But the *Oresteia* and *Hamlet* had been written already. If Harry were a man made wicked by the curse and then led by his horror of it to repent of his wilful sins, there would be the makings of a Christian play. In either circumstance the drama would require a consciously guilty hero, not one who is reassured by discovering that he is not even mad. It was grossly the wrong emphasis to extol Harry's nobility in carrying the family burden rather than to reprove the caddishness with which he does so. For the conception of guilt the Eumenides are no adequate substitute.

A close examination of the psychological problem of *The Family Reunion* will show that the apportionment of vengefulness and love between Amy and Agatha, in so far as they are both projected as the Eumenides, is really arbitrary. Agatha is as guilty as Amy, or Amy is as guiltless as Agatha. (The foregoing outline has paralleled Eliot's distinction, which was necessary for him if he was to communicate anything whatever.) The Eumenides, regarded as vehicles for the curse, do not at any time body forth the point of view of either woman exclusively, nor do they become "transformed." They only seem to change as Harry moves his allegiance to Agatha. On one level, not the naturalistic one, Amy's death shows the subsidence of the obsolete idea of domineering motherhood so that the idea of liberating motherhood may stand unimpeded. In a closely reasoned analysis of great merit C. L. Barber has complained that far from gaining his independence from the maternal "eyes" that drove him to panic, Harry defers to them by his docility to Agatha. Barber finds here a motive of infantile sexuality, a regression, and charges that Harry's Eumenides are "strange gods," because in pursuing them he is failing to attach his desire to a socially acceptable, mature object.[9] Still, a psychoanalytical critic might discern symptoms of infantile sexuality even if Harry were drowning himself in a millpond. Barber's evaluation misses the point here. On the literal level Harry *does* become independent, precisely because by accepting the Eumenides he enables them to draw him outside his psychological involvement with the family. They are more than ghosts of Amy's or even Agatha's ascendancy over him; they are the spiritual discipline guiding him to some sort of religious consummation. Besides being projections of the maternal control, associated with Amy's watchful eyes in Harry's protracted childhood and with those of the dead wife who "wouldn't leave him out of her sight," the Eumenides are the redemptive power of Harry's neurotic obsessions. If they were not, much of the point in calling them Eumenides would disappear.

But traditions associated with the Eumenides are not inclusive enough to make an audience realize what Harry is headed for. Conjecturally his destination is Christian sainthood. A remark by Agatha has given one clue: "broken stones / That lie, fang up, a lifetime's march." Harry's own words to Amy are more definite:

> . . . the worship in the desert, the thirst and deprivation,
> A stony sanctuary and a primitive altar,
> The heat of the sun and the icy vigil,
> A care over lives of humble people.

Even if Harry is not to become a missionary in the usual sense, the term is not too inaccurate. More likely Eliot thought of his being some sort of ascetic, like the Christians in the Theban desert. But to Harry the choice is not yet known. The pattern of his purgatorial trial is apparently conformable to descriptions by St. John of the Cross of the negative mystic's ascent to the divine union. Agatha in her role of Athena, having supplanted the Eumenides in the window embrasure and having there unfolded for Harry, if not for the audience, the mystery of atonement through suffering, sends him on his way to be united with the power vested in the Eumenides themselves; whether by service (action) or by death (suffering) is hardly important. Harry turns away, like the murderer in *Sweeney Agonistes*, from the things of sense, the warm human relationships sustaining other men, and perpetrates like him one final unrepented crime in order to sever himself wholly from the love of created beings. Although he has experienced what the mystics would technically call an "awakening" through Agatha, in the rose garden of reconsidered passion, it is doubtful whether he takes with him even the image of their shared emotional experience. The eyes he shall face are no longer human, the eyes of inhibition or love; they are divine, "the judicial sun / Of the final eye," under whose gaze the awful purging "evacuation / Cleanses." He has dared to cross from the "dream kingdom" of "The Hollow Men" into "death's twilight kingdom." In that realm alone, by the quasi-redemptive sacrifice of Harry as the family's Isaac, will occur the true birthday and the true family reunion. Harry, says Agatha with the same phrase Eliot used long before in "Eeldrop and Appleplex,"

> has crossed the frontier
> Beyond which safety and danger have a different meaning.
> And he cannot return. That is his privilege.
> .    .    .    .    .    .    .    .    .    .    .    .    .
> . . . Harry has been led across the frontier: he must follow.

To regard the physical sufferings of a remorseless murderer as a "privilege" is to superadd to the brutality of a *Sweeney Agonistes* the martyrdom of a *Murder in the Cathedral*.

It is curious that this negative design should subtly fulfil the ideal *affirmative* pattern outlined in Eliot's poems. Not that Harry's literal career fulfils this; for he, in turning away from Agatha, as from Mary, resigns the spiritual as he has resigned the sexual values of the human relationship. Yet he goes in search of analogous spiritual values externalized in a traditional symbol for God, "the single eye above the desert." This symbol, a kind of archetypal condensation of the Eumenides' power, is identical with the eyes in "The Hollow Men." In effect, Harry's quest is to restore him to eyes associated with the hovering Amy, and by extension with Agatha, and even Mary and Harry's wife: though through the Eumenides the eyes represent God, they are first the vigilant eyes of Harry's family. The literal aspect of *The Family Reunion* conceals this identification; but in an unconscious aspect the symbol is truly mightier than its diverse co-ordinates. Variously regarded, the eyes are whatever tortures, whatever tempts, whatever reconciles, and whatever shall redeem Harry. A play, unlike a poem, can readily split one essential value into parts, so as to show a protagonist rejecting one in favor of another. In the light of what the play un-consciously says, irrespective of the "splitting" of the ambivalent symbol, Harry's future promises a return to his past, now endowed with a new meaning. A faithful interpretation of the affirmative pattern should stress the analogy between Eliot's point of view and Dante's—the analogy between Agatha and the Beatrice of the *Vita nuova,* and between the "bright angels" and the Beatrice of the *Paradiso* conducting the aspirant toward the divine center, as in Christian theology illuminating grace draws man toward his salvation. Eliot's paradox of psychologically affirmative attainment through negative withdrawal reaches its most nearly perfect expression in the closing lines of "Little Gidding."

Since Eliot himself has decried his failures in *The Family Reunion,* one may suppose that after 1939 he perceived the dramatic limitations of his esoteric synthesis. It was probably overbold to use a ready-made theme, having psychological, anthropological, mythological, and religious meanings, for a play where all of these vie with one another on the very surface. Most of the difficulties come from inadequate differentiation of levels, from confused mixtures of the literal and the symbolic. Eliot was probably well acquainted with Gilbert Murray's "Hamlet and Orestes" (1914) in *The Classical Tradition in Poetry,* and he may consciously have embroidered the ritual analogies which Murray suggested;[10] *The Family Reunion* deals with the death-and-rebirth cycle. The time problem imposes an unnecessary hardship upon the audience; similar puzzles come close to marring *The Cocktail Party.* The treatment of levels of character makes, in one respect, an improvement upon *Sweeney Agonistes:* one feels quite sure of Harry's and Agatha's attitudes toward spiritual initiation. But the diminution of the other characters serves to extinguish them as human beings rather than to exalt by contrast the loftier sensibilities. Matthiessen observed of *Sweeney Agonistes* that the division (into sensitives and dolts) was Jamesian. One hardly detects the influence there; in *The Family Reunion* it is overwhelming. One may possibly see, besides the influence of James, that of Lewis Carroll, specifically in the rose-garden passages;[11] in atmosphere, however, the play is reminiscent of Santayana's *The Last Puritan.*

In its poetic quality *The Family Reunion* exhibits, on the one hand, its greatest success and, on the other hand, its greatest failure. The verse, if sometimes more artificial and less intense than in the choruses of *Murder in the Cathedral* and *The Rock,* and less inevitably phrased than in *Ash Wednesday*, is nevertheless fluent. Eliot has described his prosody (except in the two-stress lines of what he terms "lyrical duets") in "Poetry and Drama" as calling for "a line of varying length and varying number of syllables, with a caesura and three stresses."[12] Unlike the traditional metric principle normal to *Murder in the Cathedral*, where stress means all syllabic accentuation, this considers only the dominant stresses in each speech phrase, leaving unnoticed any inferior accents not ranking as main stresses. The new principle requires new scansion. (When scanned conservatively, many lines both in *The Family Reunion* and in *The Cocktail Party* reveal an underlying free blank-verse measure or else the four-stress rhythm of *Everyman*.) Now as Eliot acknowledges, the poetry in *The Family Reunion* is sometimes "remote from the necessity of the action."[13] He himself confines his criticism to the expressly lyrical passages, but it might justly apply to much of the remainder. The actors have to speak lines often so overburdened with cryptically associative images that no audience can be expected to follow the meaning. The poetry is not abstract: that is its whole trouble. It is too symbolically concrete, too imagistic. Phrases like "The unexpected crash of the iron cataract," "The bright colour fades," "the bird sits on the broken chimney" are good in themselves but are not closely relevant; they are "objective correlatives" for emotion that an audience wants to see justified in the plot. The connotative language should integrate with the action. Eliot's old methods of symbolism are not public enough for drama.

The defects of *The Family Reunion* should have warned Eliot away from further writing for the stage. What is permanently most valuable in his poetic technique is precisely what shuts the public out—the symbolism of his imagery. Throughout the next play, in relying less on imagery and more on plot, with more scrupulous attention to communicating a sense of realism, he was to preserve a symbolism of action which did not aggressively interfere with surface intelligibility. But in concentrating his style upon "verse," he had to throw away there the poetic gains of forty years.

The Nun's Priest of Chaucer when in danger of digressing too far into technical theology calls himself back by reminding the pilgrims that his tale is of a cock and hen. Though unable at last to refrain from reminding them also that all was written for our doctrine, he has by that time accomplished his other purpose of fooling the gullible, regaling the gay, and annoying the techy. Eliot's cock-and-hen story does much the same thing. *The Cocktail Party*, produced for the Edinburgh Festival of 1949 and staged more profitably in New York and London in 1950, is a versified drawing-room comedy.[1] In many of its incidental details it burlesques Eliot's poetic symbols; it simultaneously offers, under a satiric veneer of middle-class banter, a theme of serious spiritual quest. The plot structure, as in *The Family Reunion*, is indebted to the traditions of ritual drama.

The plot of *The Cocktail Party*, concerning domestic relations, is interesting apart from profound meanings. Edward Chamberlayne, a barrister, is estranged from his wife, Lavinia. She is in love with a young film writer, Peter Quilpe. Peter is in love with Celia Coplestone, who writes poetry. Celia is Edward's mistress and is in love with him. Edward loves nobody, and nobody loves Lavinia. At the start of the play the principal characters, except Lavinia, are attending a cocktail party in the Chamberlaynes' London flat. As is discovered a little later, Lavinia without warning has left Edward that very afternoon. He, therefore, fortified with the tale that she has had to visit a sick aunt, is acting as solitary host to Peter, Celia, and three other people of whom he knows only two—Julia Shuttlethwaite, an impertinent gossip of an age no longer certain, and Alexander MacColgie Gibbs, an eccentric amateur chef and globe-trotter in some way connected with the Foreign Office. The stranger, known until Act II only as the Unidentified Guest, is Sir Henry Harcourt-Reilly, a consulting psychiatrist or analytical psychologist. Act I is devoted to exposition, to a final severance of relations between Edward and Celia, and to a restoration of Lavinia to Edward. In scene 1, when the other guests have temporarily left after the party, Edward submits to questioning by Sir Henry, from whom he obtains a mysterious assurance that Lavinia shall come back. Afterward he listens to Peter confess his own disappointed love for Celia. In the next scene Celia breaks her emotional ties with Edward, and in scene 3, occurring on the following afternoon, Edward receives another brief visit from Sir Henry, who again makes his exit without revealing his name. Lavinia returns, and, after the departure of Celia, Julia, Alex, and Peter, who have shown up one by one in response to messages ostensibly originating from her, she and Edward renew their long-standing incompatibility.

Act II occurs several weeks later in Sir Henry's consulting room. Lavinia's departure and return have been part of a conspiracy arranged among Sir Henry, Julia, and Alex to reconcile the Chamberlaynes. Confronting Edward and Lavinia unexpectedly with each other, Sir Henry, who has been counseling Lavinia and whom Alex has tricked Edward into seeing, persuades them to have another try. In the latter part of the same long scene, after Edward and Lavinia are gone, Sir Henry in an interview with Celia encourages her to order her own life by means of a "sanatorium," which those members of the audience who know *The Family Reunion* will later associate with the pilgrimage of Harry Monchensey. Celia's choice, though she does not perceive it, constitutes a life of potential sainthood. Sir Henry's task seems to have been that rather of a father confessor than of an ordinary psychologist. At the end of Act II he, Julia, and Alex go through a little ritual of drinking one toast "for the building of the hearth" and another "for those who go upon a journey." This incident provides the only overt dramatic hocus-pocus, at any rate on the stage.

In Act III, two years later, another cocktail party is about to begin at the Chamberlaynes', who are living amicably together. The same people drop in unexpectedly: first Julia and Alex, then Peter back from film-making in California, and lastly Sir Henry, all uninvited. But not Celia. Alex brings word that Celia, having enrolled in an austere nursing order and having gone out to a remote country called Kinkanja, was stationed with two other sisters at a Christianized village there in time of pestilence. During an insurrection by the heathen, who resented the Christian natives' impiety of eating saffron monkeys, it was Celia's fate to be "crucified / Very near an ant-hill." After the shock of this news has somewhat abated, Sir Henry reveals that he foresaw she would die a violent death.

> That was her destiny. The only question
> Then was, what sort of death? *I* could not know;
>
> .   .   .   .   .   .   .   .   .   .   .
>
> *She* did not know. So all that I could do
> Was to direct her in the way of preparation.

The remainder of Act III disperses the visitors and leaves Edward and Lavinia once more alone, waiting for their cocktail party to begin.

*The Cocktail Party* is a clever, tart comedy, readily intelligible in the theater and for that reason better than *The Family Reunion*. Eliot learned in this play how to interweave easy sophistication, irresistible to one sort of audience as the work of Oscar Wilde and Noel Coward had proved, with gradual complication of problems. Scene 1, getting along without Furies and sudden illuminations, resorts to slick, superficial dialogue to beguile the attention of the audience. Nothing in the first few minutes of action prepares for any weighty message, yet by the time this comes, in the final act, it is less startling than one might imagine. In Act II the tone becomes more generally serious, and the problems (a little too jauntily) are solved. The delayed discovery of Sir Henry's occupation cannot emerge earlier, for a mystery is needed to keep the audience alert throughout the initial plot development. For this reason Eliot was well advised to put the discovery and the double climax close together. He was perhaps not quite so crafty in relying on further curiosity about the Chamberlaynes and Celia to sustain high interest into Act III. On the other hand, it would be intolerable for the audience not to know whether Sir Henry's prescriptions worked; the curiosity, though diminished, is still alive. To some, as it did to the present writer, this may take the form of hoping that the insolent Sir Henry, the center of an annoying secret, may be exposed as a quack, for having exceeded measure. The mere possibility of such an attitude means that after Act II the plot is no longer Sir Henry's—who by disclosing his name has lost his power over the spectators—but Eliot's own. What happens thenceforth is the act of superior destiny. Eliot made a pretense of giving the dramatic control back to the Chamberlaynes and, in a manner of speaking, to Celia, for her death is a result of her free choice. Sir Henry is out of it. To appease the audience after this dramatic "kick in the teeth," as Eliot is said to have pleasantly called it, the author had to vindicate Sir Henry further by re-establishing the mystery; but the lines in which Sir Henry talks of having beheld the apparition of a future dead Celia are as likely to dismay as to satisfy, even if, remembering Shaw's *Saint Joan*, the audience interprets them as a report of Galtonic visualization. It may be, however, that a feeling of hostility toward Sir Henry is exceptional.

The authority of Sir Henry, from the point of view of realism, is not that of a magistrate. Neither Celia nor the Chamberlaynes are forced to obey him, nor does he dictate their future modes of life. But in purely dramatic terms nothing can happen to them until he acts. He has greater wisdom and, as has been seen, a faculty of second sight which bears a resemblance to divine foreknowledge. He is like M. Henri, Death's harbinger in Jean Anouilh's *Eurydice*. Since Eliot's plot depends on what Sir Henry does, and since the other actors respond only to this, the relationship parallels that between God and man. This fact might not be worth comment but for the further configuration of ritual atonement, or initiation, forming the "underpattern" of the drama.

The only very conspicuous clues to its nature, apart from the analogy between Celia's death and Christ's, are the attributes and behavior, first, of Sir Henry and, second, of his adjutants Julia and Alex. These three, who compose a sort of cabal dedicated to the reordering of the other characters' mixed-up lives, are called "Guardians." Sir Henry is obviously the chief Guardian, having in charge, so to speak, both the Chamberlaynes and Celia. His function corresponds to a very ancient characterization in ritual. Eliot in 1923 wrote a review called "The Beating of a Drum," where he discussed briefly the ritual source of the fools in Shakespeare's plays. He noted that the fool, at least in the role of wise but unheeded counselor (e.g., in *King Lear*), derived from the ritual shaman or medicine man, who appears, for example, in the St. George play, the English equivalent of the Perseus legend, as the doctor who revives the dead knight.[2] That review supplied an interesting early forecast of *The Cocktail Party*. Sir Henry answers to the description both of fool and of doctor. His addiction to apparent nonsense in Act I belies the gravity of his role: he has figuratively the madness of prophecy. At different times he is referred to also as "the Devil." Lord Raglan, in *The Hero*, points out that the Mephistophelean figure, as in *Doctor Faustus*, is possibly traceable to the ritual impersonator of a god. Raglan shows also that the devil, in Egyptian ritual the horned man, was the divine king embodying fertility or, alternatively, his opponent (like the Minotaur) in a ritual combat for the right to kingship.[3] If in other circumstances, in a ritual of initiation and rebirth, a comparable figure stood by to symbolize the power acquired by the "newborn" initiate, he would be the "doctor" as well. One is certainly entitled to speculate on the ritual implications of Sir Henry's curative treatment of Edward; this devil-doctor-fool wields the power of healing. He re-creates for Edward a satisfactory relationship with his wife: that is, he effects a "ritual" marriage. In the last act of the play the common ritual term of seven years has elapsed since Edward's original union with Lavinia. It would be a simple matter, especially in view of Sir Henry's "One-eyed Riley" song, to contrive an elaborate parallel, through *The Waste Land*, with fertility myths cited by Frazer and even with the Grail legend.[4]

But since by Eliot's testimony in "Poetry and Drama" the "source" of his story was the *Alcestis* of Euripides, one need not go so far afield.[5] Sir Henry, in bringing back Lavinia like Alcestis from the grave, is cast in the part of that great boaster, drunkard, and ruffian, Hercules. Although he says,

> . . . it is a serious matter
> To bring someone back from the dead,

he has behaved as Hercules ignorantly misbehaves in the house of grief, calling for drink. The ritual origins of the myth of the savior Hercules are essentially solemn; but Hercules himself, and not only in Euripides' play, is frequently boisterous and comic. A comparable model for Sir Henry might have been Falstaff, a lineal descendant of the buffoon, "vice," or devil of the moral interludes, and perhaps also of Seneca's Hercules. Now the excuse for Sir Henry's levity is certainly to be looked for partly in the comic intentions of Eliot's plot: Lavinia, as Sir Henry very well knows, is not dead at all. His own talk of death is purely figurative, though by no means frivolous; the resurrection of Lavinia is to be no less miraculous because it is not spectacular and corporeal. It is to bring emotional reconciliation with Edward, a new life for both of them. In his adaptation, Eliot followed Euripides and went somewhat further. For, according to A. W. Verrall, a controversial student of Euripidean rationalism, the secret of the *Alcestis* is that the cowardly husband, Admetus, has hastily consigned Alcestis to her tomb without making sure whether she is dead; that the loutish Hercules, no more qualified than anybody else to work marvels, has found her rousing from her swoon and has conducted her home; that the whole point, in short, consists in Euripides' skepticism toward the mystery cults and in his determination to expose the Alcestis myth "as fundamentally untrue and immoral, before an audience who were well acquainted with the general opinions of the author."[6] As Eliot is said to have consulted Verrall's theories about the *Ion* when constructing *The Confidential Clerk*, it is fair to assume that he knew of this celebrated interpretation of the *Alcestis*. It is true, he did not emulate Verrall's Euripides by wholly dismissing the "miracle," for the action corresponding to the supposed resurrection of Alcestis, namely Lavinia's emotional cure, is perfectly genuine. Furthermore, he developed the gin-guzzling Sir Henry beyond the character of Hercules into a dispenser of sage advice. But without such a construction as Verrall puts upon the *Alcestis*, it is hard to imagine Eliot's having transferred emphasis, as he did do, to the problem of a recreant husband. If Euripides' play is "straight miracle," Admetus not only is not reprehensible but is, perhaps, even praiseworthy, a good man whom divine favor has singled out to recover his wife from the dead. On the other hand, if Euripides' play is as Verrall says, the only means by which Hercules can find Alcestis alive in the tomb is for Admetus to have conducted her funeral in huggermugger, because he was ashamed of his cowardice in letting her die for him.

What Eliot did, apparently, was to entertain Verrall's hypotheses that Alcestis was put away alive and that this action would not have been possible if her husband had loved her (both because he would not have consented to her sacrifice and because in any event he would have been more ceremonious about her funeral). Then Eliot evaluated the characters of such a husband and wife in a contemporary setting. He dispensed with the burial, since he had not Euripides' axe to grind, and undertook to arrange through Sir Henry the *rapprochement* which was outside Euripides' scope, but which a modern audience would like better. Meanwhile he dignified Sir Henry, bestowing on his own Hercules some of the attributes, though not all, that Euripides had taken away. And in the end, by Celia's martyrdom and Sir Henry's foresight of it, he reinstated the sort of thing that Euripides had spurned.

The clowning by Sir Henry and the idiocies of Alex and Julia, being largely devoid of satiric motive, should probably be considered Eliot's antidote to the gravity and problem-comedy tone of his play. They also recall Eliot's scheme, as once he outlined it in a letter to Pound, of keeping "the bloody audience's attention engaged" in order to perform "monkey tricks . . . behind the audience's back." One may agree that there are plenty of monkey tricks, "saffron" or otherwise, in *The Cocktail Party*. In some measure Eliot's use of the Euripidean material itself may have been prankish; his manner of handling it suggests that he was deliberately parodying his former practice of allusiveness. In one regard his allusions were potentially offensive. The "One-eyed Riley," thoroughly nasty in most procurable versions, bears an indirect relation here, through its slender link with Mr. Eugenides of *The Waste Land*, to a sexual deviation in pagan initiatory rites like those behind the Alcestis myth.[7] The associative process may have begun in Eliot's mind from a remark by the disgusting Dr. O'Connor in Djuna Barnes's *Nightwood*, to which Eliot wrote a Preface in 1937. O'Connor says, " '. . . the great doctor, he's a divine idiot and a wise man. He closes one eye, the eye that he studied with. . . .' "[8] But one should not try therefore to find significance in Sir Henry's being turned into Lavinia's aunt (though in a sense he is the "Charley's aunt" of the play). *The Cocktail Party*, unlike *The Waste Land*, does not require any such annotation, nor for that matter would homosexuality have any literal relevance. Eliot was baiting the critics.

In introducing the Guardians, Eliot was not being capricious.[9] The concept of guardianship, though indeed of diverse provenance, from the legal use of the term to the Stoic-Christian idea of guardian angels, recalls the Guardians in Plato's *Republic*, especially in view of the outline for the social role of the Community of Christians in Eliot's *The Idea of a Christian Society* (1939). The important thing about the Guardians here is that they initiate Celia and the Chamberlaynes into vocations according to their potentialities.[10] Celia is capable of full enlightenment; Edward and Lavinia, less gifted, remain partly blind, in the dark. The figuratively one-eyed Sir Henry and the broken-spectacled, sibyllic Julia are interpreters of light to darkness. The significance is not limited to psychological adjustment. Though Eliot mostly excluded religious terminology, the virtues that the Chamberlaynes are to practice and the martyr's death that Celia accepts constitute a spiritual discipline.

Like Anouilh's *Eurydice*, *The Cocktail Party* suggests an opposition between commonplace and heroically vital people. Of the four suffering characters two are men and two are women. They are paired so that each has an opposite of his own sex, an opposite in temperament and in what is crucial to this play—the ability to love or be loved. By nature Edward and Lavinia are alike in being dispassionately conservative; their inertia triumphs over will and imagination. Celia and Peter are imaginative and rebellious. Celia, however, is converted to patience, a quality strangely akin to conservatism, and by sublimation of will she is led to attain a nobler calling than is possible even to imagination; only Peter, upon whom the Guardians exert no present influence, still relies, at the end of the play, on his own forces of creative will. Edward defines in his conversation with Celia the two psychological elements concerned; they recall *The Master Builder*.

> The self that can say "I want this—or want that"—
> The self that wills—he is a feeble creature;
> He has to come to terms in the end
> With the obstinate, the tougher self; who does not speak,
> Who never talks, who cannot argue;
> And who in some men may be the *guardian*—
> But in men like me, the dull, the implacable,
> The indomitable spirit of mediocrity.

Will is acquisitive, but not necessarily selfish. Peter and Celia resemble each other not simply in the detail of being creative artists, though this is important, but in their common ability to affirm through love for another. This is all that Peter has, and in losing Celia he can only retreat to his film writing—connected, as Eliot's symbolism charmingly contrives it, with studying Boltwell, "The most decayed noble mansion in England," so as to reproduce its decay in California. Peter is not ready to come to terms with "the tougher self," "the *guardian*," which would establish his life more seriously. But the three Guardians who, in a manner of speaking, project the tougher selves of Edward, Lavinia, and Celia do not ban the possibility of Peter's maturing. "He has not yet come to where the words are valid," says Sir Henry; this "yet" leaves the door open to something beyond. Celia more readily, in losing Edward, upon whom she has fixed her desire, abnegates her will to the service of holiness. One thinks of Becket's words on perfection of will; for Celia in submitting to "the tougher self" accepts suffering through action.

Edward and Lavinia, the opposites of Peter and Celia, both yield to tougher selves by following the advice of Sir Henry, but they have too much the "spirit of mediocrity" to become saints. The vocation of Celia is not for them. Eliot's characterization of Lavinia is not so good as that of Edward; she is rather wooden. Edward, however, exhibits his conflict plainly. The obvious analogy is with Prufrock. Without being in love with Celia, Edward has indulged in a kind of mermaid dream of her and, out of selfishness, has simply willed their relationship. His discovery that "the tougher self" must subdue his feeble interest in her as a person is identical with what one supposes Prufrock's realization must be. For Prufrock such will (called "I" in the poem) must give way to the other self ("you") which keeps him from daring and which in the end is overwhelmed with him when they "drown." Lavinia's problem corresponds to her husband's, but rather as its converse. As loving is his masculine inability, so being loved is her feminine one. Her fancy of being at some time loved by Peter is like Edward's fancy of loving Celia. Realizing that their defects are complementary, Sir Henry calls Lavinia and Edward "exceptionally well-suited to each other." Peter and Celia are suited to each other too, but a romantic solution for them is precluded by Celia's having passed beyond such an emotional stage at the time of her disagreement with Edward. Furthermore, even though both Peter and Celia are capable of loving and of being loved, neither, until too late, sees that what he loves is only an ideal. Celia discovers the truth for herself and confesses:

> The man I saw before, he was only a projection—
> I see that now—of something that I wanted—
> No, not *wanted*—something I aspired to—
> Something that I desperately wanted to exist.

To Peter it is revealed by Lavinia after Celia's death:

> What you've been living on is an image of Celia
> Which you made for yourself, to meet your own needs.

In *The Cocktail Party*, then, Eliot depicts no human relationship which is satisfactory in itself. Those who think they love cannot marry; those who are married simply endure. Sir Henry's program for Edward and Lavinia might be disastrous, but miraculously it is not, though even he, in a momentary lapse into humanity, admits, "I have taken a great risk."

The first constructive business in the play occurs when Edward and Sir Henry, who is still the Unidentified Guest, broach the subject of Lavinia's departure. The phrases Sir Henry uses ("You no longer feel quite human / You're suddenly reduced to the status of an object— / A living object, but no longer a person."), describe Edward's plight when he becomes aware that events have made his habitual feelings inadequate to reality. Sir Henry continues with his comparison of Edward's discovery to the jolt at the bottom of the staircase.[11] His image of the Prufrockian patient stretched on the table clarifies the state of Edward's soul: he is "a piece of furniture in a repair shop," and Sir Henry is the craftsman who must reassemble his smashed life. Edward himself knows that he is a Prufrock; as he tells Celia afterward:

> I have met myself as a middle-aged man
> Beginning to know what it is to feel old.

The whole relationship between Edward and Sir Henry clarifies also the conditions under which spiritual repair is possible. Even though Sir Henry works no wonders, as a "masked actor" he cloaks the power of the spiritual surgeon—a metaphor that Eliot in "East Coker" had already applied to Christ. That the actor, being a witness like the Rock, is of necessity a sufferer, hardly comes out in the play. But Sir Henry, like the One-eyed Riley, may be wounded in some tropological sense. Now Edward's consciousness of emotional bankruptcy arises directly from Lavinia's having, as it were, withdrawn her portion from the marriage. The deficit she has left him is not, to his surprise, made up by Celia, whom now he understands he does not love. He would like to think that he does love her. As he tells her in the second scene:

> If I have ever been in love—and I think that I have—
> I have never been in love with anyone but you,
> And perhaps I still am.

But it has been only desire; and now he has "lost / The desire for all that was most desirable." Like Gerontion, he has lost his passion and has preserved nothing to fill its place. He is in process of learning that sex and love are not the same. One is not astonished when Celia, beginning to redress her own emotions, finds that he resembles a mummy, a chirping insect, or "a beetle the size of a man," like the protagonist of Kafka's *The Metamorphosis*.[12]

Sir Henry's intervention is a *fait accompli* before he ever starts to question Edward. Afterward Sir Henry makes it clear to him that since Edward has acceded to it the consequences are beyond Edward's power of reversal. What he says about "letting the genie out of the bottle" carries on Eliot's preoccupation since "Eeldrop and Appleplex" with the irreversibility of time, with the uneasy fact that what's done is done and cannot be undone. "The awful daring of a moment's surrender / Which an age of prudence can never retract" has, as Sir Henry restates it, a humiliating effect. Later, after Lavinia's return, Edward is struck aghast at having to live with the consequences of making up his mind, and, in a partial echo of some fine lines which Eliot had elsewhere quoted from Heywood's *A Woman Killed with Kindness*,[13] he exclaims in desperation:

> O God, O God, if I could return to yesterday
> Before I thought that I had made a decision.

Sir Henry, at his second visit, has pointed out that the decision to have Lavinia back is unalterable:

> You made a decision. You set in motion
> Forces in your life and in the lives of others
> Which cannot be reversed. That is one consideration.
> And another is this: it is a serious matter
> To bring someone back from the dead.

As F. Scott Fitzgerald put it, we are "borne back ceaselessly into the past."[14] We are never at one moment the same as we were in that preceding, if indeed we even *are* at all; ". . . we die to each other daily," says Sir Henry in a Pauline phrase. O'Connor in *Nightwood* says the same thing: " 'To our friends . . . we die every day, but to ourselves we die only at the end. We do not know death, or how often it has essayed our most vital spirit.' "[15] Sir Henry's poignant evocation of "affectionate ghosts": "the grandmother, / The lively bachelor uncle at the Christmas party, / The beloved nursemaid," illustrates concretely the disappearance of the earlier self into the past from which a familiar "ghost" would come as a stranger. Thus Lavinia is a stranger, her old self being dead, when she rejoins her husband. It is this fact which makes it possible for Edward, a stranger to his former self, to begin a new life with her. But, as appears also in *The Family Reunion*, the past is not so dead but that it delimits the choices of the future. The doctrine is a Hindu one.

> Only by acceptance
> Of the past will you alter its meaning.

The liberation into timelessness, into an absorption in love where time is "meaningless," lies beyond Edward's attainment.

The general implications of the scene in the doctor's consulting room are evident. Sir Henry might possibly show Edward, as an alternative to reuniting him with Lavinia, a way of spiritual rebirth, the "sanatorium." But only the saints go to the sanatorium, and Sir Henry prefers to counsel both Edward and Lavinia to rehabilitate their lives in a fashion suited to them. For Edward's acquiescence there is no explanation except that he is beginning "to feel sorry" for Lavinia, who, reappearing, has made him feel the same "oppression, the unreality / Of the role she had always imposed. . . ." All that both of them need is to submit to making the best of the past; to cease wishing for what cannot be had and thus to attain what is actually within reach—

> to avoid excessive expectation,
> Become tolerant of themselves and others,
> Giving and taking, in the usual actions
> What there is to give and take.

The reason for the distinction between Celia and the Chamberlaynes is not arbitrary. Because Edward and Lavinia cannot proceed along the way of enlightenment as Celia can, they have to stop at the point where they see themselves clearly and are willing to try to make "the best of a bad job"—just as Eliot in *The Use of Poetry* observed that the poet also must do.[16] The equivalent formula is *Datta, Dayadhvam, Damyata*. But Celia, having had the almost visional experience of timeless love— a "dream" though it may have been—has caught through it an intimation of the higher goal before her. She is ready for dedication by the sacrifice of her own will—her first martyrdom. Her second martyrdom, her sacrifice by death, simply ratifies her patient humility. But like Becket in *Murder in the Cathedral* she comes through love to humility only after consciousness of sin. Her words to Sir Henry set forth a feeling

> of emptiness, of failure
> Towards someone, or something, outside of myself;
> And I feel I must . . . atone. . . .

For the conviction of sin, alien to Edward's more limited awareness, the remedy is penitential; through action and suffering Celia may find her atonement. To atone is to reach "at-oneness"; and that is the goal of the mystic also. Eliot's previous use of St. John of the Cross explains the meaning of Celia's sacrifice. She is to enter the state of the contemplative mystic, of discipleship in the negative tradition. The "sana-torium" Sir Henry talks about is a place from which some people return, to "lead very active lives / Very often, in the world"; but it is patently also a place where others remain to proceed from illumination to contemplation and, at length, after the experience of the Dark Night, to mystical union. Celia too must pass through "the way of illumina-tion"; she is to see "projected spirits"; and, further, she "will journey blind," "towards possession." The way "between the scolding hills, / Through the valley of derision," is reminiscent of *The Ascent of Mt. Carmel.* This path of consecration "by which the human is / Trans-humanized" contrasts with the non-mystical life of average people like the Chamberlaynes. But both are ways to redemption: both are ways out of darkness through darkness.

> Each way means loneliness—and communion.
> Both ways avoid the final desolation
> Of solitude in the phantasmal world
> Of imagination, shuffling memories and desires.

Hence to Celia, as to Edward and Lavinia, Sir Henry speaks the words, "Work out your salvation with diligence," which translate the deathbed exhortation of the Buddha to his disciples.

The revelation by Sir Henry that Celia's death has come as no sur-prise to him has once more proved his superiority. The passage which he self-consciously quotes from Shelley's *Prometheus Unbound* is about second sight—the vision of the *Doppelgänger.* Here this is a projection from the future rather than, as in *The Family Reunion,* one from the past. The direct source was Charles Williams' novel *Descent into Hell,* the opening chapter of which, containing some of the same lines from Shelley, is entitled "The Magus Zoroaster."[17] The novel, with its pat-tern of simultaneity, conducts the reader into a world of the dead where all times coexist, separately present in the ordinary dimensions of space. It is not a world of frozen time; things happen in it. When by miraculous circumstance the barriers between that world and the world of modern London break down, and the two worlds perceptibly inter-sect in the same space, it is possible for certain people "here" to ob-serve what is happening "there," as in the ghost passage of "Little Gidding." One of these is a young woman who may have been a model for Celia Coplestone. There is also a strong resemblance between Julia Shuttlethwaite and Sybil, the wise woman of Williams' novel on the

Tarot, *The Greater Trumps*. Other novels by Williams, an admired friend of Eliot, may have further influenced *The Cocktail Party*.

Celia's crucifixion in Kinkanja is a grim conclusion, unalleviated by comic surprise or cynicism or any such brutal lenitives as help the case in Evelyn Waugh's *Black Mischief*. Yet the kind of comedy Eliot devised has been compared generically by some critics to Dante's *Commedia*, for in it the characters either fulfil their greatest potentialities or else are set firmly on the way toward doing so. Peter Quilpe alone waits for someone to show him his direction. It may be that Sir Henry, despite his foresight, is mistaken in thinking that Peter will "go far," unless he means only that Peter will become a successful film dramatist. This mystery the play does not expose.

# 16 HIS FATHER'S BUSINESS: "THE CONFIDENTIAL CLERK"

The characters in *The Confidential Clerk*, where Eliot sacrificed poetry even more ruthlessly than in *The Cocktail Party*, speak lines which are verse in typography but prose in cadence.[1] More rarely than in the preceding play is there a whisper of Eliot's poetic voice. Nor are there any symbolic objects like Julia's broken spectacles or Alex's eggs. There is but one verbal symbol of note—the garden— and that is a commonplace metaphor. One makes no question but that the poetic product is debased or that, on the other hand, this play seems less a theatrical oddity than the one before it. Also, its personages are more credible; Eliot dispensed with the central figure of the wise counselor round whom other characters revolve like electrons round a nucleus. No one here heals ills by recipe; the characters insist on their own diagnoses and issue their own prescriptions. In two people, Eggerson and Mrs. Guzzard, the physician type is residual, but their function is not to direct but to acquiesce and ratify. As initiator and sibyl they exhibit few pretensions. In fact, Mrs. Guzzard is a kind of fairy godmother who, after evaluating wishes, grants them if she can. As to levels of spiritual sensibility, Eliot's useful but factitious device persists, though with less than its former prominence. Mrs. Guzzard and Eggerson (the latter rather acute, as well as skilful in understanding the people he works for) are both earnest Christians. According to E. Martin Browne, director of this play as of all the previous ones, Eliot called Eggerson "the only *developed* Christian in the play."[2] But the statement is question-begging, unless it refers only to Eggerson's official connection with the Church of England. Of the characters who act out the conflict of choices, the protagonist Colby Simpkins, Sir Claude Mulhammer's new confidential clerk in succession to Eggerson, is of an alert artist type, beset with a spiritual hunger

228

similar to that of Celia Coplestone. Neither he, however, nor the minor characters, Lucasta Angel, B. Kaghan, and the baffled Lady Elizabeth Mulhammer, are other than ordinary men and women. Nobody in *The Confidential Clerk* is a genius; nobody is a saint. Even Colby has only second-rate talent; even the Christian Mrs. Guzzard and (so it seems) Eggerson himself are capable of compounding a lie. While certain of the characters co-operate to dramatize Eliot's regular themes—communication among the isolated, vocation, attainment of an ideal within the limits of actuality, freedom of choice subject to exigencies created by past time—they do so independently with a variety of attitudes. For this reason the play, apart from one tedious scene, succeeds in dramatizing its author's "struggle for harmony"—perhaps now pretty much fought to a finish—without the audience' sensing that he has somehow thrust himself onto the stage.

Having already written a pageant, a happy tragedy, a melodrama, and a comedy, Eliot made his *Confidential Clerk* a farce. It was originally produced for the sedate Edinburgh Festival in 1953, where it was instantly recognized to have serious motives. Although it uses the immemorial plot device of a mystery about a bastard's parentage, it makes this carry some weighty truths about the emotional life. Its principal source, which Eliot disclosed as the *Ion* of Euripides, contributed the germ of the story and, through A. W. Verrall's Euripidean criticism, the suggestion for an ambiguity which Eliot elaborated in his own way.

The setting is the London household of a middle-aged financier, Sir Claude Mulhammer, and his wife, Lady Elizabeth. The time is the end of winter. Act I opens with a colloquy between Sir Claude and Eggerson, his confidential clerk, just now retiring after more than thirty years' service. Before Eggerson settles down exclusively to gardening and church work at his home in rural Joshua Park, he has one more task to perform here: having already familiarized his successor, young Colby Simpkins, with the routine of being Sir Claude's secretary, he has been summoned to break to Lady Elizabeth the news of his retirement (speciously on grounds of health) and to prepare her for her first meeting with Colby. Since she is scheduled to arrive this same day from the Continent, he is to meet her plane and during the drive into London tell her enough about Colby—that he has been engaged for the position quite suddenly, and that he is "very musical"—to reconcile her to the change. What he is not to tell her, what Sir Claude is saving until her reaction to Colby becomes clear, is that the young man is Sir Claude's illegitimate son. The whole problem is the more delicate because, as she knows, Sir Claude has an illegitimate daughter, Lucasta Angel; whereas she herself, her marriage being barren, is without any child, her one son, also illegitimate, having disappeared without trace. The reason Sir Claude thinks she might be disturbed by the identity of Colby is not that the son's position is irregular but that he gives Sir Claude an unfair advantage! (She has "a strong maternal instinct.") Act I does not disclose Sir Claude's relation to Lucasta, who is a charming, whimsical, and deceptively shallow girl. Her fiancé, B. Kaghan, is a bumptious humorist with a golden future in City financial circles. B. Kaghan is to be revealed as Lady Elizabeth's long-lost child —but not till almost the end of the play.

Sir Claude's talk with Eggerson is interrupted by the entrance of Colby, presently followed by B. Kaghan and Lucasta. The dialogue is excellent, especially in the chaffing exchanges between Kaghan and the flippant Lucasta as against the punctilious dignity of Eggerson. It grows even livelier when, after the young couple depart, the inane Lady Elizabeth herself shows up ahead of schedule. She gabbles about theosophy and suchlike cults, to which she is addicted, and about which Sir Claude is a little confused. She toys with vegetarianism and numerology, flirts with doctrines of reincarnation, and judges strangers by their auras. Sir Claude is not uxorious, and poor Lady Elizabeth has had a wasted life, thwarted in her desire for children and, it appears later, in her pathetic wish to inspire an artist or a poet.

The exit of Lady Elizabeth and then of Eggerson leaves the scene to Colby Simpkins and Sir Claude. Now that Lady Elizabeth has looked Colby over, the arrangement seems satisfactory; she has even persuaded herself that it was she who interviewed and recommended him. The duologue of father and son touches a more profound note. Initiated by Sir Claude's observation that his wife ". . . has always lived in a world of make-believe," the talk takes form as Colby reveals what is to become the fundamental disagreement between himself and the older man.

> It doesn't seem quite honest.
> If we all have to live in a world of make-believe,
> Is that good for us?

In his youth, Sir Claude admits to Colby, he had no wish to imitate his own father by becoming a financier; rather, he had dreams of becoming an artist, a potter. And Colby himself at this very moment is thinking of his own disappointed ideal of becoming a musician, a great organist—an ideal he is relinquishing to become Sir Claude's confidential clerk.[3] The values perceived by each of these men in his own ideal are finely delineated by Sir Claude when he says of the potter's creations:

> To be among such things,
> If it is an escape, is escape into living,
> Escape from a sordid world to a pure one.

This is what he means when he speaks of going "through the private door / Into the real world, as I do, sometimes." But Sir Claude has not been able to live the virtually consecrated life of devotion to art; he has relegated "the real world" to a private room holding his collection of china and porcelain, things to which he may turn occasionally for

> . . . that sense of identification
> With the maker . . . an agonizing ecstasy
> Which makes life bearable.

For, stimulated by his doubt whether a man could be said "to have a vocation / To be a second-rate potter," he chose not art but business. And through this doubt he came to see that his own father, to whom business was a passion, had been right. By following his dead father's vocation he atoned to him for his former loathing of it. Lacking "the strength to impose . . . terms / Upon life," he obeyed realistically, or fatalistically, the need for accepting the terms it offered him. In the process he became, as Colby is becoming, a man adapted to facts. The substitute life, Sir Claude tells him,

> . . . begins as a kind of make-believe,
> And the make-believing makes it real.

But, it becomes obvious, the dream world of art into which Sir Claude sometimes withdraws is also make-believe, for although it is the world of his heart it is not the world of his hand. He lives "In two worlds—each a kind of make-believe." Thus, like Lady Elizabeth, he is the victim of "delusions." (Ironically, had he become an artist she might have settled down to inspiring him.) Colby's misgivings about imitating Sir Claude spring from his reluctance to be content with less than the wholly real and also from his feeling that he does not owe to

Sir Claude, always a little remote from him, the kind of emulation with which Sir Claude repaid his own father. Rebelling thus against make-believe, he is about to reject Sir Claude's fatalism along with his optimism that through acceptance of life's terms the make-believe can be "real."

Act II brings together Colby and Lucasta, clarifies the young man's own view of his vocational problem, and then complicates the plot by having Lady Elizabeth invent a hypothesis about his parentage. Lucasta, though more intuitive than she has seemed, is diffident and insecure. She has always resented being brought up poor, fatherless, under a cloud. She discloses to Colby (and to the audience) before she leaves that she is Sir Claude's daughter; hence, though she does not know it, she must be Colby's half-sister. For Colby's perplexity Lucasta thinks she has a cure—for him to retire often into the "secret garden," as she calls it, of his "inner world."

> . . . it's only the outer world that you've lost:
> You've still got your inner world—a world that's more
>     real.

In effect her advice is the same as Sir Claude's. On the other hand, Colby himself is not prepared to rest with a part-time (and actually a religious) consolation. He wants a "garden" as real as the literal one at Joshua Park, from which Eggerson fetches "marrows, or beetroot, or peas . . . for Mrs. Eggerson." To a man of Colby's sensibility, the only acceptable reality will integrate the ideal or spiritual with the actual or practical—not distinguish the garden from the vegetables.

Colby's isolated secret garden is moreover a lonely place; he longs "Not to be alone there."

> If I were religious, God would walk in my garden
> And that would make the world outside it real
> And acceptable, I think.

Mere joyous experiences of the aesthetic or spiritual are not enough: action must validate them, and more important is the sharing, whether with God or man. Colby tells Lucasta that the gate to his garden might possibly open to someone who entered spontaneously, without invitation. Yet such opening (as if into a "Burnt Norton" garden of lovers' realization) might admit also disappintment or loss. "It's not the hurting that one would mind," says Colby, "But the sense of desolation afterwards." And sharing requires understanding. Never has Eliot dealt so insistently with the problem of sympathy. Eggerson and Sir Claude, at the start of the play, talk about understanding their wives; Sir Claude and Lady Elizabeth, in Act III, deplore that they have taken too much for granted about each other; and Lady Elizabeth and B. Kaghan, in the final moments, speak of the need for understanding between the two generations of the family. And Colby and Lucasta, before she misunderstands his attitude toward her being a bastard, discuss the subject themselves. Colby asserts that "there's no end to understanding a person"; one has to keep up with the changes in him. Obviously, without understanding, one cannot even communicate from one's private world—unless perhaps with God.

After Lucasta's pettish disruption of their confidential mood, she leaves with B. Kaghan handily in attendance. Lady Elizabeth Mulhammer, appearing with some officious motherly advice, notices a framed photograph of Colby's aunt, Mrs. Guzzard, who brought him up in Teddington. Recalling that Guzzard was the name of the woman to whose care her dead lover Tony arranged to have her child intrusted, and that that Mrs. Guzzard also lived in Teddington, she concludes that Colby, being of about the right age, must be actually her own lost son. Sir Claude, however, when she tells him of her surmise, confesses the reason why her guess is wrong: Colby is the son of Mrs. Guzzard's sister—and of himself. Meanwhile poor Colby stands by, feeling at first, as he says, numb and indifferent, inclined to reject both of his would-be parents; next regretful that he never has had a father and mother, but unwilling to accept these on ambiguous terms (for then, he observes like James's Maisie Farange, he should have four instead of two); and finally eager to find out the truth, whatever it may be. To this end Sir Claude promises to summon Mrs. Guzzard as well as Eggerson, who "knows all about it." With compassionate words from Lady Elizabeth to Sir Claude, the scene ends. It has been a sparkling one from the entrance of Lady Elizabeth; its bouncing retorts and Jamesian "visions and revisions" far outdazzle the quasi-poetical *causerie* of its opening.

Act III is rapid throughout if not vivacious. Sir Claude and Lady Elizabeth begin it with an exploration of their feelings and decide that they have each abandoned a valid ideal in "obedience to the facts," though the facts amount to a misunderstanding. But then Eggerson arrives; and then Lucasta, to announce that she shall marry B. Kaghan and to learn that Colby is her half-brother; and then Colby, like a third jack-in-the-box, to be analyzed by Lucasta as either a "terribly cold" person or else one warmed by some extraordinary fire:

> You're either an egotist
> Or something so different from the rest of us
> That we can't judge you.

It may be, indeed, that Colby is of saintlike composition. Lucasta rejoices that she has found a brother and goes on her way. But in a moment she is back to announce the arrival of Mrs. Guzzard.

The first portion of Mrs. Guzzard's narrative is quite simple. Some years before, she, Sarah Guzzard, and her husband Herbert took charge of an infant left with them by an agent of one of the parents. When, later, money for the child's support was withheld, they were forced by poverty to put him out for adoption by the Kaghans, their neighbors. They had already conditionally baptized him Barnabas. In view of Lady Elizabeth's recollections about what her lover Tony did with the child, Mrs. Guzzard now believes that B. Kaghan, and certainly not Colby, must be Lady Elizabeth's son. (Lady Elizabeth, despite her uncertainty about the length of time elapsed—B. Kaghan being twenty-eight instead of twenty-five—accepts the account as probable; so does Kaghan himself.) The latter portion of Mrs. Guzzard's story is more complex. For as soon as Kaghan and Lady Elizabeth acknowledge each other, Mrs. Guzzard declares that she "should like to gratify everyone's wishes" and proceeds to ask Colby whether he had rather be the son of Sir Claude or "of some other man / Obscure and silent? A dead man. . . ." Colby, having just indicated his preference for a father never known to him but by report,

> An ordinary man
> Whose life I could in some way perpetuate
> By being the person he would have liked to be,

answers (somewhat ungratefully, one fears), "A dead obscure man." And Mrs. Guzzard immediately reveals that Colby is not Sir Claude's son but the legitimate son of herself and Herbert Guzzard, "a disappointed musician." She herself and her sister (that is, Sir Claude's mistress of many years before) were undergoing confinement at the same time; her own child was born, but owing to her sister's death the other child was not. When at length Sir Claude returned from abroad and came to inquire about his child, he supposed it to be the infant he saw. Mrs. Guzzard let him believe so: at the moment she hesitated to eclipse his evident pleasure, and afterward she decided, her husband being now dead and her poverty more severe, to prolong the fiction so that her son might be "assured of a proper start in life."

Thus the unexpected has come about. The antecedents of B. Kaghan and Colby have apparently been divulged, and the contest between Sir Claude and Lady Elizabeth for possession of Colby has been resolved with neither as the victor. This comedy of errors, however, has brought freedom to Colby. He need no longer consider himself indentured to Sir Claude's business; he can follow his own bent. Although Sir Claude would have him continue just as if their relationship had not altered, Colby chooses, as he has aspired, to claim a different inheritance. He has a chance to apply for the post of organist in the church at Joshua Park, where Eggerson is the Vicar's Warden, and to make spiritual capital out of sacred music. Eggerson predicts, in fact, that Colby will not stop in that capacity, that he will "be thinking of reading for orders":

> Joshua Park may be only a stepping-stone
> To a precentorship! And a canonry!

In the interim he may share the Eggersons' home and occupy their spare room—vacant, the audience will assume, ever since the wartime death of their son, "Lost in action, and his grave unknown." With this decision Colby becomes Eggerson's "son in spirit." Under the influence of Eggerson, who, as Eliot has commented, "cultivates his own garden, who is at peace with himself and his God,"[4] the young musician, though handicapped by admitted defects of ability, may go further yet; but whether he makes progress in his external tasks or not, he has already in his heart reached the point of destination. To him and to the others too, to Sir Claude and Lady Elizabeth, to Lucasta and B. Kaghan, Eggerson might stand as the example of entire serenity of life. Without exhorting, without coercing, but mildly and faithfully serving, he is at hand to shed the light of reasonableness whenever it is wanted. Of the characters, he alone has practiced regulating his life harmoniously through understanding. As the arbiter of common sense, he makes the final sign of assent to the choices of Colby and Lucasta, when, with a nod of his head in answer to Sir Claude's incredulous question, he affirms his belief in Mrs. Guzzard's story.

This play generates an atmosphere very different from that of its predecessors. One cause of the difference is that the plot is not dominated by the laws of guilt and atonement. The only person trying to atone for anything, namely Sir Claude, has done so in the wrong way; and he erred initially only through fatalism. Eliot's pattern wherein unhappiness brings conviction of a guilt to be expiated, and wherein surrender to the will of God through expiatory vocation brings the happiness of salvation, is not present here. *The Confidential Clerk* sets the problem how to be happy in the first place. It declares for the theory that if one seeks happiness through vocation one will be doing God's will. What one's vocation is, is not hard to discover: it is what-ever one ideally wants to do. It must, moreover, be an activity, and thus it is at once limited, defined, and fulfilled by one's relations with other people or with God. Only by self-knowledge can one elect it; and self-knowledge depends on communication with others and the under-standing of them. Without such understanding, the ideal may seem, as it did for Sir Claude, too high for attainment. But although one cannot irresponsibly accommodate the actual to the ideal, one can certainly, by comprehending the actual, extract the ideal potentially in it. The effort does not mean, as Sir Claude has unhappily supposed, submitting to the grudging terms that life seems to dictate. Quite otherwise: it means finding out what those terms really are and making certain with precisely how much of the ideal they are consonant.

And the terms of life may tolerate more of the ideal than one imagines. For actual circumstances can never confine one to but a single choice; they always permit, within inevitable bounds, the exer-tion of a creative act of will. This, and not a blindly determining past, shapes one's real future. Thus Colby Simpkins expresses his wish first and hears the secret of his parentage afterward; having the strength of will to demand his ideal, he finds an actuality amenable to it. Mrs. Guzzard merely helps him with a decision which he might make for himself: it is unimportant who his natural father is. He is, moreover, equally well off whether she is telling the truth or not (a question which, as will presently be seen, the play does not settle). Paradoxi-cally, he is enjoying a "make-believe," just as Sir Claude has tried to do. As Sir Claude piteously says,

> You want to believe it.
> Well, believe it then.

But Colby does not regard it as make-believe, and so differs from Sir Claude in being innocent of self-deception. And the rightness of his vocational choice can hardly be carped at. This play has one transpar-ently clear message: that a man must be not merely a financier but a good financier; and that to be so, he must invest his talent in the right company. If he believes that he should be about his father's business, he had better make sure who his father in spirit really is. And even if the calling to art and then to religion is intrinsically nobler than the calling to marriage or to the money market, every man's happiness lies in tilling his own field. The words of Candide sum it up: "We must cultivate our gardens."

Curbing the mystical overtones of Eliot's poetry, *The Confidential Clerk* is somewhat difficult to fit into his familiar death-and-rebirth scheme. It is not principally a play about death, but rather about life and its abundance. It reflects faintly the tension of affirmative and negative impulses as in mystical theology, inasmuch as it shows the young man rejecting the affection of human beings in favor of the life through which he may be closest to God. But if his rejection is negative in pattern, his turning toward his music is emphatically affirmative, even though he has chosen a life of service, not of mysticism through art. On the other hand, neither art nor religion contributed much more than the raw material for the play, which is about a search for vocation rather than the merits of various callings. From Eliot's own background came the alternatives of art and business: his father, a prosperous brick manufacturer, would have preferred that his son devote himself to something less visionary than poetry and criticism. The expatriate Eliot, in his turn, must often have wondered whether he fulfilled even his own artistic ambition in becoming a part-time poet, and whether he did not, after all, have a higher vocation to religion than he could satisfy as a committeeman and churchwarden. Eliot's irony must have been deliberate when he brought forth in *The Confidential Clerk* a world of self-deception, petty falsehood, and hypocrisy, in which, as always happens in the never-never land of farce, good sense and heart's desire somehow prevail.

Eliot's plot source in the *Ion* of Euripides leads to a more interesting explanation of his methods in *The Confidential Clerk* than other analogues might do. The story of the *Ion* is not in the Greek tradition of mystery drama, having apparently been made up by Euripides himself. It may be associated in general with the myth of the foundling hero, reared in ignorance of his exalted paternity. Euripides seems to have had in mind this type of myth, for he introduced Ion as the son of Apollo, in order, it is thought, to honor the Athenians, who traced their descent from Ion. A. W. Verrall had a contrary opinion both of

Euripides' real intent and of his motive; and although few scholars have yielded to Verrall's blandishments, his view is plausible.[5]

The *Ion* has a Prologue spoken by Hermes as the emissary of Apollo. According to this, the youth Ion, serving in the temple at Delphi, is the son of Apollo by the sun god's rape of Creusa, a woman of noble descent who has since become the wife of Xuthus. Upon the birth of her child, Creusa exposed him, but by order of Apollo, Hermes brought him to the shrine, where he was found by the priestess and preserved alive. The childless Creusa and Xuthus are now coming to implore the oracle's aid in acquiring children. Apollo wills that Ion be given to Xuthus as a natural son, designing to reveal the truth secretly to Creusa after the lad is taken into her house at Athens. Up to a point the god's purpose is obeyed. At the temple, as the action begins, Ion, singing a paean, purifies the entrance way with laurel boughs and menaces with his arrows the birds that would defile the sacred precincts. The chorus of handmaidens talks with Ion concerning the temple (which holds the renowned *omphalos*, the dome-shaped or egg-shaped suppliants' stone reputed to mark the center of the world); they are followed by Creusa. She explains her errand and hints at her dark secret. Later Xuthus appears, consults the oracle, and, acting on its message, hails Ion as his son. Ion, accepting the verdict of the oracle, at which he cannot demur even though preferring to remain in the god's service, accompanies Xuthus to a banquet of thanksgiving. But prematurely the chorus betrays this development to Creusa, who, shamed more than ever by the god's neglect, resolves at the instigation of an aged servant to murder Ion by poison. When the murder is thwarted, Creusa takes sanctuary upon the Delphic altar of sacrifice, where she is beset by Ion, sword of vengeance in hand. The prophetess herself now intervenes, taking from a hiding place a cradle with the tokens worn by the infant Ion when discovered. Creusa recognizes the cradle as that in which she left her own child and describes, before looking at them, the design woven in the infant clothes and the necklace of gold. Ion embraces her as his mother, whereupon she reveals to him that his father was Apollo. Ion, at this news, is about to ask the oracle which of its two pronouncements is true; but the *deus ex machina*, Athena, descends with confirmation of Creusa's story on the authority of Apollo himself. Ion, suppressing his doubt whether the god could have been guilty of double-dealing, believes because helpless to contradict.

Verrall's rationalistic interpretation of the play affected the plot of *The Confidential Clerk*. His main points may be summarized as follows: First, that Hermes and Athena cannot be trusted, because Euripides always depicted the gods as frauds. Second, that for the same reason Ion is not the son of Apollo. Third, that the tokens identified by Creusa do not constitute trustworthy evidence and that the recognition scene is stage-managed by the priestess to avert the impiety of a crime on the altar. Fourth, that although Creusa accepts the solution because it is what she wants, Ion is not her son. Fifth, that Ion is the son of Xuthus. Sixth, that the priestess knows this fact to be true because one of the temple women, perhaps herself, is Ion's mother. Euripides, in short, far from wishing to encourage the Ionians to boast that their eponymous ancestor was the offspring of a god, expected the wisest of his audience to see through the duplicities of the oracle and to be scornful of fanaticism. Unfortunately Verrall's arguments rest on unproved assumptions. The last two points are very weak. Granted that the oracle has lied once, it may just as easily have lied twice. And if Ion is not Creusa's son, there is no reason why he need be the son of Xuthus, even if he should be an illegitimate child of the priestess herself.

Now by substituting for Eliot's characters their counterparts in the *Ion*, one may see that Eliot's plot owes much to a critical reading of Verrall. Colby and Kaghan are Ion; Sir Claude, Xuthus; Lady Elizabeth, Creusa; Mrs. Guzzard, the priestess of the oracle; and Eggerson, both the aged servant and Apollo[6] (this latter role being divided, inasmuch as Kaghan is Ion, with Tony the poet). *The Confidential Clerk* pays tribute to Verrall's main argument, while ostensibly following, though with a second Ion, the conventional Euripides—everyman's Euripides. The play, having no prologue, begins with the report that "Colby-Ion" is the son of "Xuthus," who is childless in his marriage with "Creusa" (everyman's Euripides). "Creusa," wanting the son she has lost, tries on flimsy evidence to claim "Colby-Ion" for herself but fails to convince anyone (Verrall). Then the "priestess" unexpectedly awards "Kaghan-Ion" to "Creusa" (everyman's Euripides), but on no better evidence than that by which "Creusa" has laid claim to "Colby-Ion." The "priestess" next asks "Colby-Ion" whose son he wants to be; he answers, not the son of "Xuthus" (everyman's Euripides), but the son of some obscure man (Verrall criticized and improved by Eliot). Whereupon she says that he is her own son (Verrall); and he proceeds, as befits a lover of music, to behave like the son of "Apollo" (everyman's Euripides). The similarity is crucial between Verrall's and Eliot's substitution of the priestess for Creusa as the supposed mother of Ion. In calling "Colby-Ion" the son of a stranger, Eliot went one better than Verrall.

Eliot also arranged his drama so that it might be read by Verrall's methods. That is, he let the resolution depend on imperfect evidence and even on possible trickery by certain of the characters. When scrutinized, the questions of doubtful parentage permit answers far different from those believed by the leading personages and by the average audience. For example, Lady Elizabeth has had three reasons for thinking Colby her misplaced child: he looks vaguely familiar (an inconclusive fact), he is twenty-five years old (a corroborative fact, at best), and she remembers the name of Mrs. Guzzard of Teddington (a dubious fact, in view of her own absent-mindedness). And the audience readily discounts her supposition because Sir Claude denies it. Yet, prompted by Mrs. Guzzard, Lady Elizabeth believes that B. Kaghan is her son on only one of these grounds; for he seems not even slightly familiar, and he is of the wrong age. If the audience is to credit her identification along with her, it has to swallow her notion that she has heard of Mrs. Guzzard and ignore her inexplicable failure to remember how long ago the most important event of her life occurred. One suspects that B. Kaghan is not related to Lady Elizabeth at all. The case of Colby, though more intricate, gives rise to another suspicion. The "oracle," as in Euripides, has lied once. Mrs. Guzzard admits that she lied when, with a mercenary motive, she told Sir Claude that Colby was his son. Her facts in evidence seem impressive: registration of the birth of a son to herself and Herbert Guzzard and death registration for her sister, hitherto considered Colby's mother. But these do not necessarily compose evidence. Suppose that the Guzzards indeed had a child, what, beyond Mrs. Guzzard's word, is to prove that that child was Colby? And as to the death of Mrs. Guzzard's sister before her child could be born—the point is, when did she die? Sir Claude did not know that a child was expected; he was in Canada and received no message; he learned of his mistress' death only upon his return to England. Unless she died within a few months after his departure, the date of her death would not show whether her child could have been carried to term, still less whether it would have had a chance of life if born prematurely. Sir Claude does not know when it was conceived; hardly can he be expected to remember even when he went away on his voyage. The "evidence" would be consistent with the Guzzards' having had a child, and with the sister's having had a child; with the Guzzards' child's having died, and with the sister's child's having lived—and the living child, beyond cavil, is Colby. Eggerson's promise to examine the records himself does not insure that he shall find out anything important. He might, it is true, satisfy himself, if he wished, that there was no death registration for the Guzzards' son and no birth certificate for the "unborn" son of the sister. Yet, again, he might discover precisely these proofs contradicting Mrs. Guzzard. But he will not look; he believes, or affects to believe, her story.

On the other hand, if Mrs. Guzzard is truthful, her partial evidence is all she can adduce. She cannot be blamed for having so little. Nevertheless, at one time or the other, she has been a liar. And if she is truthful now, she has suddenly become eccentric. For a quarter of a century she has been committing a punishable crime for money, and just at the moment of greatest reward, for herself, her son, and the man she has been swindling, she throws away the whole game. And for what? for conscience? No: for the appeasement of Colby's whim that he had rather be the son of a dead man than of a living one!

In contrast with her admitted fraudulence, she behaves as if unaffectedly scrupulous. She is sensitive to even an imaginary suspicion of her bad faith until she proclaims it herself. To Lady Elizabeth's tactless but innocent insistence, "There is no doubt about it. / Colby is my son," she retorts, bridling:

> Your son, Lady Elizabeth?
> Are you suggesting that I kept a child of yours
> And deceived Sir Claude by pretending it was his?

She can hardly be stupid enough to raise such a question if the revelation of a real deceit, indeed almost this same deceit, is the thing she has most to fear. And she will not let the subject drop. When Lady Elizabeth reiterates, "Colby is my son," Mrs. Guzzard must allude to her dissatisfaction: "In the circumstances, I ignore that remark." A few minutes later she asserts her integrity again and, as if she had not said more than enough, comes back at length with truly a precisian's anxiety for her good name:

> I feared there might be a confusion in your mind
> Between the meaning of *confusion* and *imposture*.

Surely a woman who was insincere in this passage could not by any stretch of fancy blurt out a voluntary "confession" injurious to herself. And a woman who was sincere could have no confession to make, for she would never have perpetrated the wrong, or would have confessed it before, or, if hitherto afraid (as Mrs. Guzzard says she was), would at least explain that she had repented. But a sincere woman might have a motive to confess falsely.

That Mrs. Guzzard is sincere meets all the probabilities. A "Verrallian" inference is in order. Apparently she is a generous and good woman—even pietistic. She has never thought of deceiving Sir Claude until Colby's distress moves her to grant his wish to lead his own life in freedom. Colby is not her son; he is the son of Sir Claude and her sister. She herself had a child who died in infancy; probably he was a little older than Colby. When she lost him ("I had a child, and lost him. Not in the way / That Lady Elizabeth's child was lost"), she mothered the foster-child belonging to Sir Claude and found in him solace for the deaths of those close to her. Colby, having now gone to live in his father's house and to take up his father's work, seems unhappy. If he wants not to be Sir Claude's son, not to acquire wealth, but to go the way of the dead foster-father he never knew, the struggling musician whose poverty blighted his family's life, then Mrs. Guzzard will not hinder him. She does not agree with his choice; but what Colby desires is what he shall have. Spontaneously, therefore, she tells a brave lie, involving serious risk of detection. She performs her sacrifice. Perhaps she has sacrificed once before, when Sir Claude came to see his child and, instead of yielding to the temptation to keep Colby for herself, she told the truth which made her childless forever. (She talks of two sacrifices; they need not have been as she describes them.) Sir Claude does not believe her now, and he is right, though perhaps he does not fully understand her feelings. But Eggerson does. When he nods his head, in the gesture of final approval among gods and men, he confirms that Mrs. Guzzard's act is to receive no closer scrutiny and that Colby's search for reality, whether through make-believe or truth, is to meet no further obstacle.

The other, the more superficial, interpretation of the plot is nevertheless defensible, for in the theater it works. *The Confidential Clerk* has a true ambiguity. But the play does not harbor in this a hidden meaning. Whereas the *Ion* according to Verrall conceals a message at the heart of a devious labyrinth penetrated by a single right path,

Eliot's play sets forth its message on the far side of a labyrinth where one route is as safe as another. Eliot's labyrinth, the ambiguous explanation of Colby's parentage, can lead only to the moral validity of Colby's actual decision. *The Confidential Clerk*, as has already been noted, affirms freedom of choice. Whether the play uses a true or a false story to symbolize Colby's freedom from an imaginary obligation to Sir Claude's choice for him is immaterial; and the ambiguity of the plot itself signifies the same thing. Of course the play does not justify self-deception. But its closing scene suggests, like *The Family Reunion*, that a free approach to the meaning of one's life can redeem and remake the past. In such terms, make-believe is reality.

# V *1933–1948*

# 17 THE COMPLETE CONSORT:
"FOUR QUARTETS"

The publication, in 1932, of Part II of Eliot's unfinished *Coriolan* marks the end of his *Waste Land* period. His protracted visit to the United States, his change of domicile after returning
to London, and his engagement to write the book of words for *The
Rock*, which led in course to *Murder in the Cathedral* and to his subsequent career as a dramatist, date the start of his most distinguished
poetic activity. While in America in 1933, he wrote three short poems
called *Landscapes;* these were "New Hampshire," "Virginia," and
"Cape Ann." To them, in the year following, he added "Usk" and
"Rannoch, by Glencoe." As unpretentious as the five *Landscapes* are,
they reveal his deliverance (except for a few relapses in his plays)
from the guises of the hollow men. These are not merry poems, but
they speak with a new voice, no longer despairing or imploring but, at
its most serious, gravely meditating. "New Hampshire," somewhat
reminiscent in rhythm of juvenile "counting-out" formulas, makes an
adroit composite of children's voices and flickering birds, drawing
these together by alluding apparently to the Babes in the Wood. Guiding the speaker's self-reference ("Twenty years and the spring is over")
into the context of this allusion, it turns away from his dead self, which
he would have buried under leaves, to acclaim the exultation of
children among apple-tree boughs. Here, as in "Virginia," the pure
sound matters as much as the imagery. "Virginia" has tighter unity,
with a very faint irony for those who have read Marianne Moore's "No
Swan So Fine." The three remaining *Landscapes*, like these two, present brief vignettes. "Rannoch, by Glencoe," containing an allusion to
the massacre of the MacDonalds in 1692, underscored with a recollection of Ezekiel's valley of dry bones, and "Usk," embellished with a
quotation from Peele's *The Old Wives' Tale* not particularly appro-

priate to Monmouthshire, exhibit mild but exact symbolism. Each of
the three poems is uniform in tone except "Cape Ann," which concludes with a Pound-like flourish.

The emotional relaxation in these poems portended the philosophic
calm of *Four Quartets*. Equally, it can be seen to have indicated Eliot's
readiness for certain of the "musical" experiments in the coming mas-
terpiece. His poetry had long since discovered the vocal powers of
verse. "Portrait of a Lady," transferring through its rhythms a simple
comparison of the lady's voice to certain musical instruments into the
very perceptible whine of that voice itself, had experimented with the
music of speech cadences. Yet "music" in *Four Quartets* does not de-
note speech alone as such. It implies the sound and rhythm of spoken
words, but it also signifies the structure of interrelation among different
kinds of speech and other poetic materials. In *The Music of Poetry*
(1942) Eliot remarked, "There are possibilities for verse which bear
some analogy to the development of a theme by different groups of instruments; there are possibilities of transitions in a poem comparable to
the different movements of a symphony or a quartet; there are possibilities of contrapuntal arrangement of subject-matter."[1] As fantastical
as the first of his considerations may seem, it is valid. Although in
poetry the effect of the unison of instruments must be impossible[2]—
four layers of sound being necessary if the *Quartets* were to merit their
general title—still by "some analogy," as Eliot said, a range of effects
simulating unison may be achieved through various tonal levels or in-
tensities in the writing, extending from the prosaic to the metaphysi-
cally lyrical. Each of these levels demands perhaps a peculiar diction
and mood, a characteristic "speech." Thus the music of the *Quartets,*
as developed by "instruments," extends from the colloquial to the ora-
torical, and from the homiletical to the analytical. In it may be heard
the voices of personal reflection and discursive philosophy, the terms
of market place and inkhorn. To Eliot's own contention that, after
poetic idiom has been stabilized by a return to "speech," the time is
ripe for musical elaboration to begin,[3] one may add that such a ripen-
ing could happen only after a poet had escaped from a "speech" ex-
pressive of only a single emotional dilemma. Eliot's *Landscapes* certi-
fy his escape, if not, like the *Quartets,* his musical versatility.

Eliot's second consideration in the sentence quoted applies more
literally. Transitions between the "instrumental" passages of the *Quartets* and between whole movements are conspicuously musical. The first

movement of the quartet (that is, the first numbered section of his text), answering to the musical sonata form, is in three divisions: the two divisions at the beginning correspond to the exposition and development of the themes, the initial division being complemented or modified by the second; the third is a recapitulation. In "Burnt Norton" the first is attached to the second by a bridge passage, and the third is a brief *da capo*. In "East Coker" the second division has two parts, as in "The Dry Salvages," where the third division is wanting. The second movement, in two or more divisions, has first a lyric passage, stanzaic in the last two *Quartets*, and then a prosaic section exemplifying certain remarks in *The Music of Poetry* about shifts in intensity;[4] only in "Little Gidding" does this second division have traditional meter. The third movement, being philosophical, is more or less prosaic in contrast with the one preceding; it generally explores some theme already introduced. The fourth movement, a lyrical one, is stanzaic in each of the last three *Quartets*. It sums up and gives Christian formulation to the ideas already presented—its subject being, in the first *Quartet*, God the Father as the unmoved Mover; in the second, God the Son as Redeemer; in the third, the Virgin as Intercessor; and in the fourth, God the Holy Ghost as the voice and power of Love. A final movement contains the determination. These five movements might be distinguished as allegro, andante, minuet, scherzo, rondo, and the like, though few critics would agree as to what each was. Eliot's musical models for *Four Quartets* have not been finally isolated, but it is generally understood that he intended an analogy with Beethoven's late quartets, Op. 127–33, 135.[5] Stephen Spender, as early as 1935, had surmised that Part II of *Ash Wednesday* corresponded in structure to a movement in one of the Beethoven quartets.[6] Although it seems unlikely that Beethoven influenced *Ash Wednesday*, Spender's supposition may have influenced "Burnt Norton."

As to the third consideration introduced by Eliot, "contrapuntal arrangement of subject-matter," the *Quartets* display in abundance this quality, which is no less characteristic of poetry than of music itself. Ambivalence and ambiguity are the common linguistic heritage. The words of almost any poem reach beyond their context or bring in, from etymology and special usage, meanings to contradict or qualify their direct sense. Thus the central theme of *Four Quartets*, the union of the flux of time with the stillness of eternity (stemming from Eliot's earlier meditations on the disparity between the real and the ideal), in-

volves several philosophical meanings of "time." More important, the
supporting themes of history, poetry, love, and faith, for whose redemption the temporal seeks transfiguration in the eternal, interact to
create multileveled patterns of meaning. Such a counterpoint of themes
illustrates Eliot's method without the fourfold Dantean levels—the literal, the allegorical, the moral, and the anagogical—which some critics
detect.[7]

*Four Quartets* owe to literary allusion a type of counterpoint often
found in Eliot's work. Language is enriched by its traditional associations, not least with the verse of previous poets. Amusingly, Eliot's
*Five-Finger Exercises*, published in January, 1933, were exercises in
pure allusiveness and imitation; they give a clue to certain "music" in
the *Quartets*. (Some of the little poems salute a Yorkshire terrier, Cus-
cuscaraway, and a Persian cat, Mirza Murad Ali Beg, whose name had
been borrowed from Kipling's "To Be Filed for Reference.") Poetry
echoed in the *Exercises* includes, in the first piece, an anonymous sixteenth-century lyric, "When will the fountain of my tears be dry?"; in
the second (which recalls El Greco's stormy "Toledo"), the dirge in
*Cymbeline*, Eugene Field's "The Duel," Herrick's "Another Grace for
a Child," and (perhaps unintentionally) Du Bellay's "Épitaphe d'un
petit chien"; in the third, Tennyson's "The splendor falls," from *The
Princess*, and his line about "eft and snake" in *The Holy Grail*, Yeats's
"Host of the Air," section 4 of Baudelaire's "Le Voyage," Shakespeare's "The Phoenix and the Turtle," and Marvell's "To His Coy
Mistress"; in the fourth, Poe's "The Raven," Keats's "Ode on Melan-
choly," and, perhaps, Ralph Hodgson's "The Birdcatcher"; in the fifth,
Edward Lear's "How pleasant to know Mr. Lear." In themselves the
*Exercises* are unimportant except as specimens of the counterpoint
method.

The *Quartets*, as much by the symbols that they share as by structural and thematic homology, form a closely connected series. The
symbolism of the four seasons and of the elemental quaternion, earth,
water, air, and fire, maintains the subject of cyclical change in time,
against which Eliot posed the idea of a stable eternity.[8] Other symbolic details bring to mind the death-and-rebirth initiation pattern of
*The Waste Land*.[9] Here once more are the garden, the wounded god,
the river and the sea, death by water, fishermen, a meeting with a
ghost, blindness, the secluded chapel, the "broken king," and purgation by fire.

Each of the *Quartets* took its name from a place having for Eliot some personal or family association: Burnt Norton is a country house at Ebrington in Gloucestershire,[10] near the market town of Chipping Camden where he had stayed as a visitor in the summer of 1934; East Coker is a village in southeast Somersetshire from which the Eliot family emigrated to America; the Dry Salvages, as the note to the poem states, are "a small group of rocks, with a beacon, off the N.E. coast of Cape Ann, Massachusetts," remembered by Eliot from summer holidays in his childhood; Little Gidding, in Huntingdonshire, visited by Eliot in the spring of 1936, was the seat of an Anglican religious community established in 1625 by Nicholas Ferrar, three times visited by King Charles, and subsequently desecrated by the Roundheads. The bearing of the *Quartets* on Eliot's personal career and beliefs is sufficiently evident from their content. An indication that Eliot thought of making this fact even more obvious is that for a while he planned to use the title "The South Kensington Quartets," taken from his own place of residence. But the series began as an accident: "Burnt Norton" (1935) grew out of fragments discarded from a draft of *Murder in the Cathedral;* only in writing "East Coker" did Eliot envision the set of four.[11]

## I. *"Burnt Norton"*

Eliot's two epigraphs from Diels's edition of Heraclitus properly belong only to "Burnt Norton"[12] but would be suitable to the whole series. The first, according to Raymond Preston, attracted Eliot because of its *"poetic suggestiveness."*[13] The following paraphrases may give an idea of its breadth:

Though the law of things is universal in scope, the average man makes up the rules for himself.

Though the Word governs everything, most people trust in their own wisdom.

By applying a metaphor which Aristotle, rather than Heraclitus, would have used, one may bring the apophthegm into harmony with Eliot's most characteristic symbol:

Although there is but one Center, most men live in centers of their own.

Indeed this, though the least literal rendering, may be the best for comparison. As Elizabeth Drew has remarked in speaking of the second epigraph, Heraclitus has no concept of a "still point" at which the flux is resolved into "neither arrest nor movement."[14] Yet such a point is indispensable to the *Quartets*. The second epigraph ("The way up and the way down are one and the same") is closely related to the first. In Heraclitus it refers supposedly to the transmutation of the elements, the cycle of earth, water, air, and fire, for which later philosophers cited Heraclitus as an authority.[15] Heraclitus calls the flux "war" or "strife." The way up is from earth to fire, the way down from fire to earth; the cycle proceeds everlastingly. And since for Heraclitus the primary substance is fire, fire motivates the cycle. Indeed, in an extended sense, the cycle itself is fire. This is what Heraclitus sometimes means by his *lógos*—an equivalence, practically speaking, with the flux itself. It remained for Aristotle to introduce an idea of form and matter which placed the source of movement outside the flux—in the unmoved mover. What Eliot did in the *Quartets* was to invoke the *lógos* of Heraclitus as if it were this mover, in his own imagery, the center, round which the wheel of flux revolves forever but which "gathers" the movement into stillness. Since the flux comprehends the changes of matter and the apparent succession of time as well as the laws controlling them, the first epigraph can be deemed to relate as much to an empirically psychological point of view as to an ethical one. We each think that time passes, but in the *lógos* it is eternal. We each think that the past endures in our memory, but in the *lógos* it endures in immediate actuality.

As has been seen, Eliot in his poetry up to and including *Coriolan* was repeatedly troubled by the same "finite center" which he explored for the rationale of his poetic technique. The closed self—which, according to Bradley, is never much more than a vehicle for impressions—gave no communication with the Word. At the personal center the traces of the outside world were compacted as a duration of the horrible past. The only way of morally redeeming the past, as *The Waste Land* and *Ash Wednesday* demonstrated, was to be patient, to endure what endures. In reconsidered memories the past might acquire new meaning, the dream might become a vision. There was also a way of artistically redeeming the past: one function of art is to objectify the artist's triumph over time as he imaginatively captures memory for actuality again by giving it imperishable form. If, by the analogy which Pope develops in *The Dunciad*, the creative word of the poet shares with the all-fathering Word of the universe the glory of bringing order out of chaos, the poetic act also may be morally constructive, not alone because it is sometimes didactic, but because it proclaims the poet's victory over the darkness of death within him. In Eliot's poetic, efforts to find the word and the Word often appear identical: a poem is the concrete reward of that patience whose spiritual reward is indwelling harmony. A poem also is peace, for it, too, endows the deformed acts of the past with transfigured meaning. The maker of a poem is his own *lógos*.

The year 1934, when *The Rock* was published, seems to have been revolutionary in Eliot's thought. The Rock himself, although ostensibly an all-inclusive human consciousness, is conceived there as a super-human allegorical type. The pageant, instead of depicting events as if they were duration in the single memory, introduces an idea of time as real simultaneity. The past is preserved no longer only as memories of what has vanished, to be recovered artistically, as in the pattern of *The Waste Land*, but as an objective, eternal fact present to the mind of God. In *The Rock* Eliot did not try to exhaust this idea—long a traditional one, toward which St. Augustine had groped in Book XI of his *Confessions*[16]—but he tried to do so in "Burnt Norton." Obviously, the idea confronts one with a disturbing problem: whatever the moral or artistic redemption possible for memory, what redemption is possible for simultaneous time? None, one might answer in despair: whatever has happened, though it may change in meaning through the revaluations of the future, can never change in fact. If all times are simultaneous, then all human acts, all calamities, all miseries, tortures, death agonies, are simultaneous too. A moment in which nothing should be possible but the eternally actual could be only hell.

In the *Quartets* Eliot outlines tentatively, through poetic meditations, a concept of actual redemption for this hell of simultaneous events. The concept, as in *The Rock*, envisions the eternal presence of God, through the Incarnation, in every moment and postulates for man a liberating communion with God through meditation, action, or suffering. "Burnt Norton" concerns not so much the actuality of the past, tolerable or intolerable, as the lost potentiality never fulfilled— a problem, one recalls, that troubled Stephen Dedalus in the second episode of *Ulysses*. In simultaneity such an event could not become actual, and in *durée* it could have only phantasmal reality. But in eternity, the simultaneous as God dwells in it, an elusive good is fulfilled, "Burnt Norton" seems to be saying, not in its own potential form but in God. Not that God is its peculiar form, but that God is the pure actuality, the meaning (*lógos*), in whom all possible good has being. For "the still point," symbolizing God as the first mover, connotes simultaneity also, so that it really stands for the eternal oneness of the temporal and the eternal in a marvelous reformation of potentiality and form.

The exploratory first lines of "Burnt Norton" assert that all time may be simultaneous. If it is, then "All time is unredeemable," irremediable: this is the superficial view. Eliot proceeds, however, to what may be the "grace" redeeming simultaneity. "What might have been," according to the usual notion of time as succession, should by definition be impossible, for its moment of possible fulfilment is gone. In the dialectic of Aristotle and the Schoolmen, the potential (*dýnamis*) can achieve its perfect actuality (*entelécheia*) only by movement (*kínesis*) occurring in time, which to Aristotle is the measure of movement.[17] And it can achieve this only at the right moment (*kairós*). Here, on the other hand, since the moment of possible fulfilment is still present, "What might have been" remains perpetually possible.[18] Although in the absence of movement it continues to miss actualization, nevertheless, it does not vanish. It endures, qua potentiality (and "only" so, it is true), in some "world of speculation": simultaneity keeps it from being impossible in a speculative sense.[19] The "world of speculation" is "a wilderness of mirrors" where not only the memory of the possibility coincides with actual events but the eternal present coincides with imaginary events. (The world is also that of poetry, in which by the present poem the possible is actualized with an entelechy of the meaning that the experience might have had.)

> What might have been and what has been
> Point to one end, which is always present.

If the eternal present keeps the possibility, and the possibility "points" to an end (*télos*) which is, of course, actual, then this end in some way fulfils it. It may be that the possibility was never meant to become actual, and that its simply potential state is the fulfilment; or it may be that the end is something greater than the actuality which those who hoped for the experience could have foreseen. Eliot said in "Little Gidding":

> Either you had no purpose
> Or the purpose is beyond the end you figured
> And is altered in fulfilment.

The fact that "What might have been" points to an eternally present end recalls the imagery of the center; hence it suggests also that the end is not merely the present moment in which all times fall together but that eternal point, "the pure actuality," as Aristotle calls it, of God. With this contrapuntal meaning the reader is led, in the fifth movement, to contemplate the fact that since the experience never actual—the moment in the rose garden—was desired, and since desire, in Aristotle's definition, is movement caused by an unmoved mover, which in the Christian concept is ultimately God viewed only as Love, it follows that, being good, the thing which did not happen is eternally actual in a pure form (*eîdos*)—in Him. Time is unredeemable because it is redeemed already.

But, writing in time, a poet has to write from the point of view of a man possessing memory and having to regard what did not happen as an unreal phantasma. The lines beginning "Footfalls echo in the memory" are addressed apparently to someone with whom the experience might have occurred. They parallel in rhetoric lines 9 and 10 of this movement: "Footfalls" are "What might have been"; these echo in memory as if in the passage leading to the garden, the end eternally present.[20] The rose garden is a symbol of the moment drawing all times together and of the moment eternally here out of time, that is, the moment immediate to God. And the sentence following establishes a parallel between "words" and "footfalls" and between "mind" and "memory . . . passage . . . door . . . rose-garden":

> My words echo
> Thus, in your mind.

His words are but shadows of "What might have been," though they are now also "what has been"; and, since "echo in the memory" is equivalent to the verb "point," "your mind" is a conductor into the garden: it is even a type of the garden itself, holding by memory all the moments of the possible and the actual. The transitional lines, "But to what purpose / Disturbing the dust on a bowl of rose-leaves," retreat to a naïve reality of life in time; the garden seems but a potpourri of memories. As Shelley wrote,

> Rose leaves, when the rose is dead,
> Are heaped for the belovèd's bed;
> And so thy thoughts, when thou art gone,
> Love itself shall slumber on.

But besides the poet's words conceptually retrieving the meaning that the garden might have had actually, there are echoes in the garden itself—in the present garden of Burnt Norton, where the speaker and his companion are figured as about to go.[21] Those also are echoes of "What might have been." The pathos is deepened through allusion to Kipling's "They," a story of ghostly dream-children. Some commentators, assuming that Eliot imitated Kipling here, have regarded "them," whom the bird bids the visitors find, as either the children who might have been born of these people's love or as the visitors' own past selves. Children analogous to those in Kipling are mentioned a little later as hidden among the leaves; but it is doubtful whether these children are the same as "they," who are poised and adult-like:

> . . . dignified, invisible,
> Moving without pressure, over the dead leaves,
> In the autumn heat. . . .

"They" moved "in a formal pattern." (The shift to past tense suits the past potentiality.) It is true, the present visitors have here heeded the call of the thrush into their own "first world"; but the spectral "they" are like the man and woman in Milton's Eden, walking "Godlike erect." Turning at a "jolly corner," the interlopers have thus entered "a world of speculation," inhabited not only by dream-children "containing," suppressing, a giggling fit but apparently by the ghosts of their own selves as they might have been together there. Through what *The Family Reunion* calls a "loop in time," the bird has merged the potential in the actual. There in the garden was the music unheard now; there was the recognition of love—by "the unseen eyebeam" as in Donne's "Extasie" (with an ironical recollection of the scriptural beam in the hypocrite's eye)—in a world where roses, regarded and regarding (as in *Through the Looking-Glass*), symbolized the visitors' human gaze of love. Moving formally toward the mystic center, through maze-like box hedges, the intruders have next followed to the edge of a pool, "now" drained but instantaneously "filled with water out of sunlight."[22] In this, the innermost point of focus for past, present, and future, was revealed the vision of the rising "lotos."[23] And briefly "they were behind us, reflected in the pool"—the potential selves, mirrored in the vision as in eternity, behind the selves of the present. "Then a cloud passed, and the pool was empty." And all was present reality again. The children have remained concealed; the bird has commanded "Go." The reality that human kind cannot bear is both a vision and a loss. Since it constitutes the "one end which is always present," reality is but the actual. This fact, however, consoles no less than it disheartens: after all, "What might have been and what has been" is linked, and not only with chiasmus, to "Time past and time future." Through vision and poetry, "What might have been" has become "what has been."

In the lyric strophe at the beginning of the second movement, the first two lines, canceled from the manuscript of Eliot's "Lines for an Old Man" (1934), echo Mallarmé, to whom that poem refers. In Mallarmé's "M'introduire dans ton histoire" occurs the line "Tonnerre et rubis aux moyeux"; his "Le Tombeau de Charles Baudelaire" contains the phrase "boue et rubis." Putting them together and changing "thunder" to "garlic" and "rubies" to "sapphires," and substituting "mud" for "hubs," Eliot contrived an intricate "symbolistic" effect of his own. The axletree as Eliot had previously used it came from Chapman's *Bussy D'Ambois*; here, a few lines later, he echoed Chapman's translation of the second "Penitential Psalm" of Petrarch: "Raze, lord, my sins' inveterate scars," and "hell's horrid Boar."[24] The association of the axletree with garlic may perhaps have originated in his memory of Hotspur's rantings:

> I had rather hear a brazen canstick turn'd,
> Or a dry wheel grate on the axle-tree . . .
>
> I had rather live
> With cheese and garlic in a windmill, far. . . .[25]

When Eliot wrote "East Coker" he set a complementary passage in the second movement of that poem; "Thunder rolled by the rolling stars / Simulates triumphal cars" juxtaposes Mallarmé's "tonnerre" to the "chars" from "M'introduire."

The meaning of the two lines "Garlic and sapphires in the mud / Clot the bedded axle-tree" is difficult partly because of the reader's inability to get any sharp visual impression; if he imagines a carriage wheel mired surrealistically, he has done more than the images require. "Garlic" and "sapphires" recall the mortal sins of gluttony and avarice; "mud," filth—or flesh, the dust of the ground; "clot," blood; "bedded," embedded and put to bed; "axle-tree," the center of the wheel—hence the still point, the tree of the cross. Elizabeth Drew's conjecture that " 'bedded' and 'tree' unite manger and cross" is an excellent one; the second line draws together the Atonement, the Incarnation, and the Passion.[26] By contrast, the first line cites human interferences with the smooth turning of the wheel; they "clot" the redemptive blood.[27] There is a level also on which the cluster of images in line 2 might have a sexual connotation; this would be congruous with the double value of "blood" in the line following. The implication that opposing values need to be reconciled agrees with the remainder of the rhyming division, which points to its final line: "reconciled among the stars"—a return perhaps to the contrary overtones of "sapphire," the star gem. "The trilling wire" is the bird cry of life, whether in man's blood or in that of Christ, which, "Appeasing long forgotten wars," joyfully sings below the "inveterate scars" of sin or the wounds of the Redeemer. The movement of the blood and lymph, like the angels' "Mystical dance" in *Paradise Lost*,[28] corresponds to "the drift of stars," to the life rising in the tree, to the quanta of light playing upon "the figured leaf" (an echo of the childhood symbolism of the first movement), and even to the immemorial hunt of the boarhound and boar "below" and "among the stars," where they are reconciled in constellation. The flux of movement, of the turning wheel in its every aspect, becomes stillness. In Tennyson's phrases:

> So that still garden of the souls
> In many a figured leaf enrolls
> The total world since life began.[29]

In tone the passage in Eliot suits perfectly its abstraction of movement from the earlier blend of motion and quiet stillness. Here words and things are incessantly active, directing the reader's attention alternately downward and upward, from scars to wars, wars to dance, dance to circulation, circulation to drift of stars, stars to tree to leaf to floor, and then to stars again.

The music pauses as it reaches "the still point of the turning world." In a calmer, more peaceful passage, the antithesis, stillness, is contemplated as the point where the dance is "neither arrest nor movement."[30] The third strophe describes communion with this point; in other words, it elaborates the eternal state of consciousness presaged, indeed almost dramatized, as the vision in the rose garden. This is a condition of "freedom from the practical desire," from "movement" in an Aristotelian sense; it marks an approach to eternity not as through the intimation in the garden, which has revealed the timeless as an awakening in time, but as through mystical illumination. The other vision was poetic; this is saintlike, a "release from action and suffering," from time and the wheel; "from the inner / And the outer compulsion," from memory and desire. It bestows nevertheless "a grace of sense," of full corporeal awareness, as of the "white light" to the eyes. It is an *Erhebung*, or exaltation, which is pure entelechy, not motion; a concentration, with the full mysterious richness of the word, in which all knowledge is present.[31] All "partial ecstasy," as in the garden, is complete; all "partial horror," as in whatever suffering rules on the wheel, is resolved. Gradually the strophe leads the reader back from the distilled intensity of this illuminative condition to the state in which man, protected from the "heaven and damnation" coexistent in eternity, can make trial of reaching, as the poet has done in the first movement, toward such flashes as "the moment in the rose-garden," with its hint of mere potentiality invested with the meaning of actuality—of desire acquiring the final entelechy of love. This movement has affirmed with greater clarity than the first movement, because it has segregated the members of the dichotomy for contrast, the eternal unity of change and stillness. By the one state man may come to that which, within time, reflects the other. Memory, which is consciousness not transcending time, allows the mind, though "involved with past and future," to apprehend the simultaneous point corresponding to the eternal. The initial pessimism of the opening movement has given way here to a triumphant coda: "Only through time time is conquered."

Throughout the third movement appear further variations on the pattern of movement, concerning two kinds of life in time. The lines parallel first the initial strophe of the second movement with a consideration of human life as a sordid bondage to time, and then its final strophe with a description of negative descent as movement, and yet non-movement, into darkness, the paradoxical equivalent to motionless *Erhebung* into the "white light still and moving." Thus the beginning of the third movement shows

> a place of disaffection
> Time before and time after
> In a dim light. . . .

By "disaffection" one should understand partly the "indifference" of "Little Gidding," Part III. It is this indifference which brutalizes and stultifies the average human being; for it is neither attachment to the beauty disclosed by daylight, the transitory visions possible in a world of "rotation," the world of the wheel, nor detachment in the purgatorial darkness which cleanses affection by movement. The one would be "plenitude," which, besides implying "concentration without elimi-

nation," has (in Lovejoy's use)[32] the technical meaning of God's mani-
festing all potentiality; the other would be "vacancy," the condition
of the negative mystic which is analogous to definitions of God arrived
at by remotion. The world of hollow men is depicted in imagery that,
as Helen L. Gardner has observed, recalls the London tube, its "dim
light" and "flicker."[33] "Tumid" correlates with "sensual," and "apathy" with "disaffection." Eliot's abrupt bathos conveys the degradation of the merely normal:

> Men and bits of paper, whirled by the cold wind
> That blows before and after time.

And then the outdoor scene into which the "unhealthy souls" drift like
bats from the underworld:

> Not here
> Not here the darkness, in this twittering world.

This image parallels the description of the suitors' squeaking ghosts
in *Odyssey* xxiv.

From the negative mystics, in particular St. John of the Cross, Eliot
drew his figure of spiritual descent into the Dark Night "of perpetual
solitude."[34] This is a "World not world," for all property is gone from
it; the three psychological faculties of sense, fancy, and spirit (analogous to the Aristotelian ones), the same as those alluded to at the
end of "The Hollow Men" and at the beginning of *Ash Wednesday* and
cognates to Eliot's themes of love, poetry, and redemption, are numbed
in absolute withdrawal. Eliot seems to have had in mind here both the
active and passive Dark Night of sense and spirit, the latter being the
advanced submissive stage of the negative way. The passive Night,
because it is an involuntary purgation, is as much non-movement as
movement, even though it results from choice. Both aspects of the
Dark Night constitute "the one way," like the illuminative experience
of *Erhebung*, which "Is the same, not in movement / But abstention
from movement. . . ." Both contrast with the "world" which "moves /
In appetency," in time; appetency (Aristotle's *órexis*) involves both
concupiscence and mere appetite; it is motivation of movement. As
Raymond Preston has shown, the identity of the two ways toward the
stillness is explained by St. John's account of the "ladder of contemplation"—Eliot's "figure of the ten stairs": in the saint's words,
". . . upon this road to go down is to go up, and to go up, to go
down. . . ."[35] The verbal similarity to the second epigraph from Hera-

clitus reminds one that the way up is a way to the divine fire, but that the way down is no different, and that the flux of time and nature obeys the same law of return, of peace by strife, as the human soul: both have, as Aristotle would say, the same mover.

So far "Burnt Norton" has dealt with three stages in the mystical sequence: awakening, illumination, and aridity ("desiccation") in darkness. They all belong to the same progress; in the complete mystical life they are not alternatives but a continuous development.

As the dingy futility of the underground "metalled ways / Of time past and time future" opposes a temporal horror to the timeless ecstasy of the moment in the garden, so the mystical darkness points to "release from action and suffering" and to the "white light still and moving." The fourth movement of the poem symbolizes both this opposition (or, rather, apparent opposition) and this advance toward identity, as well as man's fall and redemption and, more obscurely, the poet's quest for the poetic word. The "day," the vision in sunlight as in the first movement, has become overcast by the "black cloud" of time and change; this, however, on the mystical level, is also what Eliot was later to call, in "East Coker," "the darkness of God." So, too, the "day" and "our first world" are Christ, and the "black cloud" is death. Or the contrast may lie between the poetic tradition and the present "wrestle / With words and meanings." (The last theme hardly appears except as weak counterpoint, though it is reinforced structurally by Eliot's having echoed in his first two lines an anonymous fifteenth or sixteenth-century lyric,

> The maidens came
> When I was in my mother's bower:
> I had all that I would.
> The bailey beareth the bell away:
> The lily, the rose, the rose I lay.[36]

The latent antithesis of the old poetry and the modern works out into a self-criticism of the poem by the poem, as is repeatedly true in the *Quartets*.) Before invoking the stillness which restores the vanished light, the poem weighs the hope of life against the terror of death. It asks whether the sunflower and the clematis (flowers associated with the Son and the Virgin) will "turn to us"—meaning rebirth; whether "Chill / Fingers of yew" will "be curled / Down on us"—meaning death.[37] Yet, as in the first movement, a bird, this time the kingfisher, seems to typify hope for communication with the vital center,[38] the vanished sun, which presently is to be introduced again as "the still point." Presumably the kingfisher is a type of Christ, but it is just as much a type of the poet; thus the Fisher King in *The Waste Land* symbolizes the "broken wings" of poetry. Here, the elusiveness of the moment that "might have been," the fading of the illuminative joy, the departure of the Savior into the weariness of time, and the failure of the poetic gift are all redeemed at "the still point" of perfection.[39]

If one has carefully threaded Eliot's maze of themes thus far in "Burnt Norton," the essential design has revealed itself as a dualism of movement and stillness, time and timelessness, potentiality and actuality, resolved partly by philosophy and partly by sheer paradox into an eternal center of union. The poem settles by means of a Christian application of Aristotle the inveterate conflict between the real and the ideal; it shows that finally there is no conflict at all. In the first movement the poet's "words," echoing in the mind of his listener, have retrieved the unfulfilled possibility of their "first world." In the last movement he meditates the relation of change and stillness to words themselves.[40] Words and music move "in time" (rhythmically); as Aristotle shows, all motion occurs "Only in time." But these are not "only living"; they do not exist in time alone but in "the silence," and as poetry, for example, or musical composition, they survive change (*kínesis*) by achieving an entelechy. This is the form (*eîdos*) or pattern (*parádeigma*) called by Aristotle the formal cause of movement.[41]

> Only by the form, the pattern,
> Can words or music reach
> The stillness, as a Chinese jar still
> Moves perpetually in its stillness.

In form as poetry, words immortalize meaning. The comparison cites "a Chinese jar," recalling Keats's Grecian urn—the static perfection acting as an unmoved mover upon the beholder and, as a modern physicist might say, existing as an entity only because it has molecular motion. Another comparison cites "the stillness of the violin, while the note lasts"; but this is inadequate, for an achieved artistic form is not only prolonged but timeless. As a form, a poem or music continues to exist, but also it has always existed and always will exist, both by "the co-existence" of time eternally present and by the eternal status, out of time, of the unmoved actuality that the form mirrors.

> Or say that the end precedes the beginning,
> And the end and the beginning were always there

THE COMPLETE CONSORT: "FOUR QUARTETS" 263

The final cause precedes the efficient cause just as the completion of a poem, because it moves the beginning, precedes that;[42] and both are simultaneous. So God as final cause, the Omega, is the Alpha or first cause. Thus to Eliot the theme of poetry itself "reaches / Into the silence" to become contemplation of God. The poet, returning to the world of movement, to the writing of these lines, comments next on the task of molding the flux into patterns and on the voices enforcing the changes that words continually undergo. With a sudden sweep of meaning upward from poetry to the eternal, "word" becomes "Word." Christ too was assailed "by voices of temptation," but the Word that was in the beginning is the Logos, the complete meaning, the pure actuality, unyielding to change. The Word is the perfection moving the poem and the poet, too, in his own empty desert. "The crying shadow in the funeral dance" and "The loud lament of the disconsolate chimera," as in St. Anthony's wilderness of temptation,[43] embody the unreason against which the poet struggles.

In a terminal strophe "Burnt Norton" reconsiders the mystery of love. The "pattern," time and its happenings, is like St. John's "figure of the ten stairs"—in detail a movement, in fulfilment a stillness.[44] Now movement toward an end is caused by that end and is called desire (*órexis, epithymía*).[45] But in contrast,

> Love is itself unmoving,
> Only the cause and end of movement.

The object as such a cause (*aitía kaì arché*) and end (*télos*), if timeless, is God, for (though not to Aristotle) God is Love; if in time, it may be incarnate in a human, intermediate mover,

> Caught in the form of limitation
> Between un-being and being,

and subject also to desire. The temporal has both actuality and potentiality; its "form of limitation" seems to be Aristotle's *sterêsis*, or "incompleteness." Its purest form, pure actuality, is the Incarnation.

Love in its highest form, the Incarnation, realizes all potentialities, and Love is the meaning of "What might have been." Since actuality is prior to potentiality, since God is prior to all that moves toward Him, the failure of a particular and only hypothetical potentiality to achieve its own actual form does not nullify its meaning. The true meaning is perpetual at the still point. And so the poem can end with its own beginning, with the shaft of eternal sunlight permanent and unaffected by the restless dust and with

> the hidden laughter
> Of children in the foliage
> Quick now, here, now, always—

forever alive, forever "still and still moving," laughter of triumph over

> the waste sad time
> Stretching before and after.

## II. *"East Coker"*

In August, 1937, Eliot visited the village of East Coker and took half-a-dozen photographs of scenes in the neighborhood. In 1940 he completed and sent to press his poem "East Coker." As he explained in a letter to H. W. Häusermann in May, 1940, "The title is taken from a village in Somerset where my family lived for some two centuries. The first section contains some phrases in Tudor English taken from 'The Governour' of Sir Thomas Elyot who was a grandson of Simon Elyot or Eliot of that village. The third section contains several lines adapted from 'The Ascent of Mount Carmel.' I think that the imagery of the first section (though taken from the village itself) may have been influenced by recollections of 'Germelshausen' [by Friedrich Gerstärker], which I have not read for many years. I don't think the poem needs or can give rise to further explanation than that."[46] Oddly, the poem needs much less explanation than many other pieces by Eliot; hence it has received more than its share. But in the framework of the *Quartets* its position is too important for it to be slighted. Here the themes of "Burnt Norton" have undergone a regrouping, so that the theme least important in the first *Quartet*, man's relation to history, is thrown into sharp relief. "East Coker" stresses time, not eternity; the way down, not the way up. Thus, although the opening and closing phrases, "In my beginning is my end" and "In my end is my beginning," recall, as they were meant to do, "the end and the beginning were always there," they scarcely imply either that the past and future are simultaneous or that eternity transcends all times. What they mean is that every moment is an end and a beginning (the view of Heraclitus) and that, on the one hand, the beginning points to the end ahead (Aristotelian finalism) and, on the other hand, the end contains the beginning from which it has come (Bergsonian duration). They express also an undeveloped hint of determinism.[47]

The key image is "succession," a cycle of building and decay, of growth and corruption. The specific symbols in the first strophe of the initial movement concern no particular place or time. They attest to the universal fact that "Houses rise and fall,"

> Old stone to new building, old timber to new fires,
> Old fires to ashes, and ashes to the earth
> Which is already flesh, fur and faeces,
> Bone of man and beast, cornstalk and leaf.[48]

Succession or flux means that nothing endures in time: everything flows.[49] As in the phrase of Sir Henry, in *The Cocktail Party*, "We die to each other daily." Echoing Ecclesiastes, chapter 3, Eliot through his image of the deserted house contrived to suggest the continuous decay of the human body. But the gloom of death is communicated here through the absence of the expressly human; the symbols connote the omnipresent, not the special, rapacity of time. And this house is any house and all houses abandoned and rotting away. The image of "the tattered arras woven with a silent motto," alludes, as Elizabeth Drew has discovered, to the motto of the Eliot family, "Tace et Fac."[50] The same image, together with the first line of the poem, recalls Mary Stuart's motto "En ma fin est mon commencement," which was embroidered on the cloth covering her royal chair of state.[51] Both mottoes, making particular historical associations, put the "beginning," at any rate of the segment of history surveyed in "East Coker," back into the sixteenth century, the time of Sir Thomas Elyot and of English humanism and nationalism, of the inception of the English Renaissance, and of the inauguration of English colonial and cultural empire. This time marked the beginning of the Eliot family as a known entity and hence of the poet's traceable ancestry, the beginning of the poetic tradition in which he has chiefly written, and the beginning of modern England. Each of these beginnings furnished themes to Eliot's poem.[52]

The second strophe, pursuing the quest for beginnings into sixteenth-century East Coker, first repeats the introductory phrases, partly to define the motto of Mary Stuart by reversing it and partly to announce a new summary with different shading and focus. The "end" is now the village, at a moment forming a beginning with respect to the past of East Coker and an end with respect to the poet's journey there. The imagery of "the deep lane / Shuttered with branches, dark in the afternoon," and of the brooding, silent heat, all pointing toward nightfall and to "the early owl," conveys the dominant movement of light to darkness, of day to night, of present to past, just as the theme of temporal succession has done.[53] But the poet does not move behind this moment, as in "Burnt Norton," Part I. The moment itself concentrates the end, which is spectrally present, not in terms of "What might have been," but of "what has been"—the villagers' dance round the midsummer fire, successor to an even more primitive "bone-fire" of primeval ritual. Theirs is a dance not of death so much as of life, the dance signified in "Burnt Norton" by the "stillness" that fulfils the promise of love in the garden. "They" here are not past selves or potential selves of the present but past counterparts, linked harmoniously, as Sir Thomas Elyot wrote, in

> daunsinge, signifying matrimonie—
> A dignified and commodious sacrament.
> Two and two, necessarye coniunction,
> Holding eche other by the hand or the arm
> Whiche betokeneth concorde.

In Gerstärker's "Germelshausen" the stranger wanders into a lost village permitted to live for but one day every century; in Eliot the hamlet is always there, accessible through a "loop in time." The lines borrowed by Eliot from *The Boke Named the Governour*[54] recapture the idiom and flavor of such an eternal "beginning." But, in time, the dance of mirth ends with the grave; those who keep time by its rhythm keep time also by the rhythm of the wheeling year.

> Feet rising and falling.
> Eating and drinking. Dung and death.

With the terminal lines of this first movement the visionary midnight has passed; the time is now dawn, which, in the French idiom, "points." So the cycle continues. Anticipating the close of the final movement, the poet refers to the sea wind—the stirrer of movement outward and forward as it was for the Eliot family—and to the concept of his being "here / Or there, or elsewhere" in his beginning, where he was in potentiality, the place of his origin.

The second movement is weaker than the corresponding one in "Burnt Norton." But in the facile opening lyric, whose subject again is succession, the symbols are clear. November represents the mature age of the poet, of English poetry, of English history, and of the moral order of the Renaissance. The lines muse questioningly on the fate of the youth past, on the destiny of its flowers of promise that have flourished and fallen, the early snowdrops, the late hollyhocks, the roses that reach to the snow of winter.[55] Answering themselves in the archaic language of weather folklore and astrology, they refer to the larger, celestial cycle of mutability within which the solar year is but an episode, to a cycle approaching the end of its own symbolic rotation. The stars move in their great year, and the thunder of their spheres

> Simulates triumphal cars
> Deployed in constellated wars.

The world of man, like the elements, is also at war. But the greatest battle is waged between the destructive and the creative in the universe, typified by the late-autumn victory of Scorpio over the sun—a victory foreshadowing the ultimate cosmic death when the sun and moon shall finally "go down." The vortex of the circling comets and showering meteors (the Leonids appear in mid-November three times a century) is but a forecast of the end of the whirling world by a fire "Which burns before the ice-cap reigns." In Heraclitus' war of the elements, fire is the beginning and the end. On the level of the moral order, both of the individual and of his culture, fire means what Eliot's fourth movement calls "fever," a fever which will be quenched for all by the "ice-cap" of death when they are

> whirled
> Beyond the circuit of the shuddering Bear
> In fractured atoms.

Some critics read the lyric strophe as a description of "chaos." But this is the chaos of Henry Adams' pessimistic view of flux, not the chaos of absolute disorder. Chaos is to be the consummation of the hurly-burly of the upward and downward, the making and unmaking, which Bergson, following Heraclitus, saw as eternally creative. Yet the fire and ice, as the fourth movement affirms, themselves typify the redemptive agony, the end enabling a beginning.

Unlike the strophes following the opening lyric of the second movement in "Burnt Norton," the remainder of this movement has no metaphysical value to pose against the tumult of change bringing all things downward. It advances, however, an ethical value. Eliot's prosaic three-stress lines return from portents of the end to a reinspection of the beginning, where the train of ruin was laid. Diddled out of its promised "autumnal serenity," the world inherits apparently only "a receipt for deceit," a knowledge no longer wanted:

> The knowledge imposes a pattern, and falsifies,
> For the pattern is new in every moment
> And every moment is a new and shocking
> Valuation of all we have been.

So Henry Adams came to believe that the science of history he had sought was a fallacy. Eliot's reworking of a problem from "Gerontion" leads through an Adams-like groping—in Dante's "dark wood" and beside the "grimpen" of Conan Doyle's *The Hound of the Basker-villes*[56]—to the stern negation found in *The Waste Land:*

> The only wisdom we can hope to acquire
> Is the wisdom of humility: humility is endless.[57]

The value accordingly triumphant over time is the purgatorial endurance of change, disappointment, and the false fire called "progress." The example of the cyclic past has nothing to contribute: "The houses are all gone under the sea. / The dancers are all gone under the hill." Eliot's double coda proclaims the littleness of human endeavor and the inconsequence of the past.

Into the declamatory first strophe of the third movement Eliot wove phrases echoing Milton's *Samson Agonistes* ("O dark, dark, dark, amid the blaze of noon"); Vaughan's "Ascension Hymn" ("They are all gone into the world of light!"); Swinburne's "The Last Oracle" ("Dark the shrine and dumb the fount of song thence welling"); Conrad Aiken's *The Jig of Forslin* ("The walls of all the city are rolled away" and "Darkness descends, more walls are rolled away . . . / Sudden, they lower the curtain on the play");[58] and, perhaps, Shakespeare's *Richard II* (Act V, scene 2, lines 23–25: "As in a theatre, the eyes of men, / After a well-graced actor leaves the stage, / Are idly bent on him that enters next"). The subject of the whole recalls "Burnt Norton," Part III. Here, too, falls the darkness of death upon the benighted leaders of society whose paths of glory end with the passage of "the vacant into the vacant"; upon all the trumpery of the *Almanach de Gotha,* the *Stock Exchange Gazette,* the *Directory of Directors;* upon the whole world as it advances in its funeral dance of time, which, because "the time of death is every moment," as Eliot was to say in "The Dry Salvages," is "Nobody's funeral, for there is no one to bury." And again, in the last strophe, a contrast offers the other darkness, the immobility of St. John's Dark Night, "the darkness of God." Eliot's three extended similes of the changing of a scene in a theater, of the pausing of a tube-train, and of the mind suspended under ether, herald, through their motif of waiting, the words of the exhortation: "I said to my soul, be still. . . ." The first simile utilizes a topical reference to the air war; the second alludes to the "time-ridden faces" of "Burnt Norton"; the third justifies the Prufrockian anesthesia as a state of curative suffering. The negative waiting in darkness, without hope or love, insures that "the darkness shall be the light, and the stillness the dancing"—not "the funeral dance" but the dance at the point. The verse modulates into the only "intimation of immortality" in the poem:

> Whisper of running streams, and winter lightning.
> The wild thyme unseen and the wild strawberry,
> The laughter in the garden, echoed ecstasy
> Not lost, but requiring, pointing to the agony
> Of death and birth.

Since in "East Coker" all is cyclical movement, ending in death, even the moment of awakening appears as only a stage on the route of privation. The matrimonial dance itself points to the way down, but through death it points harmoniously to the way up; for physical death heralds spiritual birth. The third strophe renders the gnomic summary of the negative way in *The Ascent of Mt. Carmel,* found also in a pictorial chart of the "Mount of Perfection" which the Saint himself designed to illustrate his treatise. The tenor of St. John's lines is, of course, that the way to full knowledge, possession, and joy is utter denial of the self.[59]

The supreme archetype of the downward or negative way is the Passion, Death, and Burial of Christ. Eliot's fourth movement, by an extended image of the "wounded surgeon" at work upon the soul, shows how "life's fitful fever" finds its cure through the piercing love of the Redeemer. The descent of Christ typifies that of the soul into the darkness of negation; and just as Christ's submission to death redeems man, so man's own humble submission or descent is the act of faith accepting redemption. St. John uses the metaphor of the "cure" in referring to the passive Dark Night.[60] And so does Lancelot Andrewes in a sermon on the Redemption, with a verbal conceit that Eliot may have remembered: ". . . *quis audivit talia?* The Physician slain, and of His Flesh and Blood a receipt made, that the patient might recover!" In the same place Andrewes resorts to the common Renaissance image of the world as a hospital.[61] The concluding stanza of "East Coker," Part IV, uses the symbolism of flesh and blood, but Eliot's conceit of the surgeon compares with accounts of the mystical experience of the flaming dart, as in St. John's *The Living Flame of Love*[62] or in St. Theresa's account of her raptures. The image of the surgeon was better for Eliot's poetic purposes than that of the physician, implying the ampler mystical correlation: this operation upon the soul connotes not only Christ's oblation for all men but the personal surgery of Christ's love upon the soul subjected to the Dark Night. And the image also was better with reference to the field of battle, the context being World War II. War is the hell that can become our purgatory.

The movement opens with the figure of Christ "wounded for our transgressions." Probing into the distempered soul, He wields the instrument of questioning. Yet the insistence of love, though sharp, is compassionate: the oxymoron here distils the paradox of all human spiritual suffering. It also recalls that Christ, besides enduring His Passion with bleeding hands for us, suffered along with us for the sin of Adam. Such was the "compassion of the healer's art," of the Redemption that was the meaning "beneath" the bleeding hands on Calvary. The "enigma of the fever chart" is the abnormal and, in worldly logic, inexplicable disorder of human history and the human soul. It is also the divinely willed ("resolved") good producible from that disorder and from its concomitant suffering. Now Christ "re-solves" for each man what He solved for all mankind by the Atonement. But the fever presages our salvation, inasmuch as it shall "dis-ease" and disquiet us; the awareness of evil may be the first stage of reconciliation. The disease imposes, moreover, a purgatorial trial through which we may divest ourselves of "the love of created beings" and prepare ourselves for that of God. The "dying nurse" whom we must obey is the Church, whose continuous, firm supervision and perennial anxiety is designed not to please but to instruct us. Conversely our care for the Church is intended not merely to please it or us but to remind us of our plight, "of our, and Adam's curse," original sin and exclusion from Eden. We are not yet restored to Adam's state and to spiritual health. The sickness, however, "must grow worse" before it can itself be restored, that is, cured in us and reconfined to hell; and for that it must also be restored, in our recognition, to such a place of importance that we shall deem our own cure necessary. And complete healing demands intensity of purgatorial suffering, both here and in the life to come.

If "The whole earth is our hospital," all men are equally diseased, as all equally inherit Adam's curse, and life should be for all a time of convalescence. Adam, at first a millionaire in God's economy, was ruined by disobedience: his ruin was the fall. He himself, transmitting the sickness to his posterity, paradoxically also endowed Christ's "whole earth" (flesh) for our free redemption. In this hospital of charity we have two choices. The first is to "do well" by prospering in the worldly sense, so that we shall die in consequence of our father Adam's tyrannous bequest of sin, which will not loose us but everywhere hinders and antedates us. Furthermore, if we seek temporal contentment only, we shall die in estrangement from the pure Fatherly protection of God, who will now not abandon us but by prevenient grace "prevents us everywhere." The second choice is just the opposite: to "do well" by heeding Christ, so that we shall be reborn into freedom from insolvent Adam's taint and into the co-inheritance of grace.

As Pascal said, "Fever has its cold and hot fits; and the cold proves as well as the hot the greatness of the fire of fever"; and again, "Cold is agreeable, that we may get warm."[63] Eliot made a fusion of heat and cold the symbol for both purgation and death. On the one hand, the chill of death rises through the limbs (an image reminiscent of the death of Falstaff)[64] while the mind is burning with the fever of sin. On the other, the chill and fever in which one "must freeze / And quake in frigid purgatorial fires" counteracts both the cold and the burning. The fire of divine love, "The trilling wire in the blood," warms the soul, which in this world or hereafter is chilled in the absence of God. The roses of love and the thorns of pain symbolize salvation. Here, as before, the sense of the passage is that health is attainable only through disease. The sum enlarges and intensifies the conflict of Donne's sonnet, "Oh, to vex me, contraryes meet in one."

Although (the movement continues) we are drinkers of blood and eaters of flesh, literally and figuratively predatory, "we like to think / That we are sound, substantial flesh and blood," healthy and sturdy and, in the economic sense, well-to-do, despite our impermanence. Our substance is a fluctuating union of matter and form, subject to decay. And yet we speak of "Good" Friday without considering that that day makes our values meaningless. Furthermore, our only spiritual food and drink is the body and blood of Christ; this is what we rebel against in regarding ourselves as substantial. As unregenerate natures we ought to contemplate with terror, not with liking, a fact that insures our damnation unless we let God's grace transform our animal blood. The only "sound, substantial flesh and blood" is that of Christ; He, not we as we think, is the redemptive substance: yet we still rely on secular philosophies to redeem us. But we rightly "call this Friday good," for it is the anniversary of the Atonement, which we at bottom recognize to be the eternal guarantee of our redeemed substantiality. Good Friday unites total darkness with total light. (If one is not reminded of Crusoe's savage friend at this point, perhaps one ought to be.)

A certain kinship exists between the task of the spiritual surgeon and that of the poet at his typewriter. William Blissett has quoted from a letter of Goethe to Eckermann which bears on the fact that poets may often be too conscious of their status as patients: Goethe said of certain romantics: "All these poets write as though they were ill, and as though the whole world were a hospital."[65] One is always aware in Eliot of the role which suffering has filled in shaping his poetic work and of the applicability, with reference to the emotional and spiritual life, of Edmund Wilson's thesis in The Wound and the Bow that, as Eliot himself had phrased it, art is a transmutation of "personal and private agonies."[66] Once again, "Il faut avoir un aigle." But art may turn the artist from a patient into a physician, healing not only himself but others as well. Without pressing the analogy beyond due measure, one may profitably think of "East Coker," Part IV, as to some extent an allegory of Eliot's own poetic effort as patient and surgeon. The unity of suffering and action exists here, too.

The fifth movement begins with Eliot's comment on the arduousness of this poetic toil—on the intractability of language and on the continuous flux of a medium in which, as in the flux of nature and memory, there is no permanent end to strife.

> . . . every attempt
> Is a wholly new start, and a different kind of failure.[67]

Viewed as subject to the laws of time, words "slip, slide, perish" without reaching "stillness." The poet is at war with words; the military terms "raid," "equipment," "squads," "mess," and the designation of the poetic struggle as "the fight to recover what has been lost / And found and lost again and again" call up once more the Heraclitean war of elements. To the statement at the end of the second movement, "The only wisdom we can hope to acquire / Is the wisdom of humility," the poem adds now, "For us there is only the trying. The rest is not our business." Laboring moment by moment, changing as his materials change, the poet can only acquiesce in a testing by time. The concluding strophe, like that of "Burnt Norton," recapitulates the main themes: the beginning which is the end, "Home is where one starts from"; the complication of the past as memory and history enduring not out of time but in time, "a lifetime burning in every moment / And not the lifetime of one man only / But of old stones that cannot be deciphered";[68] and time itself as *la recherche du temps perdu* of history "under starlight" and of the personal past "under lamplight / (The evening with the photograph album)." And then the profoundly sad comfort—sad because of the utter defeat needed to make it a consolation:

> Love is most nearly itself
> When here and now cease to matter.

The stillness is almost attained. But life, whether of the poet or of his society, must advance doggedly into the future, in a movement that approaches stillness only in so far as it approaches detachment and humility. It was with his family history in mind that Eliot, remembering also the poetic task of expanding the frontiers of language, wrote: "Old men ought to be explorers," as his ancestors had been when they left East Coker to cross the Atlantic.[69] Old men, old nations, however imminently faced with death, must push on across the eternally fluctuating seas of time, where each stage of the journey is "a new venture," not merely an end but a beginning.

### III. *"The Dry Salvages"*

The "What might have been" of "Burnt Norton" and the "what has been" of "East Coker" "point" through "The Dry Salvages" to the "one end" of "Little Gidding." "The Dry Salvages" (1941) even more than its immediate predecessor is a transitional poem, discovering how man can find the still point not only through fugitive insight but through ordinary action. The first movement makes use of two general symbols, the river and the sea—the former being associated by Eliot with the Mississippi, beside which he was born, and the latter with the ocean off Cape Ann, which he visited as a boy. The second movement presents a recollection of the Gloucester fishing fleet. Thus from the early history of the Eliot family the *Quartets* follow the traces of those members of it who in the seventeenth century left for America, then bring the reader to the scenes among which the poet grew up, and finally return to England, the Church of England, and Eliot's wartime London. The river, personified as a "strong brown god," connotes man's dark tide of primitive savagery—the heart of darkness. It represents also the inexorable movement of temporal history. It is rightly called both "intractable" and "patient," its dangers unheeded in the modern world, where "the builder of bridges" at his pontifical task of compelling decorum keeps it from breaking its banks, but where, at a time of crisis, it may become a destroying flood. As in the race, so in the individual, this sinister stream makes its hushed rhythm felt in the lulling serenity of civilization. The sea is the great unfathomed reservoir of the world's dateless evolution, encroaching on ordered society, continually tossing ashore "hints of earlier and other creation," and often engulfing men by reversion in its abysses. It has never been subdued, never mapped; raising not one voice but many, it cries with the voices of "many gods." And it has the similitude of eternity, into which all rivers pour. Together the river and the sea allude to the Hindu parable of the life cycle—the drop of water lifted as vapor from the sea, deposited as rain upon the Himalaya, and carried again seaward by the Ganges.

Eliot's second strophe passes, by way of "the briar rose" and "the fir trees," from the landsman's to the sailor's point of view—and to the ocean howl and yelp,

> the whine in the rigging,
> The menace and caress of wave that breaks on water,
> The distant rote in the granite teeth.

These are only the voices audible to one not venturing far from shore. The memories are merely those of the amateur sailor who makes an afternoon of sailing out to the buoy, rounding it on his homeward tack. But the bell, "rung by the unhurried / Ground swell," speaks for the far deep "that is and was from the beginning." Just as the river clocks the flow of human time, so the sea tolls the death by which each moment lapses into coexistence. Eliot's image of "anxious worried women / Lying awake, calculating the future" juxtaposes human successive time to the simultaneous. His phrase from the "De profundis" ("before the morning watch," according to the Coverdale version in the Prayer Book) points, by association with Mark, chapter 13, to the second Advent; in Christ, "time stops and time is never ending." With the clang of the bell the movement has recognized not the ancient gods of flux and caprice but Him who "was in the beginning, is now, and ever shall be, world without end."

The varying sestina of "The Dry Salvages," Part II, is arranged in questions and answers, like the lyric opening of "East Coker," Part II. The first three stanzas suggest a generalization; the other three localize it by treating of the fishermen's voyage. Eliot's initial lines, recalling the image of shattered "autumn flowers" in "East Coker" and the "soundless wailing" of the flowers' death, counter an optimistic passage in Conrad Aiken's *Preludes for Memnon:*

> Wailing I heard, but also I heard joy.
> Wreckage I saw, but also I saw flowers.[70]

The flowers, "the drifting wreckage, / The prayer of the bone on the beach" (a symbol taken apparently from Yeats's "Three Things"), symbolize an everlasting movement into death. In the face of the news of disaster, the only prayer is "unprayable." The negative answer of the second stanza, "There is no end, but addition," seems relevant to all of Eliot's principal themes. But the worst is yet to be: "the final addition" of failure and old age and the awareness of being one for whom tolls "the bell of the last annunciation." This is the grim reward of the exploration toward which the final movement of "East Coker" has looked. But the image now reveals fishermen, not explorers. Previous images in Eliot's poetry combine to enrich the symbolism: the Fisher King in quest of healing; the poet cementing a laborious mosaic of fragments; the recollection of the apostles as fishers of men. The efforts of all alike are thankless and futile, in peril of waste and of a future "liable / Like the past, to have no destination." But the poet cannot sustain the thought that life and toil are wholly without a goal; he must keep in imagination a notion of "captains courageous" persevering in their daily tasks and not think of the futility, the inherent frustration of movement into time, the betrayer of hope. But the final truth, whether tolerable or not, is that neither purpose nor conclusion exists unless in answer to "the hardly, barely prayable / Prayer of the one Annunciation"—a whispered *magnificat* for the redemptive merger of the flux with the immutable.

Eliot's discourse on the past, forming the second division of the second movement, attempts to define the meaning of the flow. Rejecting first the casual labeling of time as mere sequence, the poet is wary also of "development,"

> a partial fallacy,
> Encouraged by superficial notions of evolution,
> Which becomes, in the popular mind, a means of
> disowning the past.

The past must not be disowned. To Eliot, the ceaseless slipping-away of time is only an appearance. In the first place, the past survives in memory; he cites lost "moments of happiness" recoverable "In a different form" by "approach to the meaning." In the second place, it survives in simultaneity, the "always present." He might have said "approach to the *lógos*," for the meaning of such moments is intelligible only through the eternal order into which they fit. In eternity, the meaning grasped *now* and the experience misinterpreted *then* are coexistent. And the recovery of the past brings back "not the experience of one life only / But of many generations," even the most primordial, remembered atavistically. Yet it brings back, together with happiness, an agony "permanent / With such permanence as time has." As Eliot acutely observed, we realize this fact better when the agony, though close to us, has not been our own: "People change, and smile: but the agony abides."[71] Thus "Time the destroyer is time the preserver"; actual duration, not mere succession, gives the clue to its meaning. With a slight reminiscence of "The River" in Hart Crane's *The Bridge*,[72] the movement reintroduces the symbolism of the Mississippi, now explicitly belying the Heraclitean flux: the changing river bears flotsam from the past. And like a token of the river's cruelty is the actual duration of sin: "The bitter apple and the bite in the apple" recognized in "The backward look behind the assurance / Of recorded history. . . ." Yet though agonies abide, so does that which, itself the greatest destructive agony, constitutes the greatest preservation—the symbol of the perfected meaning, the eternal stability: "the ragged rock in the restless waters."

> In navigable weather it is always a seamark
> To lay a course by: but in the sombre season
> Or the sudden fury, is what it always was.

The third movement, before turning to the actions of the present, muses on a corollary to the actual duration of the past, that the future exists waiting for the moving "now" to reach it:

... That the future is a faded song, a Royal Rose or a lavender
    spray
Of wistful regret for those who are not yet here to regret,
Pressed between yellow leaves of a book that has never been
    opened.

If all time is simultaneous, the future is like the past in being real but inaccessible through time; in such terms "the way forward" resembles "the way back." Eliot's remark that "time is no healer: the patient is no longer here" revises the classic axiom, formulated in the *Alcestis* of Euripides ("Χρόνος μαλάξει"), time will heal.[73] The citation of Krishna, charting a passage to India, associates the idea of simultaneous time with Krishna's doctrine of consecrated momentary action. A man's career, though comprising many simultaneous moments, some of them "future," remains visible only as succession; hence the actual existence of the future does not relieve him of his duty to the present moment. In other words, he must act as if the future were nowhere existent; for, though what it is, is known to God, it results from what a man does now.

The poet of the *Bhagavad-Gita* attributed to Krishna the command to pursue ordinary activity without attachment to the fruits of action. In the poem "To the Indians Who Died in Africa" (1943), which echoes, like "Difficulties of a Statesman," Kipling's "The Story of Muhammad Din," Eliot referred pointedly to the Hindu doctrine:

Let those who go home tell the same story of you:
Of action with a common purpose, action
None the less fruitful if neither you nor I
Know, until the judgment after death,
What is the fruit of action.[74]

The life of detachment is generally called "indifference" in writings on the subject, but, since Eliot used this term in another sense in "Little Gidding," it is preferable here to say simply "detachment." In the fable unifying the *Gita* the god Vishnu, incarnate as Krishna, the charioteer of the prince Arjuna, counsels Arjuna before battle. He tells him that action need not hamper, that it is inevitable; and that the only duty of a man is to perform the obligations of his caste without interest in the profit or loss. Setting forth the way of yoga, with a sentiment from the *Upanishads*, Krishna later enunciates the other Hindu doctrine borrowed for "The Dry Salvages," to the effect that a man at death goes to that sphere of being on which his mind is then intent.[75]

From the combination of these two teachings with the idea of distinct future selves in simultaneous time it follows that devotion to God at any moment of action both takes one to Him and causes the action to "fructify in the lives of others," including one's own future selves. These selves are of course, from one point of view, already there, but their "experience" cannot exist without the "meaning" that one's present action gives. The emphasis of this movement of the poem directly reverses that of the movement preceding. This is apparently one reason why Eliot adopted the imagery of the closed book, ordinarily connoting the past, for his transition to a complementary view of the future. What looks like a synthesis with Greek thought in the latter part of the movement was probably in part derived from Buddhism. For Buddhism teaches precisely the Heraclitean conception of flux, calling it *anicca*, the impermanence of all things. Buddhism consequently emphasizes the thought and action of the present moment because these not only influence the free will to be exercised in the future but determine the heaven or hell which the totality of a man's ethical life, his karma, will produce. There is an evident connection between the doctrine of karma and Sir Henry's warning to Edward in *The Cocktail Party* about "letting the genie out of the bottle." In "The Dry Salvages" Eliot's imagery of the liner "between the hither and the farther shore" supplements that of the railway journey symbolizing the timeless, fluctuating "now." Both symbols modernize the Buddha's own references to the two "shores," desire and nirvana. (Nirvana is sometimes figured also as the ocean into which the river of life empties.) The Buddha said in the *Dhammapada:* ". . . for whom there is neither this nor that shore, nor both, him, the fearless and unshackled, I call indeed a Brāhmaṇa."[76]

Eliot's fusion of ideas from Hinduism and Buddhism, with a nod to the fortuitous parallels in Heraclitus, has an almost ironic use in the poem.[77] In both Eastern religions the goal of action or non-action is release from the Wheel. But in "The Dry Salvages" it is rather the fulfilment of the premise that only through time, time is redeemed. As the present redeems the past by renewing its meaning, so the present redeems the future by preparing a meaning for that; but only the present holds the moment of experience, and all experiences are present. Therefore the present is the "real destination" of those who "fare forward." This fact supplies commentary on the fourth and fifth stanzas of the sestina: the fishermen are *forever* "Setting and hauling"; the imaginary destinations of the future are of no significance until they become real. And redemption, although "out of time," does not exclude time, for at "the still point" all times are one.

The Lady of the fourth movement is the Virgin, in Dante's epithet "Figlia del tuo figlio," of whose human substance God was made man, the timeless taking the temporal into itself.[78] The petition calls upon her who spoke the "Prayer of the one Annunciation" to utter a prayer of intercession for those who voyage, as through time, and for those whom they leave at home,

> Women who have seen their sons or husbands
> Setting forth, and not returning.[79]

None ever comes back the same person as at his departure. The supplication has especial value in being addressed to the woman whose experience of loss was most bitter, and who might have greatest compassion for those who, Jonah-like, "Ended their voyage . . . / in the dark throat which will not reject them." Being henceforth out of time, the dead cannot hear the bell that honors the Incarnation with its perpetual, because at all times present, note of thankfulness. The only prayer that can affect them is one for the vanished—but whether for the vanished in their forever present past or in their present death the lyric does not say.

Eliot's theme of peace through strife, of ideal timelessness through time, wherein every action selflessly dedicated repairs the present agony of the past and sanctifies the present rebirth of the future, typifies the way down that is also the way up to God. The fifth movement drives onward toward clarification of the action by which the divine descent made this possible. The movement has a seriocomic tone in its first lines: the grave business of war (the occasion of Krishna's teaching), the revelation by the Ariel-like aerial voice, and the terrible voracity of "the dark throat" in the fourth movement are transformed into a derisive comment on popular enthusiasm for prying into mysteries:

> To communicate with Mars, converse with spirits,
> To report the behaviour of the sea monster.

Man's trial of his future by the numerous divinatory arts, hieratic or frolicsome, purporting to enlighten him, and his inquiry into the dark backward of his savage past by the scientific methods which "explore the womb, or tomb, or dreams," testify to his willing involvement with the dimension of time. He is most prone to such activity when, as in the prophecy of Luke, chapter 21, "there is distress of nations and perplexity." Man's other "occupation," that of sainthood, seeks

> to apprehend
> The point of intersection of the timeless
> With time. . . .

But it is not an "occupation"—sometimes a military term after all, perhaps with a side glance at "Othello's occupation"—but something both given and taken, describable as love. It is not the way of "most of us," for whom the unexpected and unregarded "distraction fit, lost in a shaft of sunlight," flashes the nearest intimation that time vouchsafes of that present eternity, here symbolized by "the wild thyme unseen," "the winter lightning," and (instead of the streams of "East Coker") "the waterfall." Eliot's unifying symbol is

> music heard so deeply
> That it is not heard at all, but you are the music
> While the music lasts.

His reference in "Burnt Norton" to the "form" by which music reaches the "stillness," along with the line "I said to my soul, be still," from "East Coker," brings the constituents of definition for the liberating detachment of such a moment. Here, however, he seems to have invoked "silent music" from the fourteenth stanza of St. John's *Spiritual Canticle,* on which the Saint commented: "In that aforesaid tranquillity and silence of the night, and in that knowledge of the Divine light . . . [the soul] seems to hear a harmony of sublimest music. . . . The Bride calls this music silent because . . . it is a tranquil and quiet intelligence, without sound of voices; and in it are thus enjoyed both the sweetness of the music and the quiet of the silence. And so she says that her Beloved is this silent music, because this harmony of spiritual music is known and experienced in Him." But the ordinary music that one hears, and the ordinary impulses of joy, one must concede, transmit "only hints and guesses"—

> the rest
> Is prayer, observance, discipline, thought and action.

The common pursuits of life also can be cultivated in detachment, and, like the occasional inspiration, they, too, point beyond time to the "hint" accorded in everyday life and to the "gift" accorded in the consecrated life of sainthood: they point to Incarnation.

There are many incarnations, many unions of matter and soul, of which Christ's is the only one reconciling time with eternity, for His Incarnation is the only one joining to the material flux absolutely pure form or actuality. When Eliot wrote,

> Here the impossible union
> Of spheres of existence is actual,

he must have meant that the union is actual not simply in Incarnation but here, at this temporal moment. The union is "impossible" both because it is beyond human comprehension and because, very literally, it is not "possible," since it is actual. A union of time and eternity, the human and the divine, has married forever the contrary partners in man's fatal dualism. By enduing time with the primal "source of movement," Incarnation has made man a partaker in that source: man, exalted to the center of action and movement, is delivered from the "daemonic, chthonic / Powers" of hell, which "otherwise" would move him as their pawn, and from the powers of his animal nature, the "strong brown god" animating the undercurrents of his blood. In every moment man, through Christ, is in eternity; and, therefore,

> right action is freedom
> From past and future also.

Man's dreary progress through time constitutes in itself a redemption. As "Burnt Norton" symbolizes the fulfilment of all potentiality in God, so "The Dry Salvages" symbolizes the incredible reconciliation of all actuality by man's concentrated unity, within time and out of it, in Christ. This is the message also of *The Rock*. The poet ends with a confession that

> For most of us, this is the aim
> Never here to be realised.

Either we shall not know the aim or we shall not accomplish it. But, in the spirit of "East Coker," we can continue our labors, "content at the last / If our temporal reversion nourish . . . / The life of significant soil"—the life whose actions fructify in others. "Temporal reversion" is too meaningful for paraphrase; the words imply not only the body of this death but the inquiry into the past, the condition of temporal life, and the very poem renewing a concept of time that most people have never heard of. All that we, including the poet, can ask is that such labor not end "too far from the yew-tree" of immortality.

Though a Buddhist might read the closing lines of "The Dry Salvages" without feeling that they were strange to his beliefs, and though he might understand by "temporal reversion" something consistent with his habitual idea of personal karma, this fact need not make "The Dry Salvages" heterodox for Christians. It is, after all, a poem; it does not affect to pronounce dogma. But most real theology, in contradistinction to commentary, was once also poetry. Eliot in "Burnt Norton" and "The Dry Salvages" reached in poetry a level which, without extravagance, one might call creative theology.

## IV. *"Little Gidding"*

The initial movement of "Little Gidding" (1942) takes up where "The Dry Salvages" leaves off, with an intense, illuminative radiance equivalent to the deeply heard music which there symbolizes the Incarnation. The imagery of the first strophe exhibits dazzling fire reflected as the sun, touching the ice of a winter afternoon, creates "Midwinter spring." This springtime comes at what Donne, in his "Nocturnall upon S. Lucies day," calls "the yeares midnight," when "The worlds whole sap is sunke." Yet, in Eliot's words, "The soul's sap quivers." For this season, "in and out of time," is an emblem of "the summer, the unimaginable / Zero summer" antipodal to it: that never described season only to be known in union with God. Meanwhile, this natural counterpart, with a blinding glare "more intense than blaze of branch, or brazier" (the allusion to the Vergilian golden bough underscores the mystery within the brilliance), "stirs the dumb spirit." Into the freezing darkness of time it bears a pentecostal flame, as into another earthly winter Christ brought the springtime of human history.[80] Unlike the spring "in time's covenant," "in the scheme of generation," this symbolic spring bears no ordinary blossom, but that "of snow,"

> a bloom more sudden
> Than that of summer, neither budding nor fading,

betokening the new covenant that unites man's spiritual winter with the eternal summer of the timeless point. And, caught up by the power pervading this experience, the poet here breaks silence. By an imagery exercising a tension between opposites, he defines the ambivalence of the spectacle and the paradox of the epiphany it connotes: pole—tropic, short—brightest, frost—fire, sun—ice, cold—heat, glare—blindness, fire—dark, melting—freezing, blossom—snow. Poetically he achieves the perfection striven after by Shelley in *The Triumph of Life* (ll. 77–79):

> . . . a cold glare, intenser than the noon,
> But icy cold, obscured with blinding light
> The sun, as he the stars.

This then is the moment, and the place is Little Gidding, whose restored chapel is a spiritual symbol analogous to the rose garden in "Burnt Norton." (A corresponding link exists between the garden and the chapel of *The Waste Land.*) The second strophe mentions as an alternative season for the journey here a time when the hedges are "White again, in May, with voluptuary sweetness"—with the may, the Glastonbury thorn, supposed always to bloom on Christmas Day. But the time, says Eliot, is unimportant: "It would be the same" whether one came secretly like King Charles, the "broken king," or like the casual visitor by day. It would be the same in purpose. And although the entelechy toward which action or movement points is never wholly known while potential, the meaning of the journey would appear in the "end"—in the final cause. To King Charles this place revealed the consummation, the meaning of the journey. For other men

> There are other places
> Which also are the world's end, some at the sea jaws,
> Or over a dark lake, in a desert or a city—[81]

places of water or earth or air, for fishermen, the airmen of war, and all others who strive,

> But this is the nearest, in place and time,
> Now and in England.

For the poet, therefore, and for all men like him in wartime England, Little Gidding holds the point of temporal access to the eternal moment. To this place one must come only for the purpose of prayer, the key to eternity. And in prayer one would attain communion with the dead who have prayed here and have become part of eternity here, and together with them one would draw closer to that full union prefigured by the pentecostal fire. When, at the conclusion of the third strophe, Eliot observes: "Here, the intersection of the timeless moment / Is England and nowhere. Never and always," he is not primarily identifying that intersection with England; rather he is saying that this place is not merely England, it is also placeless eternity, in which all times become timeless. The whole opening movement has sought a timeless value and has now isolated it by means of the historic devotional community at Little Gidding. This value is as relevant to the poet as the value glimpsed through the rose garden; but it is relevant equally to the nation. This place, once consecrated by the visit of the martyr king, enshrines memories essential to England's redemption. If England, in the fiery tribulation of war, is dedicated to these memories as symbols of the Incarnation, her agony shall become purgatorial. Such is the theme of "Little Gidding": the redemption of men and nations from the fire of hell by the fire of purgation and from the fire of purgation by the fire of love.

The second movement probes into the world of death, conceived of first as subject to decay and then as immune to it, in search of the true meaning behind man's war of life. In the Heraclitean warfare of elements governing the flux of matter, it finds no meaning but mutability;[82] but in the transcendence of time and change it finds hope at the cost of renunciation. Dealing with time as succession and afterward as simultaneity, it retraces dramatically the speculations of the earlier *Quartets*. The opening lyric of three stanzas, recalling Part V of Yeats's "Nineteen Hundred and Nineteen," borrows from a fragment of Heraclitus (alluding to the upward and downward cycle) the metaphor of elemental transmutation: that each element lives by the death of another. Here is represented only the downward tendency of material things, toward ruin. From the ashes of "burnt roses," connoting the rose garden of "Burnt Norton," the opening stanza moves to the airborne dust of house, wall, wainscot, and mouse, all from "East Coker," Part I, to characterize "the death of air," in relation to the air raids of the war. The second stanza links with "The Dry Salvages," with the savagery of flood and drought frustrating the creative effort to work a barren soil. The third stanza, after this "death of earth," depicts "the death of water and fire" through human neglect of what the past has achieved, "the marred foundations we forgot, / Of sanctuary and choir."

But the remainder of the second movement leaves Heraclitus for a device well suited to showing past time as simultaneously alive—an encounter with a ghost. Instead of the static symbolism of the quiet, sad stanzas on temporal flux, there is now the moving symbolism of a quasi-dramatic dialogue suggesting man's responsibility to the eternal. Fulfilling the first movement, the poet communicates with one of the dead whose "concern was speech" and whose utterance is "tongued with fire." There is a symbolic parallel here to three other kinds of fire, that of hell, that of purgatory, and that of aerial warfare. Whether the revenant comes from the spirit world or the actual past is unclear; perhaps Eliot aimed at ambiguity, for, he might insist, nobody knows where ghosts come from. If the ghost comes from the past—or, rather, if Eliot thought of him as still alive in a past intersecting the present— then, presumably, the rationale of the passage was indebted to James's "Jolly Corner," though it is problematical whether one can justly say that the ghost amalgamates past selves of the poet (or maybe even, as in James, potential selves only) with those of the poet's dead masters.[83] The ghost's Palinurus-like remark that he left his body "on a distant shore" implies that he is a disembodied spirit; yet the statement is ambiguous. At any rate, Eliot exhibited an intermingling of worlds and created the illusion of their visible simultaneity, if not in a physical, then, at least, in a "spiritualistic," sense. The effect is strongly sugges- tive, like the *Doppelgänger* episodes in *Ash Wednesday* and *The Cock- tail Party*, of Charles Williams' *Descent into Hell*, where the time bar- riers dissolve. For Williams' novel sets precedent for a discouraging view of the "other" world as nothing but the simultaneous presence of times.

Eliot has explained his style here by saying that he intended this passage to be "the nearest equivalent to a canto of the *Inferno* or *Purgatorio*" that he could achieve and that he meant to present "a parallel, by means of contrast, between the *Inferno* and the *Purgatorio* . . . and a hallucinated scene after an air-raid."[84] The versification, ac- cording to his own description, is a modified *terza rima*; it lacks rhyme. In the same "Talk on Dante" in which he made these observations, he quoted two lines from "Les Sept Vieillards," which he said summed up for him the significance of Baudelaire:

> Fourmillante cité, cité pleine de rêves,
> Où le spectre, en plein jour, raccroche le passant![85]

One may see the connection of this passage, as well, with Eliot's "canto." Furthermore, Eliot has great admiration for Shelley's *The Triumph of Life*, certain lines of which (ll. 176–205), quoted in his talk, he said had impressed him as long as forty-five years previously; and those same lines influenced the ghost passage by their general rhetorical pattern. A few phrases from Shelley's account of the "dance" accompanying the chariot in *The Triumph of Life* may have had a more particular impact.

Many readers will wish to distinguish the Dantean tone of Eliot's "canto" from his un-Dantean imitation of *terza rima;* for his verse is not in *terza rima* at all, in spite of its alternate hypermeters. If the lines had been printed flush with the margin, they might look more like the blank verse they are. (Eliot has published only one poem in *terza rima:* "To Walter de la Mare," which dates from 1948. It has minor poetic merit.)[86] Eliot has not said much about the astonishing phalanx of allusions and imitations concealed in his "canto." One ought not to overlook the similarity of the opening lines (after the very first, which seems to echo Kipling's "The Fabulists") to a speech in *The Atheist's Tragedy,* cited and praised by Eliot in his essay on Tourneur.[87] Nor should one ignore the probable echoes of Shakespeare's eighty-sixth sonnet ("that affable familiar ghost"); of Mallarmé's "Le Tombeau d'Edgar Poe" ("Donner un sens plus pur aux mots de la tribu"); of the account of the unpalatable fruit likened by Milton to the fruit (apples) of Sodom ("instead of Fruit / Chew'd bitter Ashes");[88] of the sad description of old age, following Milton's comparison of death to the dropping of "ripe Fruit";[89] of Swift's epitaph ("ubi saeva indignatio ulterius cor lacerare nequit");[90] of Ford's *The Lover's Melancholy* ("a lamentable tale of things / Done long ago, and ill done")[91] or Yeats's "Vacillation" ("Things said or done long years ago . . . / Weigh me down");[92] of Johnson's *The Vanity of Human Wishes* ("Grief aids disease, remember'd folly stings");[93] of *Measure for Measure* ("the delighted spirit / To bathe in fiery floods");[94] and of *Hamlet* ("It faded on the crowing of the cock").[95] But, of course, there are echoes of Dante too, the most memorable originating in the Brunetto Latini passage of *Inferno,* XV. They are mere embellishments, such as "the brown baked features," involving Brunetto's own name with the phrase "lo cotto aspetto," and "the down-turned face," alluding to "capo chino." Of less note, except as a recurrence of a persistent citation, is the reference to *Purgatorio,* XXVI, just before the ghost's disappearance, through the phrase "that refining fire." This reintroduces Arnaut Daniel.[96] The phrase "To set a crown upon your lifetime's effort" reverses the tone of Vergil's last words to Dante (*Purgatorio,* XXVII): "io te sopra te corono e mitrio"; and the ghost's remarks just after "aftersight and foresight" seem to appraise mockingly Dante's earnest discourse on old age in the *Convivio.*[97]

The incidents in the "canto" take place at dawn after a bombardment by "the dark dove with the flickering tongue"; serpent-like, the enemy has gone down whence he came. (Eliot may have been thinking of the Taube ["Dove"] aeroplane, though that would have been an anachronism.) The personal nature of the scene is best appreciated when one understands that in World War II Eliot belonged to the fire-spotting service in Kensington. The connotations of the leaves in this passage take the reader back to "Burnt Norton," Part I, and, at the same time, cause him to think of metal flak "blown" before the wind; together with the asphalt, they recall Milton's legions of the damned, "Thick as Autumnal Leaves that strow the Brooks / In Vallombrosa,"[98] and they become identified with "the leaves dead / . . . driven, like ghosts from an enchanter fleeing," in Shelley's "Ode to the West Wind." Their purpose is to introduce the ghost himself, who, "loitering and hurried," resembles them. To the poet he is half a stranger, half a familiar friend.

> So I assumed a double part, and cried
> And heard another's voice cry: "What! are *you* here?"
> Although we were not.

This "double part" forms the crux; everything depends on it. Unfortunately, there is little possibility of deciding what it means. Raymond Preston argues that it acknowledges the Dantean scene: it "is the part of Dante and the part of Eliot, and at the same time the answer seems an echo."[99] But is "another's voice" really that of Dante? Is it not that of the ghost, perhaps as a *Doppelgänger* of the poet? Apparently, at least on one level, the ghost on this occasion is entirely "someone other," for he consciously dwells in purgatory, if not hell. And it is as master and pupil that ghost and poet converse, "in a dead patrol," on their common concern with language—speech which alters as voices alter, becoming obsolete with the theories about its use: "Last season's fruit is eaten / And the fullfed beast shall kick the empty pail." (A phrase that Alexander Hamilton might have admired; but an allusion, with overtones of "Rabbi Ben Ezra," to the lament for fame in *Purgatorio*, XI.) The ghost, in words thus alien to his time and place, pronounces an icy warning to the poet desirous of the fruits of action. For old age brings sensory anesthesia, acrimony against one's fellow men, remorse for the past. The future is only hell reduplicating hell unless one accepts the fire as purgation; and the fire is here, and now, in vocation, in the activity falling to a man's lot: in the "measure" of poetry or whatever other toil. When the ghost fades "on the blowing of the horn"

by which the all clear is sounded, it is into the fire of his own purgation, one may suppose, that he returns.

As Eliot's poetry repeatedly shows, history, whether conceived of as
the life span of a nation, or as a cultural pursuit like poetry, or at the
simplest as the total acts of a man, is meaningful only in the present
instant where meaning is apprehended. The third movement, recurring
evidently to the circumstances in which the first movement concludes,
ponders the present attitude which the past should inspire and in so
doing exemplifies the detachment laid down by "The Dry Salvages" as
a rule of life. Contemplating now not merely English history but, with
the memory of the ghost before him, his personal past, the poet considers three courses as possible: attachment, detachment, and between
them "unflowering" indifference. Though attachment, clearly enough,
may be good, detachment is a way of "faring forward" without the
regret of attachment to vanished fruits or its anxiety for those that may
never ripen and without the selfish, aloof, and uncreative pride gnawing at the heart which is indifferent to life altogether. Only by detachment can one perfect the moment dividing the past from the future and
avert the danger of servile attachment by memory to the past, and to
the future by desire.

> This is the use of memory:
> For liberation—not less of love but expanding
> Of love beyond desire, and so liberation
> From the future as well as the past.

Detachment or liberation, as Eliot used the terms, permits love; attachment may vitiate it by disappointed passion, indifference by apathy.
The passage, splendidly exultant, reverses Eliot's old theme of the
tyranny of enduring memories. One begins, the poet says, with attachment to one's "own field of action" and moves toward detachment
from it without diminution of love for the country where it lies. The
past, reclaimed by memory, is no longer servitude but freedom; its fulfilment is better than its promise; it is "transfigured" with all its
ghostly "faces and places," as is "the self which, as it could, loved
them." What one shall remember is not the agony but its redemptive
meaning.

The other strophe of this movement starts with lines in which is
latent a traditional Christian version of this same teaching: the *felix
culpa* as applied to man's sins since Adam. The evil action of the past
was "behovely," that is, inevitable; but the weed of error, so to speak,

replanted in the garden of love, shall flower into perfection. As the Redemption reconciled Adam's sin by fulfilling its potentiality for good, so a man or a nation can transfigure memories by perfecting their meaning in the present. This is the curious paradox that the greatest good has come from the worst intentions—an Augustinian argument occupying the heart of *Paradise Lost*. The phrasing at the beginning and end of the strophe came in part from the *Shewings* of the fourteenth-century English mystic Dame Julian of Norwich: "Synne is behovabil, but al shal be wel & al shal be wel & al manner of thyng shal be wele." Thus the revelation of her Voice to her, and later: "I am Ground of thy beseeching."[100] In contemplating the national past as memorialized in "this place," the chapel at Little Gidding, the poet (echoing *Hamlet* again) thinks of certain men of the seventeenth century.[101] He remembers Ferrar, King Charles here and in his death, Laud, Strafford, and even perhaps Sir John Eliot, who was imprisoned before the Civil War for contumacy of the King; he remembers others such as Crashaw, who died abroad, and Milton, "who died blind and quiet";[102] and he asks once more his question: What after all is the importance of the past?

> Why should we celebrate
> These dead men more than the dying?

The "use of memory," again, is neither to "set the clock back" nor to muster forces for a vanished battle (the alarm called "ringing the bell backward" is sounded by striking a peal of bells up the scale, beginning with the bass). Nor is it "To summon the spectre of a Rose" (Sir Thomas Browne's "ghost of a rose," no doubt, in *The Garden of Cyrus:* a reminder of his speculations in *Religio Medici* on the possibility of the chemical revival, the palingenesis, of a flower from its ashes);[103] that is, sentimentally to agitate for the Stuart cause. All parties are now reconciled in death. It is rather to take from the past its lasting model of perfection, which, as a symbol, it can furnish to our own life of war. "In the ground of our beseeching," that is, in the eternal, itself the "significant soil" where our purgation, and therefore our redemption, grows by our action, the meaning and motive of the dead past have been purified—

> And all shall be well and
> All manner of thing shall be well.

The lyric fourth movement compresses the main themes of the first three movements into a "fire sermon" of tremendous energy. From the first movement comes the "flame of incandescent terror," the descent of the Holy Ghost. From the second movement, which contributes out of its initial division a reference to hope and despair, comes the image of raiding aircraft. This "death of air" does not signify merely destruction; it presents a choice between hope and despair, between the burning of purgatory and the burning of hell. Eliot's "pyre or pyre," "fire by fire," juxtaposes two forms of the same word at extremes of etymological development in different tongues. The second stanza alludes to the myth of Hercules, who, to escape the excruciating agony caused by the treacherous Nessus-shirt which his wife Deianira had given him to insure his love, lit a funeral pyre and ascended to Olympus from the consuming flames. Love prepared that agony, as Love "devised the torment" of our own agony, both in war and in the strife of emotions. This is the word received by Dame Julian from the Voice that came to her: "Wouldst thou learn thy Lord's meaning in this thing? Learn it well: Love was his meaning. Who shewed it thee? Love. What shewed He thee? Love. Wherefore shewed it He? For Love."[104] Our sufferings, the pains of longing and conflict in which we "suspire," are not removable by human power. Nor is that "intolerable shirt of flame" removable, which is God enveloping us in His love—the fire spoken of by the mystics in describing the raptures of the illuminative way, and by Pascal in describing the sensations of his conversion, and which is Christ's Passion made by His hands. These are all the same; fire is fire, and we can alter its meaning from despair to delight by recognizing its source. So in the third movement of the poem, "By purification of the motive," the fire of memory, which is "behovabil," has been transfigured as the symbolic rose.

Eliot in his terminal movement assembled the leading symbols of all four *Quartets* with their dominant themes of poetry, time and history, personal and temporal redemption, and the love that might have been and always is. The opening lines, though they paraphrase "East Coker," here have as clear an overtone of cyclical return as they have there of flux and succession. The "end" of the *Quartets* is implicit in the first movement of "Burnt Norton" just as it is explicit in this conclusion toward which the poetry has all pointed as toward its final cause. The phrases and sentences moving "in time" each make "an end and a beginning," forming in their configuration a pattern like that of time, where each moment is death and rebirth and the totality is stillness—the unity, as at the village dance in "East Coker," of love, of destiny, of Christ, "The complete consort dancing together. . . ." And at the stillness every end is at one with every beginning. But in the mood of "East Coker," too, the poet can call "Every poem an epitaph." Poetry, like all other human action, takes its beginning from the end, the death, toward which it conducts those who engage in it; the poets also, as Donne said of himself in his "Nocturnall upon S. Lucies day," are epitaphs to the past. All men are borne into the past, and thus as they die they take us with them; for, dying daily, we live by communion with what is dead and yet living. The dead "return" in our memory or otherwise—perhaps in ourselves—"and bring us with them."[105] Here, as in "A Song for Simeon," Eliot adapted the words of Heraclitus: "Those who do not die, die; those who die do not die: of one another they live the death and die the life."[106] In consequence the rose of life and the yew tree of death (with all their symbolic permutations) coexist in each moment. With the observation that

> A people without history
> Is not redeemed from time, for history is a pattern
> Of timeless moments

Eliot integrated the themes of "Burnt Norton" and "Little Gidding." The lines say that a people with history is redeemed from time, but likewise that in order to be so redeemed a people must live by the detachment beginning in attachment—not by indifference to that from which they sprang. If "history is a pattern / Of timeless moments," it is furthermore now, and since now is England "History is now and England," though "the light fails," or seems to fail, and though it is "a winter's afternoon" and the "Zero summer" of ultimate communion is far distant.

Deliberately, with a little pause before the balanced calm of the last strophe, the movement bridges its two parts with a quotation from the fourteenth-century mystical treatise *The Cloud of Unknowing*.[107] The love that draws is love of country, certainly, and probably the love in the garden too; but, as in its original context, it is chiefly the love of God; and it is the love of man for God, just as "the voice of this Calling" is the present action of the poet. The spiritual quest, the creative quest,[108] and every other endeavor in which the poet exerts himself is to be unremitting; the goal, like that in Joyce's *Finnegans Wake*, is to "know the place for the first time." Through the unopened gate, back to the Edenic origin of all man's movement, the unmoved center, "the source of the longest river" which is life itself; back to "The voice of the hidden waterfall" whose life-bearing waters (in the symbolism of Vaughan's poem) emanate from and return to God as beginning and end; back to "the children in the apple-tree" who are the unsullied eternal potentiality and fulfilment of man's freedom in paradise—this journey proceeds "in the stillness / Between two waves of the sea," at the eternal moment of the present suspended between past and future. By the discipline of action, of patience, of renunciation,

> A condition of complete simplicity
> (Costing not less than everything)

love and spiritual desire, poetry and history, out of the monstrous affliction of time all come to the best. "And all shall be well," therefore, when the fire of life is merged in the "crowned knot of fire"—a Trinity-knot, being the sailor's knot of three strands—and when suffering and love are found to be the same.[109] "For love," said St. John of the Cross, "is like fire, which ever rises upward with the desire to be absorbed in the center of its sphere."[110]

The pattern of ultimate reconciliation in *Four Quartets*, envisioning the redemption of time through knowledge of the One in the many, the eternal in the temporal, forms Eliot's most comprehensive poetic structure of ideas. Yet, though his earlier poems now seem to point to this ultimate formulation, they were individual efforts to reach it themselves, every one a separate attempt to fulfil its own potentiality. One shoots at a distant target not just to win the skill to hit it after many trials but to hit it, if possible, now. Because of their integrity, to which Eliot's varieties of technique themselves contributed, the previous poems have not been dwarfed by the *Quartets*. Some of them indeed have been magnified, for the very uniformity of Eliot's themes allows, within limits, the synthesis in the *Quartets* to be retroactive. As through Eliot's conception of the redeemability of the past through the actions of the present—an idea foreshadowed in "Tradition and the Individual Talent"—they reveal, when illuminated by the *Quartets*, the tenor of their latent meaning.

> Or say that the end precedes the beginning,
> And the end and the beginning were always there
> Before the beginning and after the end.

In the one multiplex pattern of the *Quartets*, history, art, love, and faith find a common ordering: the central problem, as now conceived, was always theodicy. Eliot has sought to vindicate the ways of God to man. The *Quartets*, a new *Essay on Man*, are poetic jottings of a philosophy holding that the world is an organ of the divine purpose. They are grounded in systems of aesthetics and physics, of psychology and epistemology, of ontology and ethics; one function of the present book has been to track down these specialities in Hinduism and Buddhism, in romanticism and symbolism, in contemporary philosophers and Aristotle, in Frazer, Bergson, and Bradley, in St. John of the Cross and St. Augustine. But more crucial than their learning is the testimony of these poems that, since all reality is at once a promise and a consummation of the divine love, all perplexities, whether social, aesthetic, personal, or intellectual, come from a need for God. In a teleological design Eliot has found the explanation for suffering and hence the remedy: to transcend by acceptance. All agonies have meaning and a use: although results of sin, they may become glorious through subjection of the human will to the divine plan. Thus, as the old disquiet induced by the bitterness of desire and by the apparent hopelessness of life has vanished from Eliot's poetry, faith in right action through humility has emerged. If the *Quartets* rather gloss over than solve the problem of sex and personal relations, still this fact would only confirm the ascetic temper of Eliot's mature work. To Eliot the one possible harmony, resulting from service to God, ideally motivates every human act but is seldom evinced in the actuality of human love.

Nobody knows how the future may judge the whole work of Eliot. Of the qualifications for permanent fame, he shows both intellectual seriousness and universality of matter. The need for "profundity" in poetry is occasionally denied. But if a poet is not to be only a writer of light verse, or, at best, a minor poet, he must not treat ideas as only an artistic resource from which to "work up" feeling. Such treatment, to be sure, is legitimate; on the other hand, ideas can never regulate poetic form without also stamping upon it the character of the poet's attitude toward them. It matters a good deal that a mysterious figure suspended head downward from a tree should really be the Hanged Man and not just a disguised possum swinging by the tail. As to universality, Eliot's death-and-rebirth theme, regardless of the stringent private necessity that it should have developed from "affirmative" quest to "negative" renunciation, is as universal a subject as a poet could aspire to. In these requirements Eliot is not found wanting. If, however, the momentousness of his pattern is not in doubt, still its moral and emotional finality very well may be. Apart from poetry by W. B. Yeats, that of Eliot may include the greatest written in the contemporary age; yet his poetry has perhaps failed in essential generosity and good humor, in steady compassion for the human lot. Nor has its austerity resulted from arid religious opinions; it was more austere before Eliot's Christian beliefs supervened, and they have been refreshing, though indeed they sprang from the brackish waste places of his young manhood.

If Eliot's poetic vision falters, it does so because of its peculiar privacy, which admits no wide sympathies. For Eliot lacks a ready power of empathy, of self-projection into the points of view of others; he lacks, therefore, in contradistinction to the great dramatists, the power of reporting a world seen from many angles, as a one-eyed man lacks stereopsis. His personages, however artfully posed in a fictitious setting or made articulate by a noble rhetoric, are too often more masks than characters, if not patently himself; and when they face one another (even, although with qualifications, in *The Confidential Clerk*), they come alive mainly to resume his inward debate. No doubt in plays, as Eliot long ago remarked, and maybe in poems too, the personages should be "somehow dramatizing, but in no obvious form, an action or struggle for harmony in the soul of the poet";[111] but if the form is not to be obvious, they should have a variety of which their archetype himself may be incapable. Eliot, though a master of the dramatic, is not a gifted dramatist, for the world he sees moves round "a center of his own" and from that center, special and confined, receives its impulse toward form—its whole order of emotional and moral values. The people of Eliot's world behave in the way Eliot has felt, and they are mostly a disenchanted lot. Few good poets, and never the greatest, have depicted only their own range of emotions; their art has rather consisted in reconstructing, imitatively, both the emotions they have had and those they have divined. In no play and in hardly more than one poem of Eliot's, the youthful "Portrait of a Lady," is there pure realization of an external character. The technical lesson of his poetry may lie in the futility of his repeated labor to reach the impersonal through dramatic camouflage; for of all expedients the dramatic monologue, so long as it draws its subject matter from interior suffering, has the least necessity or opportunity for diversifying its point of view. In the *Quartets*, apart from a few passages, Eliot circumvented the problem, for, by minimizing dramatic attitudes and by dwelling on ideas, he created here an illusion of objectivity.

Yet even at its grandest, surveying in *Four Quartets* a peopled cosmos, Eliot's strange, private vision still faces inward to the isolated self. Sometimes a poet may learn by action, by accidental experience, to bring into his craft proper the passions of all sorts and conditions of men. Eliot, great though much of his poetry is, was not this fortunate.

*NOTES AND REFERENCES*

# NOTES AND REFERENCES

Most of Eliot's poetry is contained in *Collected Poems 1909–1935* (New York, 1936), *Murder in the Cathedral* (New York, 1936), *The Family Reunion* (New York, 1939), *Four Quartets* (New York, 1943), *The Cocktail Party* (New York, 1950), *The Confidential Clerk* (New York, 1954), *The Rock* (New York, 1934), and *The Film of Murder in the Cathedral* (New York, 1952). The first five of these volumes have been reprinted as the so-called *Complete Poems and Plays* (New York, 1952), along with *Old Possum's Book of Practical Cats* (New York, 1939). All are published by Harcourt, Brace and Company and are copyrighted. Eliot's principal English publisher is Faber and Faber, Ltd., London. I have adopted at one point a variant reading from the Faber 1944 edition of *Four Quartets*.

Certain poems were first published in *Prufrock and Other Observations* (London, 1917), *Ara Vos Prec* (London, 1920), or *Poems 1909–1925* (London, 1925); others appeared in pamphlets or periodicals, concerning which see Donald Gallup, *T. S. Eliot: A Bibliography* (London, 1952).

## NOTES TO CHAPTER 1

1. T. S. Eliot, *Selected Essays 1917–1932* (New York, 1932), p. 340 (hereinafter cited as "*Selected Essays*").

2. Eliot mentions this poem in the essay "Byron (1788–1824)," *From Anne to Victoria: Essays by Various Hands,* ed. Bonamy Dobrée (New York, 1937), p. 602.

3. Probably Eliot took some time to master the intricacies of F. H. Bradley's philosophy. But he waited until June 12, 1913, to buy a copy of Bradley's *Appearance and Reality* from the Harvard Co-operative.

4. On June 26, 1915, Eliot was married to Vivienne Haigh Haigh-Wood, the daughter of the painter Charles Haigh Haigh-Wood, and from then until the end of the year he was living with Mrs. Eliot's parents in Hampstead. For some months in this period he made a trial of teaching, first at the High Wycombe Grammar School and afterward at the Highgate School, where he remained four terms. Giving up schoolmastering, he found a place in Lloyds Bank. His serious financial difficulties at that time are reported to have been somewhat alleviated through the good offices of Bertrand Russell; then also, or a little later, Russell shared with the Eliots his home in London. Until 1925, when Eliot went into the publishing firm of Faber and Gwyer (now Faber and Faber), his time was divided between the bank job and outside tasks, including extension lecturing, book-reviewing for the *Athenaeum,* the *Times Literary Supplement,* and other periodicals, and editorial work for the *Egoist* and subsequently for the *Criterion,* which he edited from 1922 to 1939. In 1927 he was

confirmed into the Church of England and in the same year became a British subject. He gave the Clark Lectures at Trinity College, Cambridge, in 1926, and lectured at Harvard in 1932–33, at the University of Virginia in 1933, and at the University of Chicago in 1950. In 1948 he received the Order of Merit and the Nobel Prize. He is said to have declined knighthood.

Mrs. Eliot, in ill health for a long period, spent her final years in a nursing home, where she died in January, 1947. Eliot separated from her in 1933.

For biographical material on Eliot see *Time*, LV, No. 10 (March 6, 1950), 22–26; Kristian Smidt, *Poetry and Belief in the Work of T. S. Eliot* (Oslo, 1949), pp. 22–45 (hereinafter cited as "Smidt"); *Harvard College Class of 1910 Twenty-fifth Anniversary Report* (Cambridge, Mass., 1935), pp. 219–21.

5. There is a brief digest by R. W. Church, "Eliot on Bradley's Metaphysic," *Harvard Advocate*, CXXV, No. 3 (December, 1938), 24–26. The dissertation remains unpublished; the final typescript, except for its missing last page, is preserved in the Houghton Library at Harvard. Since Eliot did not return to America until 1932, he did not take his degree, although the work on Bradley was acceptable.

6. Smidt, pp. 129–37.

7. Eliot, review of *Baudelaire and the Symbolists*, by Peter Quennell, *Criterion*, IX (January, 1930), 357.

8. See Eliot, "A Commentary," *Criterion*, XII (April, 1933), 469; cited by George Williamson, *A Reader's Guide to T. S. Eliot* (New York, 1953), p. 55.

9. In Paul Valéry, *Le Serpent* (London, 1924), p. 12.

10. See Eliot, "The Poetry of W. B. Yeats," *Southern Review*, VII (Winter, 1941), 446.

11. In Storm Jameson (ed.), *London Calling* (New York and London, 1942), pp. 237–38.

12. Eliot, *On Poetry* (Concord, Mass., 1947), p. 10. His use of mythology is scarcely illuminated by his review of Joyce in *"Ulysses*, Order and Myth," *Dial*, LXXV (November, 1923), 480–83, where he pointed out only a social meaning for myth.

13. Lady Charlotte Guest (trans.), *The Mabinogion* (London and New York, 1906), p. 185.

14. In his essay on Baudelaire in *Selected Essays*, p. 343, Eliot distinguished between "the romantic idea" and "the reaching out towards something which cannot be had *in*, but which may be had partly *through*, personal relations." But this precisely is "the romantic idea."

15. See Norman Nicholson, "T. S. Eliot," *Writers of To-day*, ed. Denys Val Baker (London, 1946), pp. 139–43; cf. Charles Williams, *The Figure of Beatrice: A Study in Dante* (London, 1943), pp. 8–10.

## NOTES TO CHAPTER 2

1. Cf. Jules Laforgue, "Sur une défunte," *Poésies* (Paris, 1909), pp. 330 ff. Eliot's extensive French sources have been analyzed by René Taupin, *L'Influence du symbolisme français sur la poésie américaine de 1910 à 1920* (Paris, 1929), pp. 225–32; Edmund Wilson, "T. S. Eliot," *T. S. Eliot: A Selected Critique*, ed. Leonard Unger (New York and Toronto, 1948), pp. 171–74 (this book is hereinafter cited as "Unger"); M. J. J. Laboulle, "T. S. Eliot and Some French Poets," *Revue de Littérature Comparée*, XVI (avril–juin, 1936), 389–99; Edward J. H. Greene, *T. S. Eliot et la France* (Paris, 1951); Warren Ramsey,

*Jules Laforgue and the Ironic Inheritance* (New York, 1953), pp. 192–94, 197–204; Bruce A. Morrissette, "T. S. Eliot and Guillaume Apollinaire," *Comparative Literature*, V (Summer, 1953), 262–68.

2. Cf. Tristan Corbière, "Rapsodie du sourd," *Les Amours jaunes* (Paris, 1903), p. 126:

> Bats en branle ce bon tam-tam, chaudron fêlé
> Qui rend la voix de femme ainsi qu'une sonnette. ...

Eliot's adjoining lines recall J. R. Lowell's description of the wind, in *The Vision of Sir Launfal*,

> Singing, in dreary monotone,
> A Christmas carol of its own. . . .

3. Henry James, *The Ambassadors*, chap. 5. The title "Portrait of a Lady" echoes that of a James novel. Distinctly Jamesian also is the dramatic poise of Eliot's characters, with their decorous understatements and "velleities." In *The Ambassadors* (chap. 33) Mme de Vionnet parts from Strether with the words: ". . . we might, you and I, have been friends"; Maria Gostrey repeats them in the chapter following.

4. That letter, written June 7, 1916, is now in the Houghton Library.

5. Henry James, *Maud-Evelyn, The Special Type, The Papers, and Other Tales* (London, 1923), pp. 321–61. "Crapy Cornelia" first appeared in *Harper's Magazine* in October, 1909.

6. Stephen Stepanchev, "The Origin of J. Alfred Prufrock," *Modern Language Notes*, LXVI (June, 1951), 400–401.

7. No one seems to have pointed out Eliot's apparent debt for the table image to the opening lines of Laforgue's "Complaintes sur certains temps déplacés" (*Poésies*, p. 156):

> Le couchant de sang est taché
> Comme un tablier de boucher;
> Oh! qui veut aussi m'écorcher!

—or to comparable lines in "Derniers Vers," xii (*ibid.*, p. 336). Laforgue's image recalls Baudelaire's "Harmonie du soir" in *Les Fleurs du mal:* "Le soleil s'est noyé dans son sang qui se fige."

8. Cf. Gérard de Nerval, "Les Papillons," *Poésies* (Lausanne, 1944), p. 73:

> Une toute jeune fille
> Au cœur tendre, au doux souris,
> Perçant vos cœurs d'une aiguille,
> Vous contemple, l'œil surpris. ...

9. Roberta Morgan and Albert Wohlstetter, "Observations on 'Prufrock,'" *Harvard Advocate*, CXXV, No. 3 (December, 1938), 30.

10. Perhaps an allusion to *Hamlet*, Act II, scene 2, lines 204–6.

11. A reference to cigar ends, probably; but see Nietzsche, *Also Sprach Zarathustra*, xlvi, 2.

12. John C. Pope, "Prufrock and Raskolnikov," *American Literature*, XVII (November, 1945), 213–30; "Prufrock and Raskolnikov Again: A Letter from Eliot," *American Literature*, XVIII (January, 1947), 319–21.

13. Eliot's three final lines seem to echo John Masefield's "Cardigan Bay," from *Salt-Water Ballads* (1902):

> Delicate, cool sea-weeds, green and amber-brown,
> In beds where shaken sunlight slowly filters down
> On many a drowned seventy-four, many a sunken town,
> And the whitening of the dead men's skulls.

Other sources include *Julius Caesar*, Act V, scene 2, line 103; *Twelfth Night*, Act I, scene 1, line 4; *II Henry IV*, Act II, scene 4, line 293; Chaucer's *General Prologue*, line 306; and perhaps Tennyson's *Maud*. On the last see W. K. Wimsatt, Jr., "Prufrock and Maud: From Plot to Symbol," *Yale French Studies*, No. 9, 1952, pp. 84–92. For general analyses see Morgan and Wohlstetter, *Harvard Advocate*, CXXV, No. 3, 27–30, 33–40; Cleanth Brooks, Jr., and Robert Penn Warren, *Understanding Poetry* (New York, 1950), pp. 433–44; Roy P. Basler, *Sex, Symbolism, and Psychology in Literature* (New Brunswick, N.J., 1948), pp. 203–21; Elizabeth Drew, *T. S. Eliot: The Design of His Poetry* (New York, 1949), pp. 34–36 (hereinafter cited as "Drew") ; Morris Weitz, *Philosophy of the Arts* (Cambridge, Mass., 1950), pp. 94–107.

14. Charles-Louis Philippe, *Bubu of Montparnasse* (Paris, 1932), chap. 4. See my article, "Charles-Louis Philippe and T. S. Eliot," *American Literature*, XXII (November, 1950), 254–59. Eliot's Eeldrop, in one of his conversations with Appleplex, remarks that he tests people by the way he imagines them as waking up in the morning: "Eeldrop and Appleplex. II," *Little Review*, IV, No. 5 (September, 1917), 18.

15. See Charles-Louis Philippe, *Marie Donadieu* (Paris, 1921), pp. 92–93.

16. *Ibid.*, p. 72.

17. See Philippe, *Bubu of Montparnasse*, chap. 1. Eliot's words in French were adapted from Laforgue's "Complainte de cette bonne lune" (*Poésies*, p. 74). There is a prototype of the Laforguian moon in Shelley, "The Waning Moon." The recollection referred to may be found in Eliot, *The Use of Poetry and the Use of Criticism* (London, 1933), pp. 78–79.

18. Philippe, *Marie Donadieu*, p. 93.

19. Wilde probably remembered John Heywood's *A Woman Killed with Kindness*, Act IV, scene 5:

> Astonishment,
> Fear, and amazement play against my heart,
> Even as a madman beats upon a drum.

20. Laforgue, *Poésies*, pp. 132–33.

21. Smidt, p. 95; Helen Gardner, *The Art of T. S. Eliot* (London, 1949), p. 107.

22. This line might be compared with a passage in a novel favorably regarded by Eliot, Wilkie Collins' *The Woman in White*, Part I, chap. 15: "She left the room. I turned away towards the window, where nothing faced me but the lonely autumn landscape—I turned away to master myself, before I, too, left the room in my turn, and left it for ever."

23. See Tennyson, *Maud*, especially I, 301–7, 212–15, 322.


NOTES TO CHAPTER 3

1. Ezra Pound, *Letters 1907–1941*, ed. D. D. Paige (New York, 1950), p. 142.

2. Eliot, "On a Recent Piece of Criticism," *Purpose*, X (April–June, 1938), 91–92.

3. Harriet Monroe, *A Poet's Life* (New York, 1938), p. 394.

4. Conrad Aiken, "King Bolo and Others," *T. S. Eliot: A Symposium*, ed. Richard March and Tambimuttu (London, 1948), p. 22 (this book is hereinafter cited as "March and Tambimuttu") ; Eliot, *Purpose*, X, 91, and "Ezra Pound," *Poetry*, LXVIII (September, 1946), 327.

5. Stanley K. Coffman, Jr., *Imagism: A Chapter for the History of Modern Poetry* (Norman, Okla., 1951), pp. 42–43.

6. Edward Lear, "The Story of the Four Little Children Who Went round the World."

7. Clive Bell, "How Pleasant To Know Mr Eliot," March and Tambimuttu, p. 15.

8. Eliot's title may have originated in Ford Madox Hueffer's *Mr. Apollo* (London, 1908), with some admixture with the name of M. Aronnax in Jules Verne's *Twenty Thousand Leagues under the Sea.*

9. Greene, *T. S. Eliot et la France,* pp. 63–64.

10. Wyndham Lewis, "Early London Environment," March and Tambimuttu, p. 27; Pound, *Gaudier-Brzeska* (London and New York, 1916), pp. 50–52, Pl. XXI.

11. Charles Whibley, *Studies in Frankness* (London, 1898), p. 217; Jane Worthington, "The Epigraphs to the Poetry of T. S. Eliot," *American Literature,* XXI (March, 1949), 2–4.

12. I have seen three or four lines in an unpublished letter of Pound's. See Alfred Kreymborg, *Our Singing Strength* (New York, 1929), p. 520; Aiken, March and Tambimuttu, p. 22; Pound, *Letters,* p. 171.

13. *Noctes Binanianae: Certain Voluntary and Satyrical Verses and Compliments as were lately Exchang'd between some of the Choicest Wits of the Age* (London, 1939). This hodgepodge was by Eliot, F. V. Morley, G. C. Faber, and John Hayward. Eliot contributed nine poems (*ca.* 1937–38), one being in French and one in German. The principals figure in one another's verses as the Whale (Morley), the Coot (Faber), the Spider (Hayward), and the Elephant or Possum (Eliot). An elephant's head surmounts the Eliot arms as depicted on the bookplate Eliot used while at Harvard and later; his copy of *From Ritual to Romance* contains this bookplate.

14. Laforgue, *Poésies,* p. 139.

15. Corbière, *Les Amours jaunes,* p. 234.

16. Eliot's French style was influenced by Jean de Bosschère, whose *The Closed Door,* trans. F. S. Flint (London and New York, 1917), he reviewed, *Egoist,* IV (October, 1917), 133. Indeed, his review cites a quotation from Bosschère's "Homère Mare" ("Pendant quatre saisons Homère voyage"), which forms part of a passage found by René Taupin to be comparable to the "catalogue" in "Mélange." See *L'Influence du symbolisme français,* pp. 219–20. The same passage seemingly influenced "Gerontion."

17. See my article, "Observations on Eliot's 'Death by Water,'" *Accent,* VI (Summer, 1946), 260.

18. A flagrant breach of juvenile etiquette. See M. B. DeMonvel's charming cautionary illustration in the "manners book" *Good Children and Bad* (New York, 1890), p. 29.

19. Eliot, *The Use of Poetry,* p. 69.

20. Philippe, *Marie Donadieu,* pp. 153–54.

21. Arthur Rimbaud, *Œuvres: vers et proses* (Paris, 1924), p. 61.

22. *Ibid.,* p. 63.

23. Laforgue, *Poésies,* p. 50.

24. Jules Laforgue, *Moralités légendaires* (Paris, 1909), pp. 242–49.

25. Laforgue, *Poésies,* p. 373.

26. See Byron, *Don Juan,* III, xcix.

27. Cf. Eliot, *Poetry*, LXVIII, 335.

28. Ezra Pound, *Personae* (New York, 1926), p. 189.

29. Théophile Gautier, *Poésies complètes* (Paris, 1912–16), I, 344. Cf. his "Albertus ou l'âme et le péché" (cxviii), *ibid.*, p. 182.

30. Col. 4:16; Rev. 3:14–18.

31. John Bramhall, *Works* (Oxford, 1842), I, 42–43.

32. Théophile Gautier, *Émaux et camées* (Paris, 1927), p. 115.

33. *Ibid.*, pp. 97, 99; Gautier, *Poésies complètes*, II, 9–49.

34. *Selected Essays*, p. 247.

35. Dilys Powell, *Descent from Parnassus* (London and New York, 1934), p. 68; Charles C. Walcutt, "Eliot's 'Whispers of Immortality,'" *Explicator*, VII (November, 1948), 11.

36. *Seventeenth Century Studies Presented to Sir Herbert Grierson* (Oxford, 1938), p. 242.

37. See Pound, *The Pisan Cantos*, p. 44, in *The Cantos of Ezra Pound* (New York, 1948).

38. The style of painting Eliot had in mind might be typified by Perugino's "Baptism of Christ" (Foligno). With the stanza cf. Gautier's "L'Art," *Émaux et camées*, p. 95.

39. Laforgue, *Poésies*, p. 392.

40. March and Tambimuttu, p. 21. There seems little merit to the suggestion that Sweeney may have originated in the Irish folk hero Suibhne (Sweeney) the Mad; but see Lloyd Frankenberg, *Pleasure Dome: On Reading Modern Poetry* (Boston, 1949), pp. 96–101.

41. Robert Payne, *The Great God Pan* (New York, 1952), p. 75; see E. S. Turner, *Boys Will Be Boys* (London, 1948), pp. 37–47.

42. Eliot's final stanza seems indebted to E. D. A. Morshead's translation of the boast by Clytemnestra in *The House of Atreus* (London, 1901), pp. 64–65:

> I trapped him with inextricable toils,
> The ill abundance of a baffling robe;
> Then smote him, once, again—and at each wound
> He cried aloud. . . .
>
> .  .  .  .  .  .  .  .  .  .
> And the dark sprinklings of the rain of blood
> Fell upon me; and I was fain to feel
> That dew. . . .

43. The title of this Sweeney poem, as F. L. Gwynn has pointed out, may be a parody of E. B. Browning's "Bianca among the Nightingales."

44. Eliot stated in 1949 that he had used the edition of C. F. Tucker Brooke, *The Shakespeare Apocrypha* (Oxford, 1908).

45. F. O. Matthiessen, *The Achievement of T. S. Eliot* (New York and London, 1947), p. 129 (hereinafter cited as "Matthiessen").

46. Drew, p. 45.

47. Wilson, Unger, pp. 174 ff.; Douglas Bush, *Mythology and the Romantic Tradition in English Poetry* (Cambridge, Mass., 1937), pp. 513–14. See also Drew, pp. 42–46.

48. See Hugh Ross Williamson, *The Poetry of T. S. Eliot* (London, 1932), p. 166.

49. An incidental theme of betrayal is perhaps suggested through the echo of J. G. Whittier's "Ichabod" (". . . dim, / Dishonored brow"); cited by Wilson, Unger, p. 181.

50. I. A. Richards, "The Poetry of T. S. Eliot," Unger, p. 219.

51. Wilson, Unger, p. 175.

52. Matthiessen, p. 130.

53. Villon, *Le Testament*, lines 1–2.

54. George Wyndham, *Essays in Romantic Literature* (London, 1919); Eliot, "A Romantic Patrician," *Athenaeum*, No. 4644, May 2, 1919, pp. 265–67. "A Cooking Egg" appeared in *Coterie*, No. 1, May-day, 1919, pp. 44–45.

55. See *Selected Essays*, p. 223.

56. Matthiessen, p. 92.

57. There are analyses of "Burbank" by Laura Riding and Robert Graves, *A Survey of Modernist Poetry* (London, 1927), pp. 235–42; and Drew, pp. 39–42.

58. Richards, Unger, pp. 216–17; Riding and Graves, *A Survey of Modernist Poetry*, pp. 236–37; Matthiessen, p. 53; Worthington, *American Literature*, XXI, 6–7.

59. Gautier, *Émaux et camées*, p. 18.

60. See Paul Kristeller, *Andrea Mantegna* (New York, 1901), pp. 329–31.

61. Henry James, *The Aspern Papers, Louisa Pallant, The Modern Warning* (New York, 1888), p. 7.

62. Cf. *Othello*, Act III, scene 3, lines 402–3.

63. John Marston, *Works*, ed. A. H. Bullen (London, 1887), III, 404.

64. See Eliot, "Reflections on Contemporary Poetry [IV]," *Egoist*, VI (July, 1919), 39; *Selected Essays*, p. 59; *The Use of Poetry*, p. 147.

65. Cited by Frank Wilson, *Six Essays on the Development of T. S. Eliot* (London, 1948), p. 17.

66. Gautier, *Émaux et camées*, p. 19.

67. Byron, *Childe Harold's Pilgrimage*, IV, xi.

68. Gautier, "Les Lions de l'Arsenal, à Venise," *Poésies complètes*, II, 210.

69. *Selected Essays*, p. 4.

70. See Henri Bergson, *Matter and Memory* (London and New York, 1911), chap. 3.

## NOTES TO CHAPTER 4

1. Eliot's epigraph came from *Measure for Measure*, Act III, scene 1, lines 32–34; the scene contributed other material to the poem. Reference to the following will indicate the scope of Eliot's other adaptations: Chapman, *The Tragedy of Charles Duke of Byron*, Act V, scene 3, lines 189–98; *King Lear*, Act IV, scene 1, lines 21–23; Tourneur, *The Revenger's Tragedy*, Act III, scene 4 (the passage beginning "Look you, brother"); Middleton, *The Changeling*, Act V, scene 3, line 152; *Antony and Cleopatra*, Act II, scene 2, lines 241–43; *The Merchant of Venice*, Act III, scene 1, line 128; Jonson, *The Alchemist*, Act II, scene 3, lines 195–96, and Act III, scene 2, lines 45–48; Chapman, *Bussy D'Ambois*, Act V, scene 4, lines 104–6. On the last, see Wolf Mankowitz, "Notes on 'Gerontion,'" *T. S. Eliot: A Study of His Writings by Several Hands*, ed. B. Rajan (London, 1947), p. 137 (this book is hereinafter cited as "Rajan").

2. Henri Bergson, *Creative Evolution* (New York, 1937), p. 4.

3. See Marcel Proust, *The Remembrance of Things Past*, trans. C. K. Scott Moncrieff (New York, 1934), I, 15.

4. Cf. Richards, Unger, pp. 218–19.

5. The comparison has been made by Oscar Cargill, *Intellectual America* (New York, 1941), p. 235.

6. See Hyatt Howe Waggoner, "T. S. Eliot and the Hollow Men," *American Literature*, XV (May, 1943), 101–26.

7. See *Selected Essays*, p. 5.

8. Bergson, *Matter and Memory*, chap. 3.

9. See James Joyce, *Ulysses* (New York, 1934), p. 26.

10. *Ibid.*, p. 34.

11. See Drew, pp. 51–52; Jonathan Edwards, *Works* (New York, 1843), IV, 263. Eliot's passage is sometimes compared with one in Lancelot Andrewes, *Works* (Oxford, 1854), I, 258, which remarks sarcastically, "Christ is no wildcat"; but Andrewes' context is hardly analogous. See *Selected Essays*, p. 297; William Van O'Connor, *"Gerontion* and *The Dream of Gerontius," Furioso*, III, No. 1 (Winter, 1947), 54–55.

12. Ruth Bailey, *A Dialogue on Modern Poetry* (London, 1939), pp. 15 ff.; Drew, pp. 47 ff.

13. Eliot's source here was Andrewes, *Works*, I, 204: "Signs are taken for wonders. 'Master, we would fain see a sign' [Matt. 12:38], that is a miracle. And in this sense it is a sign to wonder at. Indeed, every word here is a wonder. . . . *Verbum infans*, the Word without a word; the eternal Word not able to speak a word; 1. a wonder sure. 2. And . . . swaddled; and that a wonder too."

14. Chaucer, *The Parlement of Foules*, line 80.

15. Cf. *The Education of Henry Adams* (Boston and New York, 1918), p. 268; Matthiessen, p. 73. Eliot reviewed Adams in "A Sceptical Patrician," *Athenaeum*, No. 4647, May 23, 1919, pp. 361–62.

16. Adams, *The Education of Henry Adams*, p. 400.

17. "Cunning" evidently came from the "axletree" passage in *Bussy D'Ambois*, where "burning axletree," through an original misprint "curning," was corrupted to "cunning axletree" in the edition Eliot had: *sc., George Chapman* ("Mermaid Series"), ed. W. L. Phelps (London and New York, 1895).

18. Adams, *The Education of Henry Adams*, p. 431. The relation to "Gerontion" has been observed by Cleanth Brooks, to whom I am indebted for several sugestions here.

19. *Ibid.*, p. 451; see pp. 457–58.

20. See *ibid.*, p. 474.

21. See Hugh Kenner, "Eliot's Moral Dialectic," *Hudson Review*, II (Autumn, 1949), 426.

22. A. C. Benson, *Edward FitzGerald* (New York and London, 1905), p. 142; Matthiessen, pp. 73–74; Eliot, *Purpose*, X, 93.

23. Benson, *Edward FitzGerald*, p. 29; John Abbot Clark, "On First Looking into Benson's *FitzGerald," South Atlantic Quarterly*, XLVIII (April, 1949), 260.

24. Joseph Conrad, *Youth: A Narrative, and Two Other Stories* (London, Toronto, and Paris, 1923), p. 149.

25. Eliot was probably influenced in his "salt marsh" passage by "Heart of Darkness" (*ibid.*, pp. 49–50).

26. *Selected Essays*, p. 125.

27. Pound, *Letters*, pp. 169–72.

## NOTES TO CHAPTER 5

1. *Time*, LV, No. 10 (March 6, 1950), 24. The help of the Bel Esprit fund was mentioned by Pound in an interview to the *New York Times*, June 17, 1923, Sec. III, p. 18, col. 3. See Pound, *Letters*, pp. 172–76.

2. See Eliot, "London Letter," *Dial*, LXXII (May, 1922), 510; cf. Eliot, *Poetry*, LXVIII, 330.

3. *Tyro*, No. 1, 1922, p. 6. In April, 1922, Eliot spoke of *Tyro* as having "only just now appeared" (*Dial*, LXXII, 513).

4. Pound, *Letters*, p. 169. Elizabeth Drew is mistaken in stating (p. 91) that the proposed quotation was that later prefixed to "The Hollow Men."

5. D. G. Rossetti, *Works* (London, 1911), p. 240.

6. See Sir James Frazer, *The Golden Bough* (3d ed.; London, 1911–19), IV, 75–77.

7. W. F. Jackson Knight, *Cumaean Gates: A Reference of the Sixth Aeneid to the Initiation Pattern* (Oxford, 1936), *passim*.

8. Alfred Nutt, *Studies on the Legend of the Holy Grail* (London, 1888), p. 28.

9. See Ferner Nuhn, *The Wind Blew from the East* (New York and London, 1942), pp. 221 ff.

10. The volume (Cambridge, 1920), left unannotated by Eliot, is in the Houghton Library.

11. Colin Still, *Shakespeare's Mystery Play: A Study of "The Tempest"* (London, 1921); Eliot, Introduction to G. Wilson Knight, *The Wheel of Fire* (London, 1930), p. xix.

12. See Margaret Diggle, "The *Ancient Mariner* and *The Waste Land*," *Poetry: London*, II (1944), 195, 205–8; William C. DeVane (ed.), *The Shorter Poems of Robert Browning* (New York, 1939), p. 351.

13. Eliot, "London Letter," *Dial*, LXXI (October, 1921), 453. Eliot probably kept up with the progress of ballet for several years before writing *The Waste Land*. Mrs. Eliot had studied ballet before their marriage. See *Time*, LV, No. 10 (March 6, 1950), 23.

## NOTES TO CHAPTER 6

1. Besides those already cited, valuable commentaries on the poem include R. P. Blackmur, "T. S. Eliot," *Hound and Horn*, I (March, 1928), 187–213; Wilson, Unger, pp. 177–84; Ross Williamson, *The Poetry of T. S. Eliot*, pp. 78–150; F. R. Leavis, *New Bearings in English Poetry* (London, 1932), pp. 91–114; C. R. Jury, *T. S. Eliot's The Waste Land: Some Annotations* (Adelaide, 1932); Matthiessen; Cleanth Brooks, "*The Waste Land*: Critique of the Myth," Unger, pp. 319–48; Williamson, *A Reader's Guide to T. S. Eliot*, pp. 115–54. See also H. Reid MacCallum, "*The Waste Land* after Twenty-five Years," *Here and Now*, I (December, 1947), 16–24; Eric Mesterton, *The Waste Land: Some Commentaries* (Chicago, 1943); Derek Traversi, "*The Waste Land* Revisited," *Dublin Review*, No. 443, 1948, pp. 106–23; Drew, pp. 58–90; C. M. Bowra, *The Creative Experiment* (London, 1949), pp. 159–88.

2. Cf. Philippe, *Bubu of Montparnasse*, chap. 1: "A man walks carrying with him all the properties of his life, and they churn about in his head. Something he sees awakens them, something else excites them. For our flesh has retained all our memories, and we mingle them with our desires."

3. James Thomson, "To Our Ladies of Death," *The City of Dreadful Night, and Other Poems* (London, 1910), p. 148.

4. Cf. Rupert Brooke, *Letters from America* (New York, 1916), p. 174; Matthiessen, pp. 92–93.

5. Eccles. 12:5.

6. Ezek. 6:3–4.

7. Job 8:9, 13, 16–17.

8. Isa. 56:3.

9. Weston, *From Ritual to Romance*, pp. 62–71.

10. *Ibid.*, p. 13.

11. *Ibid.*, p. 159; Knight, *Cumaean Gates*, p. 144.

12. Frazer, *The Golden Bough*, Vol. V, Book II, chap. 7.

13. Cf. Dante, *Inferno*, XXXIV, 25: "Io non morii, e non rimasi vivo." With the phrase "heart of light," cf. *Paradiso*, XII, 28: "del cor dell'una delle luci nuove."

14. Jessie L. Weston, *From Ritual to Romance*, p. 114, says that in the Grail "ritual" the Fisher King may have been an effigy, whose place the quester filled in the course of initiation. Here, as it were, the quester becomes an effigy.

15. Ross Williamson, *The Poetry of T. S. Eliot*, pp. 93–94.

16. See Leonard Unger, "T. S. Eliot's Rose Garden," Unger, pp. 374 ff.; Louis L. Martz, "The Wheel and the Point: Aspects of Imagery and Theme in Eliot's Later Poetry," Unger, pp. 444–62.

17. Brooks, Unger, p. 323.

18. Aldous Huxley, *Crome Yellow* (London, 1921), chap. 27. See my article, "The Fortuneteller in Eliot's *Waste Land*," *American Literature*, XXV (January, 1954), 490–92.

19. Pound wrote three little poems into his correspondence with Eliot about *The Waste Land;* one of them was called "Sage Homme" (*Letters*, p. 170). I suspect no direct connection here, but the conceit is amusing: Pound was the midwife for Eliot's production. Eliot wanted (perhaps not seriously) to use the two relevant "squibs" with it, but Pound overruled the idea. The third poem did not concern Eliot. It is omitted from the bowdlerized Pound *Letters.*

20. Weston, *From Ritual to Romance*, pp. 71–76.

21. *Ibid.*, p. 75.

22. A. E. Waite, *The Pictorial Key to the Tarot* (London, 1911). I have no idea whether Eliot knew this book. One must bear in mind his statement, whatever it may have meant, that he was "not familiar with the exact constitution of the Tarot pack of cards."

23. Eliot, *Poèmes 1910–1930* (Paris, 1947), p. 140. But see Drew, p. 73.

24. Cf. North's Plutarch (*Crassus*), as quoted by Wyndham, *Essays in Romantic Literature*, pp. 173–74: "[With their] kettle drommes, hollow within . . . they all made a noise everywhere together, and it is like a dead sounde. . . . The Romans being put in feare with this dead sounde, the Parthians straight threw the clothes and coverings from them that hid their armour. . . ." Eliot noticed the passage in his review of Wyndham.

25. Brooks, Unger, p. 325.

26. Plutarch *Isis and Osiris* xxxvi.

27. Joyce, *Ulysses*, p. 47.

28. J. Rendel Harris, *The Ascent of Olympus* (Manchester, 1917), pp. 109 ff.

29. Sir James Frazer, *Folk-Lore in the Old Testament* (London, 1919), II, 381–82.

30. James Huneker, *Egoists: A Book of Supermen* (New York, 1909), p. 67.

31. On the link between Belladonna, Leonardo da Vinci, and Walter Pater see my article, "T. S. Eliot's Lady of the Rocks," *Notes and Queries*, CXCIV (March 19, 1949), 123–25.

32. Cf. Eccles. 2:14: "The wise man's eyes are in his head; but the fool walketh in darkness. . . ."

33. It was apparently this passage that recalled to Pound and caused him to paraphrase in writing to Eliot (*Letters*, p. 169) a line from Tennyson's "The Epic": ". . . mouthing out his hollow oes and aes."

34. *Aeneid* iv. 589–90. Cf. Beaumont and Fletcher, *Philaster*, Act III, scene 2:

> Thou hast overthrown me once;
> Yet, if I had another Troy to lose,
> Thou, or another villain with thy looks,
> Might talk me out of it, and send me naked,
> My hair dishevelled, through the fiery streets.

But see also Rossetti's translation of *Vita nuova*, xxiii ("Canzone," stanza 4).

35. Brooks, Unger, p. 328.

36. See Rossetti, *The House of Life*, lxiii.

37. See Weston, *From Ritual to Romance*, pp. 28–30.

38. Joyce, *Ulysses*, pp. 95, 112. Observe also the phrasing used earlier by Stephen (p. 43): ". . . pretending to speak broken English as you dragged your valise, porter threepence, across the slimy pier at Newhaven."

39. *Ibid.*, p. 89; see also pp. 102, 106.

40. Weston, *From Ritual to Romance*, chap. 9.

41. Joyce, *Ulysses*, p. 50.

42. Brooks, Unger, p. 332.

43. Eliot's "White bodies naked on the low damp ground" sounds like an echo of Walter Kittredge's "Tenting on the Old Camp Ground," though the rhythm recalls Vachel Lindsay. The "low dry garret" was perhaps suggested by Svidrigaïlov's garret in *Crime and Punishment*, Part VI, chap. 6.

44. Cf. *The Merchant of Venice*, Act V, scene 1, lines 1–6.

45. See Payne, *The Great God Pan*, pp. 144–45.

46. Bowra, *The Creative Experiment*, p. 182.

47. Bell, March and Tambimuttu, p. 16. I do not know what "Ayrian" means; Eliot could hardly have been referring to Ayr in Scotland.

48. I am obliged to the diligence of Brian Elliott, of Adelaide, who has obtained this version. A similar one, R. C. Bald informs me, was known in Australia before the first World War.

49. Traditionally the nightingale has four cries, *Fie, Jug, Nemesis,* and *Tereu.*

50. See Weston, *From Ritual to Romance*, p. 160.

51. Brooks, Unger, p. 333.

52. Guest (trans.), *The Mabinogion*, pp. 200–206.

53. Frazer, *The Golden Bough*, Vol. IX, chap. 8 and "Note."

54. For possible ritual origins see *ibid.*, VI, 257–58; IV, 82–84.

55. Cited by Nuhn, *The Wind Blew from the East*, p. 234.

56. Drew, p. 80; see Frazer, *The Golden Bough*, V, 36 ff.; VI, 264–66.

57. Drew, pp. 91–92.

58. Brooks, Unger, p. 335.

59. A partial source of her remarks may have been Conrad's "Heart of

Darkness" (*Youth*, p. 139): " 'They are simple people—and I want nothing, you know.' "

60. Except in late printings of the poem that note is incorrectly made to refer to "Death by Water."

61. Augustine *Confessions* III. i.

62. The Fire Sermon, before Eliot adopted it, had already been used by Vachel Lindsay for an epigraph to "The Fireman's Ball" (iii); see *The Congo and Other Poems* (New York, 1914), p. 28.

63. Augustine *Confessions* X. xxxiv.

64. Weston, *From Ritual to Romance*, pp. 70–71.

65. *Ibid.*, pp. 119–20.

66. *Ibid.*, pp. 169–73.

67. Cf. Rossetti, *The House of Life*, lxii.

68. Weston, *From Ritual to Romance*, pp. 44, 48.

69. See Brooks, Unger, p. 337. Cf. the phrase "to draw a blank."

70. Cf. D. H. Lawrence, *The Rainbow* (London, 1915), p. 95.

71. Frazer, *The Golden Bough*, V, 264 ff. Both the thrush and the pine trees recall Whitman's "When Lilacs Last in the Door-Yard Bloom'd."

72. Some of the imagery may have come from Kipling's *Kim*, chap. 13.

73. Cf. Whitman, "When Lilacs Last in the Door-Yard Bloom'd":

> Then with the knowledge of death as walking one side of me,
> And the thought of death close-walking the other side of me,
> And I in the middle, as with companions. . . .

The incident of the Antarctic expedition mentioned by Eliot is narrated by Sir Ernest Shackleton, *South* (London, 1919), p. 209.

74. Henry Clarke Warren, *Buddhism in Translations* (Cambridge, Mass., 1896), pp. 297–98. Cf. also the account of the cloaked stranger, of uncertain sex, in Wilkie Collins' *The Woman in White*, Part II, chap. 5.

75. Weston, *From Ritual to Romance*, p. 174.

76. For the cisterns see Eccles. 22:6 and Jer. 2:13. In Wilde's *Salome* the prophet speaks from a cistern.

77. Weston, *From Ritual to Romance*, p. 167.

78. Eliot, *Poèmes 1910–1930*, p. 155.

79. Charles de Tolnay, *Hieronymus Bosch* (Bâle, 1937), Pl. 25.

80. Cf. *Hamlet*, Act I, scene 2, lines 157–64.

81. *Brihadaranyaka Upanishad*, V, 2.

82. The close of Eliot's line echoes Tennyson, *The Princess*, IV, 75.

83. Cf. Frazer, *The Golden Bough*, V, 77.

84. See Still, *Shakespeare's Mystery Play*, pp. 242–48.

## NOTES TO CHAPTER 7

1. Lam. 2:11; 3:14, 19, 48; 4:1–2. Cf. Ps. 119:50–51.

2. See Drew, p. 95.

3. Eliot (ed.), *A Choice of Kipling's Verse* (London, 1941), p. 20.

4. *Ibid.*, pp. 11–12.

5. Eliot, "Dowson's Poems," *Times Literary Supplement*, No. 1719, January 10, 1935, p. 21. The phrase "hollow men" occurs in *Julius Caesar*, Act. IV, scene 2, line 23.

6. Thomson, *The City of Dreadful Night, and Other Poems*, p. 237; Eliot, *The Use of Poetry*, p. 156.

7. In Valéry, *Le Serpent*, p. 9.

8. Conrad, *Youth*, p. 151.

9. In Valéry, *Le Serpent*, p. 10.

10. Pierre Legouis, *Donne the Craftsman* (Paris, 1928), pp. 48–50.

11. Conrad, *Youth*, p. 150.

12. *Ibid.*, p. 131.

13. The groaning voices of Eliot's hollow men may be reminiscent of the Aeolian moans of the hollow statues in chapter 5 of Samuel Butler's *Erewhon*, the first chapter of which is entitled "Waste Lands."

14. Eliot had possibly visited the solitary column at Avenches, called *le Cigognier;* cf. Byron, *Childe Harold's Pilgrimage*, III, lxv. But see Valéry's "Cantique des Colonnes."

15. See Frazer, *The Golden Bough*, XI, 21–44.

16. Cf. Yeats's "inviolate rose" (W. B. Yeats, *Collected Poems* [New York, 1952], p. 67).

17. Genevieve W. Foster, "The Archetypal Imagery of T. S. Eliot," *PMLA*, LX (June, 1945), 567–85. Other Jungian studies of Eliot include Maud Bodkin, *Archetypal Patterns in Poetry* (London, New York, and Toronto, 1948), pp. 308–14; and Drew, *passim*.

18. See Wallace Fowlie, "Eliot and Tchelitchew," *Accent*, V (Spring, 1945), 168–69.

19. Eliot, *On Poetry* (Concord), p. 9.

20. Eliot, *From Poe to Valéry* (New York, 1948), pp. 26 ff.

21. This comparison has been pointed out to me by Lionel Trilling.

22. Eliot, *After Strange Gods* (London, 1934), p. 40.

## NOTES TO CHAPTER 8

1. Eliot, *The Use of Poetry*, p. 153.

2. Eliot, Introduction to Charlotte Eliot, *Savonarola: A Dramatic Poem* (London, 1926), p. x.

3. *Selected Essays*, p. 37.

4. Eliot, "The Need for Poetic Drama," *Listener*, XVI (November 25, 1936), 994–95; Matthiessen, p. 157.

5. Eliot, "Poetry and Drama," *Atlantic Monthly*, CLXXXVII, No. 2 (February, 1951), 31–37.

6. Eliot, *Elizabethan Essays* (London, 1934), pp. 189–90.

7. *Ibid.*, p. 194.

8. Eliot, *The Use of Poetry*, p. 153.

9. F. Scott Fitzgerald, *The Crack-up*, ed. Edmund Wilson (New York, 1945), p. 310.

10. T. H. Thompson, "The Bloody Wood," Unger, pp. 161–69.

11. Nevill Coghill, "*Sweeney Agonistes*," March and Tambimuttu, p. 86.

12. The bad-night patter; cited by Henry W. Wells, *New Poets from Old* (New York, 1940), p. 75.

13. *Selected Essays*, p. 111.

14. Eliot, "Literature and the Modern World," *America through the Essay*, ed. A. Theodore Johnson and Allen Tate (New York, 1938), p. 382.

15. Eliot, "Eeldrop and Appleplex. I," *Little Review*, IV, No. 1 (May, 1917), 9.

16. Filson Young, *The Trial of Hawley Harvey Crippen* (Edinburgh and London, 1920), pp. 90, 126.

## NOTES TO CHAPTER 9

1. *Selected Essays*, pp. 172–73.

2. Since this comment was written, Eliot has issued "The Three Voices of Poetry," *Atlantic Monthly*, CXCIII, No. 4 (April, 1954), 38–44, in which he recognizes the problems referred to here.

3. *Poetry by T. S. Eliot* ("University of Chicago Round Table," No. 659, broadcast November 12, 1950), p. 9.

4. "The Cultivation of Christmas Trees" is dissimilar in mood to the early "Ariel Poems" and, because of the slackness of its verse, it has less appeal than those. Its relation to "Animula" is a corrective one. It envisions that the child's wonder and gladness in the presence of "the first-remembered Christmas tree" can be treasured up untarnished and be increased by repetitions, so that in his old age "accumulated memories of annual emotion / May be concentrated into a great joy / Which shall also be a great fear." It thus implies, recalling "The Dry Salvages," that by "approach to the meaning" his vitalizing experiences may assume new form. In this, "a great joy" would be expected, "a great fear" perhaps not; yet, as Eliot suggests by alluding to the second chapter of Acts (in which "fear came upon every soul"), such experience is a type not only of the Epiphany, or "first coming," but of Pentecost, prefiguring a "second coming." And, in the eyes of an old man nearing death, the affirmative symbol of Birth and Crucifixion offers a reminder of how close he stands to the Power that numbers his days.

The poem does not explain by what means wonder can survive "the bored habituation, the fatigue, the tedium, / The awareness of death, the consciousness of failure." Prayerfully, it only adopts a posture of hope that the child may keep his freshness: "Let him continue in the spirit of wonder. . . ." It substitutes for the pessimism of "Animula" the possibility of emotional health. This, for the poet himself, seems to be correlated with still another symbol. Mentioning the oblivion of "reverence and gaiety" under "the piety of the convert / Which may be tainted with a self-conceit," Eliot adds:

(And here I remember also with gratitude
St. Lucy, her carol, and her crown of fire).

The naïve story of the early martyr, whom the executioner's fire would not burn and whose feet the Roman troops could not stir, seeks an audience possessing a sincerity equal to its own. But the innocence of St. Lucy's carol of faith and praise can evoke an aesthetic emotion approximating such sincerity. And an understanding of the story's meaning, combined with the reiterated aesthetic emotion, can yield the joy and fear of which Eliot has written.

For the legend of St. Lucy see Sigebert of Gembloux, *Passio Sanctae Luciae Virginis*, ed. Ernest Dümmler, in "Abhandlungen der Königlichen Akademie der Wissenschaften zu Berlin (philosophische und historische)" (Berlin, 1893), I, 23–43.

5. Eliot, *For Lancelot Andrewes* (London, 1928), p. ix.

6. *Selected Essays*, p. 402. In making his choice, Eliot is said to have reacted specifically against Bertrand Russell's *A Free Man's Worship* (*Time*, LV, No. 10 [March 6, 1950], 24).

7. See Drew, pp. 118–19.

8. Andrewes, *Works*, I, 257; *Selected Essays*, p. 297.

9. St.-J. Perse, *Anabasis: A Poem*, trans. T. S. Eliot (London, 1930), pp. 42–47.

10. Eliot, *The Use of Poetry*, p. 148; cited by Louis MacNeice, *The Poetry of W. B. Yeats* (London, New York, and Toronto, 1941), p. 138.

11. Cf. *Othello*, Act V, scene 2, line 351: "Set you down this." See *Selected Essays*, p. 111.

12. Eph. 3:2. This occurs in the Book of Common Prayer, Epistle for the Epiphany.

13. Isa. 53:3.

14. Cf. Conrad, "Heart of Darkness," in *Youth*, p. 48: ". . . the foreign shores, the foreign faces"; cf. also Swinburne, "Itylus."

15. Matt. 8:20.

16. Mark 13:14.

17. Eliot perhaps picked up the name "Boudin" from the Eumaeus episode of Joyce's *Ulysses*, p. 610, where it is appropriate as a sly allusion to Mr. Bloom's appetite (as a common noun it generally means black pudding). Eliot overlooked this connotation.

18. Cited by Drew, p. 124.

19. Possible sources for the theme of "Animula" include Baudelaire, "Le Voyage" (cited in *Selected Essays*, p. 249); Tennyson, *In Memoriam*, xlv; Cardinal Newman, *The Idea of a University* (New York and London, 1927), pp. 331–32 (Preface to "Elementary Studies"); and *The Education of Henry Adams*, p. 460. The last has been noticed by Robert A. Hume, *Runaway Star: An Appreciation of Henry Adams* (Ithaca, N.Y., 1951), p. 37.

20. E. M. Stephenson, *T. S. Eliot and the Lay Reader* (London, 1946), p. 49.

21. *Ibid.*

22. See Drew, p. 127.

23. Cf. *Pericles*, Act V, scene 1, lines 154–56:

> But are you flesh and blood?
> Have you a working pulse, and are no fairy?
> Motion?

24. Cf. Sidney Lanier, "The Marshes of Glynn," lines 101–3:

> . . . who will reveal to our waking ken
> The forms that swim and the shapes that creep
> Under the waters of sleep?

25. Cited with reference to "Burnt Norton" by Helen L. Gardner, *"Four Quartets:* A Commentary," Rajan, p. 62.

26. Cited by Frank Wilson, *Six Essays on the Development of T. S. Eliot*, p. 39.

27. Eliot, *After Strange Gods*, p. 28.

## NOTES TO CHAPTER 10

1. For criticism of the poem see Drew, pp. 98–117; Leonard Unger, *"Ash Wednesday,"* Unger, pp. 349–73; E. E. Duncan Jones, *"Ash Wednesday,"* Rajan, pp. 37–56; Mario Praz, "T. S. Eliot and Dante," Unger, pp. 296 ff.; my article in *Notes and Queries,* CXCIV, 123–25; Allen Tate, extract from *Reactionary Essays,* Unger, pp. 289–95; Frederick A. Pottle, *The Idiom of Poetry* (Ithaca, N.Y., 1946), pp. 96–99.

2. See Eliot's essays "Dante" and "Baudelaire," in *Selected Essays,* and "Baudelaire in Our Time," in *Essays Ancient and Modern* (New York, 1936), for conceptions of love fundamental to *Ash Wednesday.*

3. Unger, pp. 350 ff.

4. Cf. St. John of the Cross, *The Ascent of Mt. Carmel,* I, xi, 3–4; I, iv, 1–2; II, viii, 3. For convenience I have used the edition of E. Allison Peers (London, 1934).

5. On the life of mysticism see Evelyn Underhill's comparative study, *Mysticism* (London, 1911).

6. Rendered from a quotation in Charles Du Bos, *Approximations* (Paris, 1922), p. 221; see Eliot, *Essays Ancient and Modern,* p. 69.

7. Cf. the Anglican Commination Service in the Book of Common Prayer, Pss. 80:3 and 126, and Lam. 5:21.

8. Andrewes, *Works,* I, 354.

9. St. John of the Cross, *The Dark Night of the Soul,* II, xiii, 11.

10. St. John of the Cross, *The Ascent of Mt. Carmel,* III, xvi–xxxii.

11. Pascal, *Pensées,* 139. Mrs. Duncan Jones (Rajan, p. 43) points out that Eliot's "vans" recall the winnowing of chaff. It is possible that in terming the air "thoroughly small and dry" Eliot was obliquely reintroducing the problem of artistic creativity: according to T. E. Hulme's *Speculations* (New York and London, 1924), p. 131, "neo-classic verse" must seek beauty "in small, dry things." Through Pound, some of Eliot's early verse had been influenced by Hulme's theories. On the aridity of the mystical passive Dark Night see *The Dark Night of the Soul,* I, xi, 1; II, vi, 4–5, and on "sitting still" see Lam. 3:26–28.

12. Dante, *Vita nuova,* iii; cf. xi.

13. *Ibid.,* iii.

14. Émile Mâle, *L'Art religieux de la fin du moyen âge* (Paris, 1908), p. 355.

15. Unger, pp. 357–58.

16. St. John of the Cross, *The Dark Night of the Soul,* III, vi, 1; III, vi, 3.

17. Cf. Rossetti, *The House of Life,* xxix: "Lady, I thank thee for thy loveliness."

18. Cf. *Antony and Cleopatra,* Act I, scene 4, line 27: "Full surfeits and the dryness of his bones. . . ."

19. There is a whimsical commentary in an unpublished letter from Ezra Pound to Eliot (April 12, 1940): ". . . mebbe you is TOUGH. The leopards done tried to ate you and then bent their goddam tin teeth. At least I had the helluva argument as to whether 'reject' meant spit out. I sez trown back; I sez as to food it CAN mean that the animal just leaves it on the plate or desert sand and DONT TRY to eat it. No sez the lady [*sc.* Mrs. Pound], it means spit it out. Waaal, I sez, I will ASK the author. No, she sez, DONT. however. . . ."

20. Cited by W. Y. Tindall, *Forces in Modern British Literature 1885–1946* (New York, 1947), p. 271.

21. Mrs. Duncan Jones (Rajan, pp. 46–47) points out that the Lady also represents the Church (the Rose of saints in *Paradiso*, XXXI) and that the Rose of Sharon is an epithet applied to Christ. Eliot's deletion of the line "With worm-eaten petals," following "The single Rose" in the original printing of Part II, averts a slur. The line is traceable to Herbert's "Church-rents and Schisms"; it recalls also Blake's "O Rose, thou art sick." Other omitted lines are "Spattered and worshipped" after "Rose of forgetfulness," and "For the end of remembering / End of forgetting" after "Grace to the Mother." The litany passage probably owes several phrases to *Paradiso*, XXXIII, 1–39.

22. St. John of the Cross, *The Dark Night of the Soul*, II, xvii, 6.

23. *Selected Essays*, p. 5.

24. Eliot, *The Use of Poetry*, p. 108.

25. With the lines cf. Rossetti, "Love's Nocturn":

> Ah! might I, by thy good grace
> Groping in the windy stair
> (Darkness and the breath of space
> Like loud waters everywhere),
> Meeting mine own image there
> Face to face,
> Send it from that place to her!

26. Cf. *Macbeth*, Act IV, scene 1, lines 23–24: ". . . maw and gulf / Of the ravin'd salt-sea shark. . . ."

27. Cf. Conrad Aiken, *The Charnel Rose*, III, i (Boston, 1922), p. 92:

> Bright hair, tumbled in sunlight, and sunlit feet,
> Light hands lifting in air,—
> They are gone forever; they are no longer sweet. . . .

On the poignant associations of lilac see Eliot, "A Commentary," *Criterion*, XIII (April, 1934), 451–54. See Smidt, p. 34.

28. See *Selected Essays*, p. 222. Since Eliot's syntax in Part IV has given pause to commentators, it is not amiss to point out that the "Who" at the beginning is a relative pronoun with its antecedent in the subject of "Sovegna"; the structure is periodic. Eliot's first line is perhaps an echo of Poe's "The viol, the violet, and the vine" ("The City in the Sea"), quoted in *The Use of Poetry*, p. 57.

29. Drew, p. 112.

30. Cf. Conrad Aiken, *Senlin*, I, iii, in *The Charnel Rose*, p. 12:

> By a silent shore, by a far distant sea,
> White unicorns come gravely down to the water.

—and I, iv, p. 13:

> . . . he turns his eyes
> To regard white horses drawing a small white hearse.

Aiken told me in 1949 that the resemblance to *Ash Wednesday* had previously been noticed by Mrs. E. F. Piper. See also Yeats's "Meditations in Time of Civil War," vii.

31. Speaking of courtly love, Elizabeth Drew remarks (p. 112): "The first sign of the Lady's grace to her lover was mere wordless inclination of the head, which nevertheless pledges her to him." The technical name for an accompanying gesture was "la main."

32. Cf. Aiken, *The Jig of Forslin*, IV, iv (London, 1921), p. 69: "The fountain splashed by the blue yew-trees."

33. The symbolism of the Dark Night is exhaustively developed in *The Dark Night of the Soul*, II, xvi. Cf. Ps. 22:2 and Heb. 12:17.

34. Cf. St. John of the Cross, Commentary on *The Spiritual Canticle*, xxviii.

35. Rendered from Du Bos, *Approximations*, pp. 181–82.

36. Eliot, *The Sacred Wood* (London, 1920), p. 150.

37. Eliot, *Essays Ancient and Modern*, p. 69.

38. Dante, *Paradiso*, III, 85. See Matthew Arnold, *The Study of Poetry*.

39. Eliot, *The Use of Poetry*, pp. 30–31; Byron, *Don Juan*, IV, v.


## NOTES TO CHAPTER 11

1. *Poetry by T. S. Eliot* ("University of Chicago Round Table," No. 659), p. 10.

2. Useful commentaries on *Coriolan* include Drew, pp. 132 ff.; Earl Daniels, *The Art of Reading Poetry* (New York, 1941), pp. 406–9; Donald F. Theall, "Traditional Satire in Eliot's 'Coriolan,'" *Accent*, XI (Autumn, 1951), 194–206; Ross Williamson, *The Poetry of T. S. Eliot*, pp. 180–85; Foster, *PMLA*, LX, 583–84.

3. Cited by Matthiessen, pp. 82–83.

4. Richard Eberhart, "Homage to T. S. Eliot," *Harvard Advocate*, CXXV, No. 3 (December, 1938), 19.

5. Edmund Husserl, *Ideas*, trans. W. R. B. Gibson (London and New York, 1931), p. 127.

6. General Erich F. W. Ludendorff, *The Coming War* (London, 1931), p. 67.

7. W. B. Yeats, *A Vision* (London, 1925), p. 188.

8. Cf. *Selected Essays*, p. 216.

9. Vergil *Georgics* i. 378.

10. The pun was probably intentional. Eliot's source was presumably Massinger, *The Roman Actor*, Act IV, scene 1: "Here he comes, / His nose held up; he hath something in the wind," and Webster, *The Devil's Law-Case*, Act V, scene 4: ". . . weave but nets to catch the wind." Other sources for the poem include lines that Eliot has quoted from T. L. Beddoes in "The Three Voices of Poetry," *Atlantic Monthly*, CXCIII, No. 4 (April, 1954), 42:

> . . . bodiless childful of life in the gloom
> Crying with frog voice, "what shall I be?"

—and, as Eliot has informed me, the epigraph to Kipling's "The Story of Muhammad Din": "Who is the happy man? He that sees in his own house at home little children crowned with dust, leaping and falling and crying."


## NOTES TO CHAPTER 12

1. A slip prepared for insertion in copies of the first English edition of *The Rock* (London, 1934) reads as follows: "In the Iconoclasm scene, all the incidents are taken from London history. St. Uncumber's statue was divested of its 'gay gown and silver shoes'; the Maypole from St. Andrew's Undershaft was destroyed by Puritans who objected to the name of the church being derived from it; the Rood of St. Paul's was broken up in the street and the head desecrated. The sermons are extracts from those of Latimer and others."

2. Robert Graves, *The Common Asphodel* (London, 1949), p. 289.
3. Cited *ibid.*, p. 288.
4. D. W. Harding, *Scrutiny*, III (September, 1934), 182.
5. Some of the lines spoken by the Rock immediately after this recall Augustine's *Confessions* XI. xi: ". . . they strive to comprehend things eternal, whilst their heart fluttereth between the motions of things past and to come, and is still unstable" (trans. Pusey). On Augustine's view of eternity see *The City of God* XI. xxi.
6. J. W. Dunne, *An Experiment with Time* (London, 1927).

## NOTES TO CHAPTER 13

1. Critical appraisals are numerous; among the most useful are Francis Fergusson, *The Idea of a Theatre* (Princeton, N.J., 1949), pp. 210 ff.; Theodore Spencer, "On 'Murder in the Cathedral,' " *Harvard Advocate*, CXXV, No. 3 (December, 1938), 21–22; Leo Shapiro, "The Medievalism of T. S. Eliot," *Poetry*, LVI (July, 1940), 202–13; D. S. Bland, "The Tragic Hero in Modern Literature," *Cambridge Journal*, III (January, 1950), 214–23; Martz, Unger, pp. 444–62; Grete and Hans Schaeder, *Ein Weg zu T. S. Eliot* (Hameln, 1948), pp. 93 ff.
2. Eliot and George Hoellering, *The Film of Murder in the Cathedral*, p. 14.
3. Ashley Dukes, "T. S. Eliot in the Theatre," March and Tambimuttu, p. 113.
4. E. A. Abbott, *St. Thomas of Canterbury* (London, 1898).
5. See *Selected Essays*, pp. 87–88.
6. E.g., by Malcolm Cowley, "Afterthoughts on T. S. Eliot," *New Republic*, LXXXVII, No. 1120 (May 20, 1936), 49.
7. Orestes has just arrived at the temple of Artemis; he laments:

> I slew my mother; I avenged
> My father at thy bidding; I have ranged
> A homeless world, hunted by shapes of pain,
> And circling trod in mine own steps again.

—and, almost immediately after, speaks lines apparently echoed in *The Family Reunion*, p. 29:

> . . . these miseries, wherein I reel
> Through Hellas, mad, lashed like a burning wheel.

8. Spencer, *Harvard Advocate*, CXXV, No. 3, 21–22.
9. Fergusson, *The Idea of a Theatre*, pp. 210 ff.
10. There is an abhorrent hypothesis, fostered by Margaret Alice Murray and developed in Hugh Ross Williamson's *The Arrow and the Sword* (London, 1947), that Becket died as the sacrifice in a witch cult of the Cathar heresy! See Maud Bodkin, *Studies of Type Images in Poetry, Religion, and Philosophy* (London, New York, and Toronto, 1951), pp. 131–35.
11. *De Anima* iii. 10 (trans. J. A. Smith).
12. *De Generatione et Corruptione* i. 7. Cf. Plato *Theaetetus* 156–57.
13. Rom. 8:28.
14. The last lines of the alternating speeches were apparently derived from the passage in Montaigne's *Apology for Raimond Sebond* beginning ". . . ce furieux monstre."

15. Eliot, *Atlantic Monthly*, CLXXXVII, No. 2, 34.
16. See my article, "T. S. Eliot and Sherlock Holmes," *Notes and Queries*, CXCIII (October 2, 1948), 431–32. This source, which Eliot has since acknowledged, was first noted, I think, by Elizabeth Jackson.

## NOTES TO CHAPTER 14

1. The outstanding analyses are by C. L. Barber, "T. S. Eliot after Strange Gods," Unger, pp. 415–43; Maud Bodkin, *The Quest for Salvation in an Ancient and a Modern Play* (London, New York, and Toronto, 1941) ; Roy W. Battenhouse, "Eliot's 'The Family Reunion' as Christian Prophecy," *Christendom*, X (Summer, 1945), 307–21; Anne Ward, "Speculations on Eliot's Timeworld: An Analysis of *The Family Reunion* in Relation to Hulme and Bergson," *American Literature*, XXI (March, 1949), 18–34. See William Montgomerie, "Harry, Meet Mr. Prufrock (T. S. Eliot's Dilemma)," *Life and Letters To-day*, XXXI (November, 1941), 115–28; Rudolf Stamm, "The Orestes Theme in Three Plays by Eugene O'Neill, T. S. Eliot and Jean-Paul Sartre," *English Studies*, XXX (October, 1949), 244–55; and the analytic study by John Peter, " 'Family Reunion,' " *Scrutiny*, XVI (September, 1949), 219–30. Some of the names in the play (Ivy, Violet, and Monchensey) have been discovered by Harold F. Brooks in the epigraph to Browning's drama *Colombe's Birthday*, the lines having been quoted from Sir John Hanmer's *Fra Cipollo and Other Poems:*

> Ivy and violet, what do you here
> With blossom and shoot in the warm spring weather,
> Hiding the arms of Monchensey and Vere?

See " 'The Family Reunion' and 'Colombe's Birthday,' " *Times Literary Supplement*, LI (December 12, 1952), 819. (Browning spelled the surname "Monchenci"; Eliot's English spelling is closer to the "Mounchensey" of *The Merry Devil of Edmonton.*)
2. According to Eliot in a letter to E. Martin Browne; see the extract in Matthiessen, pp. 167–68.
3. Ward, *American Literature*, XXI, 26 ff.
4. Alessandro Pellegrini, "A London Conversation with T. S. Eliot," *Sewanee Review*, LVII (Spring, 1949), 289.
5. Eliot, *Atlantic Monthly*, CLXXXVII, No. 2, 36.
6. Dostoevsky, *Crime and Punishment*, Part IV, chap. 1.
7. Neither in *The Family Reunion* nor in *Four Quartets* did Eliot explore a theory of serial time, such as Dunne's in *An Experiment with Time* or P. D. Ouspensky's in *A New Model of the Universe*. He must nevertheless have known of these writers' speculations, which have received wide currency, in part through J. B. Priestley's *Midnight on the Desert* (1937) and *Rain upon Godshill* (1939). Ouspensky's sixth dimension, where the unactualized possibilities of the fourth (that is, of time, whose simultaneous duration in a fifth dimension is eternity) are finally actualized, would have helped solve the problem of "what might have been" in "Burnt Norton."
8. Matthiessen, pp. 175–76.
9. Barber, Unger, pp. 433 ff.

10. Gilbert Murray, *The Classical Tradition in Poetry* (Cambridge, Mass., 1927), chap. 8.

11. Cited by Martz, Unger, p. 448.

12. Eliot, *Atlantic Monthly*, CLXXXVII, No. 2, 35.

13. *Ibid.*

## NOTES TO CHAPTER 15

1. On this play see John J. McLaughlin, "A Daring Metaphysic: *The Cocktail Party*," *Renascence*, III, No. 1 (Autumn, 1950), 15–28; William Arrowsmith, "*The Cocktail Party*," *Hudson Review*, III (Autumn, 1950), 411–30; W. K. Wimsatt, Jr., "Eliot's Comedy," *Sewanee Review*, LVIII (Autumn, 1950), 666–78; Foster Hailey, "An Interview with T. S. Eliot," *New York Times*, April 16, 1950, Sec. II, p. 1, cols. 5–7; p. 3, cols. 4–6; Robert B. Heilman, "*Alcestis* and *The Cocktail Party*," *Comparative Literature*, V (Spring, 1953) 105–16.

2. Eliot, "The Beating of a Drum," *Nation and Athenaeum*, XXXIV (October 6, 1923), 11.

3. Lord Raglan, *The Hero* (London, 1936), chap. 26, and *passim*.

4. See Leo Hamalian, "Mr. Eliot's Saturday Evening Service," *Accent*, X (Autumn, 1950), 195–206, and Sandra Wool, "Weston Revisited," *Accent*, X (Autumn, 1950), 207–12.

5. Eliot, *Atlantic Monthly*, CLXXXVII, No. 2, 36–37.

6. A. W. Verrall, *Euripides the Rationalist* (Cambridge, 1913), pp. 1–137.

7. An old innocuous version, different in words and tune from Eliot's, may be found in B. A. Botkin, *A Treasury of American Folklore* (New York, 1944), p. 838.

8. Djuna Barnes, *Nightwood* (New York, 1937), p. 40.

9. An interesting primitive code of initiatory guardianship is described in John Layard's fascinating study on the northern New Hebrides, *Stone Men of Malekula*, Vol. I (London, 1942), with which Eliot is acquainted. I strongly suspect that this book influenced the play. It contains, incidentally, an arresting parallel to the initiation pattern of death and rebirth which Knight, in *Cumaean Gates*, traces in the *Aeneid*. And I think that the *Aeneid*, too, may have been in Eliot's awareness at his time of writing. See Eliot, "Vergil and the Christian World," *Listener*, XLVI (September 13, 1951), 411–12, 423–24.

10. See McLaughlin, *Renascence*, III, No. 1, 15–28.

11. Brendan Gill has suggested to me that this image, with others, was perhaps borrowed by Eliot from John Macmurray's *Reason and Emotion* (London, 1935). Eliot knows the book but does not concede that he was consciously influenced by it. See *Reason and Emotion*, pp. 33, 58, 63–64, 136.

12. There is a similar image in Henry James, *The Sense of the Past* (New York, 1917), p. 12.

13. John Heywood, *A Woman Killed with Kindness*, Act II, scene 6:

O God! O God! that it were possible
To undo things done; to call back yesterday!

14. This is the last sentence of Fitzgerald's *The Great Gatsby* (New York, 1925).

15. Barnes, *Nightwood*, p. 122.

16. Eliot, *The Use of Poetry*, p. 45.

17. Charles Williams, *Descent into Hell* (New York, 1949), p. 15.

## NOTES TO CHAPTER 16

1. Some interesting American reviews include those of John Beaufort, " 'The Confidential Clerk' on Broadway," *Christian Science Monitor*, February 20, 1954, p. 10, cols. 1–2; Spencer Brown, "T. S. Eliot's Latest Poetic Drama," *Commentary*, XVII (April, 1954), 367–72; Sam Hynes, "Religion in the West End," *Commonweal*, LIX (February 12, 1954), 475–76; Walter F. Kerr, "T. S. Eliot Strolls the Same Garden," *New York Herald Tribune*, February 21, 1954, Sec. IV, p. 1, cols. 3–6.

2. Burke Wilkinson, "A Most Serious Comedy by Eliot," *New York Times*, February 7, 1954, Sec. II, p. 1, col. 7.

3. Colby's problem is very similar in detail to the one lamented by the painter Constable in a letter to J. T. Smith (March, 1797), quoted by Andrew Shirley, *The Rainbow: A Portrait of John Constable* (London, 1949), p. 47: "I must now take your advice and attend to My Father's business, as we are likely soon to lose an old servant (our clerk), who has been with us eighteen years; and now I see plainly it will be my lot to walk through life in a path contrary to that in which my inclination would lead me."

4. Eliot quoted in Wilkinson, *New York Times*, February 7, 1954, Sec. II, p. 1, col. 7; p. 3, col. 4.

5. Verrall, *Euripides the Rationalist*, pp. 138–76; *The Ion of Euripides* (Cambridge, 1890), pp. xi–xlv.

6. Because Colby tells Eggerson, "It's reassuring / To know that I have you always at my back," some readers may want to imagine an allusion to "time's wingèd chariot," the car of the sun-god, in Marvell's "To His Coy Mistress." If the echo is present, it is more trivial even than the analogy between Ion's and Colby's bird-watching.

## NOTES TO CHAPTER 17

1. Eliot, *The Music of Poetry* (Glasgow, 1942), p. 28.

2. Cf. the ingenious theory of H. Reid MacCallum, *Time Lost and Regained: The Theme of Eliot's Four Quartets* (Toronto, n.d.).

3. Eliot, *The Music of Poetry*, p. 27.

4. *Ibid.*, p. 18.

5. See, for an analysis of "East Coker" as a musical quartet, D. Bosley Brotman, "T. S. Eliot: 'The Music of Ideas,' " *University of Toronto Quarterly*, XVIII (October, 1948), 20–29.

6. Stephen Spender, *The Destructive Element* (London, 1935), pp. 149–51; see Stanley E. Hyman, *The Armed Vision* (New York, 1948), p. 90.

7. Cf. Sister M. Cleophas, "Notes on Levels of Meaning in 'Four Quartets,' " *Renascence*, II (Spring, 1950), 102–16.

8. John M. Bradbury, "*Four Quartets:* The Structural Symbolism," *Sewanee Review*, LIX (Spring, 1951), 254–70.

9. The parallel with the Grail legend, noted by Wallace Fowlie (*Accent*, V, 166–70), is limited in validity by meagerness of narrative in the *Quartets*. But see Fowlie, *The Clown's Grail* (London, 1947).

10. For the early history of Burnt Norton, which derived its epithet from a fire set by its owner, Sir William Keyte, in October, 1741, see the *Gentleman's Magazine*, XLIV (1774), 171–72.

11. John Lehmann, "T. S. Eliot Talks about Himself and the Drive To Create," *New York Times Book Review*, November 29, 1953, p. 5.

12. The best commentary on the first *Quartet* is that of Charlie Masters, "Some Observations on 'Burnt Norton,'" *American Prefaces*, VI (Winter, 1941), 99–112; *ibid.*, Spring, 1941, pp. 212–31. On the series of four, see Drew, pp. 140–200; Raymond Preston, *"Four Quartets" Rehearsed* (New York, 1946) ; Gardner, Rajan, pp. 57 ff., and *The Art of T. S. Eliot*, chap. 7; Elizabeth Vassilieff, "The Quiddity of *Four Quartets*," *Direction* (Melbourne), No. 1, May, 1952, pp. 34–45; notes by John Hayward in Eliot, *Quatre Quatuors* (Paris, 1950), pp. 127–56; Anon., *On the Four Quartets of T. S. Eliot*, with a Foreword by Roy Campbell (London, 1953) ; Hideo Funato, "T. S. Eliot's Idea of Time," *Rikkyo Review* (Tokyo), No. 16, 1955, pp. 19–51.

13. Preston, *"Four Quartets" Rehearsed*, p. viii; cf. Stephenson, *T. S. Eliot and the Lay Reader*, p. 80.

14. Drew, p. 148; Philip Wheelwright, "Eliot's Philosophical Themes," Rajan, pp. 99–100.

15. Diogenes Laertius, for example. For the cycle see *Timaeus* 49c; cf. *Physics* iv. 5.

16. Cited by Martz, Unger, pp. 451–52.

17. *Physics* iv. 11; see also *Physics* viii. 1.

18. The only critic ever to throw much light on this passage was the late Willy Schenk, "The Experience and the Meaning," *Humanitas* (Manchester), I, No. 4 (June, 1947), 23–27.

19. On the problem see *Metaphysics* β.6.

20. F. R. Leavis, *Education and the University* (London, 1943), p. 95.

21. The literary echoes are of *Alice's Adventures in Wonderland*, as Eliot revealed to Louis L. Martz, and probably also of *Through the Looking-Glass*, where Alice meets some self-conscious flowers. Martz detects the influence of D. H. Lawrence's "The Shadow in the Rose Garden" and of Joyce's "The Dead"; see Martz, Unger, pp. 447–50. The fascination of a little door into a walled garden obsessed Eliot later in *The Family Reunion*. A good analogue is seen in H. G. Wells's story, "The Door in the Wall"; cf. also Arthur Machen's "Opening the Door," in *The Cozy Room*, and William Morris' "The Nymph's Song to Hylas."

22. Eliot's phrase "accepted and accepting" recalls Bishop Andrewes' "Let us then make this so accepted a time in itself twice acceptable by our accepting, which He will acceptably take at our hands" (*Works*, I, 84).

23. The lotos is a familiar Hindu symbol; among the ancient Egyptians it was sacred to Horus, the child sun-god, daily born anew; in Buddhist art the Buddha is depicted, like Horus, seated in the midst of its petals. It is also, as in the *Odyssey*, associated with dreams.

24. John Shand, "Around 'Little Gidding,'" *Nineteenth Century*, CXXXVI (September, 1944), 126.

25. *I Henry IV*, Act III, scene 1, lines 131–32, 161–62.

26. Drew, p. 155.

27. Wheelwright, Rajan, pp. 100–101.

28. Milton, *Paradise Lost*, V, 620–22.

29. Tennyson, *In Memoriam*, xliii.

30. Eliot was indebted for his image of the dance at the still point to the dance of the Tarot in Charles Williams' novel *The Greater Trumps;* cited by

Hayward in Eliot, *Quatre Quatuors*, p. 132; Gardner, *The Art of T. S. Eliot*, p. 161.

31. With Eliot's style here cf. Pound's " 'The Age Demanded,' " *Personae*, p. 202.

32. Arthur O. Lovejoy, *The Great Chain of Being: A Study of the History of an Idea* (Cambridge, Mass., 1936), p. 52.

33. Gardner, Rajan, p. 59.

34. St. John of the Cross, *The Dark Night of the Soul*, II, vi, 4.

35. *Ibid.*, II, xviii, 2; Preston, *"Four Quartets" Rehearsed*, p. 20. Cf. St. John of the Cross, *The Ascent of Mt. Carmel*, II, i, 1.

36. Cited by Mark Reinsberg, "A Footnote to *Four Quartets*," *American Literature*, XXI (November, 1949), 343–44.

37. Cf. Tennyson, *In Memoriam*, ii; xxxix.

38. Cf. Conrad Aiken, *Preludes for Memnon*, li (New York, 1931), p. 90.

39. On the symbolism of this movement see Arthur O. Lewis, Jr., "Eliot's *Four Quartets: Burnt Norton* IV," *Explicator*, VIII (November, 1949), 9.

40. Cf. George A. Knox, "Quest for the Word in Eliot's *Four Quartets*," *Journal of English Literary History*, XVIII (December, 1951), 310–21.

41. See *Physics* ii. 3.

42. See *Metaphysics* $\theta$.8.

43. Gustave Flaubert, *La Tentation de Saint-Antoine*, chap. 7.

44. St. John of the Cross, *The Dark Night of the Soul*, II, xvii–xix.

45. *De Anima* iii. 10.

46. H. W. Häusermann, " 'East Coker' by T. S. Eliot," *English Studies*, XXIII (August, 1941), 109–10.

47. The paraphrases would run thus: "In my beginning is *foreseen* my end" (finalism) ; "In my beginning is *caused* my end" (determinism). Likewise, "In my end is *fulfilled* my beginning" (finalism) ; "In my end is *presupposed* my beginning" (determinism).

48. Ward, *American Literature*, XXI, 29, cites for comparison a passage from T. E. Hulme's *Speculations* (p. 227): "The eyes, the beauty of the world, have been organized out of the faeces. Man returns to dust. So does the face of the world to primeval cinders."

49. Cf. *Herakleitos von Ephesos*, ed. Hermann Diels (Berlin, 1909), Frag. 12, 49*a*, 91.

50. Drew, p. 165.

51. James Johnson Sweeney, *"East Coker:* A Reading," Unger, p. 399. There are numerous analogues to the Queen's motto, which contains a paradox going all the way back, as Sweeney points out, to Heraclitus (Frag. 103 in Diels) ; cf. my article, "Tourneur and *Little Gidding;* Corbière and *East Coker*," *Modern Language Notes*, LXV (June, 1950), 420–21.

52. On the significance of the sixteenth century for the poem see Sweeney, Unger, pp. 395 ff., and the equally illuminating article by Curtis Bradford, "Footnotes to *East Coker:* A Reading," *Sewanee Review*, LII (Winter, 1944), 169–75.

53. See the excellent impressionistic reading by Dom Sebastian Moore, "East Coker: The Place and the Poem," *Focus Two*, ed. B. Rajan and Andrew Pearse (London, 1946), pp. 91–103.

54. Sir Thomas Elyot, *The Boke Named the Governour*, Book I, chap. 12.

55. Literary associations are plentiful here. Cf. Swinburne's "Before the Mirror," Shirley's "The glories of our blood and state," Campion's "There is a garden in her face" ("They look like rosebuds filled with snow"), and Cowley's "Anacreontiques" on drinking—the last containing a possible model for the Sun-and-Moon line.

56. Sweeney, Unger, p. 404.

57. Cf. Andrewes, *Works*, I, 171.

58. Aiken, *The Jig of Forslin*, V, vi, in *The Charnel Rose*, pp. 94–95.

59. St. John of the Cross, *The Ascent of Mt. Carmel*, I, xiii, 11.

60. St. John of the Cross, *The Dark Night of the Soul*, II, xvi, 10; see Sweeney, Unger, pp. 409–10.

61. Andrewes, *Works*, I, 113; cf. p. 112.

62. Cited by Sweeney, Unger, p. 410.

63. Pascal, *Pensées*, 354, 355.

64. Eliot's description is of course typical; cf. also the *Phaedo*.

65. William Blissett, "The Argument of T. S. Eliot's *Four Quartets*," *University of Toronto Quarterly*, XV (January, 1946), 118.

66. See Lionel Trilling, "Art and Neurosis," in *The Liberal Imagination* (New York, 1950).

67. Cf. Eliot, "John Donne," *Nation and Athenaeum*, XXXIII (June 9, 1923), 332: "A style, a rhythm, to be significant, must embody a significant mind, must be produced by the necessity of a new form for a new content."

68. Hayward, in Eliot, *Quatre Quatuors*, p. 138, says that Eliot was thinking of the "old stones" of the village churchyard at East Coker.

69. See Eliot, *The Music of Poetry*, p. 23.

70. Aiken, *Preludes for Memnon*, xiv, p. 27.

71. Cf. Byron, *Childe Harold's Pilgrimage*, II, xxxii.

72. Hart Crane, *Collected Poems* (New York, 1946), p. 17.

73. Euripides, *Alcestis*, line 1085.

74. In *Queen Mary's Book for India* (London, Toronto, Bombay, and Sidney, 1943), p. 61; cf. *Bhagavad-Gita*, II, 47.

75. *Ibid.*, VIII, 6.

76. *Dhammapada*, stanza 385 (trans. F. Max Müller).

77. At the time of writing I had not seen the valuable article by Harold E. McCarthy, "T. S. Eliot and Buddhism," *Philosophy East and West*, II (April, 1952), 31–55.

78. Dante, *Purgatorio*, XXXIII, 1.

79. Cf. Tennyson, *In Memoriam*, vi. The shrine on the promontory is unidentified; Eliot possibly had in mind the Portuguese church of Our Lady of Good Voyage, at Gloucester, Massachusetts.

80. The conceit of spring at Christmas is common in seventeenth-century poetry, occurring in Crashaw, Traherne, and Herrick. Eliot once quoted an example of it, from Herrick's "A Christmas Carroll" in *Noble Numbers*, as a Christmas-greeting verse.

81. John Hayward, in Eliot, *Quatre Quatuors*, p. 149, gives a surprising and perhaps useless, because quite non-functional, series of associations for this passage. The "sea jaws" he associates with Iona and St. Columba and with Lindisfarne and St. Cuthbert; the "dark lake" with the lake of Glendalough and St. Kevin's hermitage in County Wicklow; the "desert" with the Thebaid and St. Anthony; the "city" with Padua and St. Anthony of Padua.

82. With Eliot's use of the elements here cf. Matthew Arnold, *Empedocles on Etna*, II, 331 ff. Eliot had already in 1940 used the symbolism of the four elements, in a more subdued fashion, in his broadside "Defense of the Islands," reprinted in *Britain at War*, ed. Monroe Wheeler (New York, 1941), p. 8. (This incidentally contains a partial echo of Simonides' epitaph on the Lacedemonians.)

83. Cf. Hermann Peschmann, "The Later Poetry of T. S. Eliot," *English*, V (Autumn, 1945), 185.

84. Eliot, "A Talk on Dante," *Kenyon Review*, XIV (Spring, 1952), 181.

85. *Ibid.*, p. 180.

86. In *Tribute to Walter de la Mare on His Seventy-fifth Birthday* (London, 1948), pp. 106–7.

87. *Selected Essays*, p. 164; see my article in *Modern Language Notes*, LXV, 418–20.

88. Milton, *Paradise Lost*, X, 565–66. The tradition is ancient, being instanced in Josephus and Tacitus.

89. Milton, *Paradise Lost*, XI, 535 ff.; Gardner, Rajan, p. 74.

90. John Hayward assumes credit for having suggested to Eliot the word "laceration," remarking at the time (he informs me on a postal card) that the obvious allusion to Swift's epitaph would give the hungry grubs something to feed on. Eliot informed Maurice Johnson that he in his own mind associated it with Yeats (who versified it into English, and whose play *The Words upon the Window Pane* is about Swift's ghost); see Johnson, "The Ghost of Swift in 'Four Quartets,'" *Modern Language Notes*, LXIV (April, 1949), 273.

91. Ford, *The Lover's Melancholy*, Act IV, scene 2.

92. Yeats, *Collected Poems*, p. 246.

93. Johnson, *The Vanity of Human Wishes*, line 117.

94. *Measure for Measure*, Act III, scene 1, lines 121–22.

95. *Hamlet*, Act I, scene 1, line 157. The beginning of Eliot's "canto" recalls Thomson's *The City of Dreadful Night*, xviii, p. 38:

> I wandered in a suburb of the north,
> And reached a spot whence three close lanes led down. . .

96. See Preston, *"Four Quartets" Rehearsed*, pp. 56–57.

97. Dante, *Convivio*, IV, xxvii.

98. Milton, *Paradise Lost*, I, 301–3.

99. Preston, *"Four Quartets" Rehearsed*, pp. 57–58.

100. Julian of Norwich, *Revelations of Divine Love*, ed. Grace Warrack (London, 1901), pp. 56, 84; see Gardner, Rajan, p. 76, and James Johnson Sweeney, "*Little Gidding*: Introductory to a Reading," *Poetry*, LXII (July, 1943), 217. With the first quotation Helen Gardner compares the beginning of the final chorus of *Samson Agonistes*.

101. Cf. Gardner, Rajan, p. 75.

102. With Milton, Eliot has more than once associated Joyce in his blindness; e.g., in the lecture *Milton* (London, 1947), p. 12.

103. Sir Thomas Browne, *Works* (London, 1852), II, 562, 394–98. Cf. Bulwer-Lytton, "The Haunted and the Haunters." Eliot's phrasing was doubtless influenced by Gautier's "Le Spectre de la rose"; this title recalls also the Nijinsky ballet.

104. Julian of Norwich, *Revelations of Divine Love*, p. 202; Gardner, Rajan, pp. 76–77.

105. There is an echo here of Pound's "The Return," *Personae,* p. 74; I believe that it was first pointed out in 1942 by Mary T. Shea.

106. Heraclitus, Frag. 62; cf. Yeats, *A Vision* (1925), p. 183.

107. Cited by Gardner, Rajan, p. 76.

108. Eliot gave a gloss on this in his "Leçon de Valéry," *Paul Valéry Vivant* (Marseille, 1946), pp. 78, 80: "The proper end of the romantic is to achieve the classic—that is to say, every language, to retain its vitality, must perpetually depart and return upon itself; but without the *departure* there is no return, and the *returning* is as important as the arrival. We have to return to where we started from, but the journey has altered the starting place: so that the place we left and the place we return to are the same and also different."

109. One recalls Dante's vision of the three circles in *Paradiso,* XXXIII. For the knot cf. *The Cloud of Unknowing* (chap. 47): ". . . to help thee to knit the ghostly knot of burning love betwixt thee and thy God, in ghostly onehead and according of will" (cited by Drew, p. 199).

110. St. John of the Cross, *The Dark Night of the Soul,* II, xx, 6.

111. *Selected Essays,* p. 173.

*INDEX*

# INDEX

à Becket, Thomas; *see* Becket, St. Thomas à

Abbott, E. A., *St. Thomas of Canterbury*, 182

Action, 5, 64, 68, 103, 107, 232, 236, 273, 277–78, 279, 280, 281, 283, 287, 288, 289, 291, 292, 295; *see also* Will

Action and suffering, 15–16, 17, 23, 33, 71, 99, 114, 125, 178–79, 182, 185, 186, 187–91, 192, 193, 195, 196, 199, 203, 210, 221, 223, 225, 272, 293; *see also* Purgation; Will

Adams, Henry, 267, 268; *The Education of Henry Adams*, 62–63, 313

Aeschylus: *Agamemnon*, 45, 46–47, 85, 304 (Morshead, trans.); *Choephoroi*, 116, 201; *Eumenides*, 201, 206; *Oresteia*, 201, 203, 209

Affirmative way; *see* Negative and affirmative ways, the

Aiken, Conrad, 9, 30, 31, 34, 44, 114; *The Charnel Rose*, 315; *The Jig of Forslin*, 268, 316; *Preludes for Memnon*, 275, 322; *Senlin*, 315

Alain-Fournier; *see* Fournier, Henri Alain

Andrewes, Lancelot, 122, 123, 139, 141, 269–70, 306, 321

Anouilh, Jean, *Eurydice*, 217, 220

Apocrypha, 183

Apollinaire, Guillaume, *Les Mamelles de Tirésias*, 67, 76

"Apteryx" (T. S. Eliot), 141

Aquinas, St. Thomas, 107, 190

Aristophanes, 112; *The Acharnians*, 161; *The Knights*, 161

Aristotle, 107, 178, 186, 190, 251, 252, 254–55, 258, 260, 261, 262, 263, 264, 293; *De Anima*, 188; *De Generatione et Corruptione*, 188

Arnold, Matthew: "The Buried Life," 12;

"Dover Beach," 96; *Empedocles on Etna*, 98, 324; "The Scholar Gipsy," 140

Asceticism, 7, 90, 92–93, 106, 146, 210, 293

Augustine, St., 91, 189, 289, 293; *Confessions*, 90, 253, 317

Augustine of Canterbury, St., 91, 183

Babbitt, Irving, 4

Barber, C. L., 209–10

Barham, R. H., *The Ingoldsby Legends*, 3

Barnes, Djuna, *Nightwood*, 87, 220, 224

Barrie, Sir James, *The Admirable Crichton*, 115

Baudelaire, 257; "Au Lecteur," 79, 98; "Femmes damnées," 183; "Harmonie du soir," 301; "L'Invitation au voyage," 157; "Recueillement," 32; "Les Sept Vieillards," 78, 285; "Le Voyage," 250, 313

Beaumont and Fletcher: *The Maid's Tragedy*, 47, 48; *Philaster*, 73, 309

Becket, St. Thomas à, 181–95

Beddoes, T. L., 48, 316

Beethoven: *Coriolan*, 167; late quartets, 249

Bel Esprit fund, 68

Bellay, Joachim du, "Épitaphe d'un petit chien," 250

Bennett, Arnold, 113

Benson, A. C., 63

Bentley, E. C., 172

Bergson, 4, 24–25, 26, 54, 59, 176, 198, 253, 264, 267, 293; *Creative Evolution*, 23, 58; *Matter and Memory*, 22; *see also* Time

*Bhagavad-Gita*, 277, 279

Bible, 20, 32, 39, 44, 60, 72, 73, 81, 84, 90, 93, 96, 100, 106, 124, 125, 126, 132, 139, 140, 141, 142, 143, 144, 145, 146, 148, 153, 154, 160, 161, 165, 173, 181–82, 184–85, 202, 247, 265, 274–75, 279, 280, 306, 309, 310

Blake, 172; "An Ancient Proverb," 151; "Auguries of Innocence," 60; "London," 151; "O Rose, thou art sick," 315; "The Poison Tree," 61; "The Tyger," 60
Blavatsky, Mme H. P., *The Secret Doctrine*, 49
Blissett, William, 272
Boccaccio, *Decameron*, 46
Book of Common Prayer, 72, 73, 76, 78, 124, 139, 142, 157, 174, 175, 193, 274–75; see also Catholic prayers and ritual
Bosch, Hieronymus, 94–95
Bosschère, Jean de, "Homère Mare," 303
Bowra, C. M., 86
Bradley, F. H., 4, 5, 68, 252, 293
Bramhall, John, "Answer to the Epistle of M. de la Milletière," 40
Brooke, Rupert, *Letters from America*, 308
Brooks, Cleanth, Jr., 82, 85
Browne, E. Martin, 171, 228
Browne, Mrs. E. Martin, 181
Browne, Sir Thomas: *The Garden of Cyrus*, 289; *Hydriotaphia*, 145; *Religio Medici*, 289
Browning, E. B., "Bianca among the Nightingales," 304
Browning, Robert, 15; "Childe Roland," 70, 95; *Colombe's Birthday*, 318; "Rabbi Ben Ezra," 287; "A Toccata of Galuppi's," 52, 53
Buddhism, 78, 90, 91, 92, 93–94, 191, 226, 278, 282, 293
Bulwer-Lytton, Edward, "The Haunted and the Haunters," 324
Burbank, Luther, 51
Burne-Jones, Sir Edward, 148
Butler, Samuel, *Erewhon*, 311
Byron, 3, 84, 117, 129; *Cain*, 65; *Childe Harold's Pilgrimage*, 4, 52, 53, 311; *Don Juan*, 158, 303

Campion, Thomas, "There is a garden in her face," 323
Canaletto, Antonio, 53
Carlyle, 171
Carroll, Lewis, 31, 212; *Alice's Adventures in Wonderland*, 321; *Sylvie and Bruno*, 40; *Through the Looking-Glass*, 68, 256, 321
Catholic prayers and ritual, 130, 139, 142, 143, 145, 148, 153, 154–55, 157; see also Book of Common Prayer
Catullus, "Hymen o Hymenaee," 37
Cavalcanti, Guido, 152; "Perch' io non spero," 140, 143, 154

Chapman, George, 57; *Bussy D'Ambois*, 53, 183, 257, 305, 306; "Penitential Psalms" (Petrarch), 257; *The Tragedy of Charles Duke of Byron*, 305
Charles I, 251, 283, 284, 289
Chaucer, 88; *General Prologue to the Canterbury Tales*, 302; *Nonne Preestes Tale*, 214; *The Parlement of Foules*, 61
Chesterton, G. K., 61
Chopin, 11
Chrétien de Troyes, 73
Church, the, 39–40, 43, 77, 95, 122, 137, 139, 146, 161, 171, 172, 173, 175, 176, 177, 178, 181, 183, 184, 187, 189, 194–95, 270, 274
Cicero, *Somnium Scipionis*, 61
Clairmont, Clare, 52
Classicism, 3, 28
*Cloud of Unknowing, The*, 291, 325
Coghill, Nevill, 114
Coleridge: "Dejection: An Ode," 108; "The Rime of the Ancient Mariner," 70
Collins, Wilkie, *The Woman in White*, 302, 310
Columbus, 33
Conrad: "At the End of the Tether," 63; "Heart of Darkness," 63, 68, 89, 101, 102, 103–4, 106, 166, 306, 309–10, 313; "Youth," 58
Constable, John, 320
Corbière, Tristan, 36; "Épitaphe," 35; "Rapsodie du sourd," 301; "Le Renégat," 35
Coverdale, Miles, 274–75
Coward, Noel, 216
Cowley, "Anacreontiques," 323
Cowper, *Olney Hymns*, 40
Crane, Hart, *The Bridge*, 276
Crashaw, 289
Crippen, Dr. H. H., 118

Dante, 6, 99, 134, 138, 151, 153, 250; *Commedia*, 7, 16–17, 49–50, 68, 78, 89, 96, 97, 103, 105, 106, 109, 117, 129, 130, 137, 141, 143, 144, 145, 147, 148–49, 150, 153, 156, 157, 165, 176, 190, 212, 227, 268, 279, 285, 286, 287, 308, 315, 325; *Convivio*, 286; *Vita nuova*, 7, 75, 137, 143–44, 145, 212, 309 (Rossetti, trans.)
Dark night, mystical; see John of the Cross, St.; Mysticism
Darley, George, *Thomas à Becket*, 183–84
Day, John, *The Parliament of Bees*, 85
De Quincey, Thomas, "On the Knocking at the Gate in *Macbeth*," 118

de Vere, Aubrey, *St. Thomas of Canterbury*, 184
Death and rebirth, 6, 12, 18, 20, 60–61, 65, 66, 69–70, 71, 72, 74, 77–78, 82, 90, 92, 93, 94, 95, 108, 116, 122–23, 124, 125–26, 128, 130, 131, 134, 141, 144–45, 151–52, 153, 156, 166, 186, 187, 190, 193, 196, 203, 207, 208, 210, 212, 217–19, 225, 237, 250, 261, 269, 271, 279, 291, 293, 312; *see also* Initiation; Primitive ritual and religion
Defoe, *Robinson Crusoe*, 272
Democritus, 144
DeMonvel, M. B., 303
Detachment, 273, 277, 280, 288, 291
*Dhammapada*, 278
Dickens: "A Christmas Carol," 205; *Nicholas Nickleby*, 33
Diels, Hermann, 251
Donne, 40, 41, 42; "The Extasie," 145, 256; "A Lecture upon the Shadow," 73; "A Nocturnall upon S. Lucies day," 282, 291; "Oh, to vex me, contraryes meet in one," 271
*Doppelgänger*, 16, 17–18, 148, 188, 204–5, 226, 285, 287
Dostoevsky, 26, 111; *Crime and Punishment*, 20, 117, 204, 309
Doyle, Sir A. Conan: *The Hound of the Baskervilles*, 130, 268; "The Musgrave Ritual," 194
Drama, poetic, 110–11, 121, 171, 179, 193–94, 213, 220
Dramatic monologue, 3, 6, 9, 10, 15, 16, 27, 57, 59, 99–100, 102–3, 109, 121, 122, 125, 133, 135, 159–60, 294–95
Drew, Elizabeth, 89, 151, 163, 251, 257, 265
Du Bos, Charles, 140, 154
Duchamp, Marcel, 185
Dukes, Ashley, 181
Dunne, J. W., 177, 205

Eckermann, J. P., 272
Edwards, Jonathan, 60
Eliot, Charlotte, *Savonarola*, 110
Eliot, Henry Ware, 237
Eliot, Henry Ware, Jr., 30
Eliot, Sir John, 289
Eliot, T. S., poetry
   *Anabasis* (Perse), 123, 160
   *Ara Vos Prec*, 37, 39, 40, 45, 299
   "Ariel Poems," *121–34, 312*
      "Journey of the Magi," *121–24,* 125, *126–28,* 132

"A Song for Simeon," 122, *124–28,* 129, 291
"Animula," 122, *127–30,* 133, 156, 312
"Marina," 7, 99, 122, *130–34*
"The Cultivation of Christmas Trees," 122, *312*
*Ash Wednesday,* 7, 8, 35, 39, 61, 68, 99, 107, 116, 130, 132, 134, *135–58,* 164, 165, 166, 208, 249, 252, 260, 285, 314
"Aunt Helen," 21, *31–32*
"Ballade of the Fox Dinner," 30
"The Ballade of the Outlook," 30
"The *Boston Evening Transcript,*" 21, *31–32*
"Burbank with a Baedeker: Bleistein with a Cigar," *50–54,* 57, 60, 65, 305
*The Cocktail Party,* 69, 87, 115–16, 127, 212, 213, *214–27,* 228, 229, 265, 278, 299
*Collected Poems 1909–1935,* 40, 174, 299
*Complete Poems and Plays,* 299
*The Confidential Clerk,* 219, *228–43,* 294, 299
"Conversation Galante," 9, *26–27*
"A Cooking Egg," *48–50,* 129, 305
*Coriolan,* 106, 122, *159–67,* 247, 252
   "Triumphal March," 99, 121, 122, *159–64*
   "Difficulties of a Statesman," 159, 160, 161, 163, *164–67,* 277
"Cousin Nancy," *31–32,* 35, 47
"Dans le Restaurant," 35, *36–37,* 49, 75, 79, 85, 91, 129–30
"The Death of Saint Narcissus," *34–35,* 64, 68, 73
"Defense of the Islands," 324
"Le Directeur," *35*
"Doris's Dream Songs," 100
"Eyes That Last I Saw in Tears," *100–101*
"A Fable for Feasters," 3, 9
*The Family Reunion,* 7, 61, 85, 106, 127, 175, *196–213,* 214, 215, 216, 224, 226, 256, 299, 317, 321
"La Figlia che Piange," 9, *27–28,* 30, 101
*The Film of Murder in the Cathedral,* 180, 299, 317
*Five-Finger Exercises,* 250
*Four Quartets,* 6, 8, 39, 108, 127, 194, *247–95,* 299; *Quatre Quatuors,* 322–23
   "Burnt Norton," 7, 31, 61, 99, 106, 107, 108, 134, 138, 190, 249, *251–*

*64*, 266, 267, 268, 269, 273, 280,
281, 282, 283, 284, 287, 290
"East Coker," 127, 249, 251, 257, 261,
*264–73*, 275, 280, 281, 284, 290,
291
"The Dry Salvages," 92, 151, 177, 208,
249, 251, 268, *273–82*, 284, 288,
312
"Little Gidding," 31, 149, 208, 212,
226, 249, 251, 254, 259, 273, *282–
92*
"Gerontion," 6, 29, 35, 39, *57–66*, 67, 75,
99–100, 103, 122, 123, 124–25, 126–
27, 130, 144, 152, 176, 199, 223, 254,
268, 303, 305–6
(Harvard Class) "Ode," 9
"The Hippopotamus," *39–40*, 43
"The Hollow Men," 7, 8, *99–109*, 123,
125, 126–27, 128, 132, 135, 137, 146,
147, 149, 161, 173, 201, 211, 247, 260
"Humoresque," 9
"Hysteria," 33
"King Bolo and His Great Black Queen,"
33, 115
*Landscapes*, 173, *247–48*
"New Hampshire," 37, 106, 247
"Virginia," 247
"Usk," 33–34, *247–48*
"Rannoch, by Glencoe," *247–48*
"Cape Ann," *247–48*
"Lines for an Old Man," 257
"The Love Song of J. Alfred Prufrock,"
6, 9, 10, *15–20*, 21, 22, 25, 28, 29,
31, 33, 37, 39, 50, 54, 57, 59, 63, 65,
89, 99, 103, 107, 114, 117, 142, 148,
164, 222, 223, 269, 301–2
"Lune de Miel," *35–36*, 40
"Mélange Adultère de Tout," 35
"Mr. Apollinax," 29, 31, *32–33*, 35, 47
"Mr. Eliot's Sunday Morning Service,"
29, *43–45*, 47, 51, 54, 65, 108, 166,
304
"Morning at the Window," *30–31*
*Murder in the Cathedral*, 35, 110, 114,
126, 127, *180–95*, 197–98, 211, 212,
213, 247, 251, 299
*Noctes Binanianae*, 33, 303
"Nocturne," 9
"A Note on War Poetry," 5
"Ode," *37–38*, 86, 107
*Old Possum's Book of Practical Cats*,
33, 299
*Poèmes 1910–1930*, 308, 310
*Poems 1909–1925*, 40, 100, 299
*Poems Written in Early Youth*, 34

"Portrait of a Lady," *9–15*, 25, 28, 31,
39, 248, 294
*A Practical Possum*, 33
"Preludes," 9, *20–23*, 24, 25, 26, 30
*Prufrock and Other Observations*, 9, 30,
299
"Rhapsody on a Windy Night," 9, 21,
*23–25*, 30, 72
*The Rock*, *171–79*, 180, 187, 193, 195,
212, 223, 247, 253, 275, 281, 299
"Song to the Opherian," 68, 100, 101
"Spleen," 9
*Sweeney Agonistes*, 45, 47, 99, 100, *110–
18*, 171, 187, 194, 196, 210–11, 212
"Fragment of a Prologue," 113, *114–
15*
"Fragment of an Agon," 113, 114,
*115–18*, 176
"Sweeney Erect," 45, *47–48*, 85, 100,
109, 114, 115
"Sweeney among the Nightingales," *45–
47*, 50, 85, 304
"To the Indians Who Died in Africa,"
277
"To Walter de la Mare," 286
*The Waste Land*, 4, 6, 8, 10, 20, 29, 33,
34–35, 57, 58–59, 60, 63, 65–66,
67–71, *72–98*, 99, 100, 101, 102, 103,
104, 105, 106, 109, 114, 115, 117,
118, 122, 125, 126–27, 130, 132, 134,
135, 136–37, 141, 143, 144, 146,
148, 149, 150, 154, 157, 160, 164,
166, 174, 175, 176, 187, 191, 196,
208, 218, 220, 250, 252, 253, 262,
268, 275, 283
"Whispers of Immortality," 7–8, *40–42*,
47, 106, 147
"The Wind Sprang Up at Four O'-
Clock," 68, 100, *101*

Eliot, T. S., prose
*After Strange Gods*, 108, 133, 311, 313
"Baudelaire," 300, 314
"Baudelaire in Our Time," 157, 314
*"Baudelaire and the Symbolists"* (Quen-
nell), 300
"The Beating of a Drum," 217, 319
"Byron (1788–1824)," 299
*A Choice of Kipling's Verse*, 310
Clark Lectures, 7
"A Commentary" (April, 1933), 300
"A Commentary" (April, 1934), 315
"Cyril Tourneur," 286
"Dante," 151, 314
"A Dialogue on Dramatic Poetry," 110

"Dowson's Poems," 310
"Eeldrop and Appleplex. I," 117–18, 211, 312
"Eeldrop and Appleplex. II," 302
*Egoists* (Huneker), 79
*Elizabethan Essays,* 311
*Essays Ancient and Modern,* 314, 316
"Experience and the Objects of Knowledge, in the Philosophy of F. H. Bradley," 4, 300
"Ezra Pound," 302, 304
*For Lancelot Andrewes,* 122, 313
*From Poe to Valéry,* 311
"Hamlet and His Problems," 65
*The Idea of a Christian Society,* 220
"John Donne," 323
"John Ford," 121, 229, 294
"John Marston," 111, 112, 138, 187
"Leçon de Valéry," 325
"Literature and the Modern World," 117, 311
"London Letter" (October, 1921), 71, 307
"London Letter" (May, 1922), 307
"The Metaphysical Poets," 41
*The Music of Poetry,* 248–49, **320, 323**
"The Need for Poetic Drama," 110–11, 311
*Nightwood* (Barnes), Preface to, **220**
"A Note on Two Odes of Cowley," 41
*On Poetry,* 6, 108, 300, 311
"On a Recent Piece of Criticism," 302, 306
"The *Pensées* of Pascal," 185
"Poetry and Drama," 111, 193–94, 204, 213, 218, 311, 318, 319
*Poetry by T. S. Eliot,* 121–22, 159, 312, 316
"The Poetry of W. B. Yeats," 5, 300
"Reflections on Contemporary Poetry. II" (Bosschère, *The Closed Door*), 303
"Reflections on Contemporary Poetry [IV]," 305
"A Romantic Patrician," 50, 305, 308
*The Sacred Wood,* 156, 316
*Savonarola* (Charlotte Eliot), Introduction to, 110, 311
"A Sceptical Patrician," 306
*Selected Essays 1917–1932,* 299, 304, 305, 306, 311, 312, 313, 314, 315, 316, 317, 324, 325
*Le Serpent* (Valéry), Introduction to, 5, 102, 300, 311

"Shakespeare and the Stoicism of Seneca," 116
"A Talk on Dante," 285, 324
"The Three Voices of Poetry," 312, 316
"Tradition and the Individual Talent," 5, 54, 57, 59, 147, 292
"*Ulysses,* Order and Myth," 300
*The Use of Poetry and the Use of Criticism,* 24, 36, 101, 110, 112, 123, 147, 158, 302, 303, 305, 311, 313, 315, 316, 319
*The Wheel of Fire* (Knight), Introduction to, 307

Eliot, Vivienne (Mrs. T. S. Eliot), 135, 299, 300, 307
Elyot, Simon, 264
Elyot, Sir Thomas, 265; *The Boke Named the Governour,* 264, 266
Emerson, "Self-reliance," 48
Empson, William, *Seven Types of Ambiguity,* 40
Eternity, 61, 128, 162, 175, 176, 177–79, 187, 190, 199, 200, 204–5, 208, 224, 226, 249, 252–55, 256–57, 258–61, 262–64, 266, 269, 273, 274–77, 278–79, 280–85, 288–89, 290–92; see also Time
Euripides: *Alcestis,* 218–19, 220, 277; *Ion,* 219, 229, 237–40, 242, 320; *Iphigenia in Tauris,* 183 (Murray, trans.), 186, 317 (Murray, trans.)
*Everyman,* 194, 213

Fawkes, Guy, 103, 105
Fergusson, Francis, 185
Ferrar, Nicholas, 251, 289
Field, Eugene, "The Duel," 250
"Fire Sermon, The" (Buddha), 90
FitzGerald, Edward, 63, 67; *The Rubáiyát of Omar Khayyám,* 3
Fitzgerald, F. Scott, 224; *The Great Gatsby,* 113–14
Flaubert: "Un Cœur simple," 32; *La Tentation de Saint-Antoine,* 263
Fletcher; see Beaumont and Fletcher
Fletcher, John Gould, 31
Flint, F. S., 21
Fokine, Michel, *Narcisse,* 35
Ford, Ford Madox; see Hueffer, Ford Madox
Ford, John, 121; *The Lover's Melancholy,* 175, 286
Foster, Genevieve W., 106
Fournier, Henri Alain, 4
Frazer, Sir James, 293; *Folk-Lore in the*

Old Testament, 79; The Golden Bough, 6, 65, 66, 70, 71, 74, 87, 105, 163
Fry, Roger, 67

Galen, 144
Galsworthy, 171
Galton, Sir Francis, 217
Gardner, Helen L., 260
Gardner, Mrs. Jack, 32
Gaudier-Brzeska, Henri, 33
Gautier: "Albertus ou l'âme et le péché," 304; "L'Art," 304; "Buchers et Tombeaux," 40; "Carmen," 40, 42; La Comédie de la mort, 40; Émaux et camées, 38; "L'Hippopotame," 39; Poésies diverses, 39; "Le Spectre de la rose," 324; "Variations sur le Carnaval de Venise," 51, 53
Gerstärker, Friedrich, "Germelshausen," 264, 266
Gide: Les Faux Monnayeurs, 108; Le Prométhée mal enchaîné, 36, 141, 272
Gilbert, W. S., Iolanthe, 116
Goethe, 272
Goldsmith, Oliver, The Vicar of Wakefield, 88
Gosse, Sir Edmund, 118
Gourmont, Remy de, 59; "Les Litanies de la Rose," 145
Grail legend, 6, 65, 66, 69–70, 71, 73 ff., 102, 104, 132, 149, 164, 218, 320
Graves, Robert, 172
Greco, El, 250
Greene, E. J. H., 33
Grimm, Jacob, "The Juniper Tree," 144, 145
Griswold, Rufus, 79
Groser, Father John, 181

Hadrian, 129
Häusermann, H. W., 264
Hale, Emily, 197
Hamilton, Alexander, 287
Harding, D. W., 174
Harris, J. Rendel, 79
Harrison, Austin, 31
Hawthorne, "Feathertop," 105
Hayward, John, 323, 324
Heraclitus, 39, 94, 251–52, 260–61, 264, 267, 272–73, 276, 278, 284, 291, 294
Herbert, George, "Church-rents and Schisms," 315
Herodotus, 76
Herrick: "Another Grace for a Child," 250; "A Christmas Carroll," 323

Heywood, John: Hercules Furens (Seneca), 183; A Woman Killed with Kindness, 224, 302
Hinduism, 95, 97, 98, 108, 224, 274, 277–79, 293
History, 7–8, 59, 60, 61, 62, 64, 65, 108, 122, 176, 264, 265, 273, 276, 288–89, 290, 291, 292, 293
Hobbes, 172
Hodgson, Ralph, "The Birdcatcher," 250
Hoellering, George, 181, 194
Hogarth, 45
Hueffer, Ford Madox, 33; Mr. Apollo, 303
Hulme, T. E., 21, 198; "Complete Poetical Works," 34; "Conversion," 34; Speculations, 314, 322
Huneker, James, Egoists: A Book of Supermen, 79
Husserl, Edmund, Ideas, 161–62
Huxley, Aldous, Crome Yellow, 76
Huysmans, J. K., A rebours, 101

Ibsen, The Master Builder, 221
Ignatius, St., "Epistle to the Trallians," 39
Imagism, 21, 34, 100
Impersonality in poetry, 3, 5, 28, 133, 294–95
Incarnation, the, 43–44, 122, 136, 152, 177–79, 253, 263, 279, 280–81
Initiation, 6, 69–70, 71, 73–75, 76, 79, 93, 94–96, 104, 145, 149, 153–54, 217–18, 220, 228; see also Death and rebirth; Grail legend; Primitive ritual and religion
Isaacs, J., 112

James, Henry, 26, 31, 212; The Ambassadors, 12; The Aspern Papers, 51–52; "The Beast in the Jungle," 60; "Crapy Cornelia," 15; "The Jolly Corner," 205, 256, 285; The Portrait of a Lady, 301; The Sense of the Past, 319; What Maisie Knew, 233
John the Baptist, St., 6, 19, 32, 183
John of the Cross, St., 7, 99, 118, 137–38, 143, 145, 149, 157, 210, 225, 263, 269, 293; The Ascent of Mount Carmel, 116, 123, 138, 142, 226, 264, 269; The Dark Night of the Soul, 138, 141, 144, 146, 147, 246, 269, 292; The Living Flame of Love, 270; The Spiritual Canticle, 280; see also Mysticism; Negative and affirmative ways, the

Johnson, Samuel, *The Vanity of Human Wishes*, 286
Jonson, 57; *The Alchemist*, 64, 305
Jourdain, Eleanor, *An Adventure*, 205
Joyce, 33, 67, 324; "The Dead," 321; *Finnegans Wake*, 7, 51, 291; *Ulysses*, 58, 59–60, 79, 84–85, 253, 313
Julian of Norwich, 289, 290
Jung, C. G., 59, 70

Kafka, *The Metamorphosis*, 223
Keats: "Ode on a Grecian Urn," 262; "Ode on Melancholy," 250; "Ode to a Nightingale," 88
Kipling: "At the End of the Passage," 101, 105, 201; "The Ballad of East and West," 53; "The Broken Men," 101; "Danny Deever," 101; "The Explorer," 123; "The Fabulists," 286; *Kim*, 310; "Mandalay," 101; "La Nuit Blanche," 101; "The Story of Muhammad Din," 277, 316; "They," 132, 256; "To Be Filed for Reference," 250; "A Truthful Song," 172
Kittredge, Walter, "Tenting on the Old Camp Ground," 309
"Krutzsch, Gus" (T. S. Eliot), 68
Kyd, *The Spanish Tragedy*, 97–98

Laforgue, 5, 9–10, 11, 15, 23, 24–25, 27, 29, 31, 33, 39, 54; "Autre Complainte de Lord Pierrot," 26; "Ballade," 44; "Complainte de cette bonne lune," 302; "Complainte du vent qui s'ennuie la nuit," 35; "Complaintes sur certains temps déplacés," 301; "Cythère," 37–38; "Hamlet," 83; "Persée et Andromède," 37, 38; "Pétition," 28; "La Première Nuit," 37; "Salomé," 32; "Sur une défunte," 300
Lanier, Sidney, "The Marshes of Glynn," 313
Lanman, Charles, 108
Latimer, 172
Laud, William, 289
Lawrence, D. H.: "Hymn to Priapus," 40; *The Rainbow*, 310; "The Shadow in the Rose Garden," 321
Layard, John, *Stone Men of Malekula*, 319
Lear, Edward, 31; "How pleasant to know Mr. Lear," 250
Legouis, Pierre, 103
Leibniz, 189, 190

Leonardo da Vinci; *see* Vinci, Leonardo da
Lewis, Wyndham, 68
Lindsay, Vachel, 309; "The Daniel Jazz," 182; "The Fireman's Ball," 310
"London Bridge" (song), 96–97
Lovejoy, Arthur O., 259–60
Lowell, J. R., *The Vision of Sir Launfal*, 301
Lucian, 92; "Zeuxis or Antiochus," 33
Lucy, St., 282, 291, 312
Ludendorff, Erich F. W., *The Coming War*, 162

*Mabinogion, The*, 6, 87
Machen, Arthur, "Opening the Door," 321
Macmurray, John, *Reason and Emotion*, 319
Maeterlinck, 111, 112
Magnus Martyr, St., 89, 90, 96
Mallarmé: "M'introduire dans ton histoire," 257; "Le Tombeau de Charles Baudelaire," 257; "Le Tombeau d'Edgar Poe," 286
Mantegna, Andrea, 51, 53
Marlowe: *Doctor Faustus*, 118, 217; *The Jew of Malta*, 14, 43, 44
Marston, 111, 112, 138, 187; *Entertainment*, 52, 53
Martz, Louis L., 184
Marvell, "To His Coy Mistress," 19–20, 41, 84, 250, 320
Mary, Queen of Scots, 265
Matthiessen, F. O., 45, 48, 50, 160, 205, 212
Maugham, W. S., *The Moon and Sixpence*, 115
Maurras, Charles, *L'Avenir de l'Intelligence*, 160, 164
Meinong, Alexis, 4
Memory and memories, 16, 22–23, 24–25, 50, 57–59, 64, 67–68, 72, 103, 146–49, 151, 154–55, 176, 187, 208, 252, 255, 259, 272, 273, 276, 288, 289, 290
Menotti, Gian-Carlo, *The Telephone*, 113
Meredith, George, "Lucifer in Starlight," 32
Merry, W. W., 161
*Merry Devil of Edmonton, The*, 318
Meynell, Alice, "Unto us a Son is given," 132
Michelangelo, 18
Middleton, 57; *The Changeling*, 305; *Women Beware Women*, 81

Masefield, "Cardigan Bay," 301
Massine, Léonide, 71
Massinger, *The Roman Actor,* 316
Milton: *Areopagitica,* 190; "Lycidas," 40, 92; *Paradise Lost,* 192, 256, 258, 286, 287, 289; *Samson Agonistes,* 117, 184, 268, 324
"Mrs. Porter" (song), 85, 90, 115
Moberly, Anne, *An Adventure,* 205
Molière, 63
Monro, Harold, 31
Monroe, Harriet, 15, 31
Montaigne, *Apology for Raimond Sebond,* 317
Moore, Marianne, 31; "No Swan So Fine," 247
Morris, William, 171; "The Hollow Land," 101; "The Nymph's Song to Hylas," 321
Morshead, E. D. A., *Agamemnon* (Aeschylus), 304
"Mulberry Bush, The" (song), 106–7
Murray, Gilbert: "Hamlet and Orestes," 212; *Iphigenia in Tauris* (Euripides), 183
Music of poetry, 110–11, 174, 248–50
Mysticism, 5, 6, 7, 71, 94, 99, 106, 113, 116, 117, 118, 123, 127, 137–39, 142–43, 147, 149, 157, 210–11, 225–26, 237, 258, 260–61, 270; *see also* Negative and affirmative ways, the; John of the Cross, St.

Negative and affirmative ways, the, 7, 93, 99, 103, 106, 116, 123, 127, 137–39, 140, 142, 143, 156, 157, 164, 166, 167, 178, 195, 210–12, 221, 225–26, 237, 259–60, 268–69, 293–94; *see also* Death and rebirth; Initiation; John of the Cross, St.; Mysticism
Nerval, Gérard de: "El Desdichado," 97; "Les Papillons," 301
Newman: "The Dream of Gerontius," 63; *The Idea of a University,* 313
Nietzsche, 177; *Also Sprach Zarathustra,* 301
Nijinsky, 324
*Noctes Binanianae,* 33

O'Donnell, Stephen, 44
*Odyssey,* 47–48, 67, 83, 89, 260
"One-eyed Riley, The" (song), 87, 218, 220, 223
O'Neill, Eugene, *Mourning Becomes Electra,* 201

Origen, 29, 43–44, 45, 51, 65, 108
Ovid, *Metamorphoses,* 88

*Palatine Anthology, The,* 36
Pascal, 185, 290; *Pensées,* 143, 271
Patanjali, 108
Pater, Walter, 309
Paul, St., 72, 127, 148, 150, 183, 189
Payne, Robert, 44–45, 86
Pearson, Karl, 62
Peele, George, *The Old Wives' Tale,* 247–48
"Peredur," 6, 87
*Perlesvaus,* 91
Perse, St.-J., 100; *Anabasis* (Eliot, trans.), 123, 160
Perugino, Pietro, 304
*Pervigilium Veneris,* 97
Peter, St., 73, 95, 172, 175, 183
Petrarch, "Penitential Psalms" (Chapman, trans.), 257
Petronius Arbiter, *Satyricon,* 69
Philippe, Charles-Louis: *Bubu de Montparnasse,* 20–21, 23–24, 26, 307; *Marie Donadieu,* 21, 24, 36–37
*Physiologus,* 40
Plato, 134; *Phaedo,* 323; *Republic,* 220; *Theaetetus,* 317
Plutarch: *Crassus* (North, trans.), 308; *Isis and Osiris,* 308
Poe, 79; "The City in the Sea," 315; "The Murders in the Rue Morgue," 47; "The Raven," 250
Pope, 189; *The Dunciad,* 107, 252; *An Essay on Man,* 293; *The Rape of the Lock,* 79–80, 115
Potentiality and the possible, 107, 199, 208, 220, 236, 253–55, 256, 257, 259, 262, 263, 266, 281, 289, 292
Pound, 30, 34, 220, 248; *A Lume Spento,* 34; abridgment of *The Waste Land* (Eliot), 65, 68, 102, 308; "The Age Demanded," 322; "The Bath Tub," 31; *Cathay,* 38–39; *The Cantos,* 59, 67, 304; "Exile's Letter," 123; "A Girl," 34; "Homage to Sextus Propertius," 38–39; "Hugh Selwyn Mauberley," 31, 38–39; letters, 31, 33, 65, 68, 308, 309, 314; *Lustra,* 32; "Les Millwin," 31; "Phyllidula," 31; *Quia Pauper Amavi,* 38–39, 67; "The Return," 31, 34, 325; *Ripostes,* 34; "The Seafarer," 34; "The Tree," 34
Prest, T. P., 45
Preston, Raymond, 251, 260, 287

Primitive ritual and religion, 65, 66, 69–70, 71, 82, 87, 88, 95, 98, 104, 107, 125, 130, 161, 163, 178, 203, 212, 214, 217–18, 219; *see also* Death and rebirth; Grail legend; Initiation
Proust, 59, 67; *A la recherche du temps perdu*, 58
Purgation, 71, 94, 97, 99, 106, 116, 117, 127, 137, 138, 140, 142, 147, 149, 165, 196, 198, 200, 203, 208, 210, 250, 260, 268, 269, 270–71, 284, 285, 287–88, 289, 290; *see also* Action and suffering

Quinn, John, 30, 68

Raglan, Lord, *The Hero*, 217–18
*Raigne of King Edward the Third, The*, 45, 46
Richards, I. A., 48, 58
*Rig-Veda*, 95
Rimbaud, 35, 39; "Le Bateau ivre," 33; "Le Cœur volé," 37; "Les Effarés," 35; "Les Pauvres à l'église," 43; "Les Poètes de sept ans," 36–37
Rossetti, D. G.: "The Ballad of Dead Ladies" (Villon), 50; "The Blessed Damozel," 3, 28, 50, 101; *The House of Life*, 314; "I saw the Sibyl at Cumae" (Petronius), 69; "Love's Nocturn," 315; *Vita nuova* (Dante), 309
Royce, Josiah, 4
Ruskin, 50
Russell, Bertrand, 4, 32, 299

Sadler, Sir Michael, 131
St. George play, 217
St. Patrick's purgatory, 94
Sandburg, "Fog," 19
Santayana, *The Last Puritan*, 212
Sappho, "Hesperus," 88
Schumann, Robert, *The Merry Peasant*, 86
Sebastian, St., 34, 51, 53
Seneca, 218; *Hercules Furens*, 52–53, 131, 133, 183 (Heywood, trans.)
Sesostris, 76
Shackleton, Sir Ernest, *South*, 310
Shakespeare, 57; *Antony and Cleopatra*, 52, 53, 80, 89, 305, 314; *Coriolanus*, 37, 38, 96, 160, 164; *Cymbeline* 80, 250; *Hamlet*, 16, 17, 20, 28, 81, 83, 171, 209, 286, 289, 301, 310; *I Henry IV*, 208, 218, 257; *II Henry IV*, 302; *Henry V*, 271; *Julius Caesar*, 37, 38, 102, 302, 310; *King Lear*, 81, 82, 112, 125, 186,

198, 217, 305; *Macbeth*, 37, 38, 118, 269, 315; *Measure for Measure*, 286, 305; *The Merchant of Venice*, 52, 53, 305, 309; *Othello*, 52, 53, 82, 116, 280, 305, 313; *Pericles*, 130–31, 133, 172, 313; "The Phoenix and the Turtle," 52, 250; *Richard II*, 268; *Romeo and Juliet*, 11, 102; *Sonnets*, 140–41, 192, 286; *The Tempest*, 70, 81, 82, 84–85, 89, 91, 98, 279; *Twelfth Night*, 302
Shaw, *Saint Joan*, 194, 217
Shelley: "Music, when soft voices die," 255; "Ode to the West Wind," 287; *Prometheus Unbound*, 226; *The Triumph of Life*, 48, 282–83, 285; "The Waning Moon," 302
Shirley, James, 'The glories of our blood and state," 323
Sigebert of Gembloux, *Passio Sanctae Luciae Virginis*, 312
Simonides, 324
Smidt, Kristian, 4
Smith, George Joseph, 118
Sophocles, 185; *Oedipus at Colonus*, 45, 46, 184; *Oedipus the King*, 175–76
Spencer, Theodore, 185
Spender, Stephen, 249
Spenser, 53; *The Faerie Queene*, 83, 151; "Prothalamion," 84
Spinoza, 176, 189
Stephenson, Ethel M., 130
Stevenson, R. L., "Requiem," 88
Still, Colin, *Shakespeare's Mystery Play*, 70, 84
Strafford, first Earl of, 289
Stravinsky, *Le Sacre du printemps*, 71
Stream of consciousness, 57–59, 67; *see also* Memory and memories
Swift, 286
Swinburne, 174–75; "Before the Mirror," 323; "Itylus," 313; "The Last Oracle," 268; "Tiresias," 88
Symons, Arthur, *The Symbolist Movement in Literature*, 5

Tarot pack, 76, 77, 78–79, 87–88, 97
Tennyson, 83; *Becket*, 183–84; *The Holy Grail*, 250; *In Memoriam*, 258, 313, 322, 323; *Maud*, 28, 302; *The Princess*, 250, 310; "The Sisters," 52; "Tiresias," 67, 88; "Ulysses," 61
Tennyson, Frederick, 63
Theresa, St., 270
Thompson, Francis, "The Kingdom of God," 175

Thompson, T. H., 114
Thomson, James: "Art," 101; *The City of Dreadful Night*, 324; "To Our Ladies of Death," 72
Time, 11, 18, 24, 57–59, 61, 68, 128, 134, 142, 146–47, 151, 156, 175, 176–79, 187, 190, 193, 198, 200, 204–5, 207, 208, 212, 224, 226, 229, 243, 249, 252–55, 256–57, 258, 259, 260–61, 262, 263, 264–68, 269, 273, 274–77, 278–82, 283, 284, 285, 288, 289, 290, 291, 292; *see also* Memory and memories
Tourneur, 57, 62; *The Atheist's Tragedy*, 286; *The Revenger's Tragedy*, 111

Unger, Leonard, 137, 144
*Upanishads*, 95, 97, 98, 277

Vail, Laurence, 20
Valéry, 35, 103, 108; "Cantique des Colonnes," 102, 311; "Le Cimetière marin," 102; *Le Serpent*, 5, 102
Vaughan, Henry: "Ascension Hymn," 268; "The Night," 44; "The Retreat," 129; "The Waterfall," 292
Vergil, 165–66, 286; *Aeneid*, 27, 69, 76, 80, 82, 83, 91, 105, 282, 285, 319; *Georgics*, 166
Verdenal, Jean, 9
Verlaine, "Parsifal," 86, 87
Verne, Jules, *Twenty Thousand Leagues under the Sea*, 303
Verrall, A. W., 218–19, 229, 237–38, 239–40, 242
Versification, 38, 57, 174–75, 193–94, 212–13, 228, 285–86
Villon: "The Ballad of Dead Ladies" (Rossetti, trans.), 50; "Épitaphe Villon," 142–43; *Le Testament*, 49, 50
Vinci, Leonardo da, 36, 309
Voltaire, *Candide*, 49, 237

Wagner: *Götterdämmerung*, 89, 90; *Parzival*, 70, 76–77, 86; *Rheingold*, 90; *Ring*, 70, 90; *Siegfried*, 70; *Tristan und Isolde*, 70, 75–76, 83, 96

Waite, A. E., *The Pictorial Key to the Tarot*, 77
Ward, Anne, 198
Warren, H. C., *Buddhism in Translations*, 93–94
Waugh, Evelyn, *Black Mischief*, 227
Webster, John, 42; *The Devil's Law Case*, 81, 316; *The White Devil*, 40–41, 78, 79, 96
Wells, H. G., "The Door in the Wall," 321
Weston, Jessie L.: *From Ritual to Romance*, 66, 70, 71, 74, 76, 77, 87, 91, 92, 94, 95, 149; *The Quest of the Holy Grail*, 66
Whibley, Charles, *Studies in Frankness*, 33
Whitman, 37, 165; "When Lilacs Last in the Door-Yard Bloom'd," 310
Whittier, "Ichabod," 304
Wilde, 216; "The Ballad of Reading Gaol," 24; *Salome*, 310
Will, 16, 92–93, 97, 108–9, 117, 127, 129, 138, 156, 157, 181, 184, 185, 186, 188–91, 192, 196, 198, 200, 220, 236, 293; *see also* Action and suffering
Williams, Charles, 112; *Descent into Hell*, 226, 285; *The Greater Trumps*, 226–27, 321–22
Wilson, Edmund, 48; *The Wound and the Bow*, 272
Winslow, Richard, 113
Wolfram von Eschenbach, *Parzival*, 85
Wood, James, 108
Wordsworth: "Ode on Intimations of Immortality," 129, 142; "The Reverie of Poor Susan," 34
Wyndham, George, *Essays in Romantic Literature*, 50

Yeats, 112, 149, 205, 294; "The Host of the Air," 250; "Meditations in Time of Civil War," 315; "Nineteen Hundred and Nineteen," 284; "Sailing to Byzantium," 105; "The Secret Rose," 311; "Three Things," 275; "Vacillation," 286; *A Vision*, 163, 325; *The Words upon the Window Pane*, 324